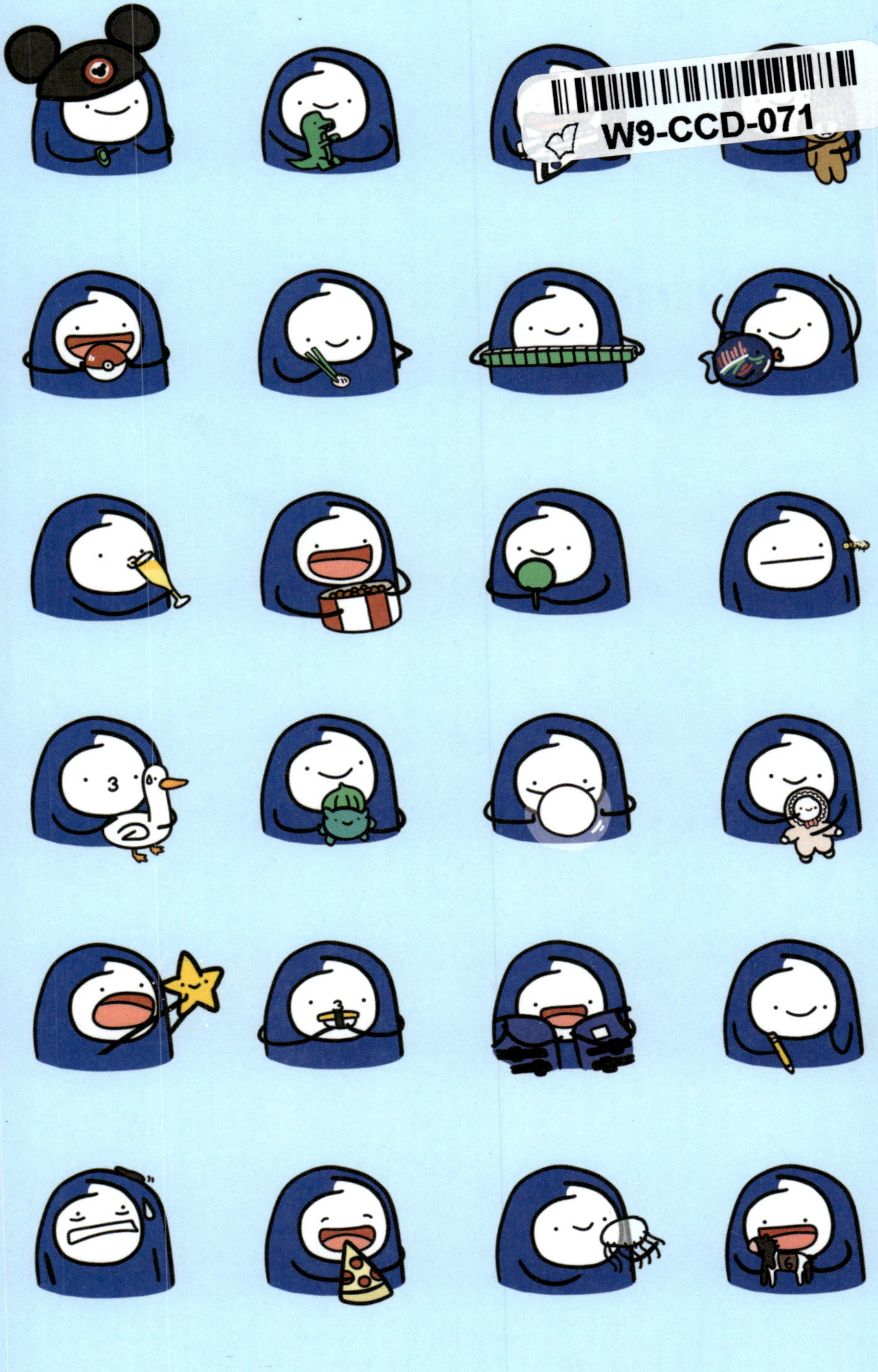

# BARELY FUNCTIONAL ADULT

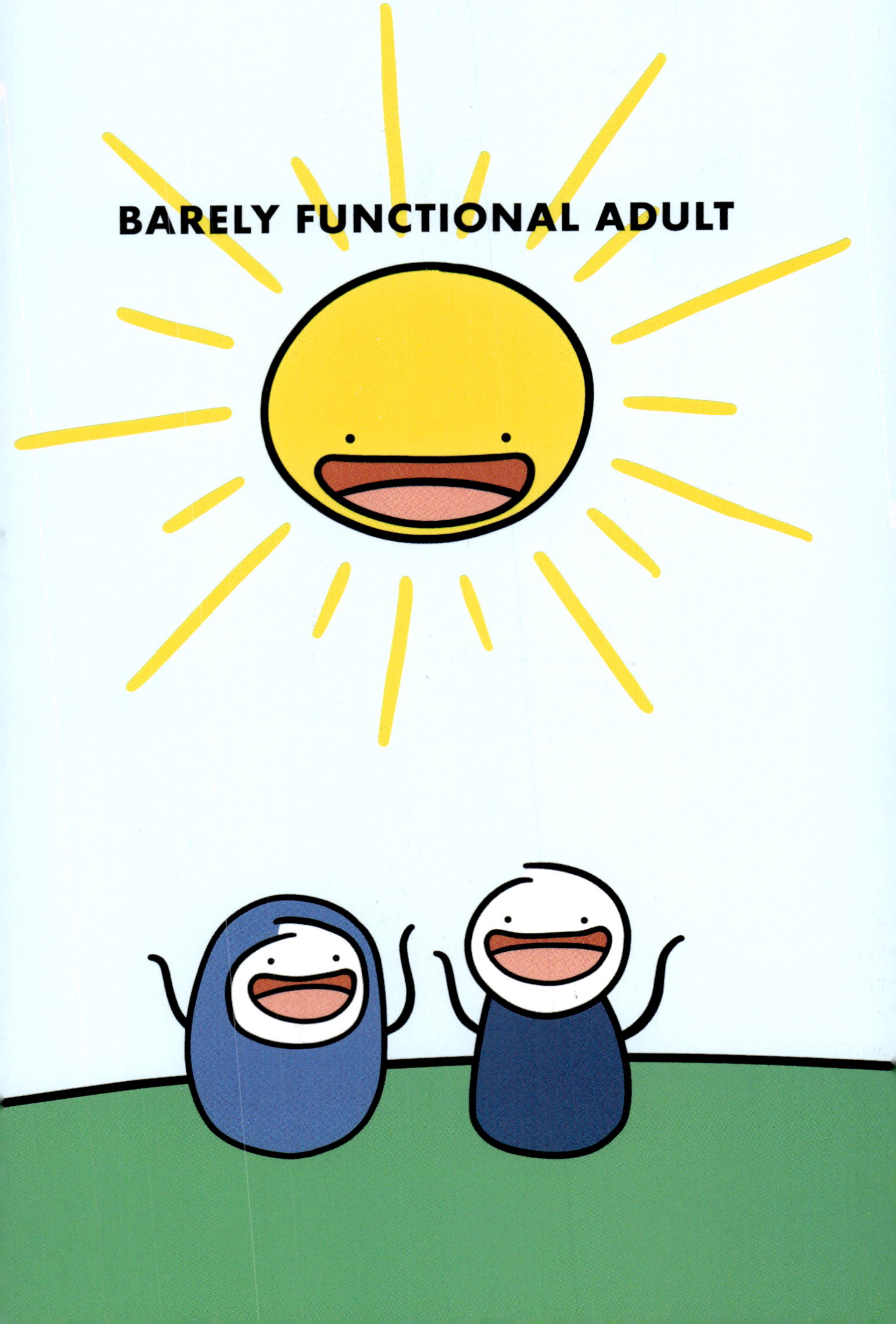

# BARELY FUNCTIONAL ADULT

## IT'LL ALL MAKE SENSE EVENTUALLY

## MEICHI NG

HARPER PERENNIAL

NEW YORK • LONDON • TORONTO • SYDNEY • NEW DELHI • AUCKLAND

HARPER ⬤ PERENNIAL

HarperCollins books may be purchased for educational, business, or sales promotional use. For information, please email the Special Markets Department at SPsales@harpercollins.com.

FIRST EDITION

*Designed by Jen Overstreet*

Library of Congress Cataloging-in-Publication Data has been applied for.

ISBN 978-0-06-294559-4

20 21 22 23 24  LSC  10 9 8 7 6 5 4 3 2 1

For the people I love,
Who tolerate my nonsense on a regular basis.

For Mum,
Who has supported every ridiculous
dream I've ever pursued.

For Dad,
Who taught me how to be brave
in the face of darkness.

For Jenny,
Who was my very first therapist.

•  •  •

& for all the Barely Functional Adults out there,
Who ought to know they're not alone.

Don't forget.
We write our own stories.
And we can write whatever the hell we want.

# CONTENTS

# INTRODUCTION

There is a strange but potent comfort in the discovery that someone else in the universe has experienced the *exact* same feelings as we have.

And seeing these feelings—the ones we previously thought were unique to us—perfectly articulated by someone else always comes as a bit of a surprise.

It makes me wonder whether all our stories are more or less the same—that there is a fixed number of emotions to be had in this world, and despite the distinctive notes that separate your stories from mine, the underlying feelings that we experience—even the most deeply isolating ones—are actually much more universal than we think.

In writing this book, I spent a lot of time looking back. And in doing so, I came to discover that my perspective on my own stories has shifted significantly since many of these events transpired. Perhaps this is a result of having experienced the same stories play out with different people over the years and finding myself playing new parts every time. It's hard not to look back with increased objectivity once you've been the other person. I'd like to think that this impartiality has given me more clarity to make sense of it all, but that is simply something I like to think.

Here you will find the stories I needed to read at different points in my life—I didn't get to read them when I needed to, but I hope these stories will come to you at a time when you do.

And while these stories are my own, I hope they will feel familiar to you in all the right ways.

# BARELY FUNCTIONAL ADULT

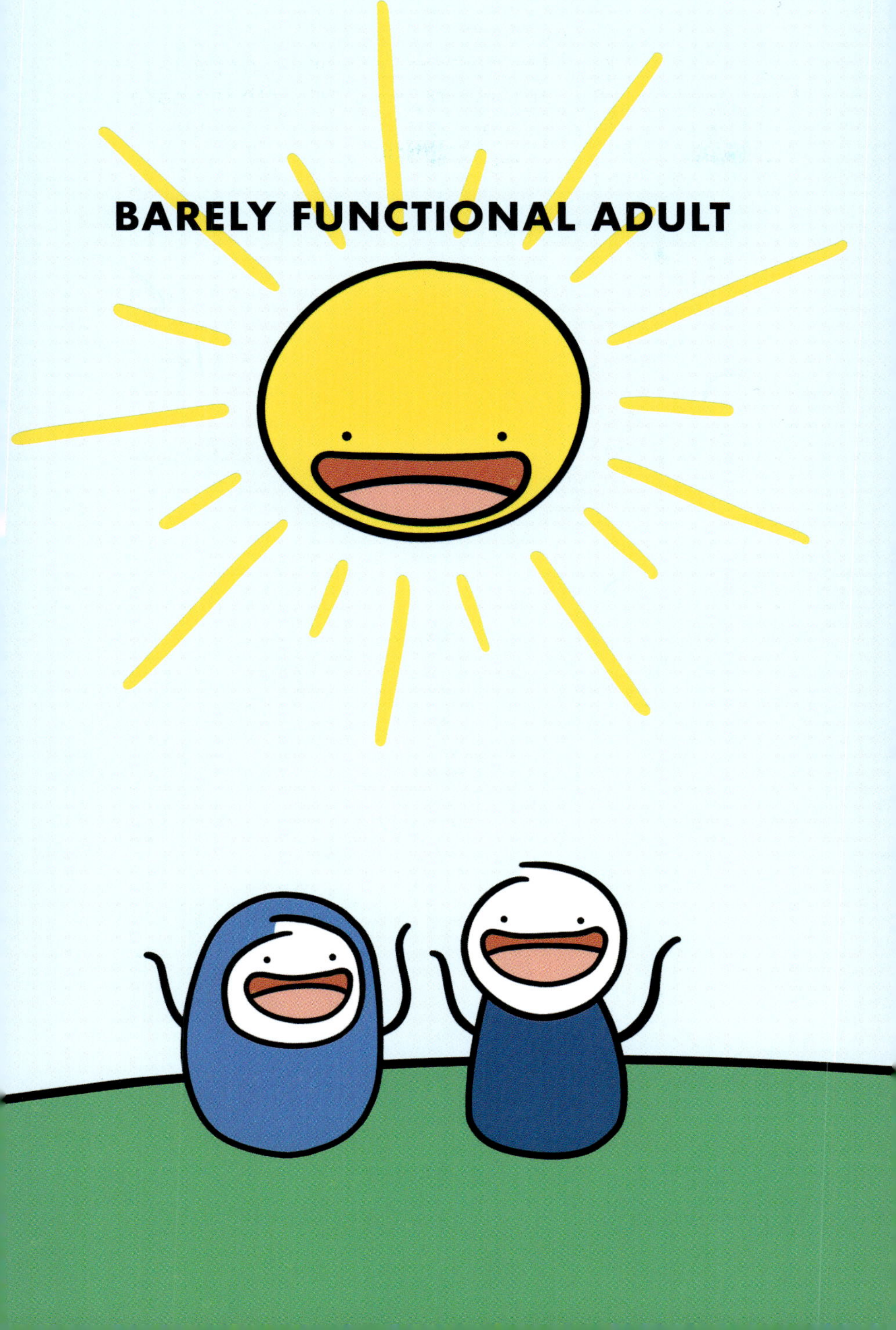

# CHAPTER 1

# MY PET FISH

**S**hortly after becoming a strong, independent adult, I decided it was finally time to start a family.

So, I bought a fish.

OTHER FAMILIES
HUMAN
+
HUMAN
=
BORING SAME-SPECIES OFFSPRING

MY FAMILY
HUMAN
+
EXCITING FISH OFFSPRING

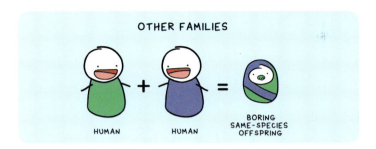

My fish adventure began like all my adventures, with a single impulsive idea prancing through my brain, followed by an almost immediate compulsion to act on it. There's only a small sliver of time to follow through on your fun, impractical notions before that pesky voice of reason reels you out of it—so you gotta act fast. This is the logic that led me to text my best friend at 6:28 a.m. on a Saturday morning with the following message:

> Me: *NEED A FISH BABY!!! CAN YOU PLEASE GIVE ME A RIDE?*

Eleven words. No further context. I realized I had accidentally nicked the caps lock, but I liked how it aptly communicated the sense of urgency in the situation, so I left the message as-is. Two minutes later, a response came through.

Best friend: *Sure.*\*

I was ecstatic, a state that would be preserved for the next three and a half hours because, as we would later learn, the pet store doesn't open until ten.

· · ·

My best friend is used to my nonsense, which is why we are best friends, I suppose, so it came as no surprise to her that I was texting in all caps at the crack of dawn about fish babies. Now that I think of it, she didn't even ask any further questions before heading over to meet me. What a remarkably tolerant human being.

If I could drive, I would. And technically I *can* drive! After all, I *am* a strong, independent adult with a driver's license. But instead of that license being proof of my competence as a driver, all it proves is that it's much too easy to get a license. I've never held any of the core competencies one would want of a driver—like the ability to focus—so as a courtesy to the world, I do not drive.

---

\* A notably more composed response than my initial text.

SELF-AWARENESS.
IT'S IMPORTANT, KIDS.

Getting my license wasn't a complete waste though, because I, like so many before and after me, simply got a driver's license as proof of age. Besides, I've always preferred being in the passenger seat of a car. I like the luxury of letting my mind wander, of being in my own pocket dimension of consciousness untethered from the world, and of being pleasantly brought back to earth at the driver's melodic announcement of "We're hereeeeee!" There's comfort in knowing you can be on your way to somewhere good even if you're not always in control of it all.

•  •  •

When we arrived at the pet store, my friend asked me why I wasn't getting a dog or a cat. People always assume it's one or the other when you declare your intention of acquiring a pet. It really throws off their worldview when your pet species goes beyond the fourth letter of the alphabet.

SO WHY
AREN'T YOU
GETTING A
CAT OR
DOG?

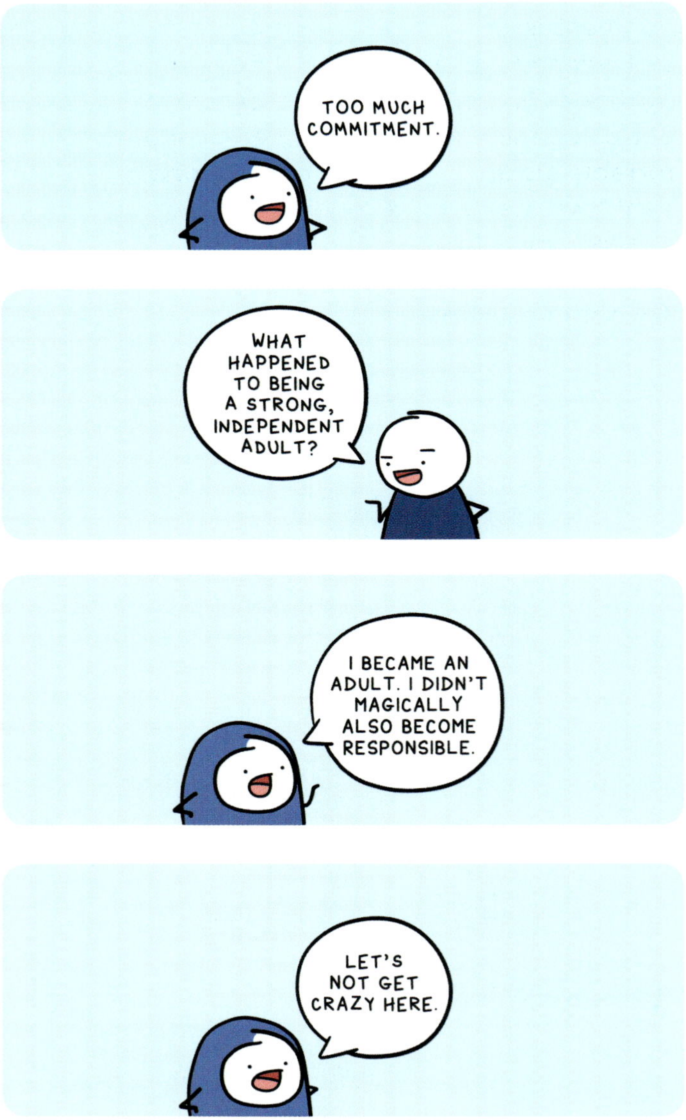
TOO MUCH COMMITMENT.
WHAT HAPPENED TO BEING A STRONG, INDEPENDENT ADULT?
I BECAME AN ADULT. I DIDN'T MAGICALLY ALSO BECOME RESPONSIBLE.
LET'S NOT GET CRAZY HERE.

In fairness, I love both cats and dogs. But it was important for me to get a pet that didn't have abandonment issues. I didn't want a pet that would be sad whenever I left for work; I have enough guilt in my life as is. So instead, I focused my search on a pet companion that would love me—but at a comfortable distance. The kind of emotionally independent love that is there when you need it, but won't swallow you whole.

Try not to psychoanalyze that.

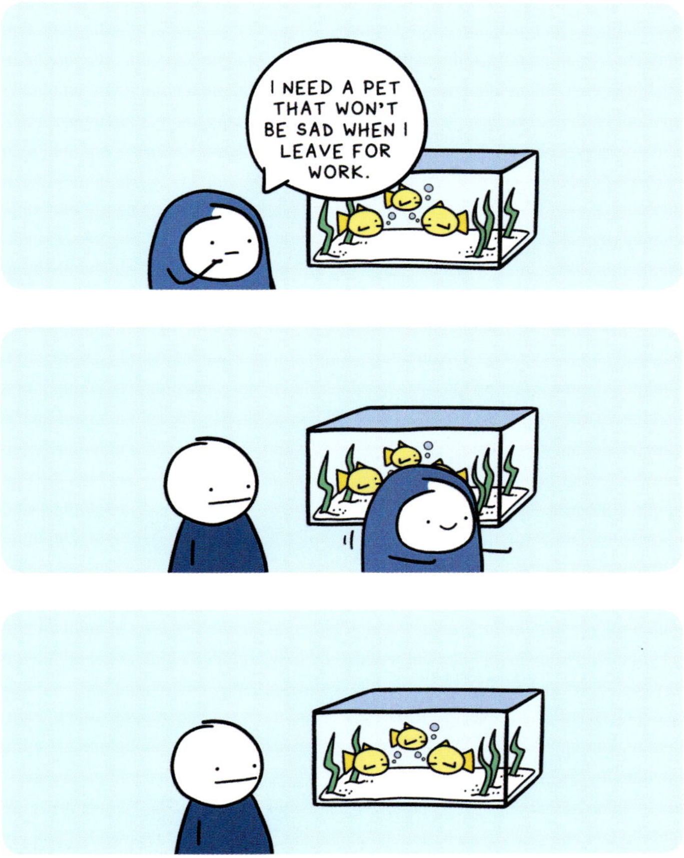
I NEED A PET THAT WON'T BE SAD WHEN I LEAVE FOR WORK.

YOU SEE! THE FISH DON'T CARE IF I COME OR GO. THEY'RE THE PERFECT COMPANIONS!

I MEAN, I GUESS... IF INDIFFERENCE IS WHAT YOU'RE LOOKING FOR IN A COMPANION.

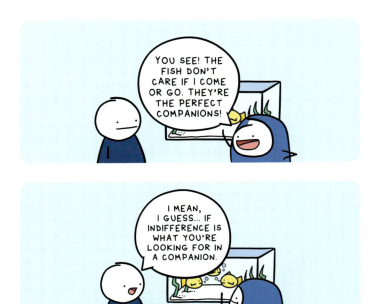

After deciding on a species, I started to look for the fish that was *the one*. I didn't know what I was looking for exactly, but somehow, I knew I would know it when I saw it. The power of choice went to my head almost immediately.

WHO AMONG YOU SHALL I GIVE THE GIFT OF LIFE?

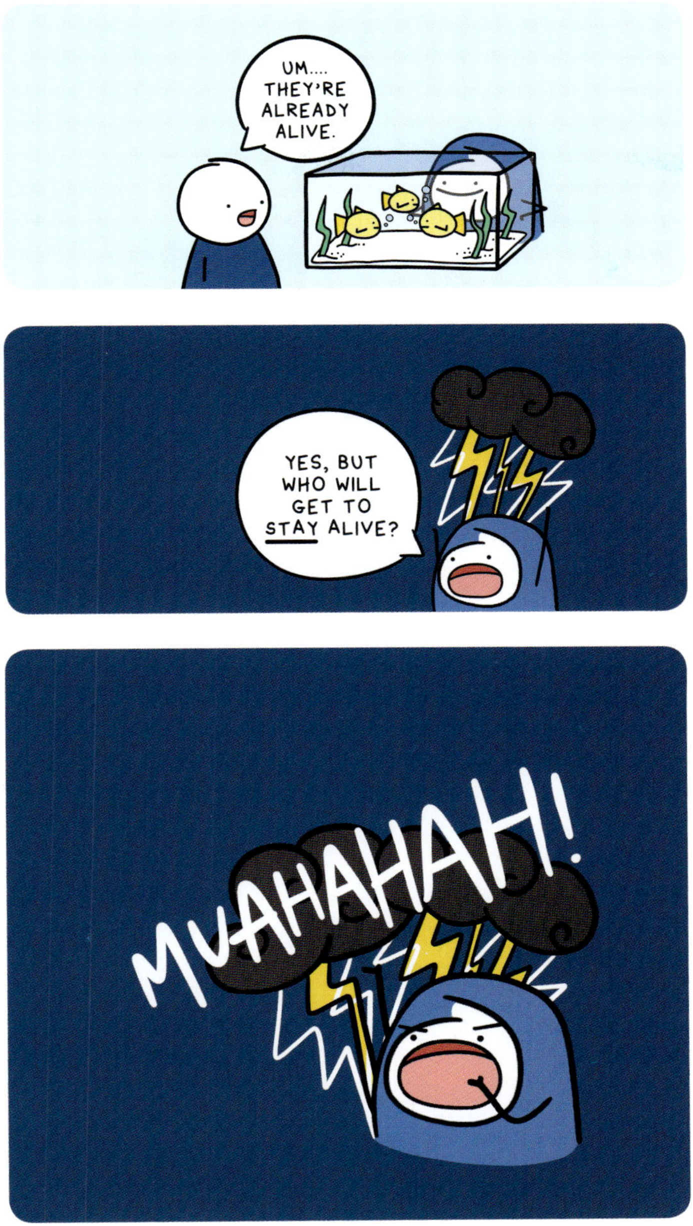
UM.... THEY'RE ALREADY ALIVE.
YES, BUT WHO WILL GET TO STAY ALIVE?
MUAHAHAH!

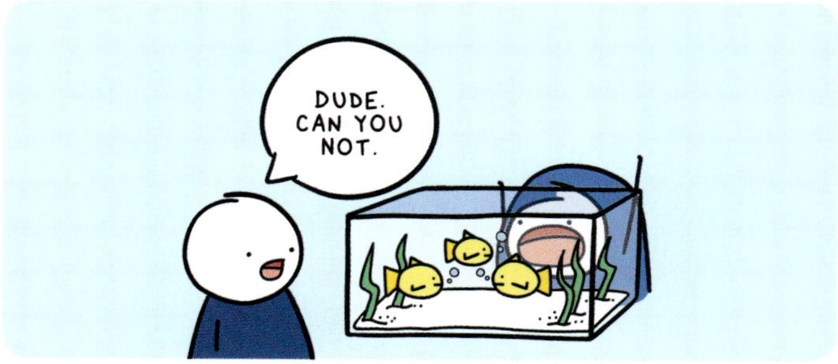
DUDE. CAN YOU NOT.

Upon initial review, all I found were normal-looking fish bathing peacefully. They were much too perfect for us to realistically get along. But just as I was about to give up, I saw it—*the one*. Tucked away in the back corner of the tank, there was this ostracized, peculiar-looking fish quivering quietly behind a thin strand of plastic kelp. It was as though he was the lone, unwitting survivor from a game of hide-and-seek that the other fish had long finished without him.

I felt a deep and immediate connection.

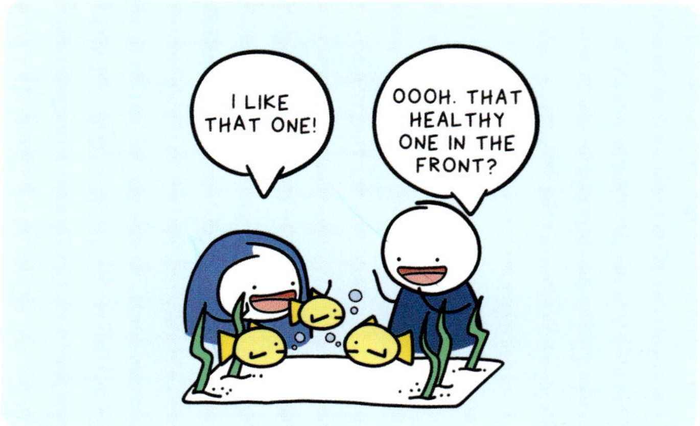
I LIKE THAT ONE!
OOOH. THAT HEALTHY ONE IN THE FRONT?

NO, THAT WEIRD LOOKING ONE TWITCHING IN THE BACK!
UH...
THIS ONE.
I THINK THERE'S SOMETHING WRONG WITH IT. ALL THE OTHER FISH SEEM TO BE AVOIDING IT...
NOPE. THAT'S THE ONE!

"Why *this* fish?" my friend asked, understandably concerned by my ever-growing list of questionable life decisions.

"Sometimes you just know it when you feel it," I explained matter-of-factly with a smile, knowing that this was exactly the type of vague, incontestable response that settles any argument.

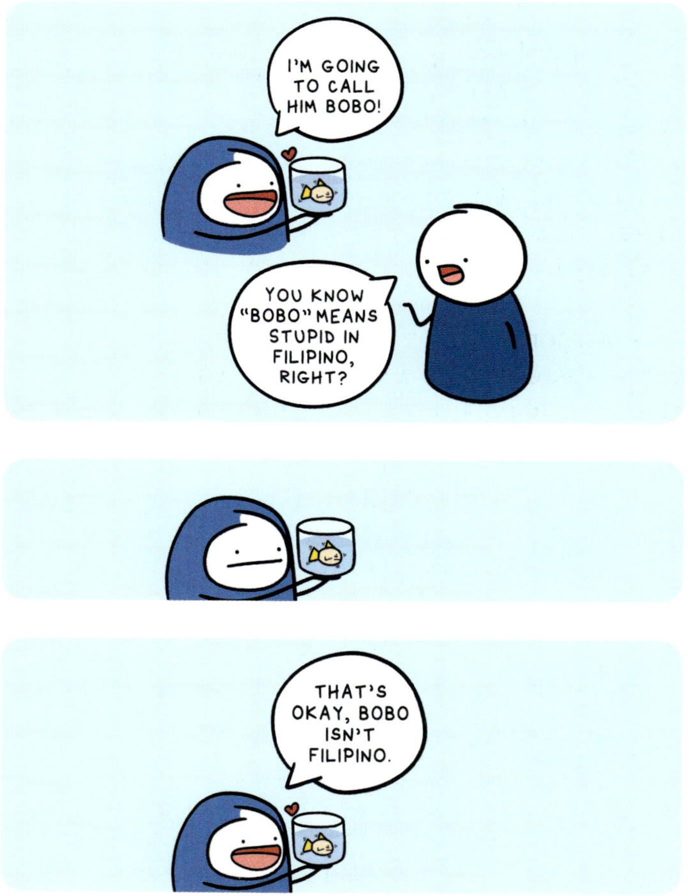
I'M GOING TO CALL HIM BOBO!
YOU KNOW "BOBO" MEANS STUPID IN FILIPINO, RIGHT?
THAT'S OKAY, BOBO ISN'T FILIPINO.

It's easy to love things that are beautiful, but Bobo was far from beautiful. While the other fish in his tank had shimmering, buttercup-yellow scales that effortlessly glistened with every movement in the water, Bobo's coat was more of a dull mustard color. Even as he anxiously darted from one corner of the tank to the other, his scales shimmered half-heartedly, as though they had long given up on the facade of beauty.

This simply made me adore him even more.

"Well you see, he's *ugly* cute," I would later explain to people who never asked. It was a label that acknowledged his homely looks, but also insisted there was some redeeming beauty to be slowly uncovered, like an acquired taste for your eyes.

As a welcome gift to his new home, I bought Bobo some tasteful aquarium decor—shamrock-green, clear plastic aquarium plants and a rock with a hole in it—no expense was spared.

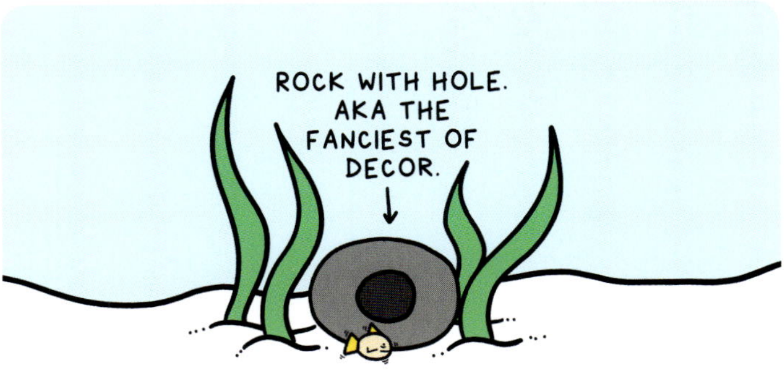
ROCK WITH HOLE.
AKA THE
FANCIEST OF
DECOR.

I was weirdly obsessed with the idea of Bobo swimming inside the rock for naps, but he never actually ended up doing so. That's the thing with pet fish—they tend not to care about what you want them to do. They also don't really do anything at all.

Nevertheless, I was enamored.

FISH DOING NOTHING.

STILL DOING NOTHING.

STILL NOTHING.

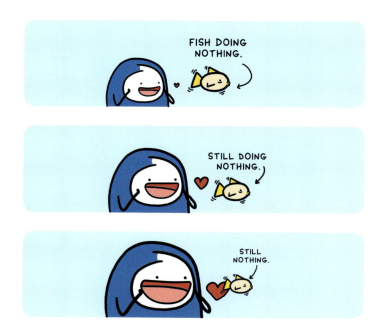

On the first night of his arrival, I read Bobo a bedtime story.

MR. AND MRS. DURSLEY OF NUMBER FOUR, PRIVET DRIVE, WERE PROUD TO SAY THAT THEY WERE PERFECTLY NORMAL, THANK YOU VERY MUCH.

On the second day, I played him his favorite music—the soundtrack from *Harry Potter and the Sorcerer's Stone*.

On the third day, Bobo died.

BOBO! I BOUGHT YOU BOTH PELLETS AND FLAKES BECAUSE I DIDN'T KNOW WHICH ONE YOU LIKE MORE...

BOBO?! BOBO?!?
DEADEST LOOKING FISH.

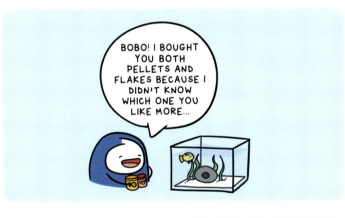

DEAD.
FLEETINGLY CONSIDERS CPR.
STILL DEAD.
DECIDES AGAINST IT.
DEAD BUT RELIEVED.

After hearing about Bobo's untimely demise, my friend suggested that I bring Bobo back to the store to get a refund. They had a policy that if your pet dies within seven days or less, you can return it. No questions asked. But the idea of bringing a dead Bobo back to the store in a little Ziploc bag depressed me. I didn't want to feel Bobo's lifeless body slipping around in a clear plastic bag designed for peanut butter and jelly sandwiches. And the idea that people brought dead pets back to the store at all saddened me even further. Bobo deserved better than that.

So instead, I sent him back to the ocean.

I DON'T THINK YOU'RE SUPPOSED TO FLUSH YOUR DEAD FISH.

BOBO WOULD HAVE WANTED THIS.
FLUSH

I spent the next thirty days grieving Bobo with an empty aquarium.

HEY, YOU KNOW WHAT WOULD BE FUN? GETTING A PET.

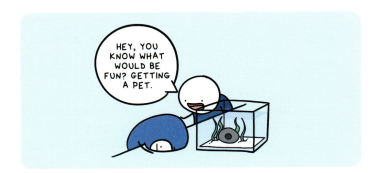

I ALREADY HAVE ONE.
EMPTY TANK

LET'S GO. YOU NEED SOMETHING TO LOVE.

When we returned to the store, I reluctantly walked towards their fish aisle. None of the fish were good enough—they all swam normally.

UPPITY LITTLE...

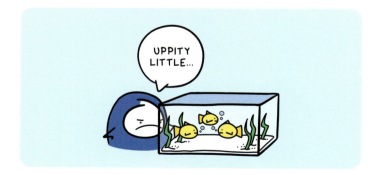

It was as though merely by existing, the fish offended me.

Seeing that I was hell-bent on being an unreasonable judge of fish character that day, my friend beckoned me to a neon purple-and-green tank in the middle of the store. The tank must have been new, because I hadn't seen it before, or maybe I just never really looked.

COME LOOK! THEY HAVE AFRICAN DWARF FROGS!
I DON'T CARE ABOUT FROGS.

UGH. THIS ONE WEIRD FROG KEEPS DARTING AROUND AND SWIMMING CRAZY.
WHERE? SHOW ME!

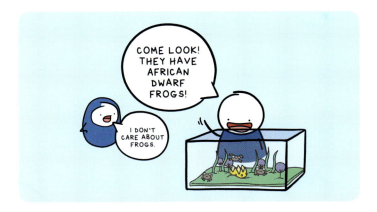

At first glance, the tank came off a bit ostentatious. Upon second glance, it most definitely was. *Strike*

*one*, I thought to myself. The water in the tank was surprisingly clear despite the large army of speckled greyish-brown African dwarf frogs that occupied it. The sign next to the tank explained that these were aquatic frogs, meaning they're the type of frogs that live underwater—they were basically fish, but not fish.

My friend really wanted me to move on from being a weirdo with an empty tank, so she started selling me hard on the idea of getting a pet frog.

"You know . . . the frogs are actually *cheaper* than Bobo!" she offered with a helpful smile.

My friend didn't get it. It wasn't about *the money*—after all, things that matter rarely ever are—and as I opened my mouth to present this rebuttal, the frog that had previously been darting around gleefully suddenly hurled its chubby little body against the glass walls of the tank with a tiny but dramatic *flop*.

*How peculiar*, I thought.

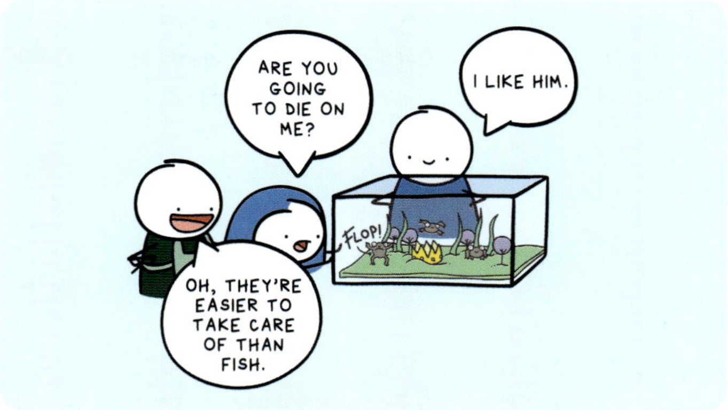
OH, THEY'RE EASIER TO TAKE CARE OF THAN FISH.
FLOP!
ARE YOU GOING TO DIE ON ME?
I LIKE HIM.

When I brought the peculiar frog home, I was determined not to love him. It's hard to give your heart to something when you're not sure how long things will last. The pain of Bobo's untimely death was still fresh in my mind and I just wasn't ready to read Harry Potter bedtime stories again—not yet at least.

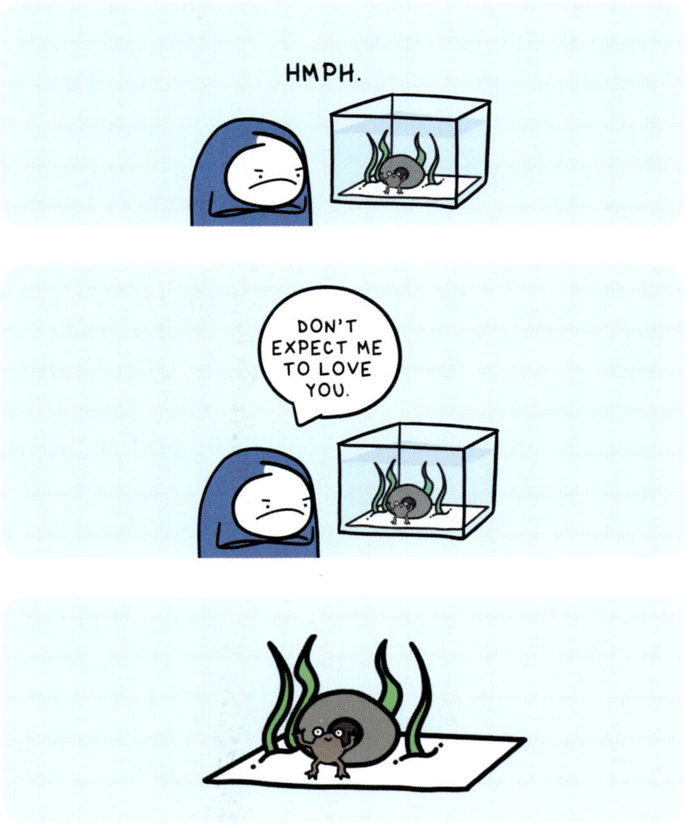
HMPH.
DON'T EXPECT ME TO LOVE YOU.

But the frog proved to be much hardier than Bobo, and over time, this endeared him to me. After a few weeks, I gave in and named him Harry.

I realized Harry was a male frog after some research because he had subdermal glands—little bumps that protruded behind his front legs. Beyond that, there was little to no literature available on African dwarf frogs. Most of the information available online was from websites or blogs created by pet owners or enthusiasts and the "facts" fluctuated wildly from source to source.

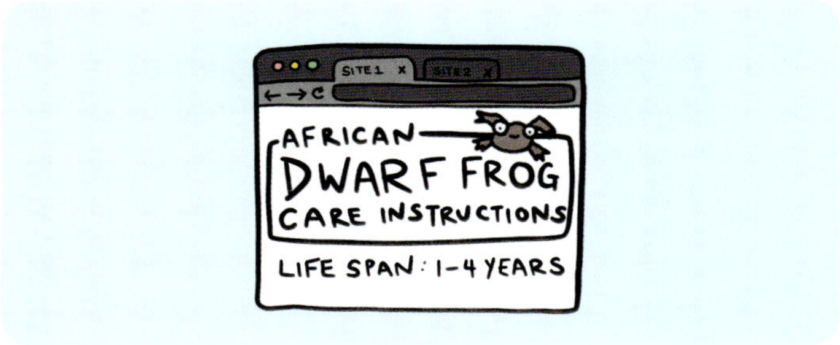
SITE 1
SITE 2
AFRICAN
DWARF FROG
CARE INSTRUCTIONS
LIFE SPAN: 1-4 YEARS

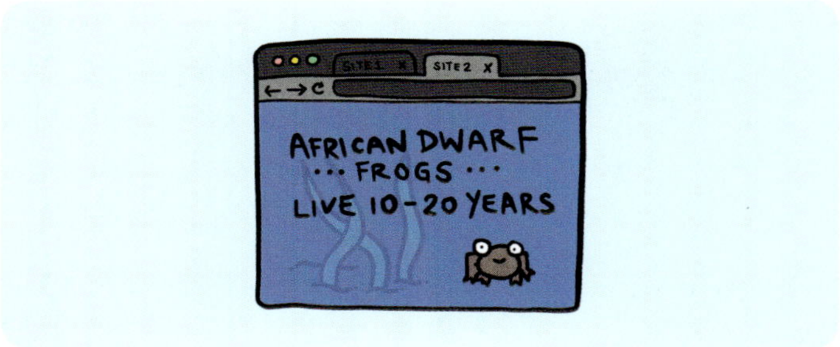
SITE 1
SITE 2
AFRICAN DWARF
... FROGS ...
LIVE 10-20 YEARS

It had been a long time since I had discovered a topic that the internet knew little to nothing about, and the novelty of this excited me. For once, I didn't know things with absolute certainty. It was humbling and riveting in the nerdiest sense. Without a single source of truth to rely on, I simply chose to believe in the good things. Because why not?

HARRY! YOU'RE GOING TO LIVE 1-20 YEARS!

Within two months, I had become obsessed with Harry—the same way owners of cats, dogs, or children often are. I had become that which I mocked, a doting parent beguiled by their child, and Harry became the rising star of my Instagram.

@BARELYFUNCTIONALADULT
HARRY BEING CUTE
@BARELYFUNCTIONALADULT
HARRY STANDING CUTE
@BARELYFUNCTIONALADULT
HARRY EXISTING CUTE

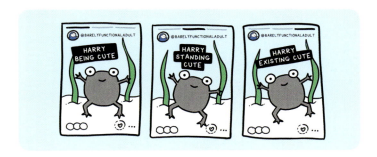

As with most updates of pets and children, it was all mostly the same repetitive nonsense.

Through further research and observation, I learned that African dwarf frogs are tiny when they're young, and remain minuscule as they mature. Unlike human offspring, who are too often prone to outgrowing their charm as they move through adolescence, Harry was adorable as a froglet and promised to remain as such even through adulthood. Something about this level of consistency and predictability felt comforting to me.

Harry also stood up a lot, as though he were about to say something truly profound. But of course, after capturing my undivided attention, he never quite managed to say anything at all. Wondering if this was just his way of asking for my affection, I would put my finger against the tank to remind him that he always had it. At night, like most male African dwarf frogs, Harry would sing. I often wondered if he wanted backup singers, so at times, I would play Backstreet Boys for him.

He probably hated it.

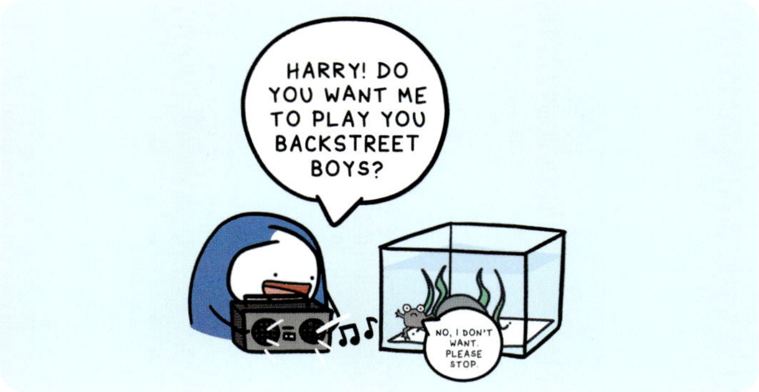
HARRY! DO YOU WANT ME TO PLAY YOU BACKSTREET BOYS?
NO, I DON'T WANT. PLEASE STOP.

After a few weeks of hearing Harry's poignant melodies, I started to worry if Harry was lonely—a type of lonely that even Backstreet Boys couldn't cure. I wanted to buy Harry a female frog, but I didn't want to constantly deal with an influx of frog babies. Something told me I wouldn't exactly thrive as a frog grandparent.

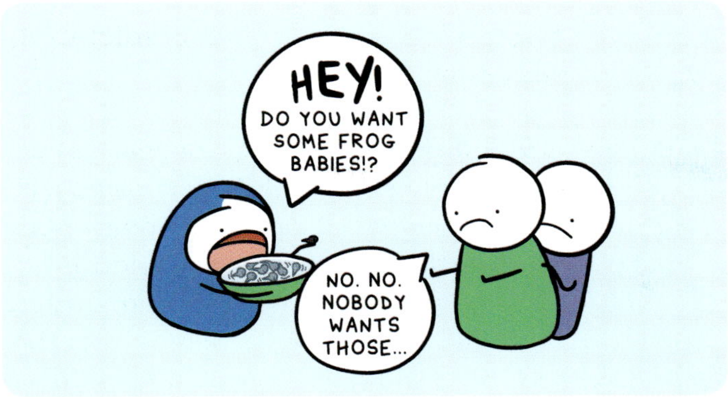
HEY! DO YOU WANT SOME FROG BABIES!?
NO. NO. NOBODY WANTS THOSE...

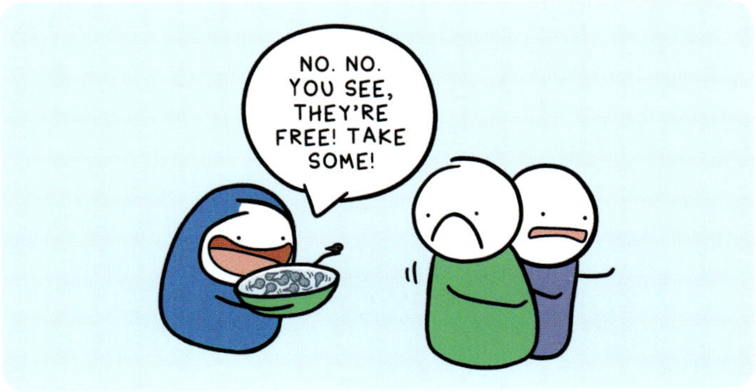
NO. NO. YOU SEE, THEY'RE FREE! TAKE SOME!

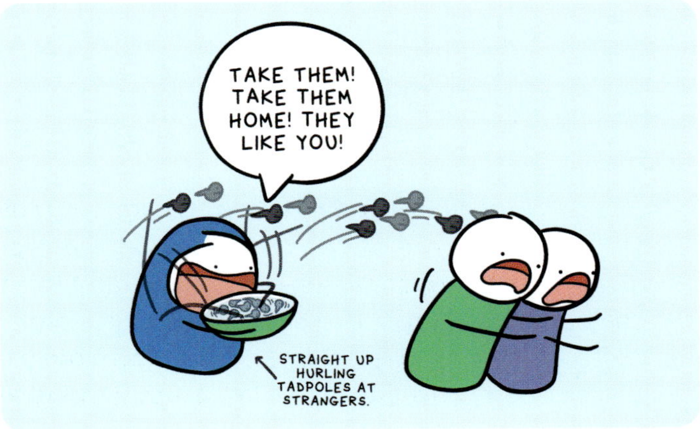
TAKE THEM! TAKE THEM HOME! THEY LIKE YOU!
STRAIGHT UP HURLING TADPOLES AT STRANGERS.

So instead, I bought Harry a boyfriend.

The new frog proved problematic from the start. Upon taking him home from the pet store, I saw that he had suddenly developed reddish legs—so I googled it.

> Forum 1 Diagnosis: *"Probably dying or contagious . . . or both."*
> Forum 2 Diagnosis: *"He's probably already dead."*
> Me: *"But he seems alive."*
> Forum 2 Diagnosis: *"Naw, he's dead."*

Unsurprisingly, the internet diagnoses gave me little clarity, and a lot of anxiety. To be safe, I decided to put the new frog in a separate tank just in case.

*WHISPERS* MAYBE YOU SHOULD JUST RETURN IT.
BUT THEY'LL KILL HIM! I'M SCARED HE'LL INFECT HARRY THOUGH.
NEW FROG IN TEMPORARY HOUSING.

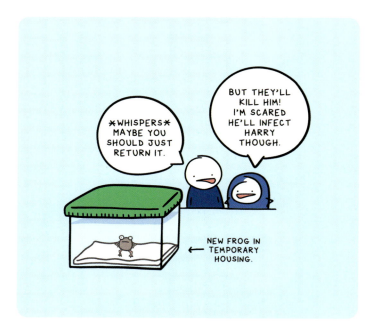

WELL, DO YOU WANT TO KILL HIM?
NOBODY IS KILLING ANYTHING!

I started to wonder if I had made a terrible mistake. Maybe it was wrong of me to get a second frog. Maybe one was enough. Maybe I had Icarus'ed and flown too close to the sun. I started to wonder if my parents felt the same way when they had me.

LICK

HEHE.

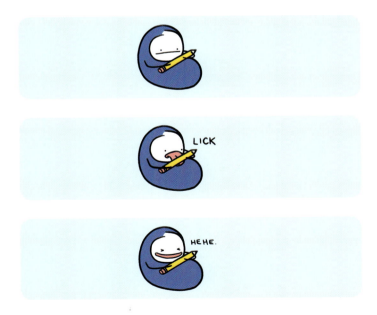

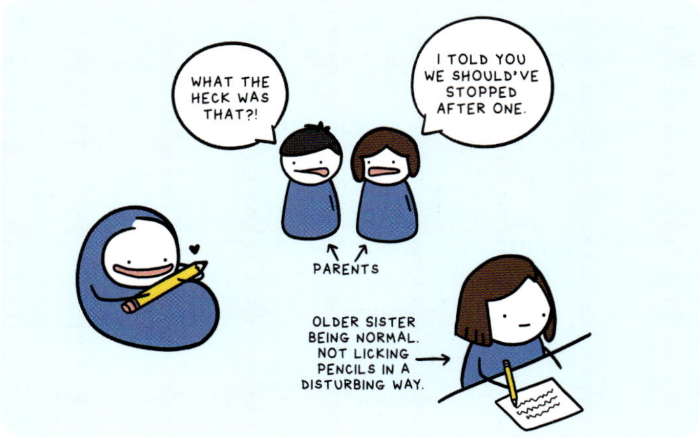
WHAT THE HECK WAS THAT?!
I TOLD YOU WE SHOULD'VE STOPPED AFTER ONE.
PARENTS
OLDER SISTER BEING NORMAL. NOT LICKING PENCILS IN A DISTURBING WAY.

I named the new frog "Vlad" and continued to monitor him while he lived in the intensive care unit I had designed specifically for his inscrutable needs. Every day for a week, I waited for Vlad to die from his internet-diagnosed infection. But when he remained very much alive after two weeks of obsessive observation, I modified his "dying" status to "actually perfectly healthy," and made plans to introduce him into Harry's tank. It was a miracle, or a total misdiagnosis, one of those two things.

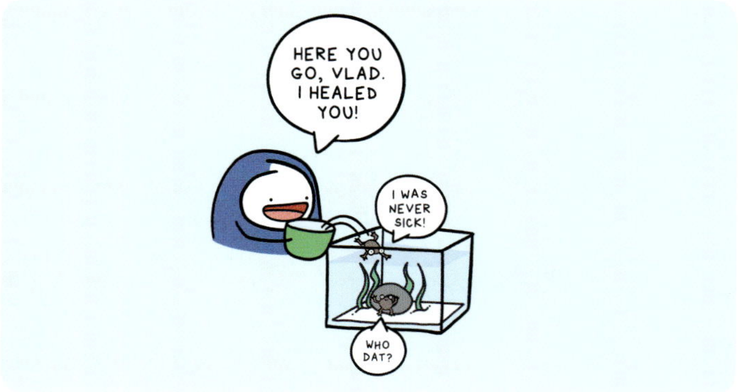
HERE YOU GO, VLAD. I HEALED YOU!
I WAS NEVER SICK!
WHO DAT?

In the week following Vlad's integration into Harry's tank, everything was perfect. There was no longer redness to be seen in Vlad's legs, I could tell the two of them apart based on a special pattern that only Harry had on his arm, and Vlad would even occasionally swim into the rock with the hole, only to charmingly pop his head out when I called out his name. For one glorious week, I had a clean break from my parental anxieties.

On the second week, however, Vlad decided to pull this little rabbit out of his hat.

VLAD TOTALLY FINE.
SUDDEN REDNESS APPEARS.
REDNESS BECOMES BULGE.
SUPER GIANT RED BUTT GROWTH.

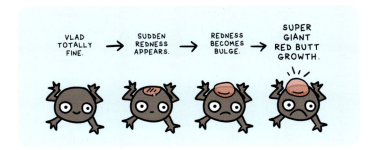

I panicked. I panicked hard. The way one does when one's previously healthy pet frog spontaneously decides to develop a noxious, sizeable red growth on its butt.

HARRY
VLAD

IS VLAD INFECTIOUS? IS HE GOING TO GET HARRY SICK? SHOULD I TAKE HIM OUT OF THE TANK?

WELL IF HE IS, HARRY WOULD ALREADY BE SICK.

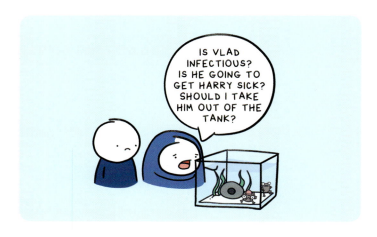

I tried to find a specialist for Vlad, but none of the vets I called knew how to care for African dwarf frogs—they were simply too low on the totem pole of life. I considered moving Vlad back to his ICU, but he looked weak, as though he was already nearing the end of it. Without better options available, I decided to keep Vlad in the main tank so that he could at least die next to a friend. It was Bobo all over again, but this time in slow motion.

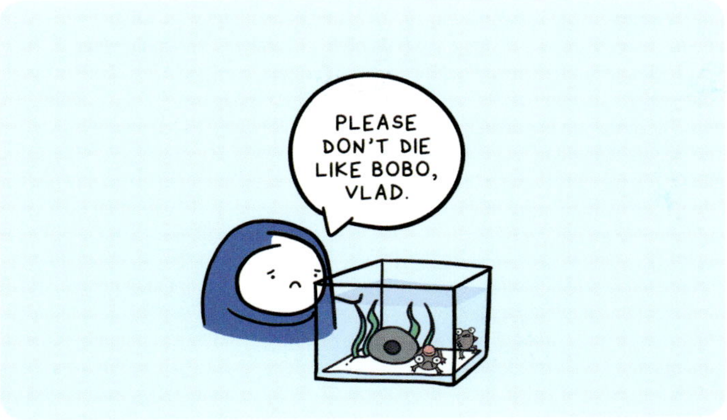
PLEASE
DON'T DIE
LIKE BOBO,
VLAD.

Over the next few days, the growth on Vlad's butt got bigger and bigger. It would've been funny had he not been dying so visibly in front of me. Within a week, Vlad stopped eating altogether and began floating around a lot. Not in the adorable, buoyant sprawl African dwarf frogs often drift in, but in a worrisome way, more reminiscent of Bobo's final moments. At times, Vlad would simply collapse near Harry and sit quietly at his side. I think he enjoyed Harry's company.

But Harry was a bad boyfriend.

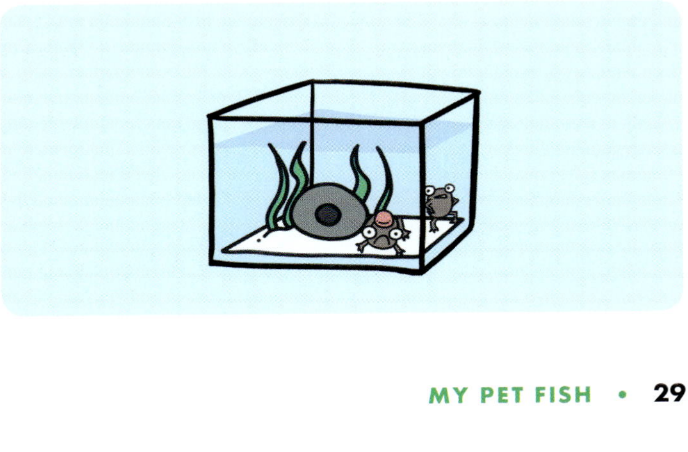

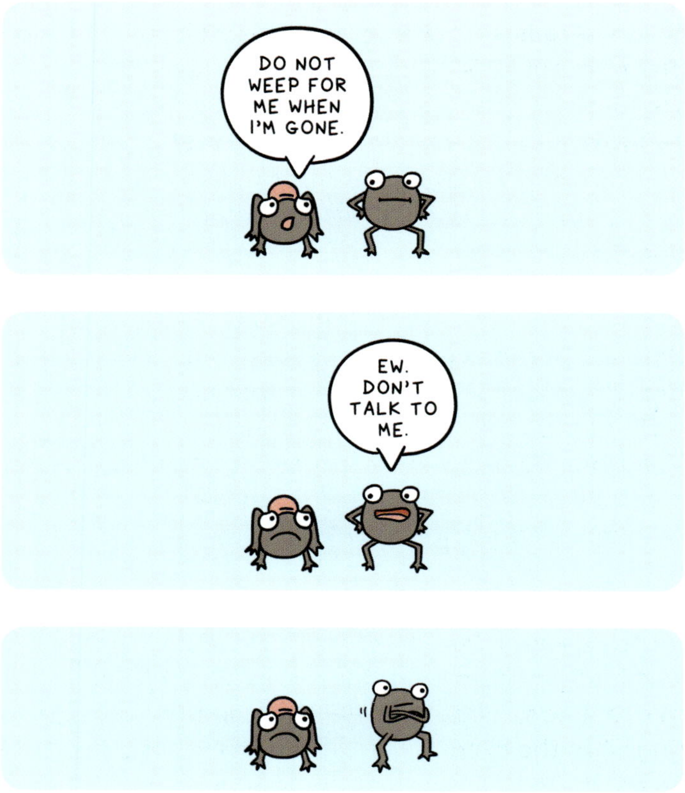
DO NOT WEEP FOR ME WHEN I'M GONE.
EW. DON'T TALK TO ME.

Vlad seemed lonely as he awaited his imminent death. I would often find him sitting by himself in the back corner of the tank, veiled in a stillness that worried me. In an attempt to alleviate his suffering, I put Harry's stuffed frog, Potter, next to Vlad in hopes of making him feel better. Potter was a small, National Geographic McDonald's Happy Meal plushie my sister had given me a while back. It was the kind of gift that might have felt like junk to someone else, but to me, it was a reminder that she fundamentally understood who I was as a person. There is something to be said about the people who are able to give us the exact kind of junk we love. Not the expensive gifts, because anyone can give those, but the inexpensive ones, the crap no one would steal if we left it out in our cars, the worthless but priceless totems that remind us we are seen.

Vlad appreciated Potter, but it felt childish to think that a stuffed frog could soften his suffering. It broke my heart a little to know that no gift, however well-intentioned, would really make a difference for Vlad. But I didn't know how else to help, so Potter, carefully propped up against the side of Vlad's tank, became his guardian angel.

Every night, I sat next to Vlad and read him a chapter from *Harry Potter and the Half-Blood Prince*—it was his favorite out of the series. When Vlad swam out to listen, I would pet him by gently moving my finger on the other side of the glass in parallel to his head. At this, Vlad would always muster a feeble smile. I didn't know how to make him feel better or less scared in his final moments, but it felt important to remind him he wasn't alone.

At the end of it all, Vlad's cryptic growth was more than a third of his total body mass. One evening, I came home to discover Vlad floating morbidly still at the top of the tank. I thought knowing that this moment would come would somehow lessen the pain of it when it did—but it didn't. I took a breath to steady myself before moving to fish Vlad out with a net. It was time. He looked very dead.

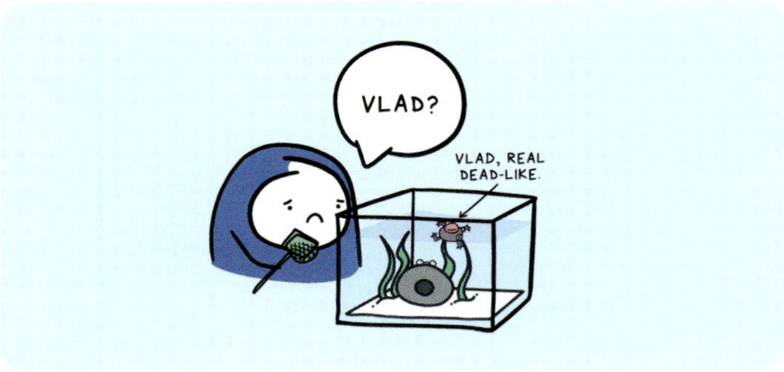
VLAD?
VLAD, REAL DEAD-LIKE.

But as I was fishing Vlad out, he suddenly jolted alive, and scurried down to the bottom of the tank.

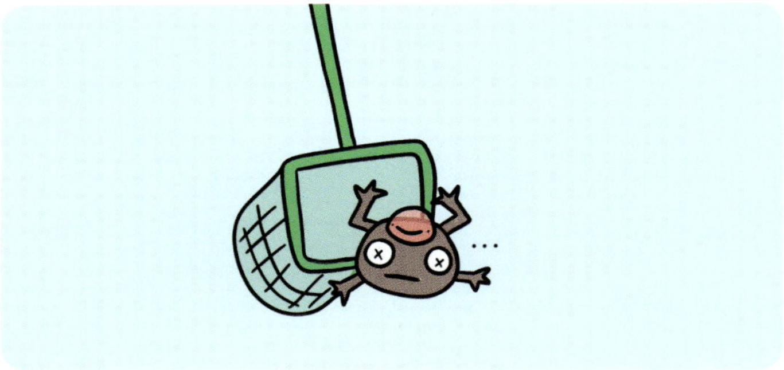
...

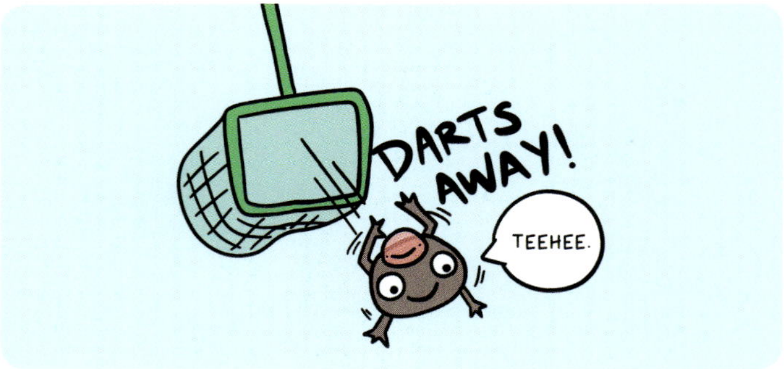
DARTS AWAY!
TEEHEE.

What happened next, I can never unsee.

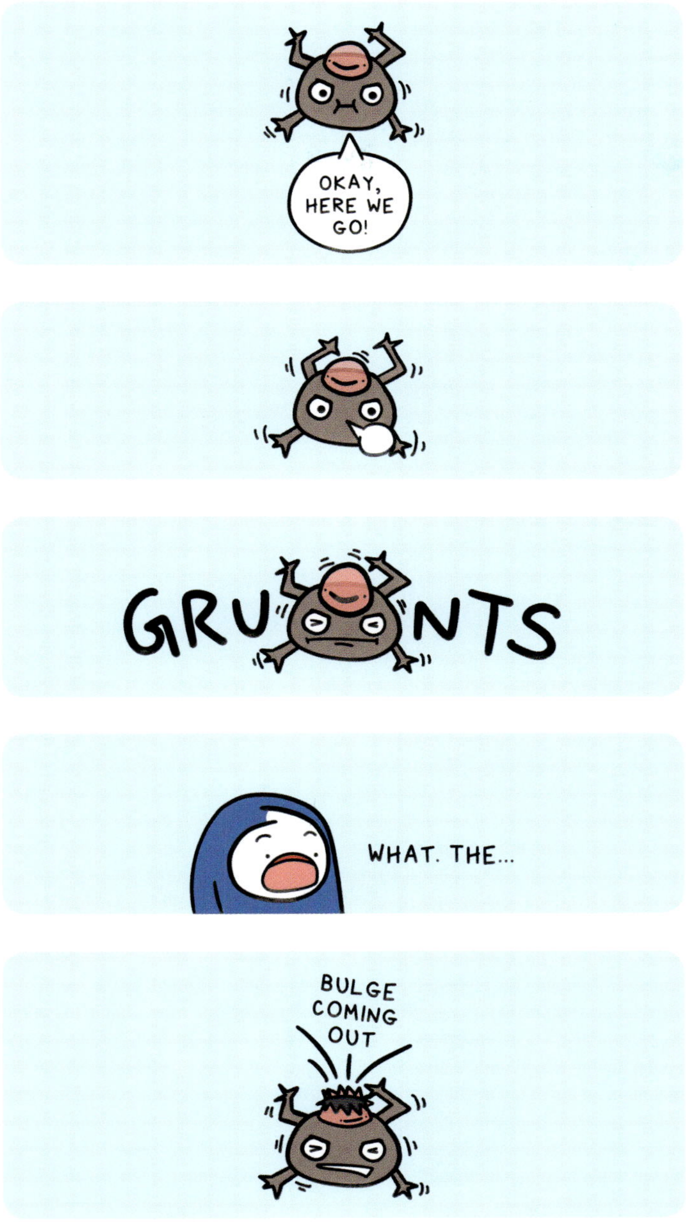
OKAY, HERE WE GO!
GRUNTS
WHAT. THE...
BULGE COMING OUT

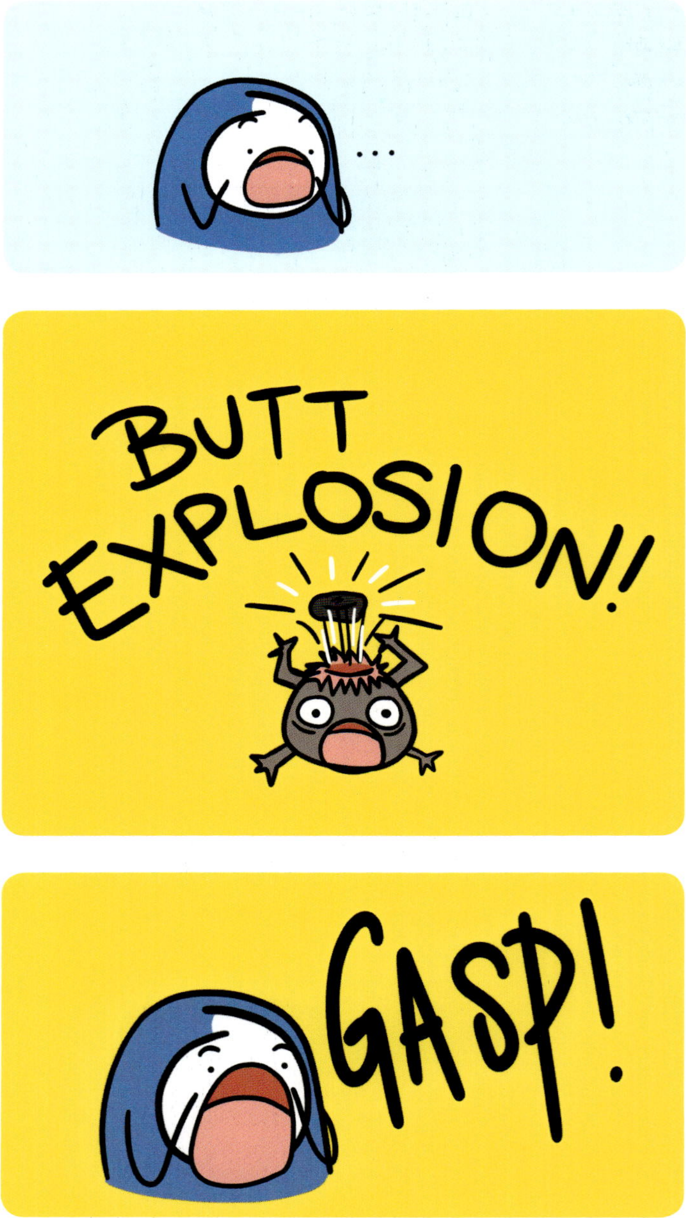
...
BUTT EXPLOSION!
GASP!

SPEECHLESS
PEBBLE THAT WAS IN BUTT MOMENTS AGO.
RECTUM DESTROYED.
ME AND HARRY.
VLAD SUPER PLEASED WITH SELF.

SPEECHLESS

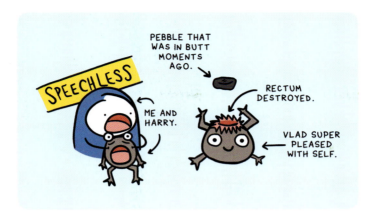

After I recovered from the trauma of witnessing this display of . . . whatever it was that I had just witnessed, I started to string together the series of events that must have led to my pet frog having a sudden and horrifying rectal explosion.

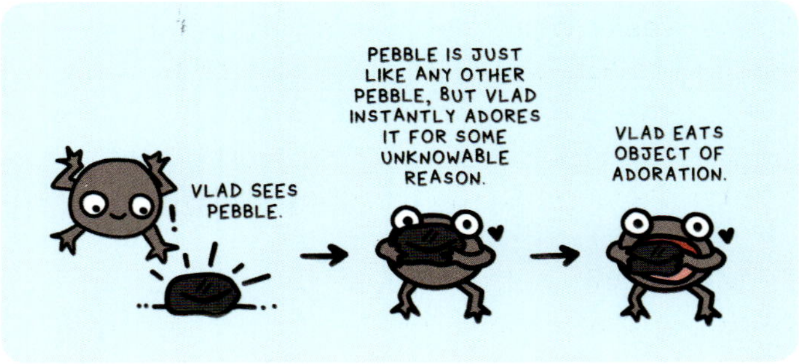
VLAD SEES PEBBLE.
PEBBLE IS JUST LIKE ANY OTHER PEBBLE, BUT VLAD INSTANTLY ADORES IT FOR SOME UNKNOWABLE REASON.
VLAD EATS OBJECT OF ADORATION.

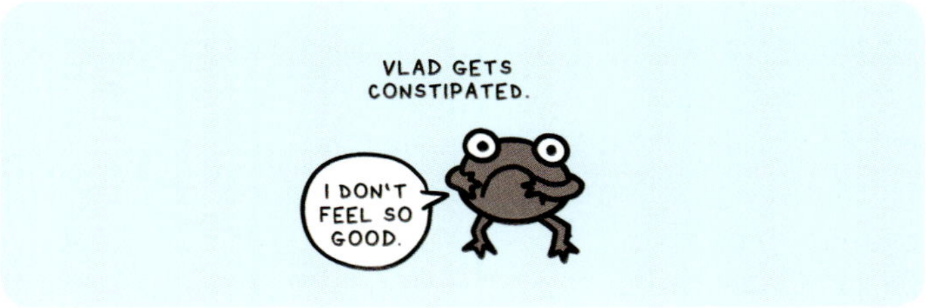
VLAD GETS CONSTIPATED.
I DON'T FEEL SO GOOD.

And the rest is . . . going to be discussed extensively in therapy.

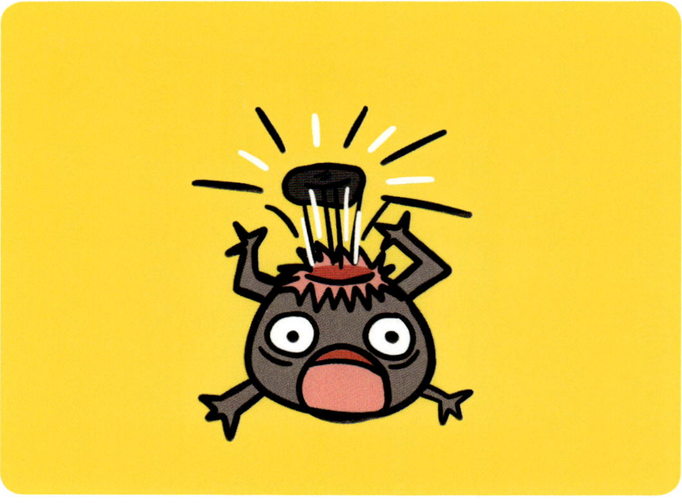

In the weeks when I was at my peak stress levels tending to Harry and Vlad, I would often dream of a life where I had done it all differently. A beautiful parallel universe where I had simply chosen a normal-looking fish that first day at the pet store.

"*Wow.* I can't believe you're actually choosing a healthy, normal-looking fish," my friend would say to me in this parallel universe fantasy. She is impressed by my uncharacteristically responsible decision-making. I acknowledge her praise with a smile as I gesture towards one particularly normal-looking fish at the front of the tank. The staff member helping us nods in approval of my choice and moves to fish it out. The fish I've chosen is swimming effortlessly with shimmering, buttercup-yellow scales that glisten with its every movement in the water. It is, in all respects, the perfect fish. In this version of events, I take home the rectal explosion–free pet and live a normal, peaceful, rectal explosion–free life. I imagine it to be a nice life.

But the problem with daydreaming about parallel-universe narratives is that you can never be certain how great alternate timelines would have played out. Would normalcy really have been that wonderful? Or would it have been unbearably dull? Would I *really* have been happy with this "perfect" normal-looking pet companion? Who knows. But something tells me that life has a habit of never quite panning out as planned. It's fickle, it's messy, and sometimes there are frog rectal explosions.

You just gotta roll with it.

Here are two photos of Vlad and Harry taken years after the rectal-explosion incident (they're both doing fine now by the way). The photo on the right makes them look like Anna Kendrick and Rebel Wilson getting worked up for a riff off—a pose they seem partial to as they are often found in this state.

And you wouldn't look for it without first hearing the story, but Vlad actually has a barely perceptible tiny white scar at the root of his butt. It is a symbol that he is at once a survivor, and an idiot.

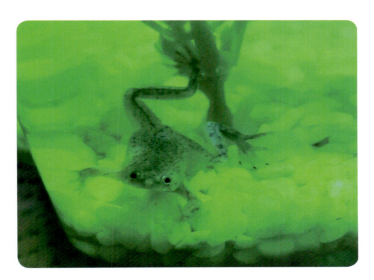

# CHAPTER 2

# GUM

At some point in my life, I found a piece of gum stuck on me.

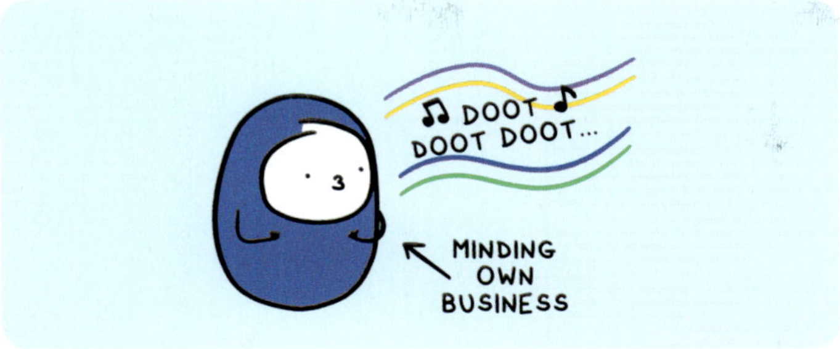
♫ DOOT ♪
DOOT DOOT...
MINDING
OWN
BUSINESS

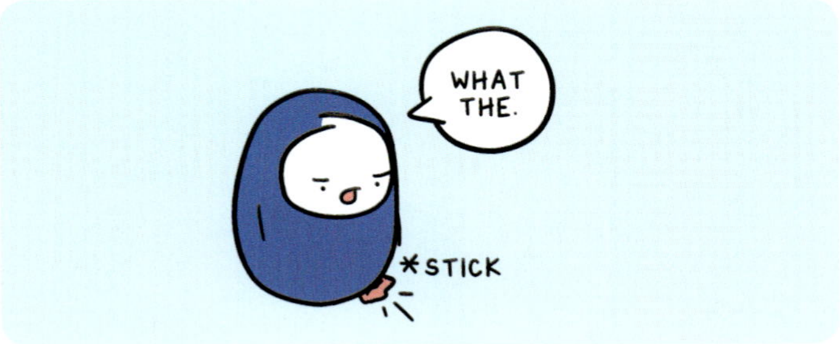
WHAT
THE.
*STICK

At first, the gum was merely stuck on my shoe.

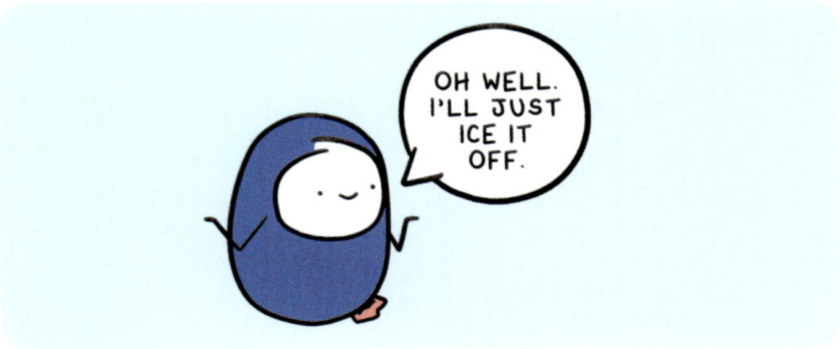
OH WELL.
I'LL JUST
ICE IT
OFF.

So I didn't think much of it.

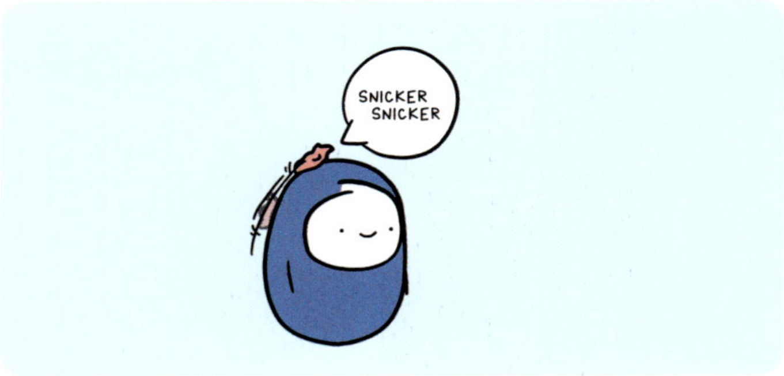
SNICKER
SNICKER

But then the gum got stuck in my hair.

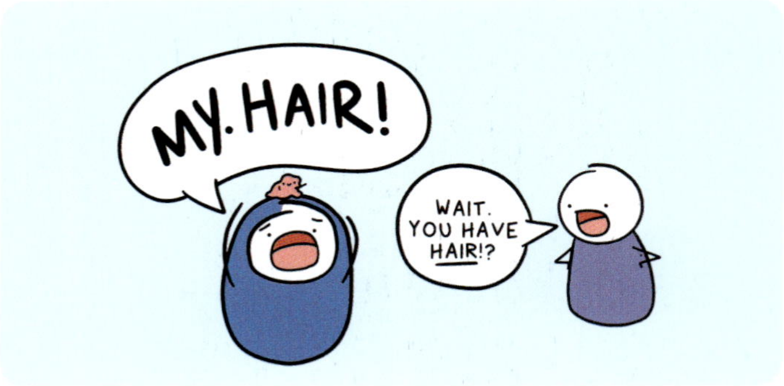
MY. HAIR!
WAIT.
YOU HAVE
HAIR!?

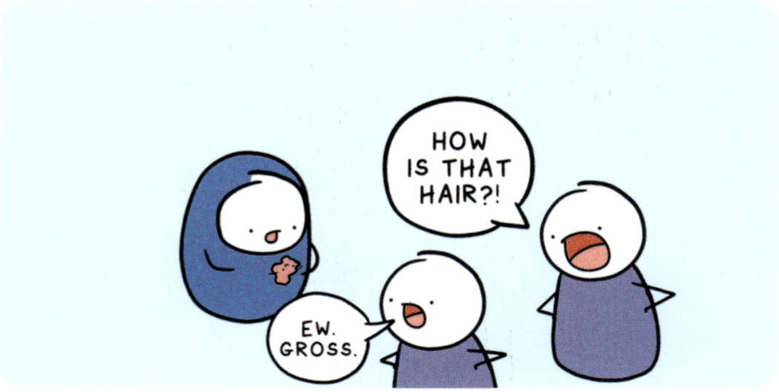
HOW
IS THAT
HAIR?!
EW.
GROSS.

This piece of gum is also known as my ex.

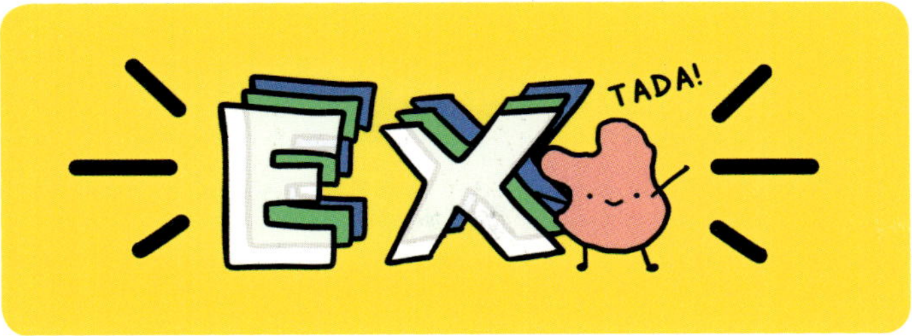
EX
TADA!

And not just any ex, *the* Ex, the Ex with the capital E. The kind of Ex whose name you don't like to hear said out loud. Most people have at least one of these.*

Over the course of our lives, most of the people we meet don't really play that big of a part in our story.

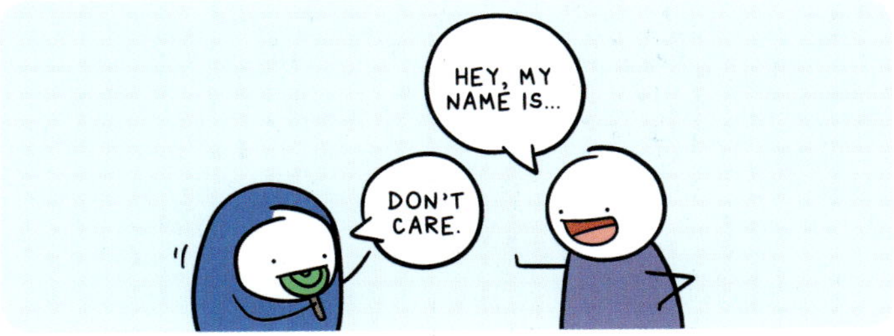
HEY, MY NAME IS...
DON'T CARE.

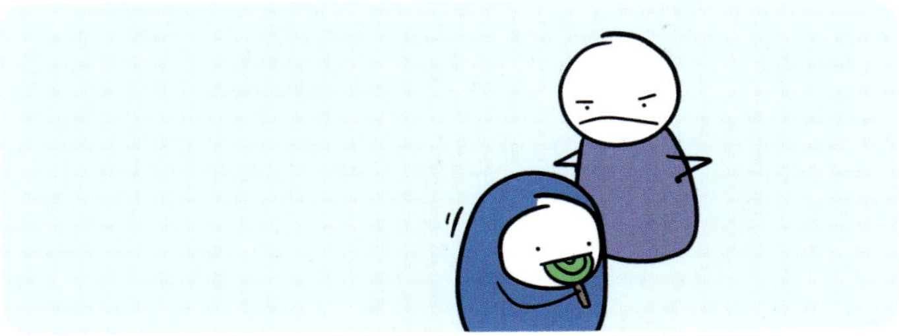

---

* If you have somehow magically lived your life without ever getting any gum stuck on you, then I wholeheartedly congratulate you on this feat, you majestic unicorn.

Even when it comes to relationships, there are some exes we never really think about—the ones who come and go after a mere three-episode arc, unremarkable and forgettable to say the least. But every now and then, someone sticks.

Gum was one of those people.

• • •

Like most first loves, the love I had for Gum was the kind of love that felt effortless. I arrived empty-handed, no emotional baggage in sight, and dove head-first into our relationship without a second thought. When Gum told me, "I'll love you forever," I believed it. Because when your first love tells you they love you, there's no reason to doubt it. And when I responded, "I'll love you forever too," I meant it in equal measure.

I LOVE YOU.
THANKS, I LOVE YOU TOO.
PEW! PEW!

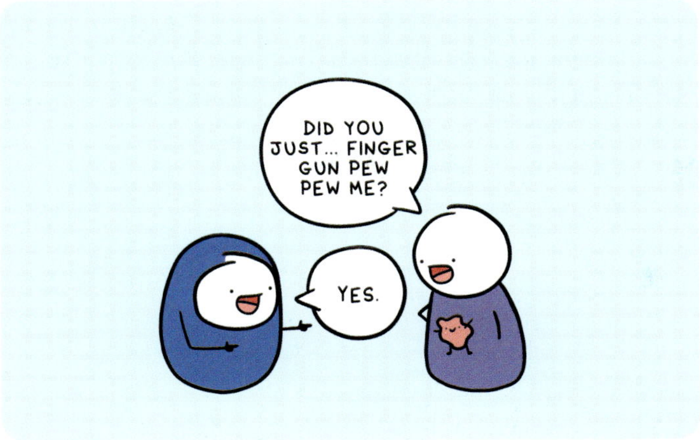
DID YOU JUST... FINGER GUN PEW PEW ME?
YES.

My love for Gum was instant. It's easy to fall in love when you've never been heartbroken before. After all, I was emotionally invincible, a quality I never fully appreciated at the time. Every feeling with Gum felt so uncalibrated—the highs were so high, and the lows were so low—I don't think we ever get that back. That unparalleled high that only comes with first loves. It's the kind of high you could spend your life chasing.

In total, Gum and I dated for maybe half a year? That's barely the gestation period for an anaconda. Six. Measly. Months. But oh, the damage that can be done in six measly months. I spent the years that followed feeling silly that someone was able to make such a lasting impact on my life in such a short period of time, but I've since learned that time and impact are disturbingly uncorrelated when it comes to the people we love.

Gum and I broke up on a Friday. I remember this because I spent the next three days sobbing into my pillow while listening to Bruno Mars on repeat.

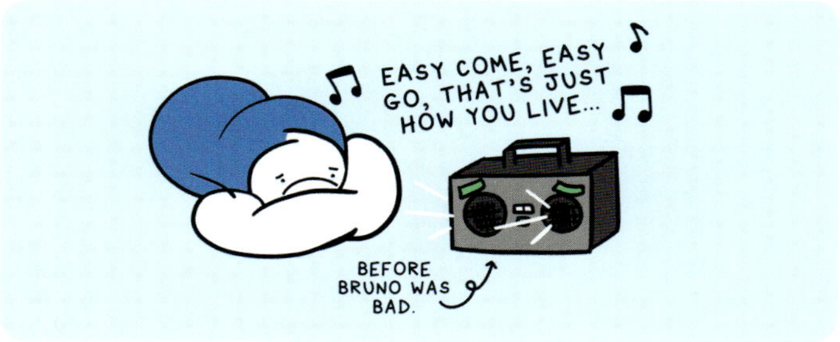
EASY COME, EASY GO, THAT'S JUST HOW YOU LIVE...
BEFORE BRUNO WAS BAD.

Oh, the melodrama of youth.

It was a breakup that was mutually agreed upon, but just because a breakup is mutual doesn't mean it hurts any less. Some breakups are indiscriminately destructive—everyone gets hurt regardless of the part they played. After a week of heartbreak, I started doing the math—Relationship Math.

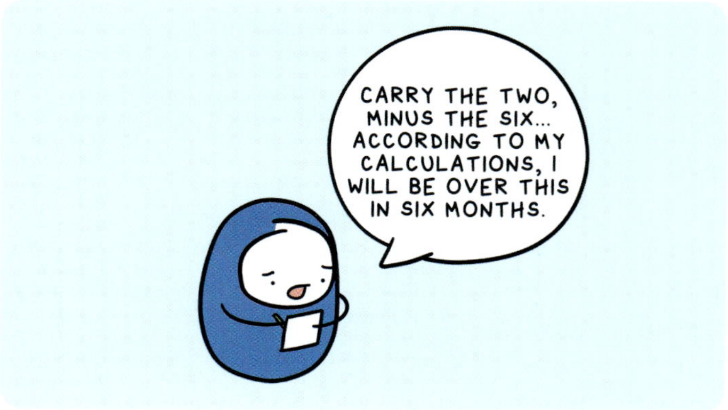
CARRY THE TWO, MINUS THE SIX... ACCORDING TO MY CALCULATIONS, I WILL BE OVER THIS IN SIX MONTHS.

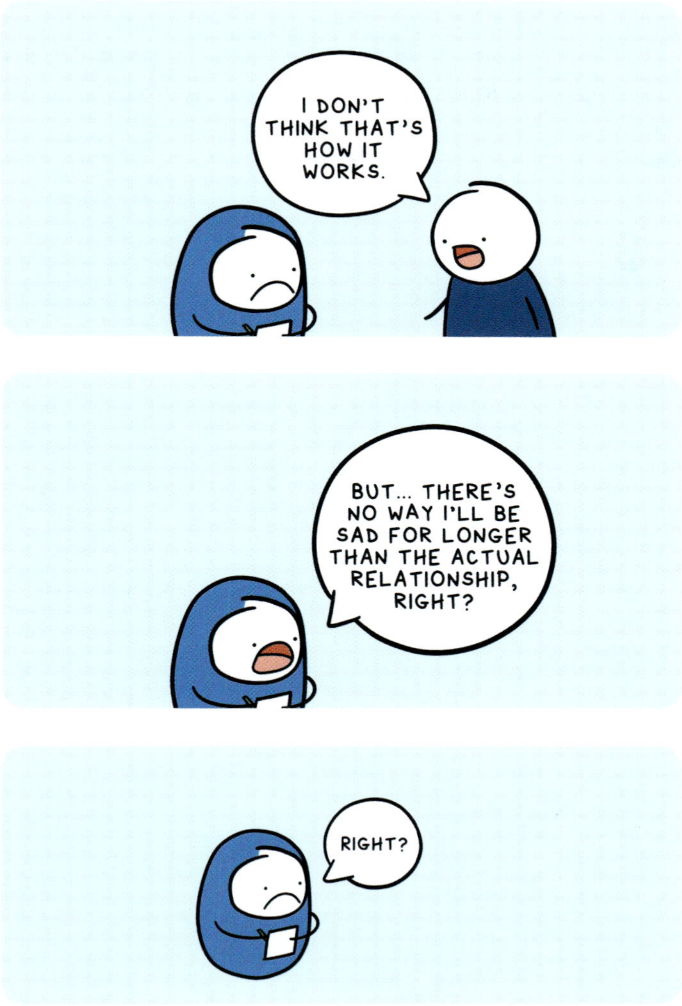
I DON'T THINK THAT'S HOW IT WORKS.
BUT... THERE'S NO WAY I'LL BE SAD FOR LONGER THAN THE ACTUAL RELATIONSHIP, RIGHT?
RIGHT?

For six months, I was devastated. For six months, I grieved our relationship. Gum grieved too. But grief presents itself as different monsters for different people. For me, grief came in the form of pretending everything was okay even when it was clearly not. It was as though I was trying to trick myself into feeling better. *If I outwardly act okay, I might inwardly feel okay.* It was a noble aspiration but fell short of its mark in execution.

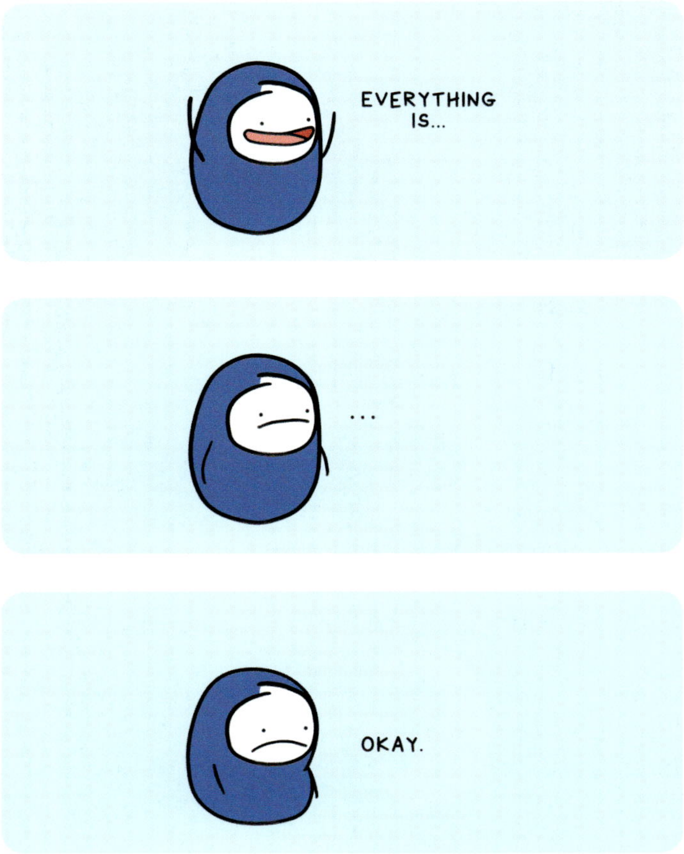
EVERYTHING IS...
...
OKAY.

For Gum, grief came in the form of rallying the village people to burn me at the stake for the demise of our relationship. In Gum's narrative, I was the villain.

So much for mutual.

I was young and ill-equipped to handle the gaslight-ing that was about to ensue. On a post-breakup call, Gum planted a small, but insidious, seed: "I'll love you forever . . . but you don't deserve to be loved."

And then Gum hung up before I could respond.

At first, I recognized it was only Gum's grief speak-ing. *People say things they don't mean when they're hurt*, I reminded myself. But as time passed, I lost this shield of reason, and the seeds of doubt started to take root. *Was Gum right? Was I undeserving of love? Was this the only person who would ever love me? Was I to blame for the demise of it all?*

When you are repeatedly told a lie by someone you love, your grasp on the truth tends to weaken.

TRUTH.
TRUTH
LIES
LIES
LIES
TRUTH
LIES
TRUTH?
LIES
LIES

Six months passed, but I didn't feel any better. I had failed in my Relationship Math (just like real math, I guess). If anything, I was somehow feeling *worse*.

Gum was still stuck on me. Or maybe it was I who was now stuck on Gum. Everywhere I went, I was reminded of our relationship.

When our songs came on the radio, I would find Gum in my ears.

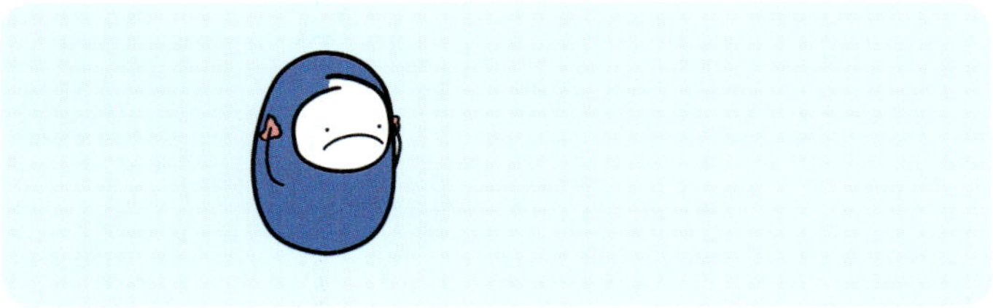

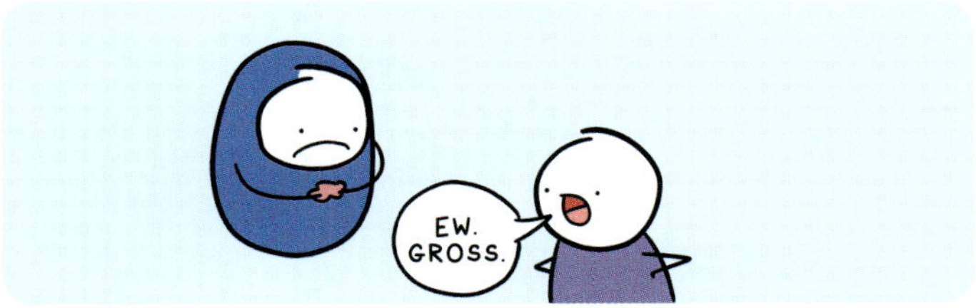
EW. GROSS.

When I went to my favorite place in the city, I would be reminded of all the times Gum and I had gone there too.

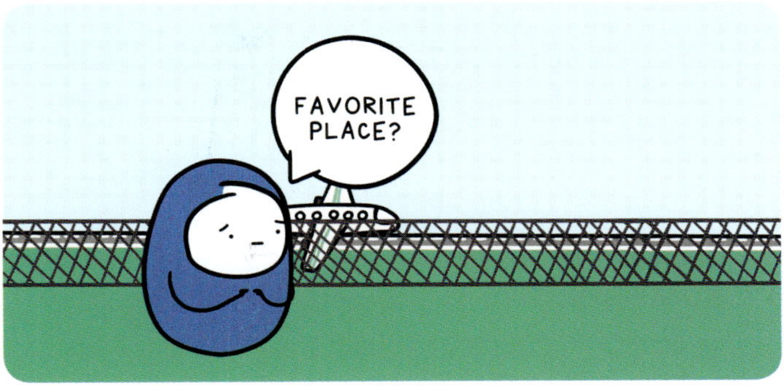
FAVORITE PLACE?

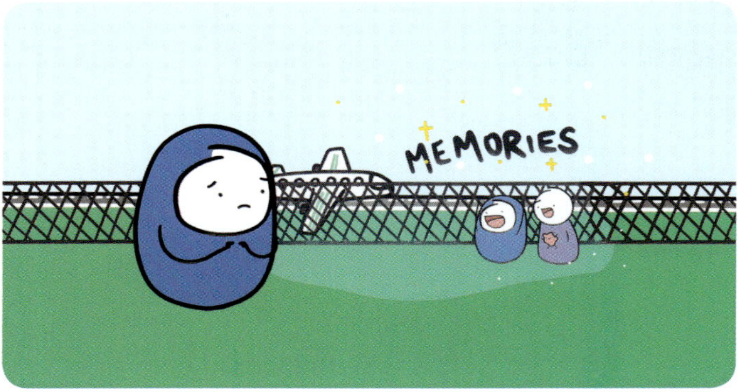
MEMORIES

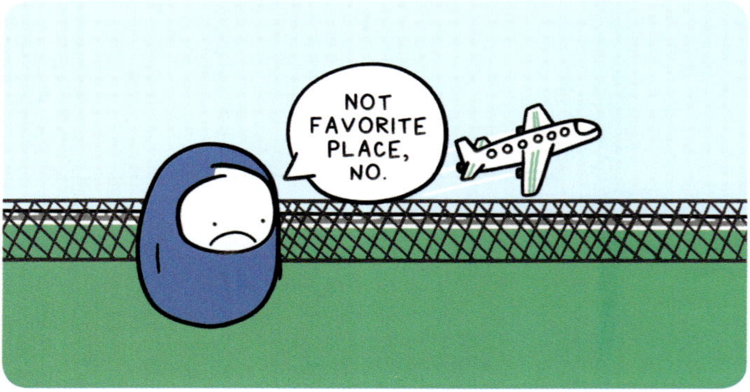
NOT FAVORITE PLACE, NO.

Even drive-in movies were ruined.

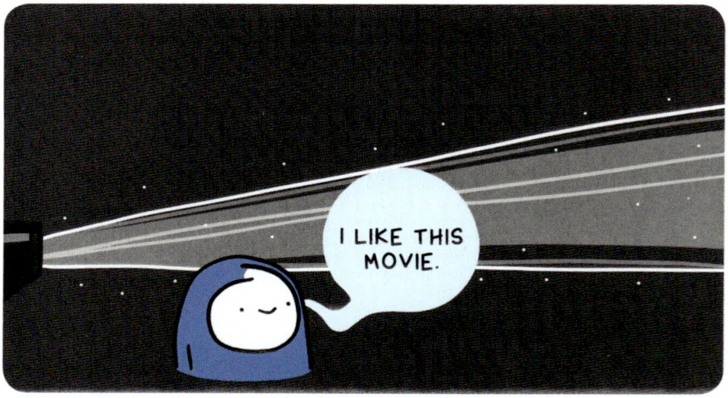
I LIKE THIS MOVIE.

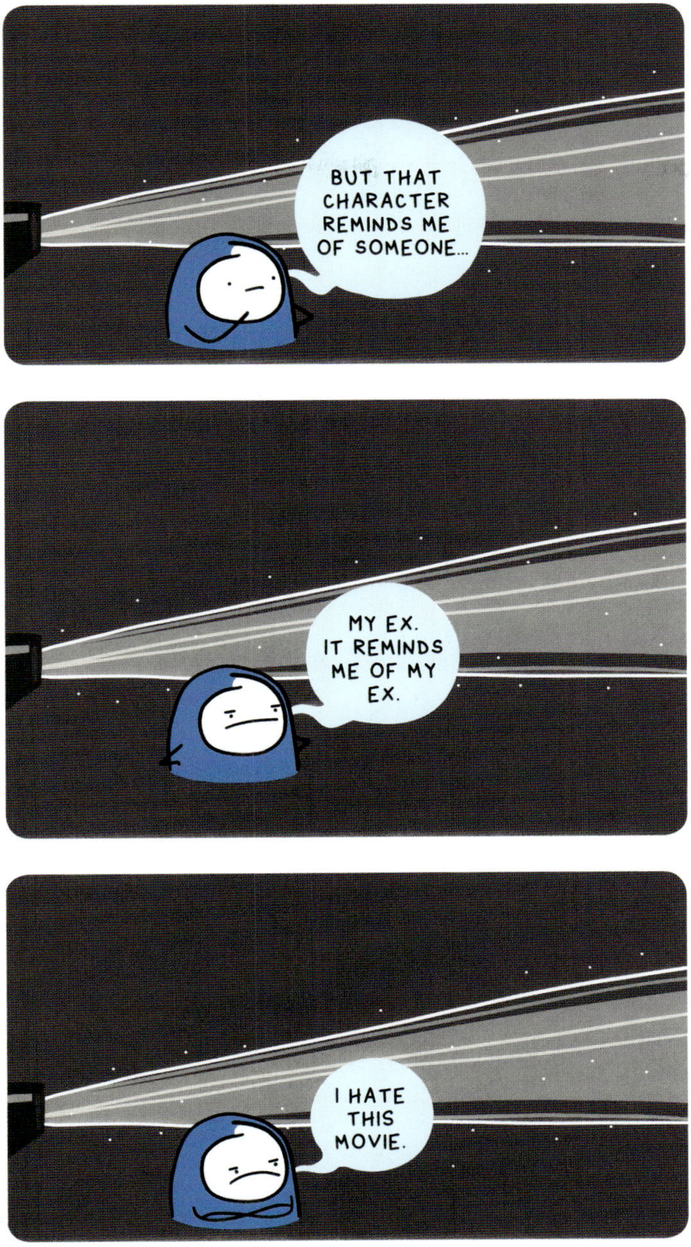
BUT THAT CHARACTER REMINDS ME OF SOMEONE...
MY EX. IT REMINDS ME OF MY EX.
I HATE THIS MOVIE.

After a while, I started to question how normal this sustained period of grief was. To determine what "normal" was, I asked a friend for some sage advice.

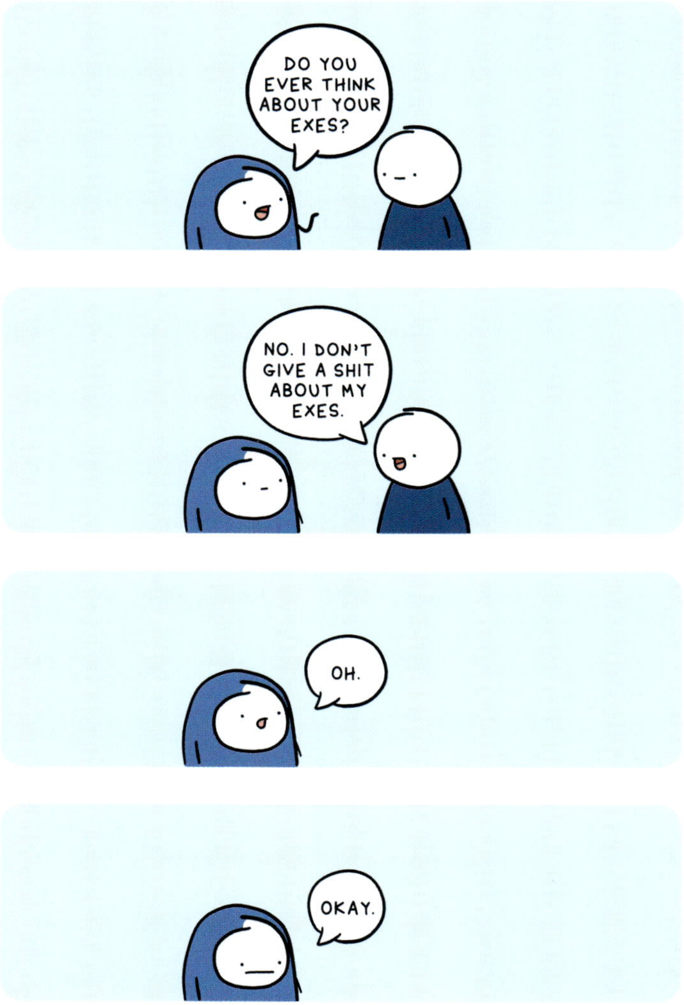
DO YOU EVER THINK ABOUT YOUR EXES?
NO. I DON'T GIVE A SHIT ABOUT MY EXES.
OH.
OKAY.

It was decided that this was not normal.

### ONE YEAR LATER

Gum and I hadn't spoken in a while. A "happy birthday" text became the only form of communication between the two of us in an otherwise barren conversation thread.

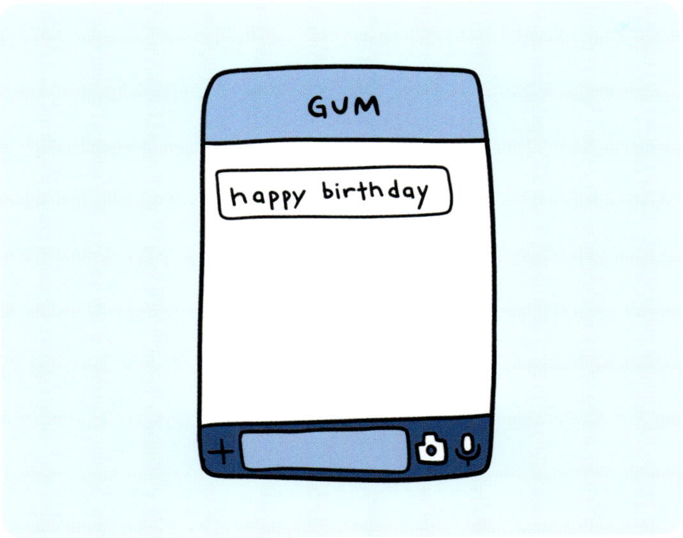
GUM
happy birthday

*happy birthday*

Gum couldn't even be bothered to capitalize that shit. Gum *knew* I hated lazy capitalization.

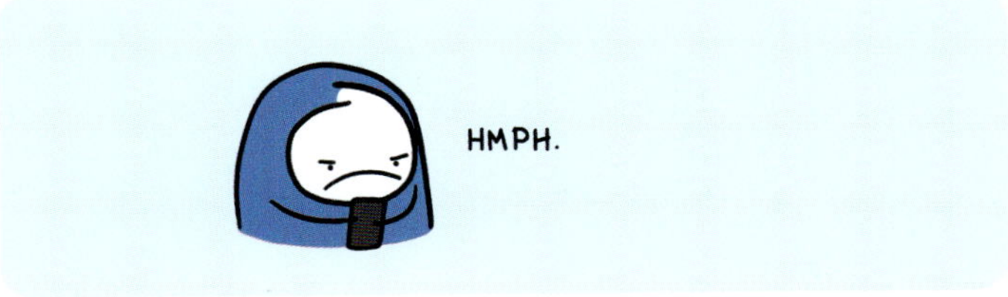
HMPH.

*thank you*

I wrote back.

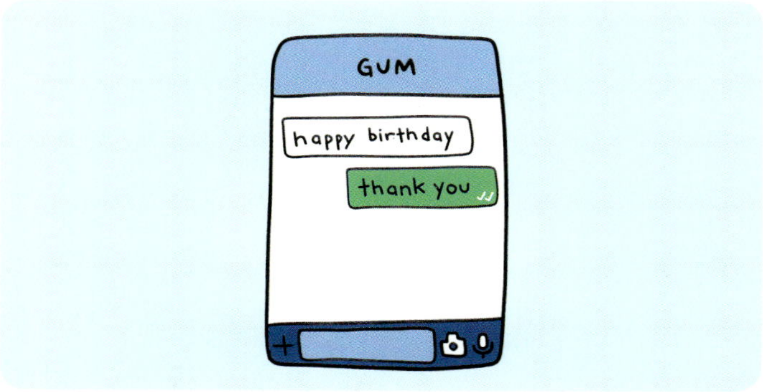
GUM
happy birthday
thank you

Also uncapitalized.

**TWO YEARS LATER**

I was dating someone new and so was Gum. I found out because a mutual friend of ours simply loved subjecting me to unsolicited updates about my ex.

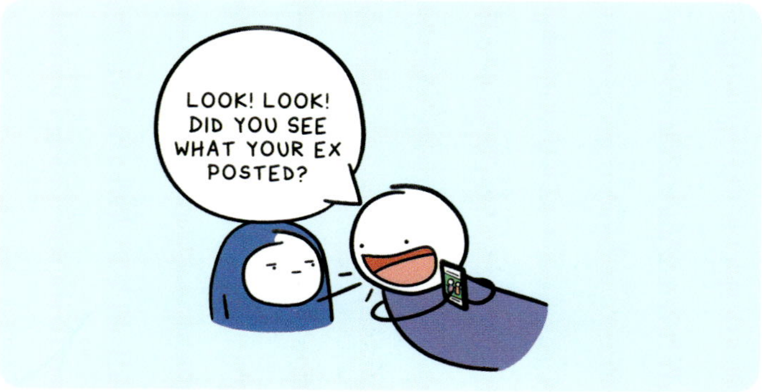
LOOK! LOOK! DID YOU SEE WHAT YOUR EX POSTED?

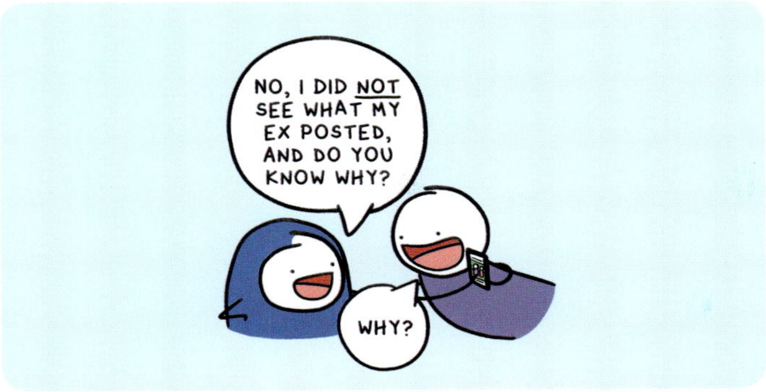
NO, I DID NOT SEE WHAT MY EX POSTED, AND DO YOU KNOW WHY?
WHY?

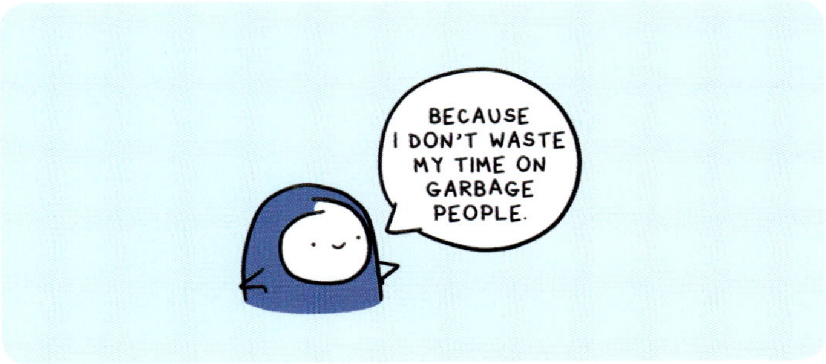
BECAUSE I DON'T WASTE MY TIME ON GARBAGE PEOPLE.

**THREE YEARS LATER**

Gum was an unwelcome yet constantly recurring motif in my life. Every time I thought I was over it, I wasn't.

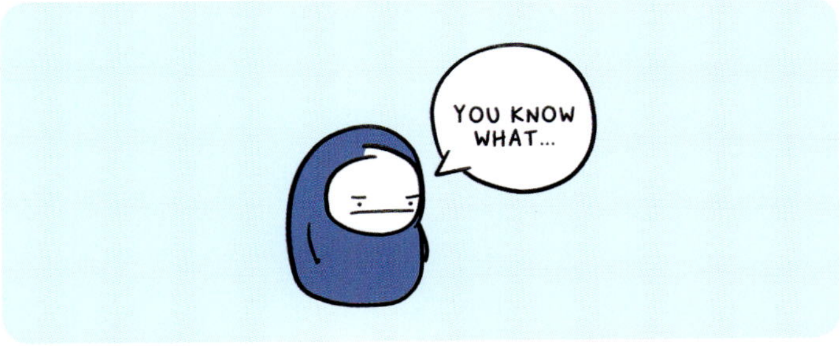
YOU KNOW WHAT...

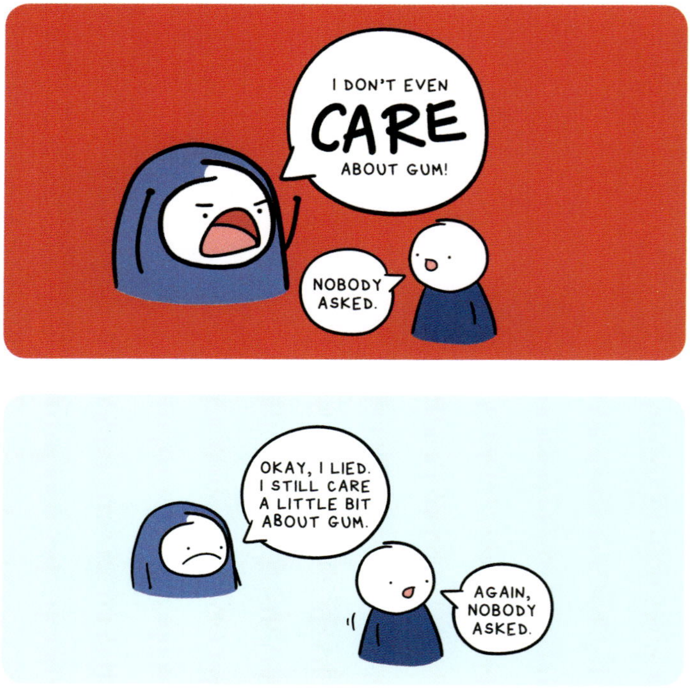
I DON'T EVEN CARE ABOUT GUM!
NOBODY ASKED.
OKAY, I LIED. I STILL CARE A LITTLE BIT ABOUT GUM.
AGAIN, NOBODY ASKED.

**FOUR YEARS LATER**

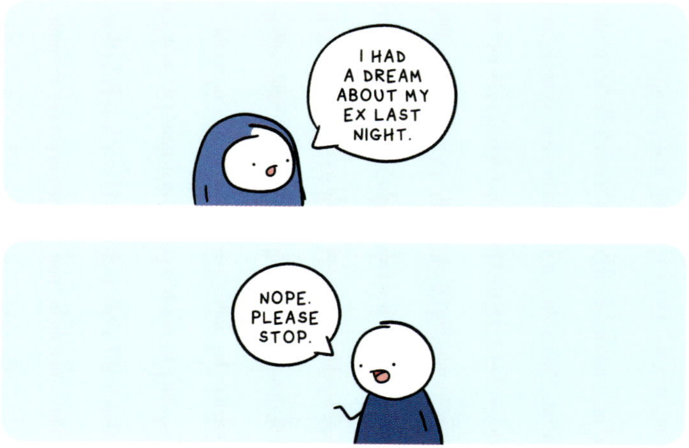
I HAD A DREAM ABOUT MY EX LAST NIGHT.
NOPE. PLEASE STOP.

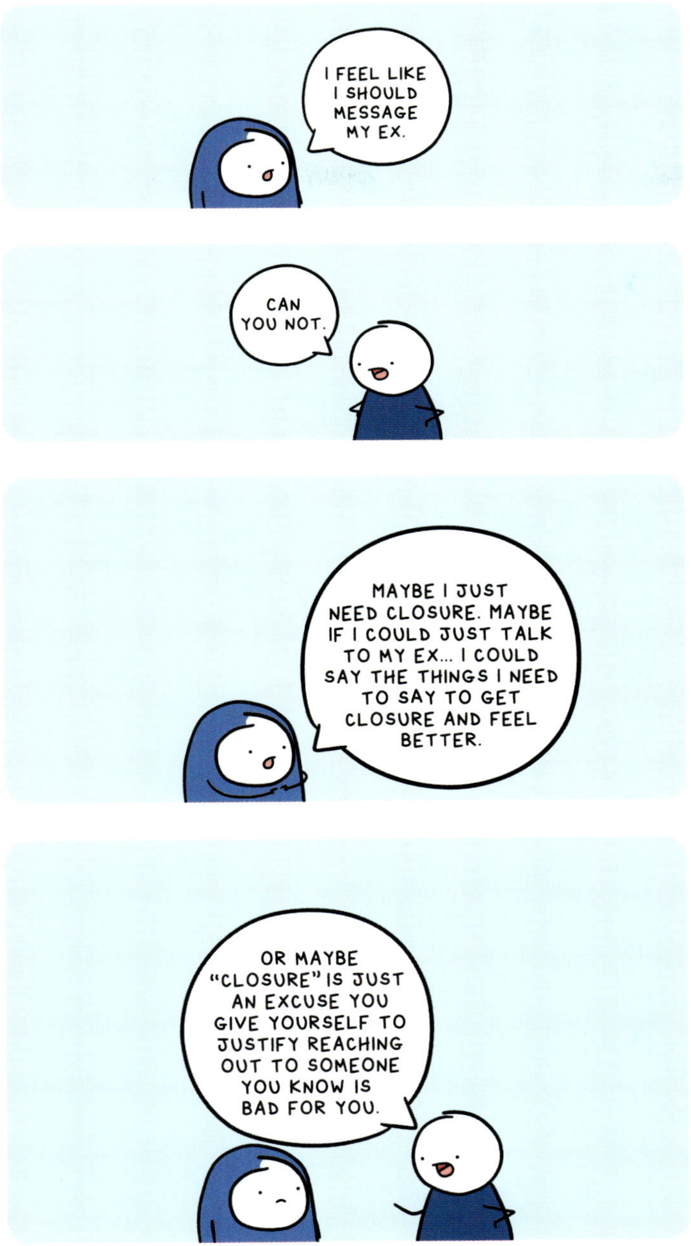
I FEEL LIKE I SHOULD MESSAGE MY EX.
CAN YOU NOT.
MAYBE I JUST NEED CLOSURE. MAYBE IF I COULD JUST TALK TO MY EX... I COULD SAY THE THINGS I NEED TO SAY TO GET CLOSURE AND FEEL BETTER.
OR MAYBE "CLOSURE" IS JUST AN EXCUSE YOU GIVE YOURSELF TO JUSTIFY REACHING OUT TO SOMEONE YOU KNOW IS BAD FOR YOU.

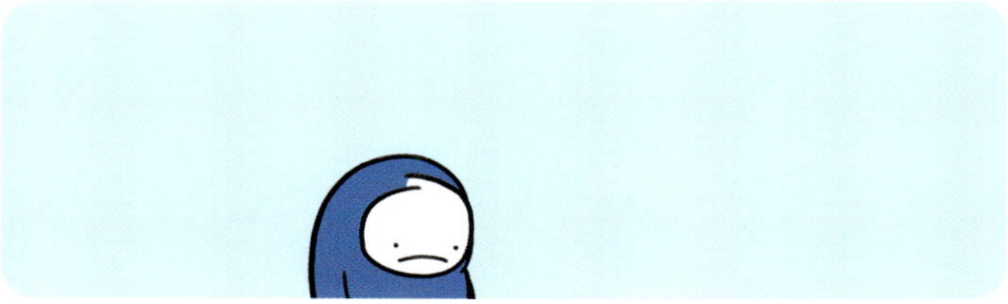

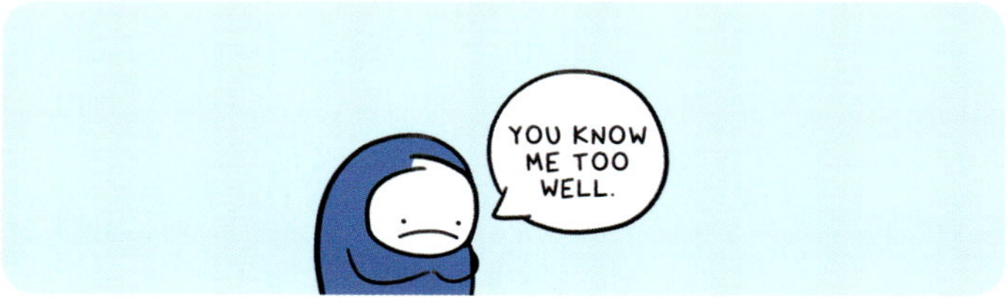
YOU KNOW ME TOO WELL.

When you first break up, your friends are there for you. They're there because they love you, and more importantly, they're there because they need to talk shit about your ex and this is the window of opportunity they've been patiently waiting for.

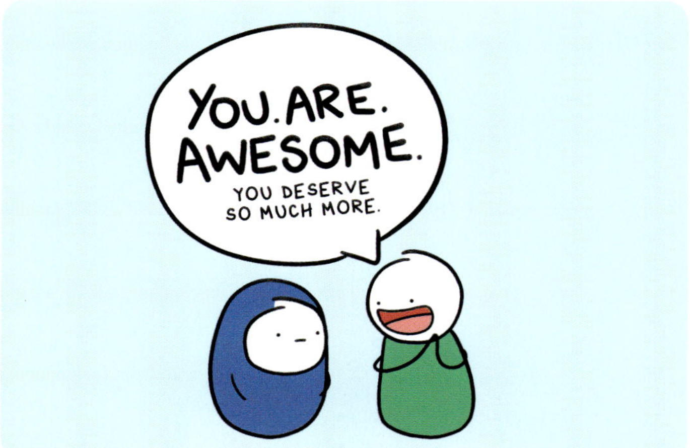
YOU. ARE. AWESOME.
YOU DESERVE SO MUCH MORE.

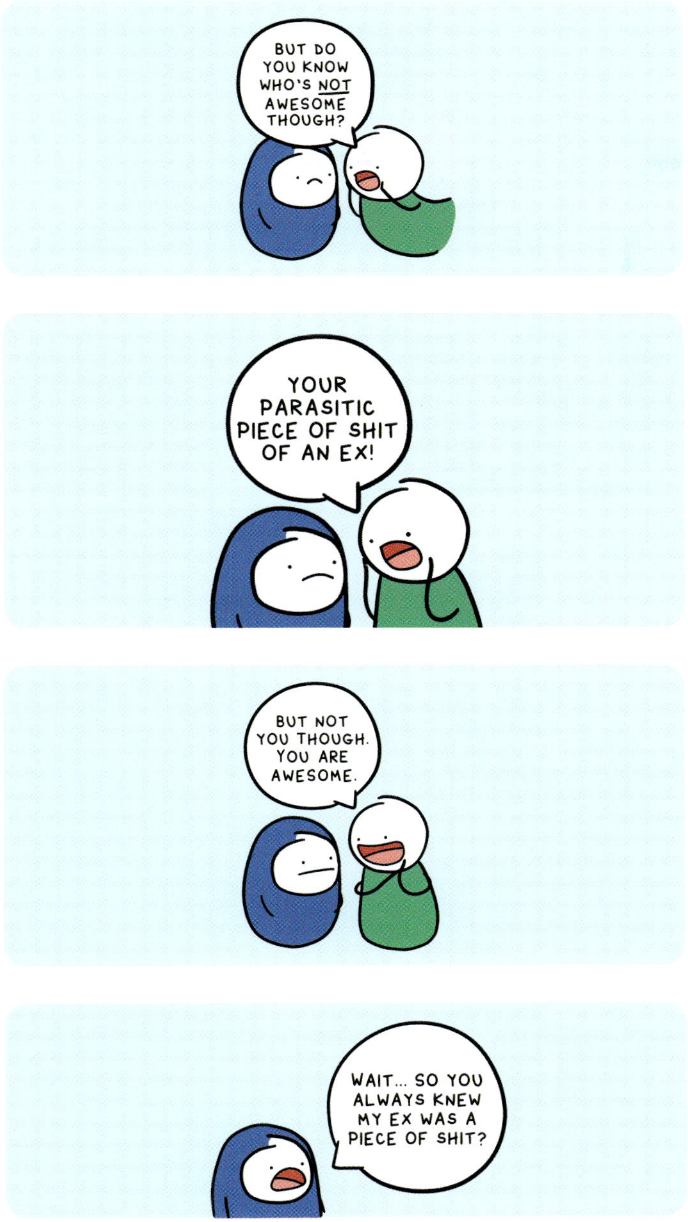
BUT DO YOU KNOW WHO'S NOT AWESOME THOUGH?
YOUR PARASITIC PIECE OF SHIT OF AN EX!
BUT NOT YOU THOUGH. YOU ARE AWESOME.
WAIT... SO YOU ALWAYS KNEW MY EX WAS A PIECE OF SHIT?

My relationship grief wasn't at its peak right after the initial breakup. It stayed much longer, and peaked much later—years after our split, long after every drop of socially acceptable sadness had been spent. It was an emotional hangover that no amount of Gatorade could cure.

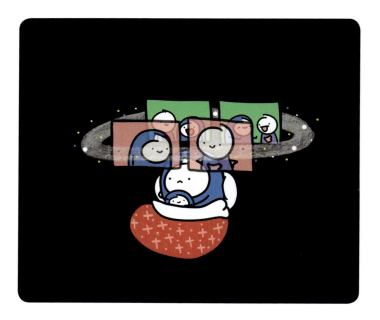

In time, I got used to feeling permanently heartbroken. Or maybe just broken. It was hard to differentiate between the two. That version of me before

Gum—that happy, carefree version—seemed like such a distant memory, so far away I could barely remember its existence.

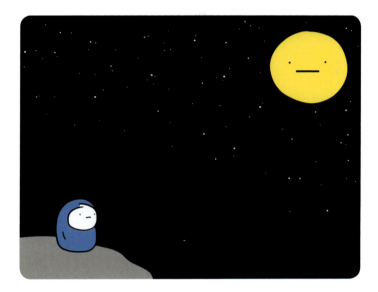

My friends started out sympathetic, but there is a limit to the sympathy of friends when it comes to heartbreak.

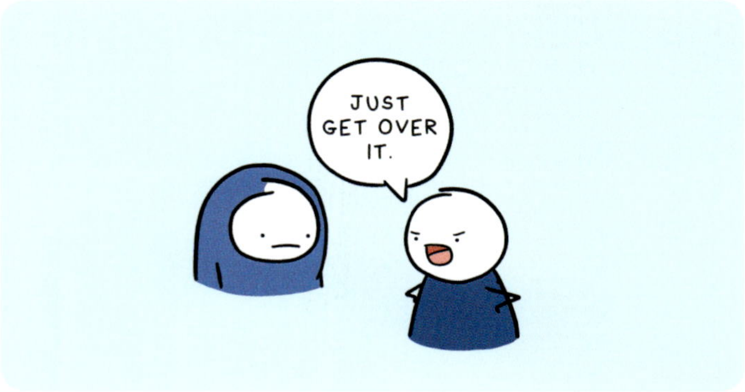
JUST GET OVER IT.

Trying to get over someone you can't get over is like seeing a bridge and knowing full well that the only thing that separates you from eternal happiness is that *one* bridge.

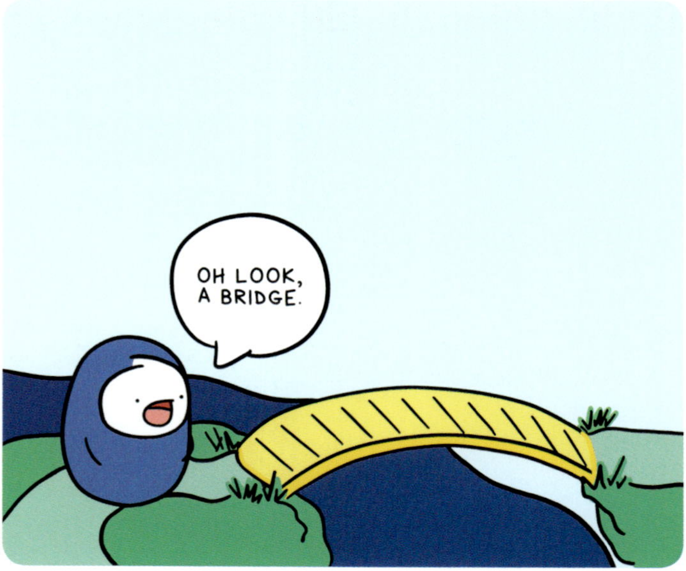
OH LOOK, A BRIDGE.

In theory, you recognize you can simply "get over it."

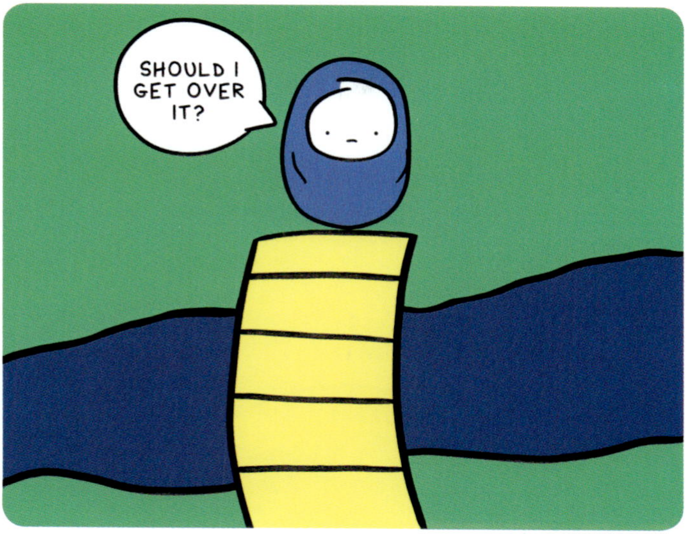
SHOULD I GET OVER IT?

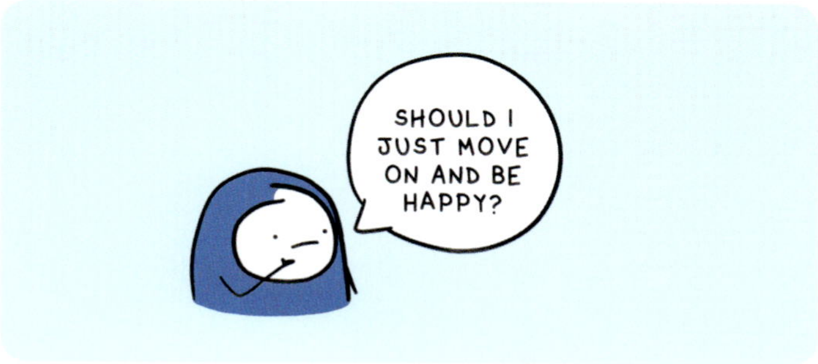
SHOULD I JUST MOVE ON AND BE HAPPY?

But despite our best intentions, it never quite pans out as easily in execution.

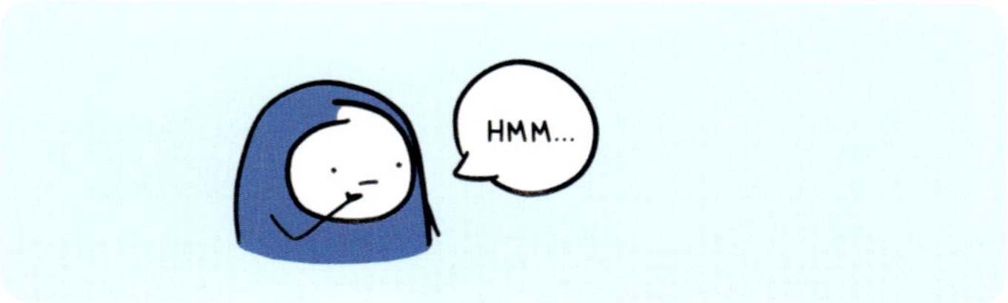
HMM...

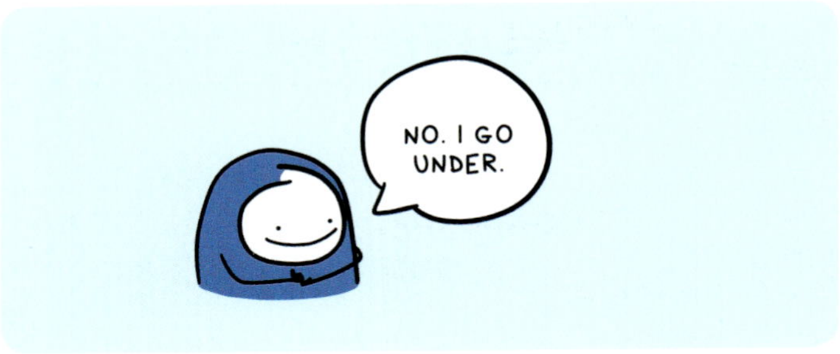
NO. I GO UNDER.

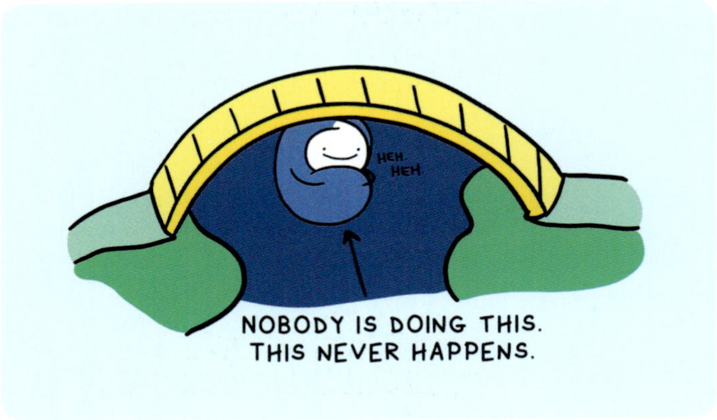
HEH. HEH
NOBODY IS DOING THIS. THIS NEVER HAPPENS.

Nobody *chooses* to be stuck on someone. They just are. So if you're telling someone to "just get over it," odds are, you're being a bit of a pill.

Most people are trying, even if it doesn't always look like it.

• • •

As the years passed, I got new jobs and new friends, dated new people, fell in love, fell out of love . . . I lived my life. And from the surface, you might not even notice I was broken at all.

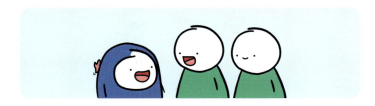

But there was always a part of me that knew Gum was still there. Gum was always there, and I grew to resent this.

The rational part of me knew this was misdirected anger. I didn't *hate* Gum, I just hated the *hold* Gum had on me.

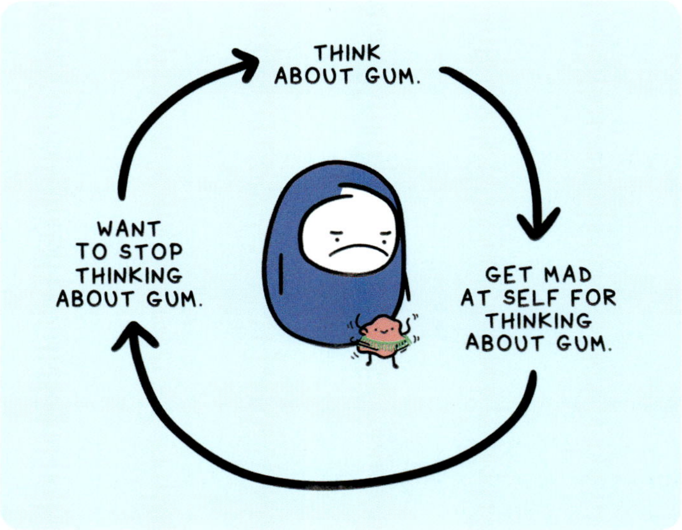
THINK ABOUT GUM.
GET MAD AT SELF FOR THINKING ABOUT GUM.
WANT TO STOP THINKING ABOUT GUM.

And then there was the guilt. That heavy, sinking guilt I had for comparing everyone to Gum. The guilt of having to ask every new and wonderful person in my life to please accept their lease on my heart—but ignore that unbecoming piece of Gum smushed on the side of it.

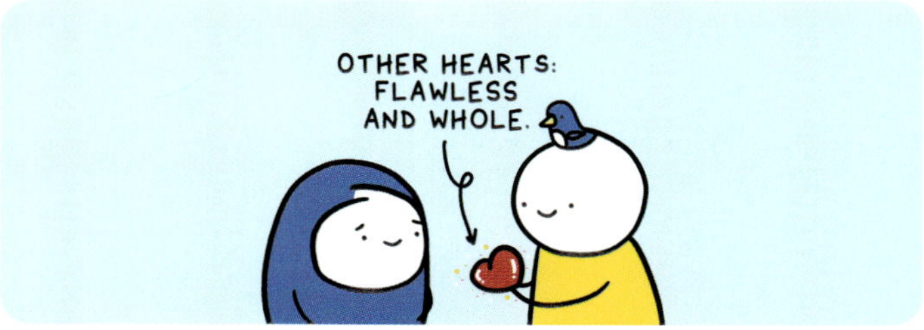
OTHER HEARTS: FLAWLESS AND WHOLE.

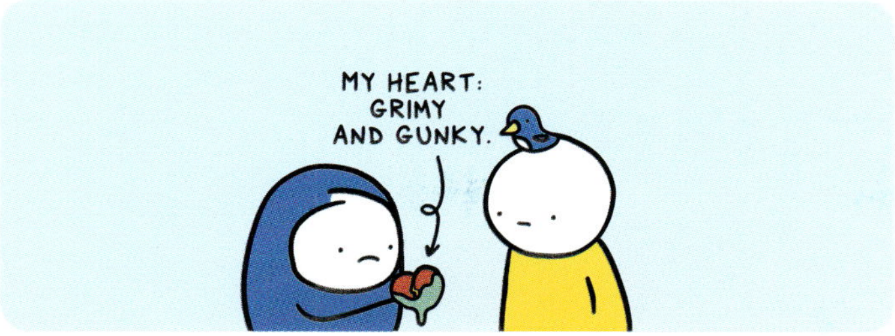
MY HEART: GRIMY AND GUNKY.

I wasn't even comparing them to someone real anymore. Gum was just an idyllic by-product of rosy retrospection, more memory than human, a piece of nostalgia I just couldn't shake.

• • •

Some unmeasured amount of time later, a friend of mine asked me to visit her at a convention. She was an exhibitor and thought I'd enjoy the event. When I arrived at the convention hall, it was packed with people jostling to get to different booths.

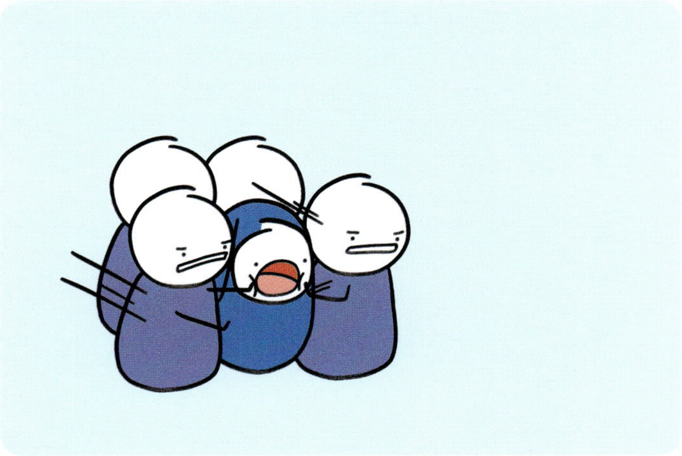

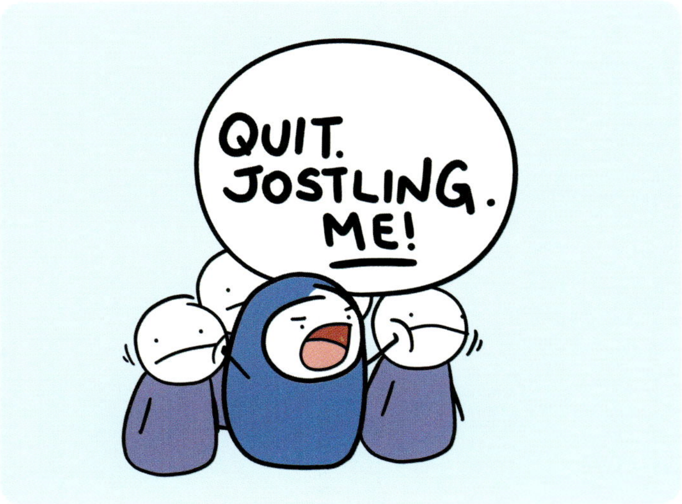
QUIT. JOSTLING. ME!

After finding an exhibition map, I started scanning for my friend's name and booth number. As I thumbed through the list, something caught my eye—Gum's name was there.

The Gum I knew didn't work in this field. But something told me it was the same Gum. *I mean, how many people are named Gum?* I looked up the booth number: J19.

*No big deal. I'm not scared.*

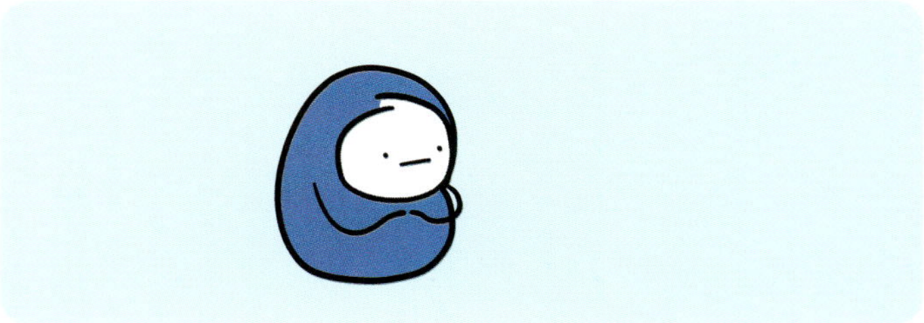

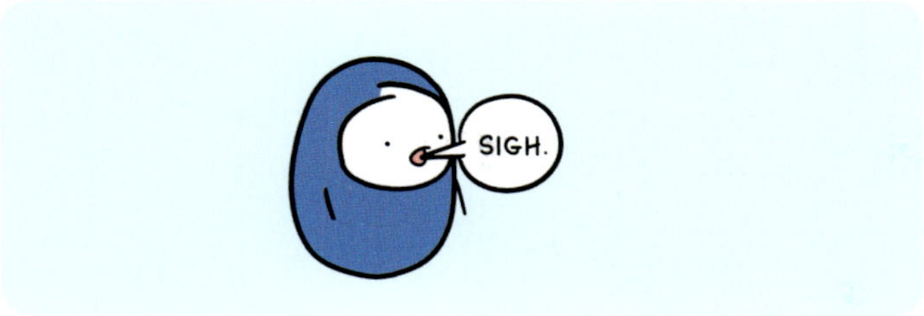
SIGH.

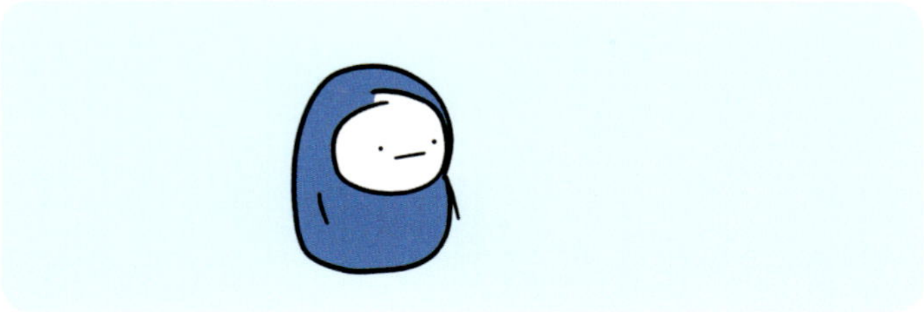

After visiting my friend's booth on the opposite side of the space, I found myself walking mindlessly towards J19. I was determined to be nonchalant. But of course, fixation on being nonchalant is the best way to ensure you are anything *but* nonchalant. The tightness in my chest and the lump in my throat were telling reminders that I wasn't anywhere near as apathetic as I ought to be after all this time. I didn't know what to do with my hands, so I started fidgeting with my hair.

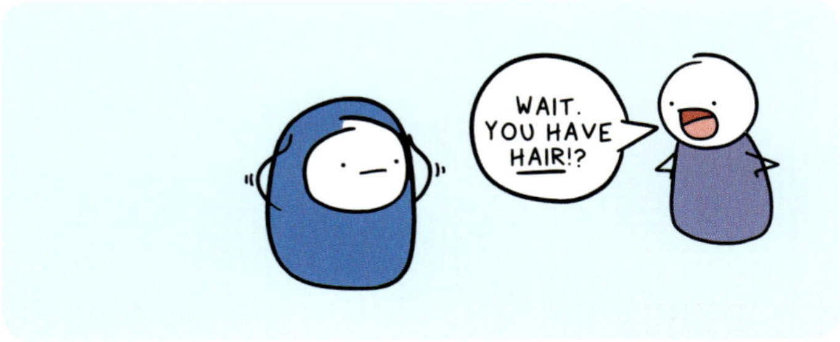
WAIT. YOU HAVE HAIR!?

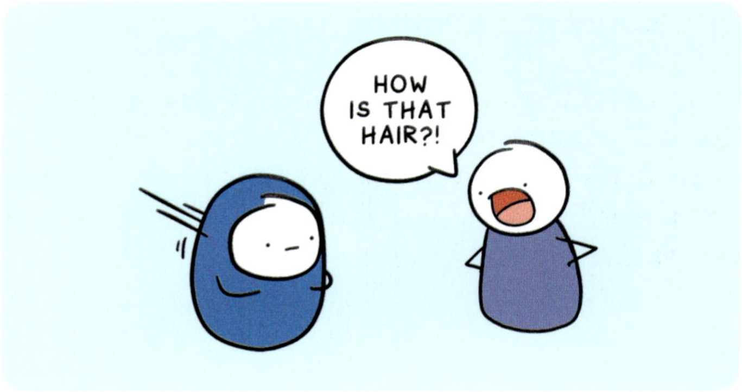
HOW
IS THAT
HAIR?!

And then I saw Gum—the person I had painstakingly avoided but also secretly hoped to run into all these years—standing in the distance, like a ghost back from the dead.

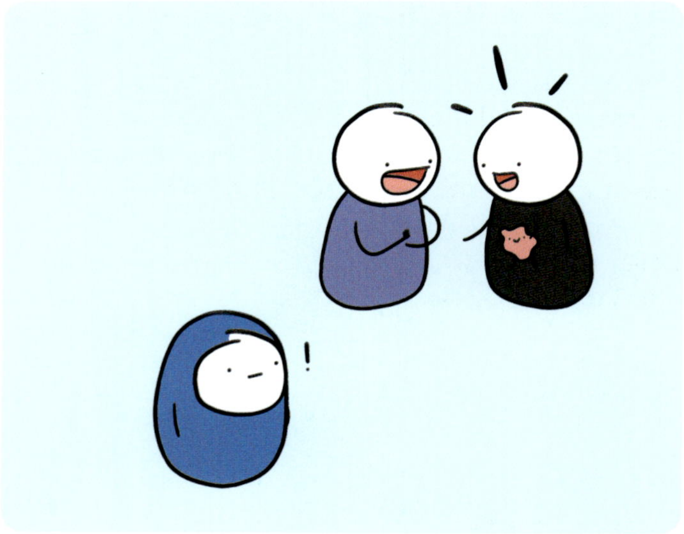

In that moment, I felt a pang of something. Excitement? Anxiety? Dread? Perhaps a bit of everything.

Gum looked so . . . different.

It's a strange feeling, seeing the effects of time on someone you once knew. It's this juxtaposed sense of closeness and unfamiliarity that is at once wistful and unsettling. Gum was older, and for some illogical reason, this surprised me.

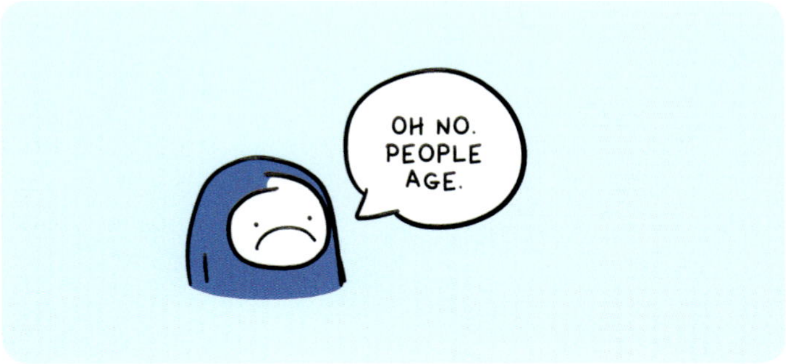
OH NO. PEOPLE AGE.

The rational part of me knew this was normal. But the sentimental, delusional part of me—the part that had always conjured up memories of Gum at the static age at which we met—was rattled by this reality.

*Wait. Was Gum wearing a black T-shirt?* Since when did Gum wear or even *own* black?

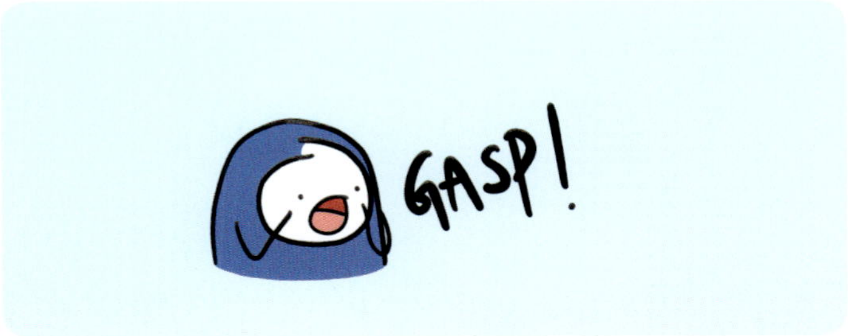
GASP!

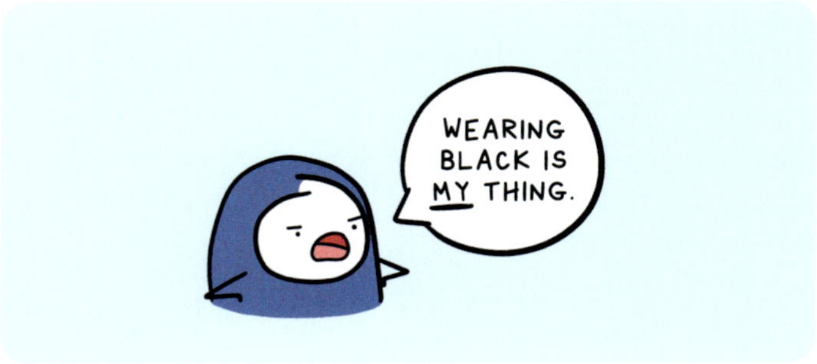
WEARING BLACK IS MY THING.

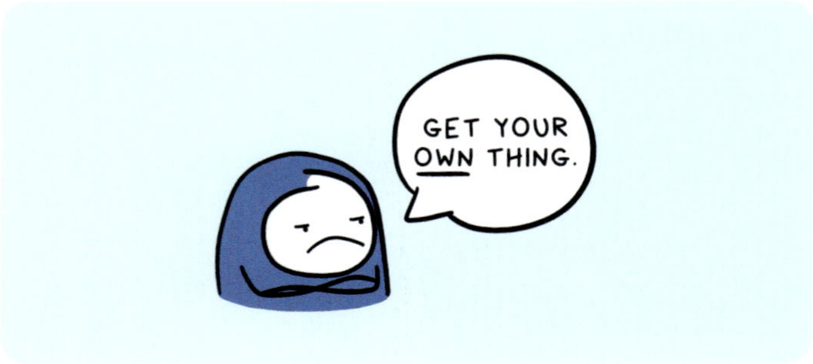
GET YOUR OWN THING.

Then again, based on Gum's presence at this very event, a significant career shift had also occurred in my absence. I saw hints of wrinkles around Gum's eyes, and for the briefest of moments, I felt a fleeting sense of petty glee.

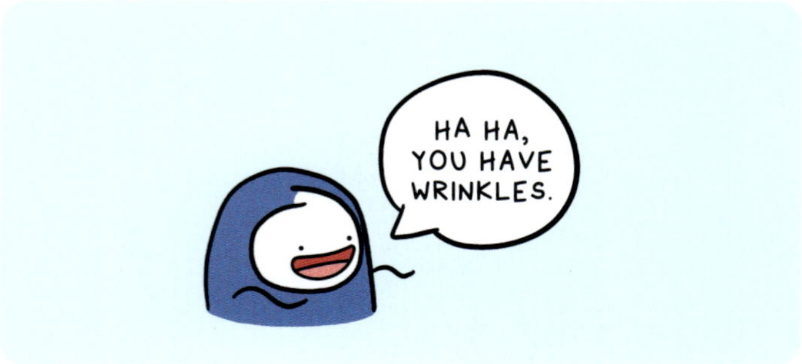
HA HA, YOU HAVE WRINKLES.

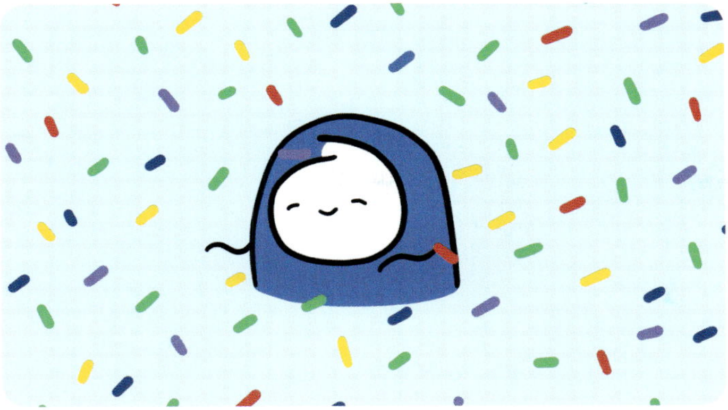

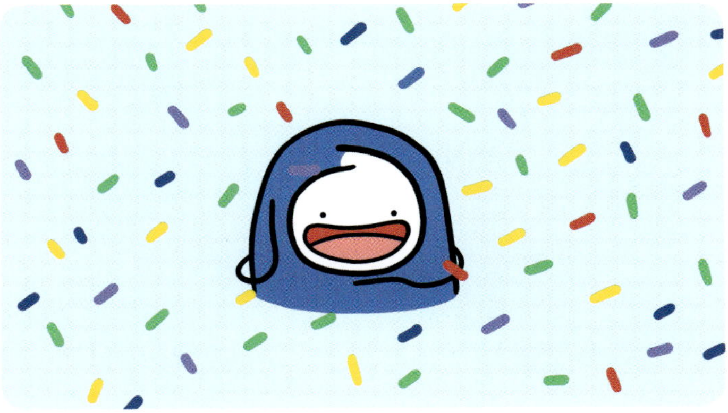

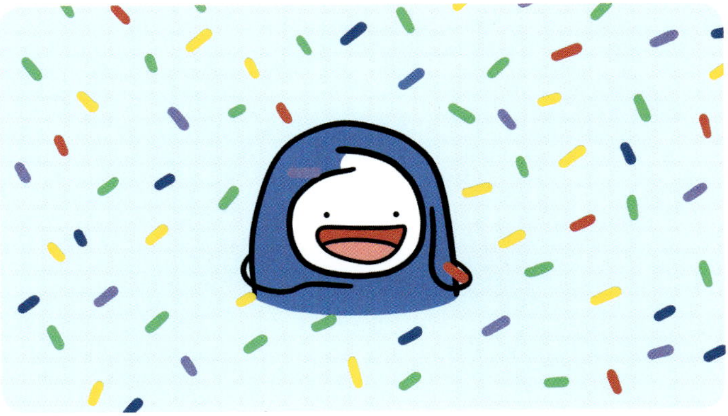

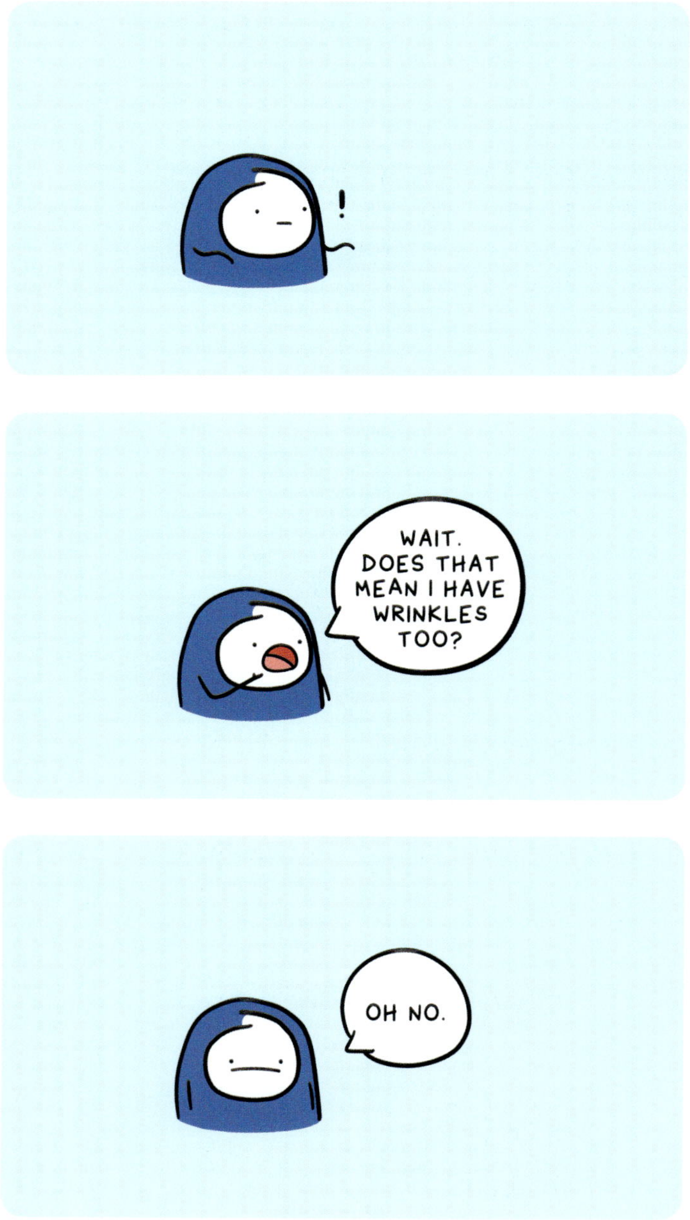
!
WAIT. DOES THAT MEAN I HAVE WRINKLES TOO?
OH NO.

I made a mental note to check for wrinkles later.

Gum's wrinkles were happy wrinkles—the kind you get from smiling too earnestly. I found a surprising sense of comfort towards this observation. Cradling a small silver trophy, Gum was wearing a bright smile while deep in conversation with someone from a neighboring table.

At least the smile was still the same.

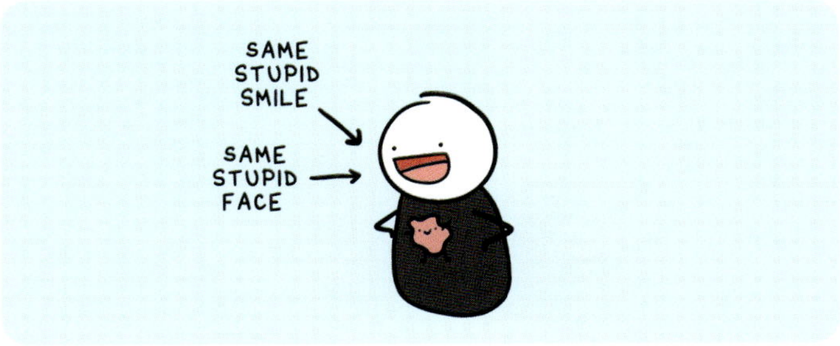
SAME STUPID SMILE
SAME STUPID FACE

In that moment, I realized two things:

1. I'm being *very* creepy and should probably leave before I get arrested by the Creep Police.

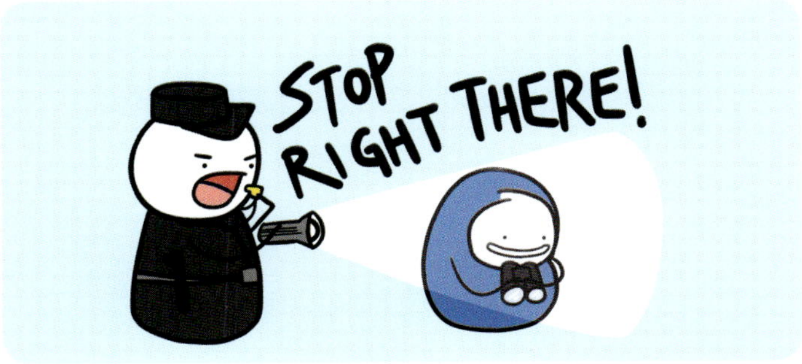
STOP RIGHT THERE!

2. The Gum I knew didn't exist anymore.

And then I felt it. The slow, deep rumbling of Gum's pedestal crashing down.

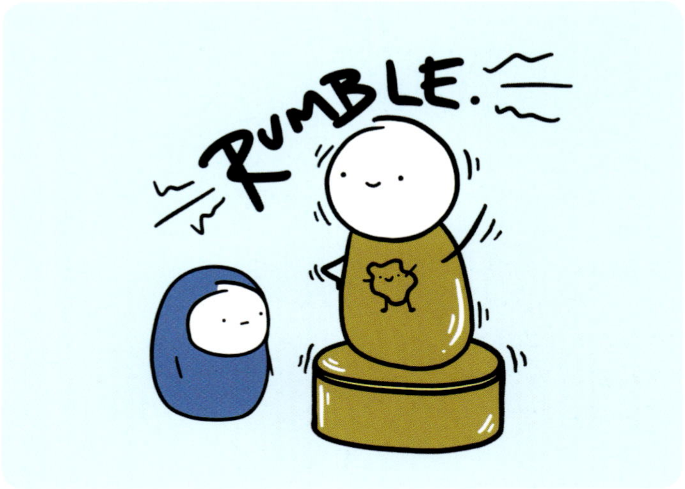
RUMBLE.

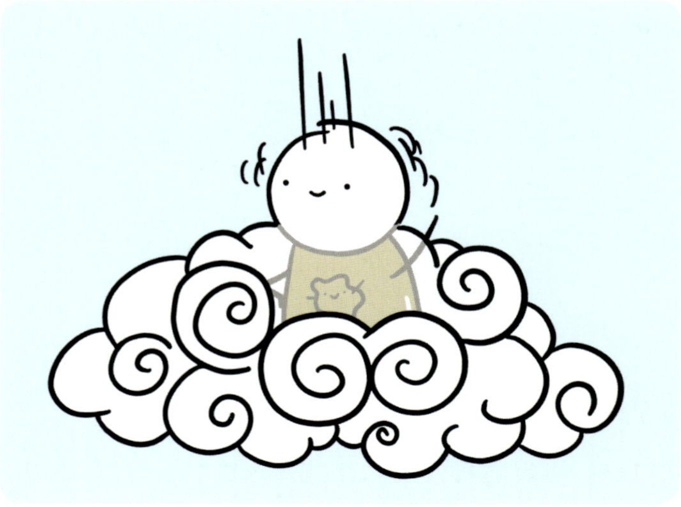

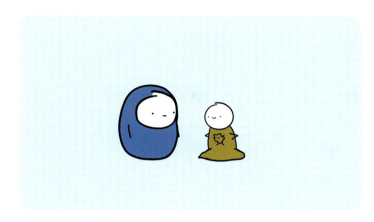

No longer a flawless memory, Gum had finally returned to human form. A real person who went on
to live a radically different life after our paths had
diverged. Why I had to see Gum in person in order
to realize this, I couldn't say.

For one reckless moment, I considered walking over
to say hi. *Maybe I could say a casual congratulations,*
I thought.

Maybe a casual congratulations *AND* finger guns. You know, to keep things real casual.

CONGRATS!
PEW! PEW!
BUT WHY.

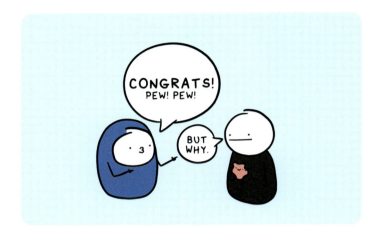

But something told me it was time to go.

NAW, FINGER GUNS ARE NEVER A GOOD IDEA.

Some people are best left in our memories.

• • •

That was the last time I ever saw Gum.

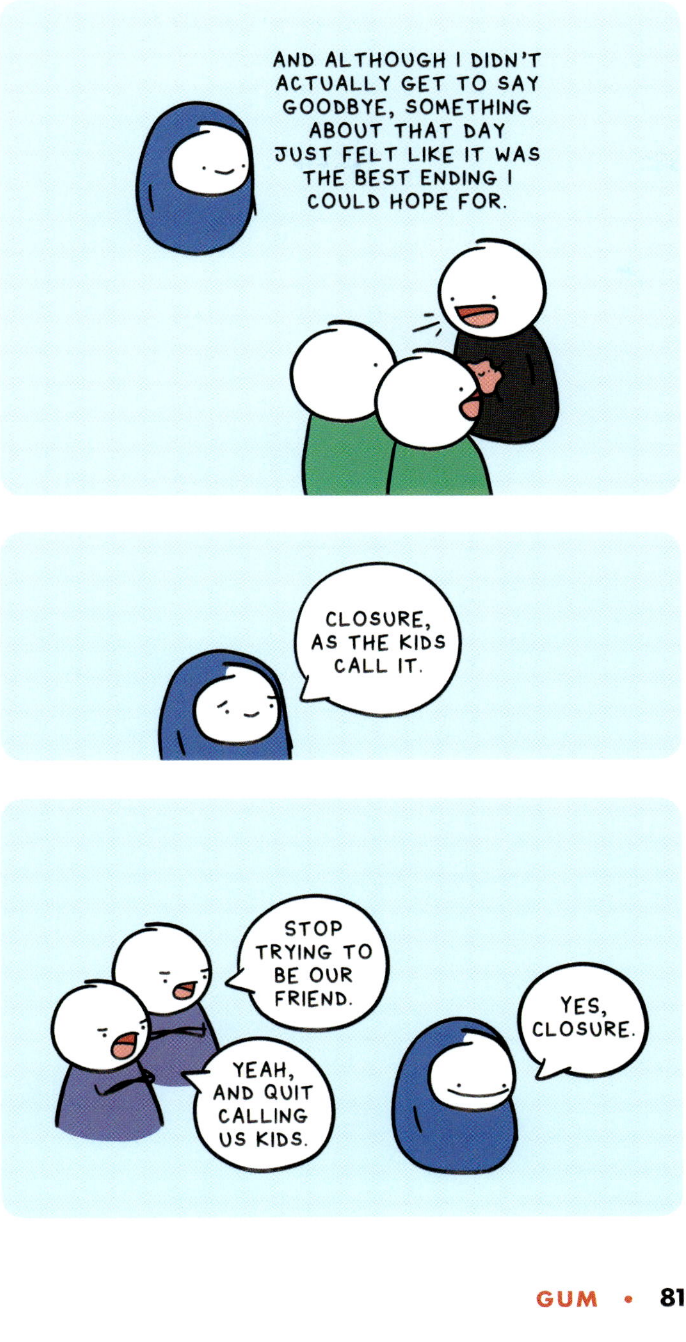
AND ALTHOUGH I DIDN'T ACTUALLY GET TO SAY GOODBYE, SOMETHING ABOUT THAT DAY JUST FELT LIKE IT WAS THE BEST ENDING I COULD HOPE FOR.
CLOSURE, AS THE KIDS CALL IT.
STOP TRYING TO BE OUR FRIEND.
YEAH, AND QUIT CALLING US KIDS.
YES, CLOSURE.

Looking back, I still can't pinpoint what it was about that day. But something inside me changed—something was set free. Maybe it was the realization that the Gum I knew didn't exist anymore, that this memory of a person I had frozen in time was only just that—a memory. Maybe it was the surprise of finding myself genuinely happy for someone I had spent so much of my life both loving and resenting. Or maybe it was just the petty delight of discovering that I had fewer wrinkles than my ex.

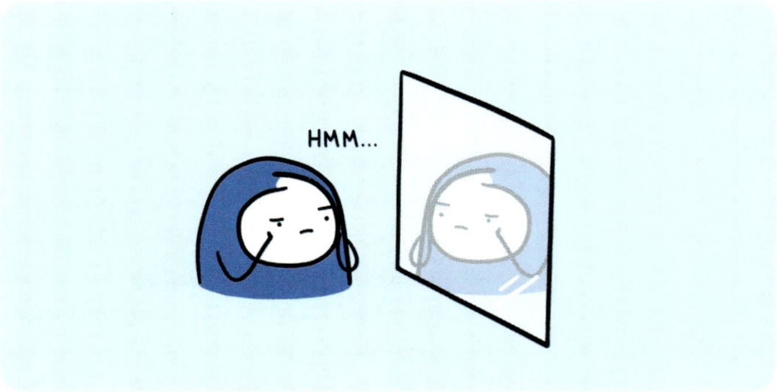
HMM...

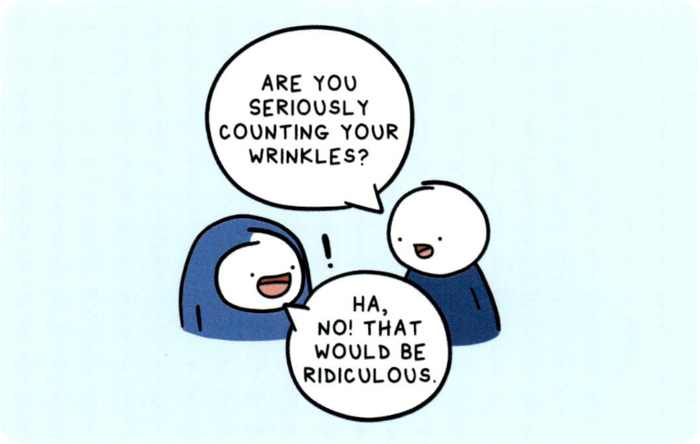
ARE YOU SERIOUSLY COUNTING YOUR WRINKLES?
!
HA, NO! THAT WOULD BE RIDICULOUS.

TEEHEE, NO WRINKLES!

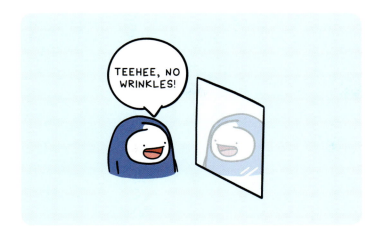

Whatever magic it was, it worked. After that day, I moved on.

• • •

For the longest time, I considered "moving on" to be synonymous with the absence of feeling. That's the goal, right? To remove the significance of someone from our past? The prized, delicious trophy of having successfully moved on?

I AM OVER YOU.

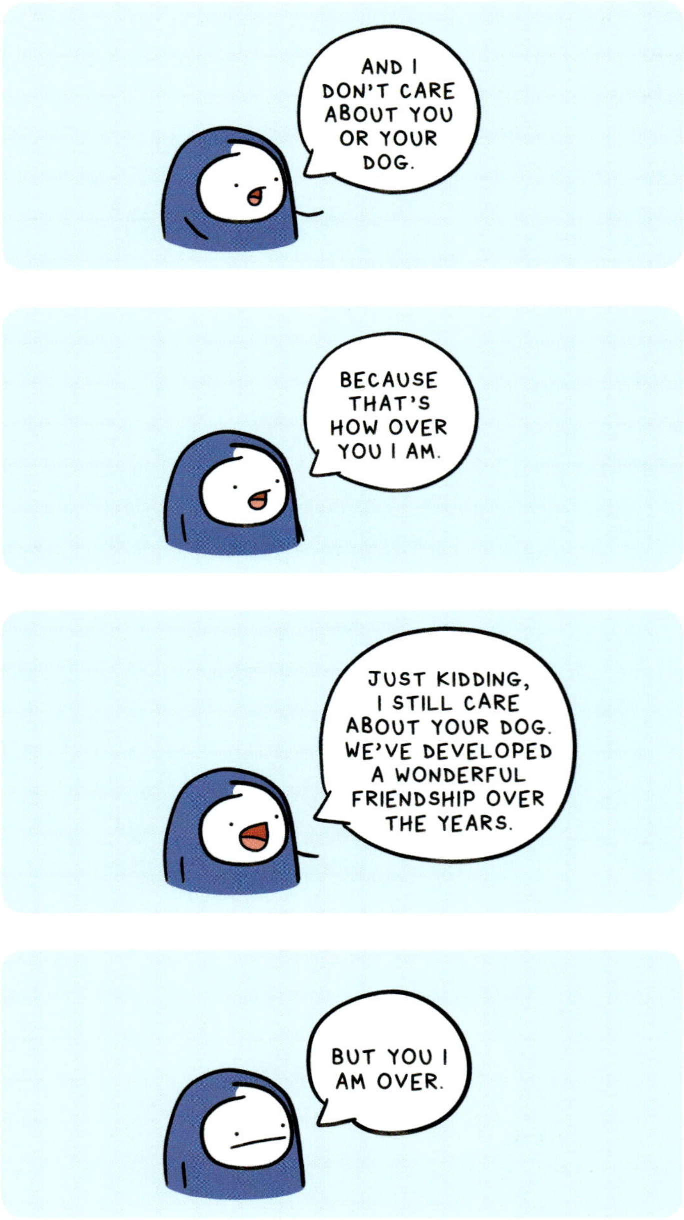
AND I DON'T CARE ABOUT YOU OR YOUR DOG.
BECAUSE THAT'S HOW OVER YOU I AM.
JUST KIDDING, I STILL CARE ABOUT YOUR DOG. WE'VE DEVELOPED A WONDERFUL FRIENDSHIP OVER THE YEARS.
BUT YOU I AM OVER.

But the truth is, some people just stick. Maybe they were there for your formative years. Maybe they played a significant part in your story. Or maybe you still care simply because you're just fundamentally someone who cares.

There are worse things to be.

. . .

I think inside each of us is an archive of our past selves.

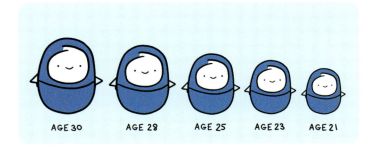

AGE 30    AGE 28    AGE 25    AGE 23    AGE 21

And in each past self, we loved and cared for different people. People who, for better or for worse, became the groundwork for our future selves. And although we evolve into older and wiser versions of ourselves in time, I don't think we ever lose those past selves. I don't think we ever really forget the people we once loved.

After I stopped berating myself for thinking about Gum, I found that our memories came up much less frequently. Eventually, they stopped bothering me altogether.

**BEFORE**

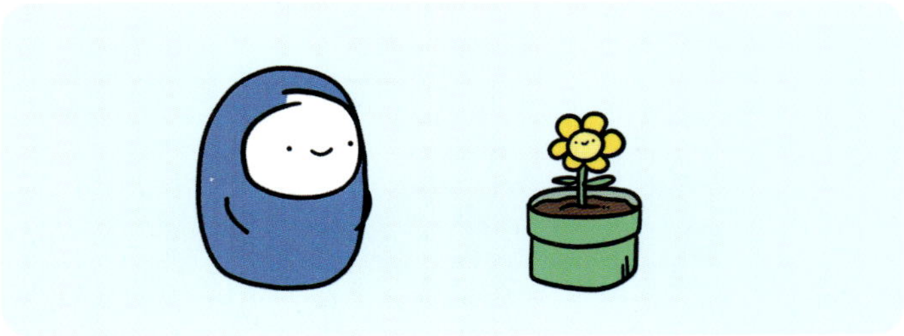

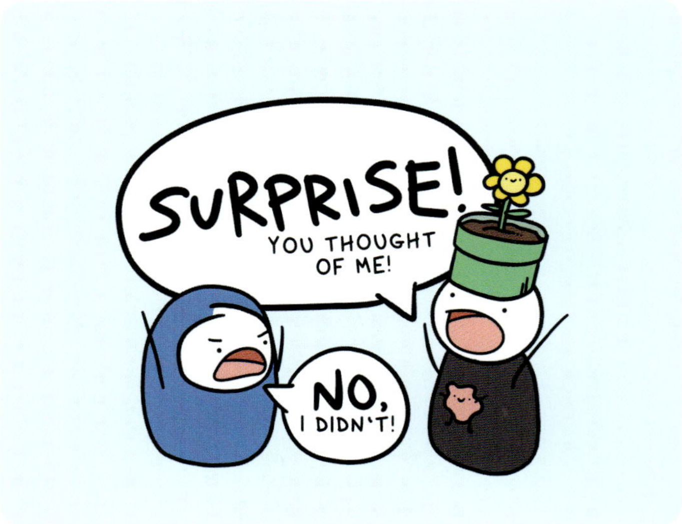
SURPRISE!
YOU THOUGHT OF ME!
NO, I DIDN'T!

AFTER

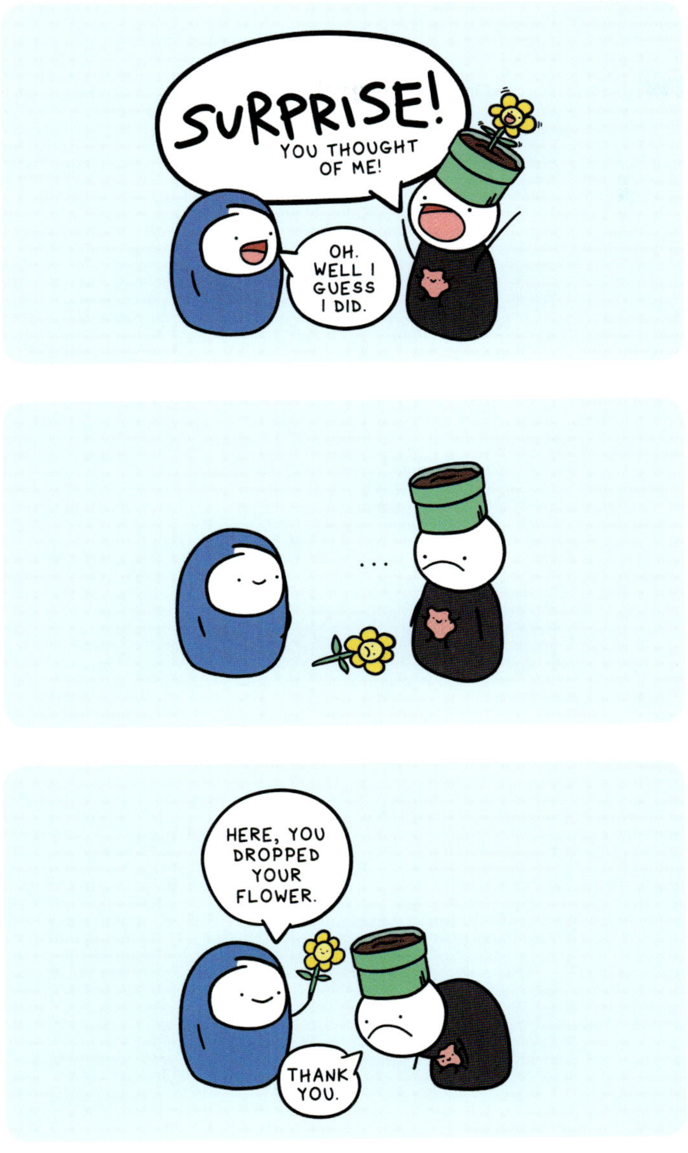
SURPRISE! YOU THOUGHT OF ME!
OH. WELL I GUESS I DID.
...
HERE, YOU DROPPED YOUR FLOWER.
THANK YOU.

I've since taken up the habit of holding on to three good memories for every person who has played a significant part in my life.

"Why *three* good memories?" my friend asks as I share this secret with her. "Why not one? Or two? Or ten!" she exclaims, as though she is excited by the mere existence of the number ten.

"Well," I said thoughtfully, "ten memories would be too hard. I mean . . . who the heck has ten good memories of someone just off the top of their head?"

My friend nods vigorously in agreement; she has already forgotten that the whole ten memories thing was her suggestion. I continue,

"I think one memory is too easy. You don't really have to look for that. In fact, you probably already have one memory that you frequently cycle back to. Same goes for two. But *three* good memories? You gotta reach for that. You have to dig around a bit. And I guess . . . I just like the idea of having to look back in search of good things."

At this, my friend nods twice before slowly moving her gaze to something in the distance. I can tell she's already gone in search of good memories.

• • •

I used to begrudge the fact that I was preserving memories that the other person had likely long forgotten. *Why am I such a sucker?* I would think to myself, conflicted and annoyed by the fond memories I still had for people I was no longer fond of. But perhaps the benefit of time has given me the distance to understand that holding on to the good parts of our stories is something we do for ourselves, and not for other people. When I look back today, I can appreciate the good moments without feeling conflicted, just as I am able to recall the bad ones with quiet objectivity.

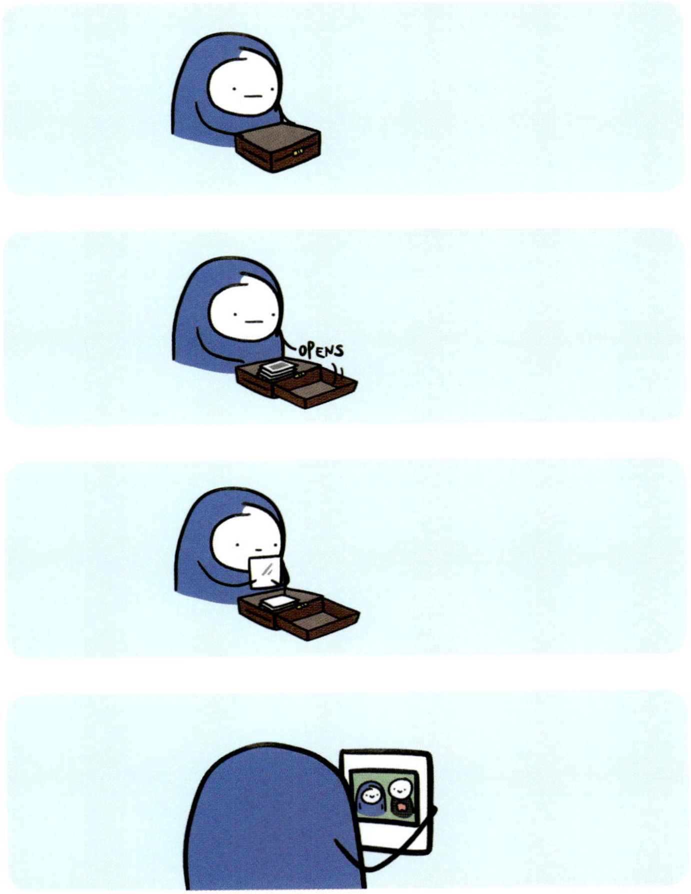
OPENS

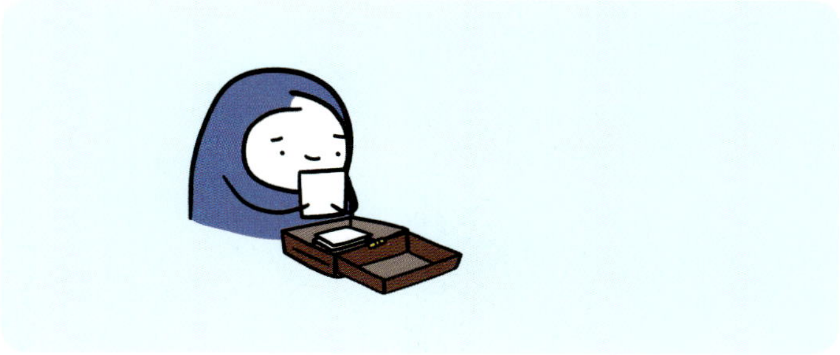

My understanding of "moving on" has shifted substantially over the years. I no longer consider moving on to be synonymous with not caring. I think it's more complex than that. I think moving on is about allowing ourselves to remember the good *and* the bad, to distinguish the past from the present, and to accept who we are, who we were, and everyone we met along the way.

• • •

The other day, I found a little piece of Gum stuck in my heart.

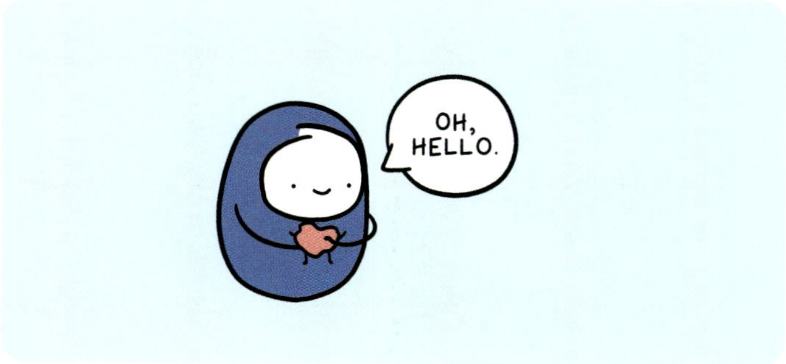
OH,
HELLO.

I took it out, I smiled . . .

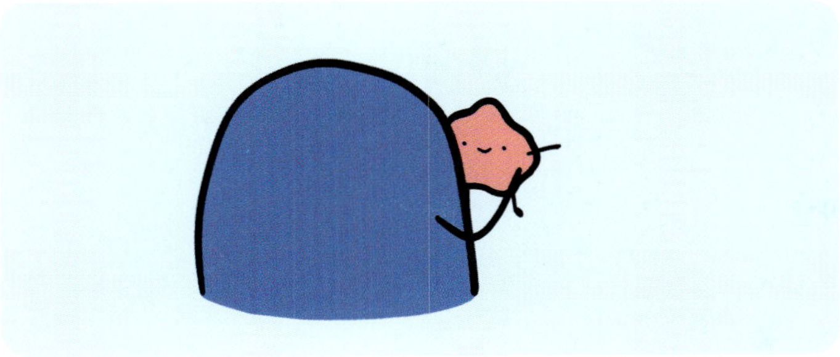

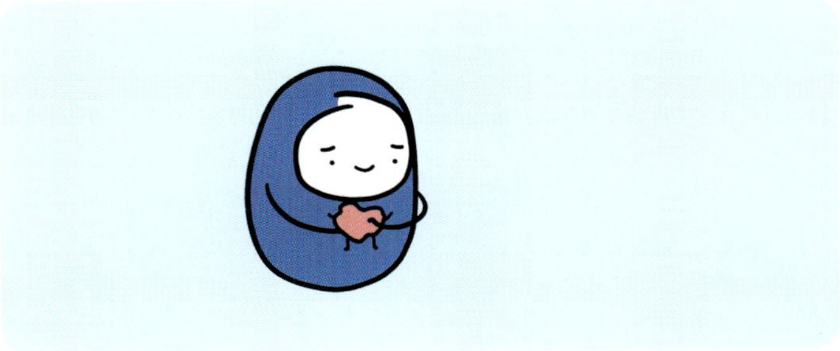

And then I put it back.

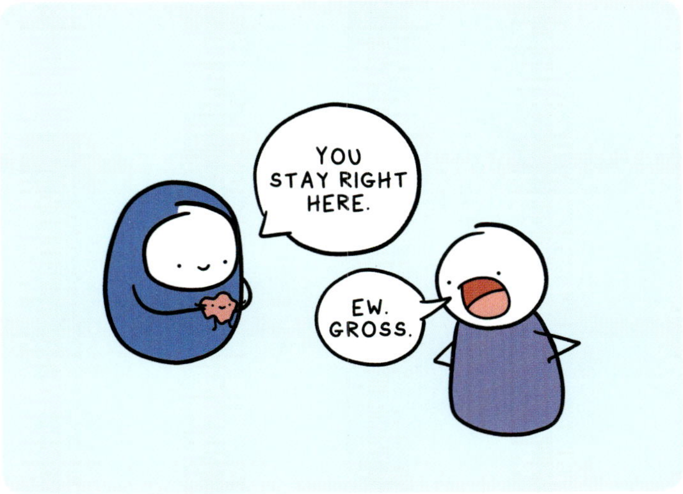
YOU STAY RIGHT HERE.
EW. GROSS.

# CHAPTER 3

# THE GLORY OF QUITTING

The summer before graduation, I was tricked by some friends to go to a patio lunch at a pretentious Vietnamese restaurant. I hate pretentious food, but I have pretentious food friends, so this kind of duplicity happens a lot.

While my friends ordered fancy fusion plates, I ordered regular pho. I always order regular pho—one does not trifle with perfection.

AND WOULD YOU LIKE SOMETHING FANCY TODAY?

NO, I JUST WANT UNPRETENTIOUS REGULAR FOOD.

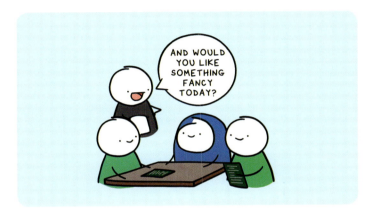

When my pho arrived, I was delighted. I had skipped breakfast that morning and was in desperate need of sustenance.

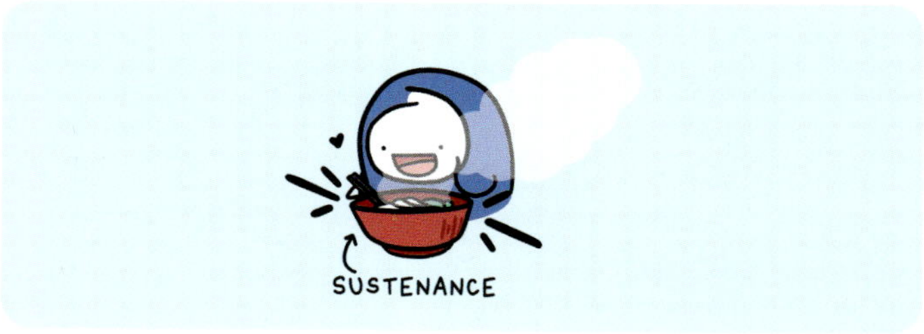
SUSTENANCE

But as I was about to take my first bite, a wasp landed on my chopsticks.

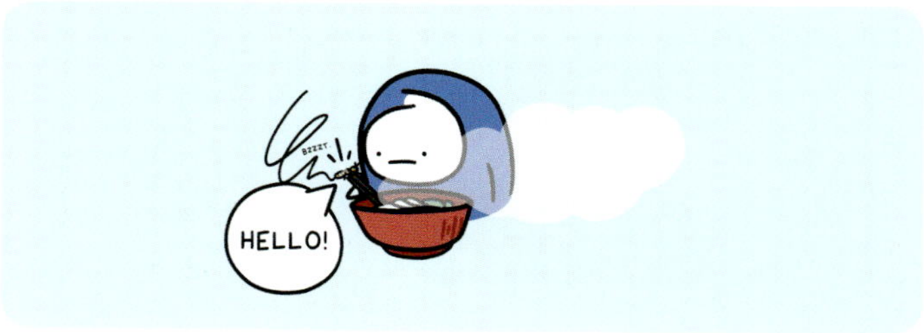
HELLO!

*How unusual*, I thought, waving it away. But as if on cue, another wasp flew onto my napkin.

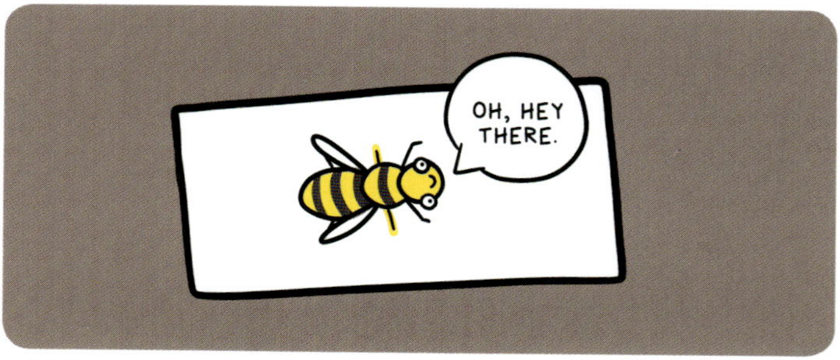
OH, HEY THERE.

And then another on my lap.

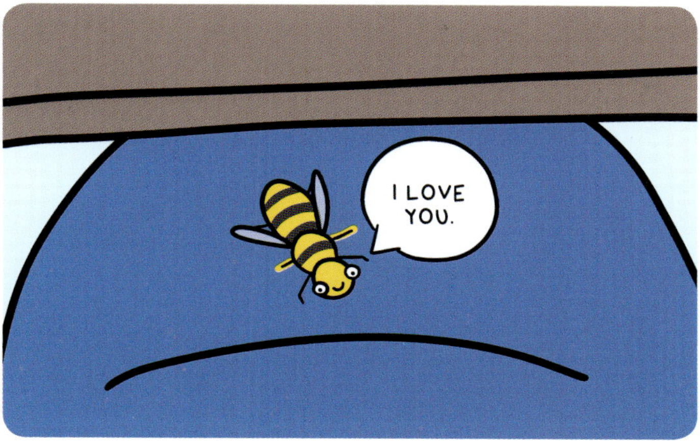
I LOVE YOU.

And then another on my face. Yes, my *fricking face.*

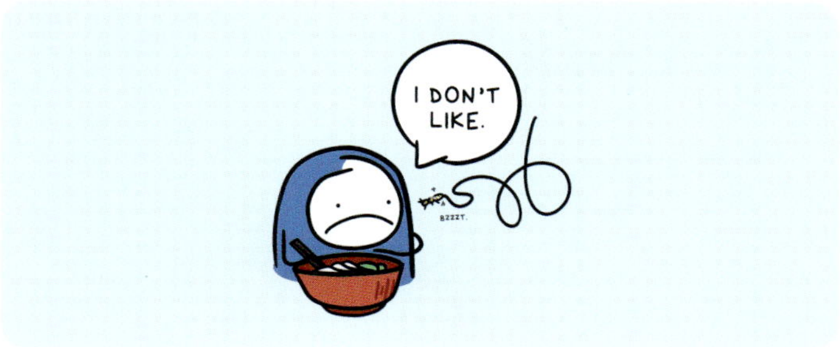
I DON'T LIKE.
BZZZT.

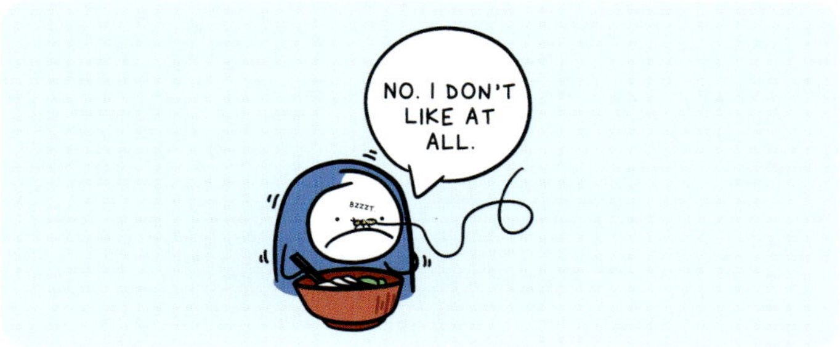
NO. I DON'T LIKE AT ALL.
BZZZT.

I tried to remain stoic.

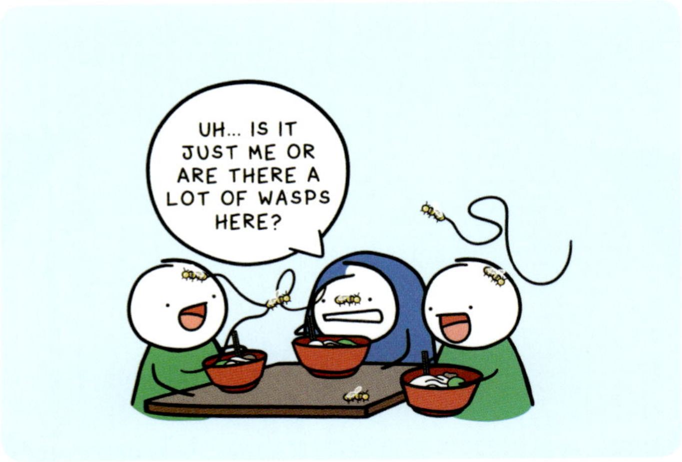
UH... IS IT JUST ME OR ARE THERE A LOT OF WASPS HERE?

But to my dismay, my friends were strangely unperturbed by the legion of wasps that had aggressively descended upon us.

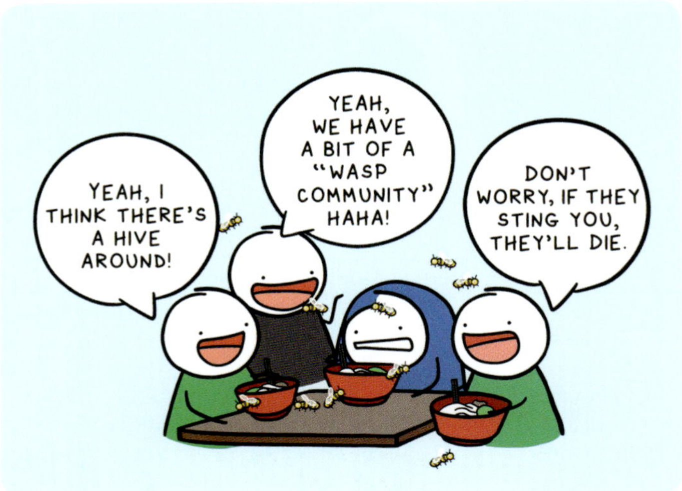
YEAH, I THINK THERE'S A HIVE AROUND!
YEAH, WE HAVE A BIT OF A "WASP COMMUNITY" HAHA!
DON'T WORRY, IF THEY STING YOU, THEY'LL DIE.

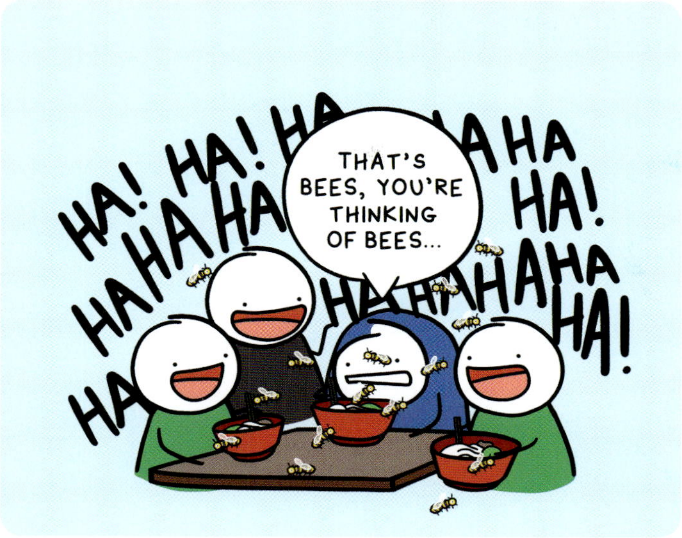
HA! HA! HA
HAHAHA
HAHA
HA
THAT'S BEES, YOU'RE THINKING OF BEES...
AHA HA
HA!
HAHAHA
HA!

My friends were disturbingly delighted.

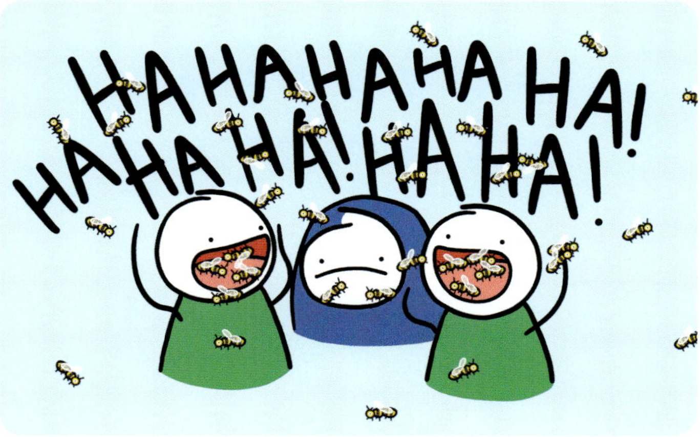
HAHAHAHAHA HA HA!
HAHA HA! HA HA HA!

And yet, their inability to demonstrate the basic human emotion of panic somehow made me wonder if *my* panic was misplaced.

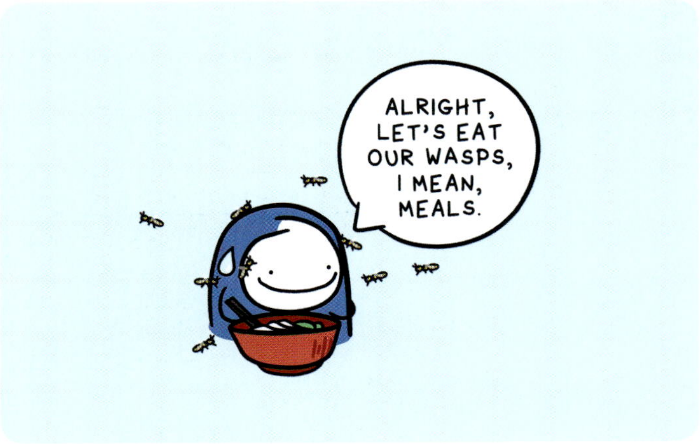
ALRIGHT, LET'S EAT OUR WASPS, I MEAN, MEALS.

Maybe I was wrong. Maybe it's fine to eat with wasps everywhere. Maybe if everyone else is okay with it, I should learn to be okay with it too.

*Maybe I'm allergic to wasp stings.*

And at that thought, a wasp suddenly shot out of nowhere, kamikazed into my soup, and drowned itself.

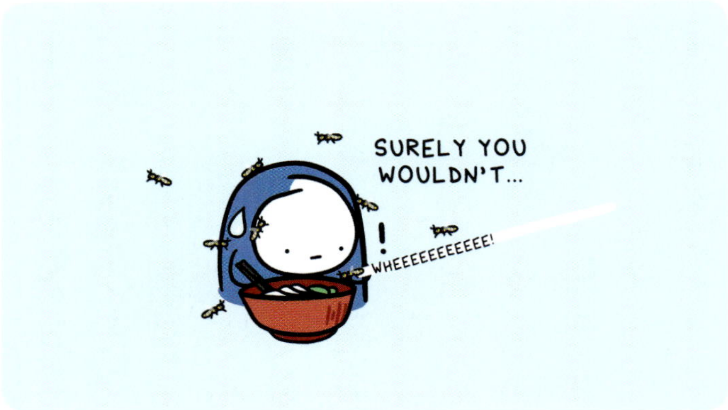
SURELY YOU WOULDN'T...
!
WHEEEEEEEEEEE!

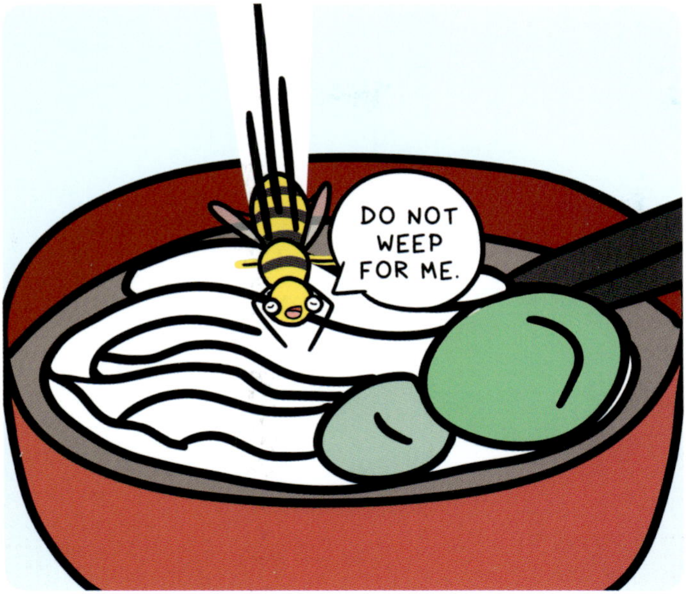
DO NOT WEEP FOR ME.

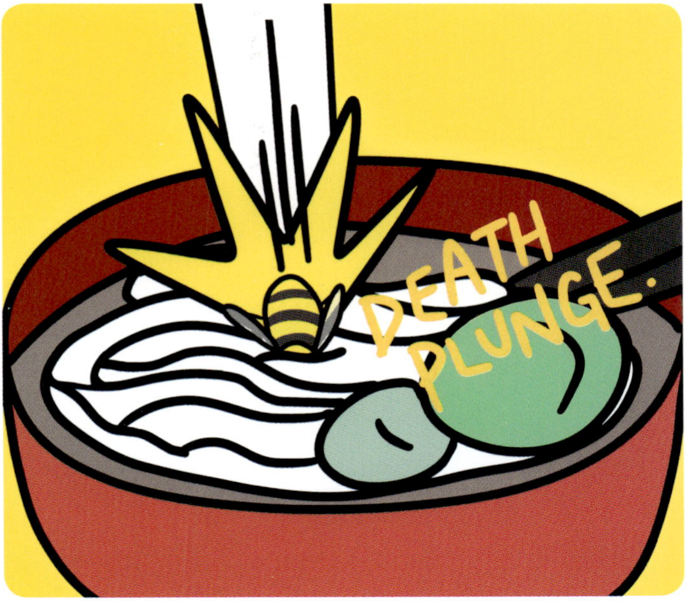
DEATH PLUNGE.

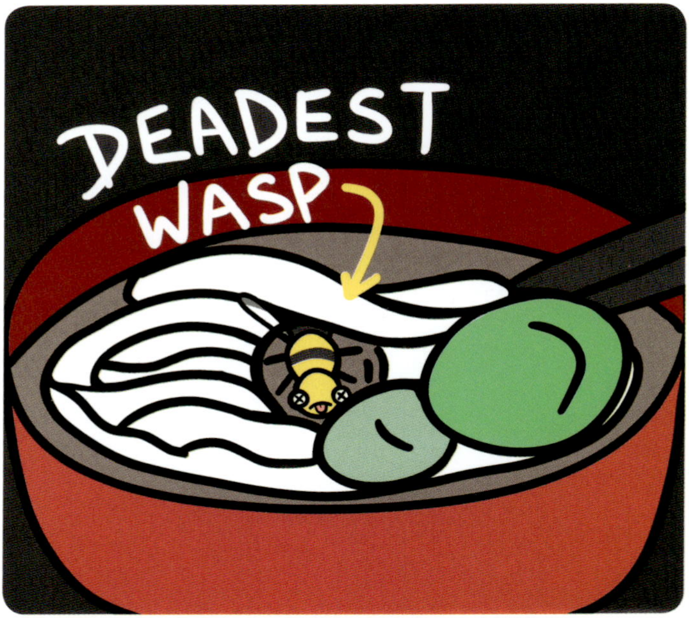
DEADEST
WASP

Looking at the dead wasp now floating at the center of my soup, I knew I was done.

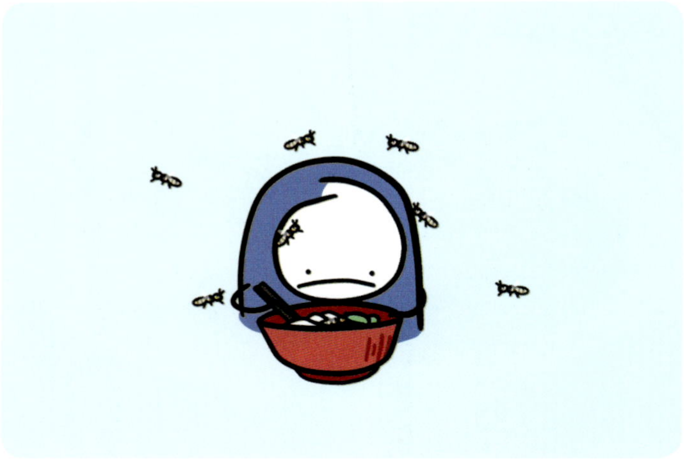

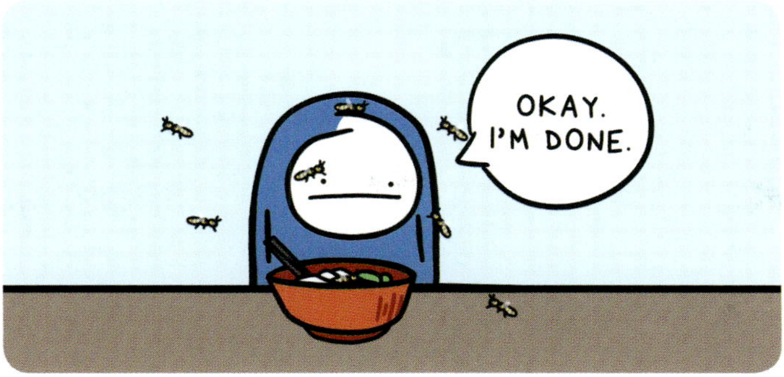
OKAY.
I'M DONE.

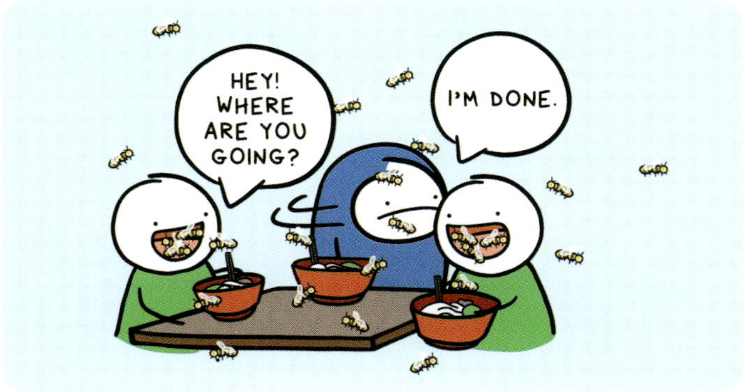
HEY!
WHERE
ARE YOU
GOING?
I'M DONE.

I don't particularly like talking about the years I spent in school. The dull parts were kind of dull, and the fun parts have been sworn to secrecy, so there's really not all that much left to say. And to be honest, most of my memories from school, including the things I learned, have long faded from lack of recall. But there are two things I still distinctly remember about graduation.

1. The graduation cap looks atrocious no matter how you position it.

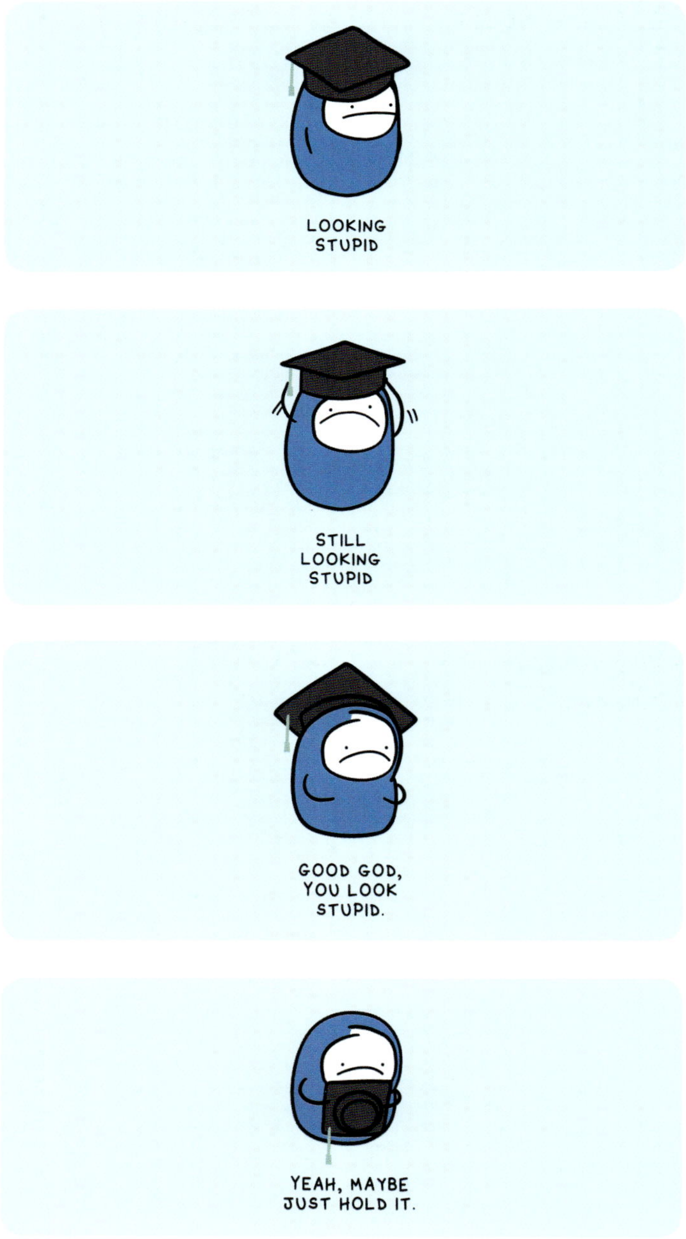
LOOKING STUPID
STILL LOOKING STUPID
GOOD GOD, YOU LOOK STUPID.
YEAH, MAYBE JUST HOLD IT.

2. Everyone is hell-bent on asking you this *one* question.

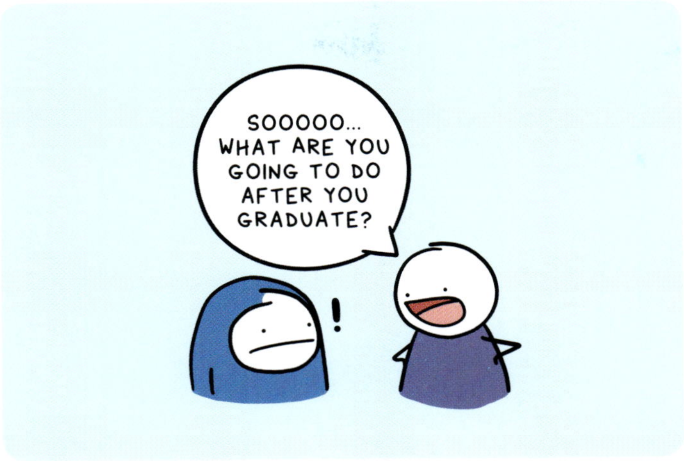
SOOOOO...
WHAT ARE YOU GOING TO DO AFTER YOU GRADUATE?
!

"What are you going to do after you graduate?" The million-dollar question that prompts equally fun, anxiety-inducing follow-up questions such as:

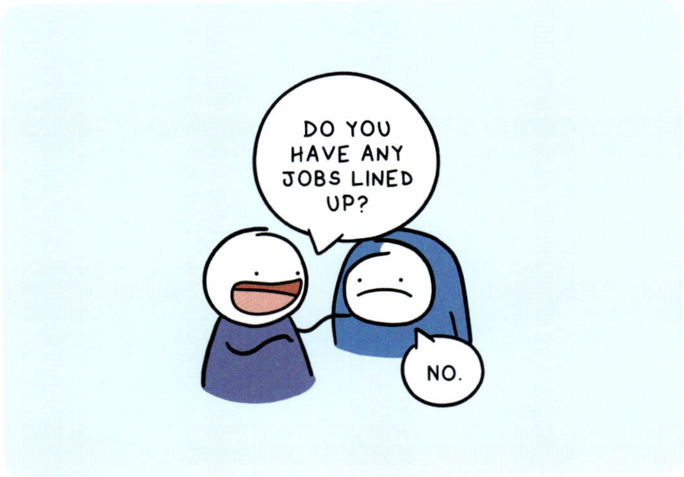
DO YOU HAVE ANY JOBS LINED UP?
NO.

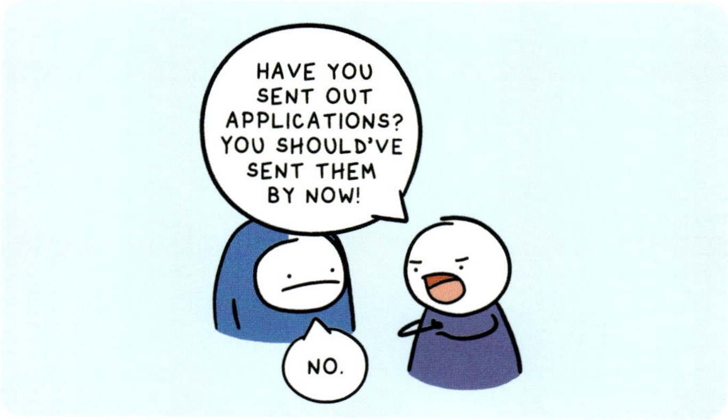
HAVE YOU SENT OUT APPLICATIONS? YOU SHOULD'VE SENT THEM BY NOW!
NO.

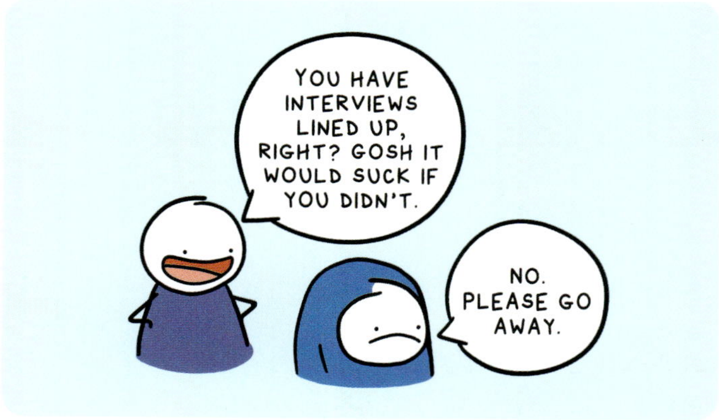
YOU HAVE INTERVIEWS LINED UP, RIGHT? GOSH IT WOULD SUCK IF YOU DIDN'T.
NO. PLEASE GO AWAY.

Never ask a new grad if they have any jobs lined up. It's sort of mean—it's like asking someone who was recently fired when they think they'll get promoted. Life is stressful enough without foolish questions.

The realization that I was ill-prepared for life set in remarkably quickly after graduation. So quickly, in fact, that I almost felt as though I deserved praise for my high level of self-awareness. Sadly, no one ever rewards me for my self-awareness.

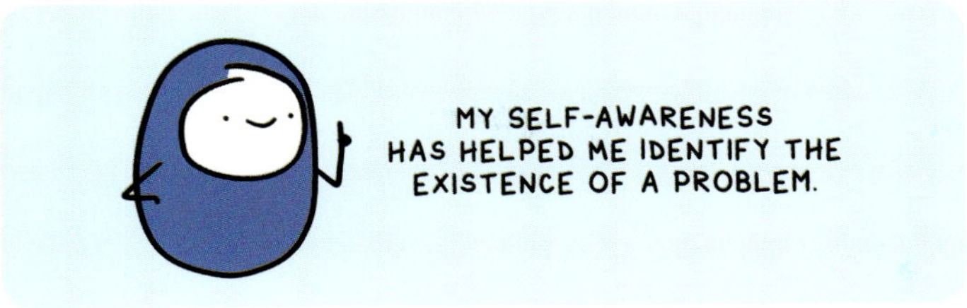
MY SELF-AWARENESS HAS HELPED ME IDENTIFY THE EXISTENCE OF A PROBLEM.

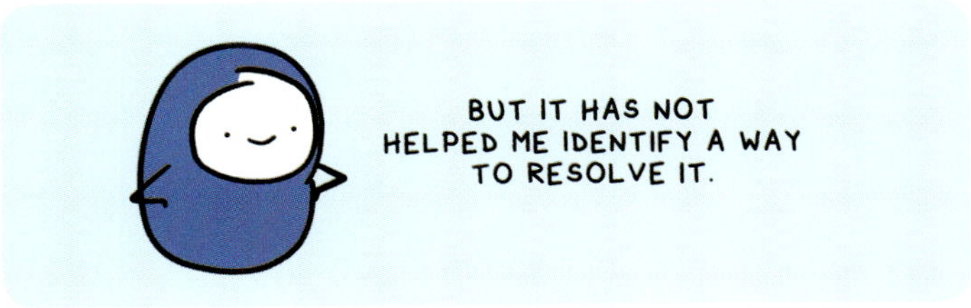
BUT IT HAS NOT HELPED ME IDENTIFY A WAY TO RESOLVE IT.

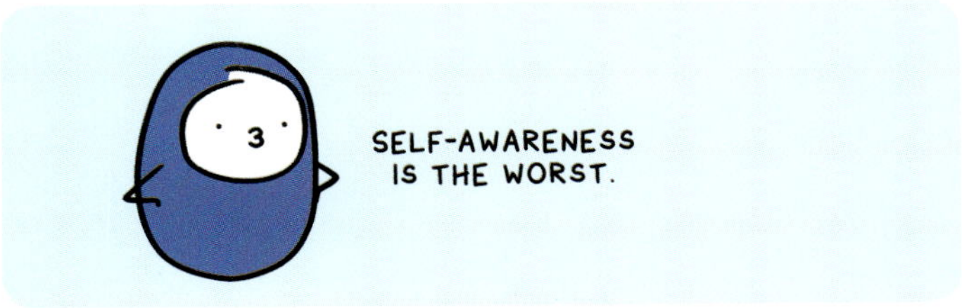
SELF-AWARENESS IS THE WORST.

While life before graduation was smooth, effortless, and brimming with positive affirmation, the real world proved to be much less generous. Having spent the better part of my life bracing for graduation, you'd think I would have been more prepared for what came after.

Tragically, I was not.

I had no plans or clue as to what I would be doing postgraduation, so I did what everyone else seemed to be doing: I started planning a postgraduation trip.

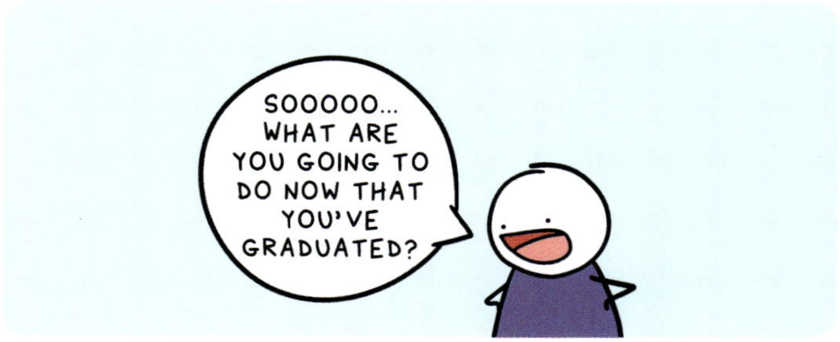
SOOOOO...
WHAT ARE
YOU GOING TO
DO NOW THAT
YOU'VE
GRADUATED?

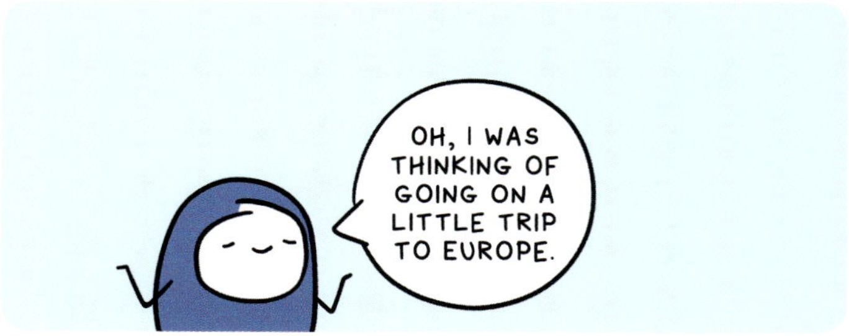
OH, I WAS
THINKING OF
GOING ON A
LITTLE TRIP
TO EUROPE.

A "postgraduation trip" is a glorified escape plan one hatches in order to run away from the fact that they have no idea what they want to do with their lives now that they've been tossed off the conveyor belt of formal education. My solace, however, was quickly dismantled.

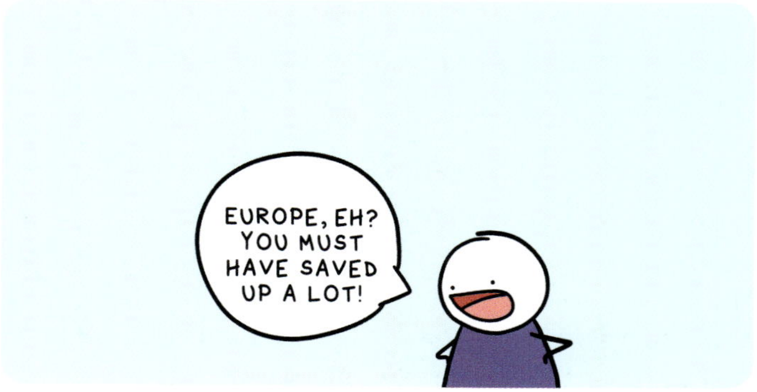
EUROPE, EH?
YOU MUST
HAVE SAVED
UP A LOT!

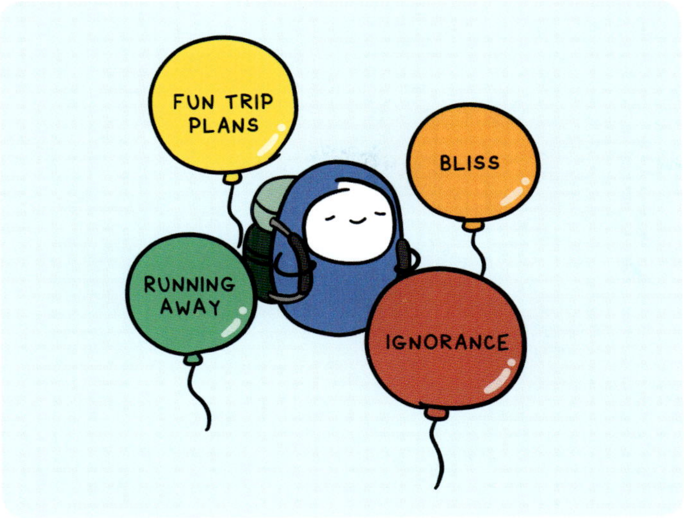
FUN TRIP PLANS
BLISS
RUNNING AWAY
IGNORANCE

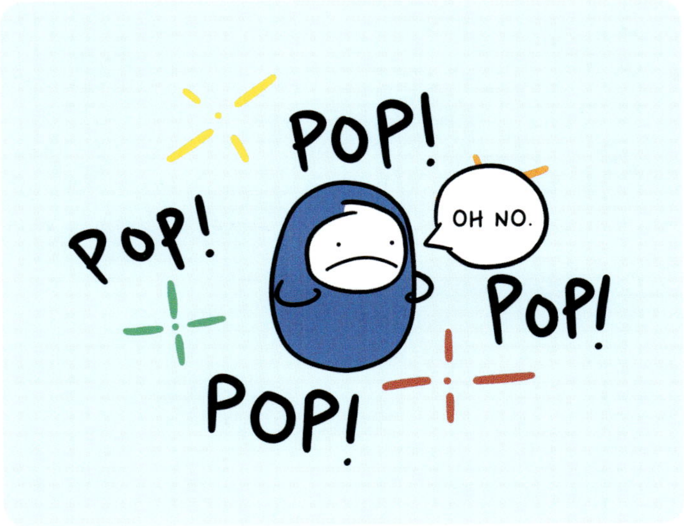
POP!
POP!
OH NO.
POP!
POP!

Money? I had no *money*. After all, what little money I had earned while working part-time during school had gone entirely into my tuition.

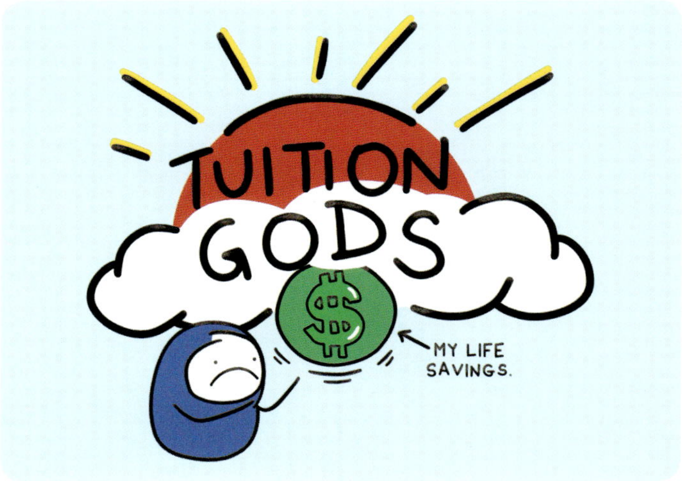
TUITION GODS
MY LIFE SAVINGS.

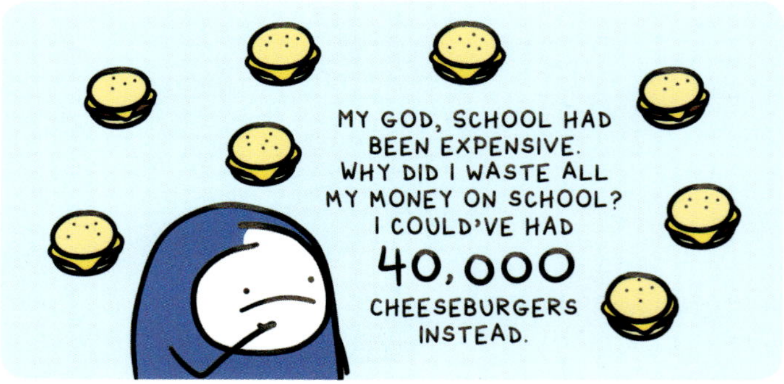
MY GOD, SCHOOL HAD BEEN EXPENSIVE. WHY DID I WASTE ALL MY MONEY ON SCHOOL? I COULD'VE HAD 40,000 CHEESEBURGERS INSTEAD.

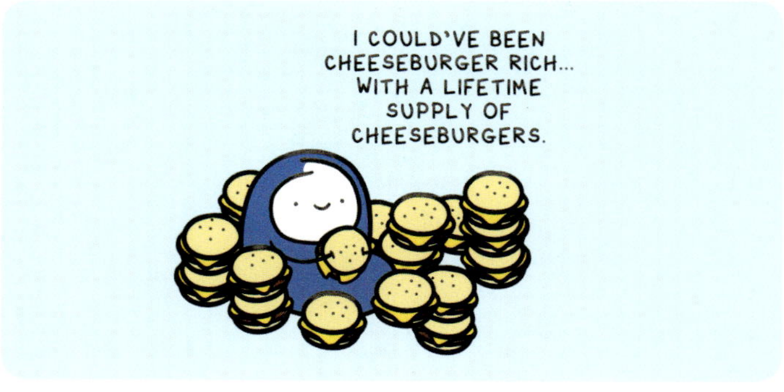
I COULD'VE BEEN CHEESEBURGER RICH... WITH A LIFETIME SUPPLY OF CHEESEBURGERS.

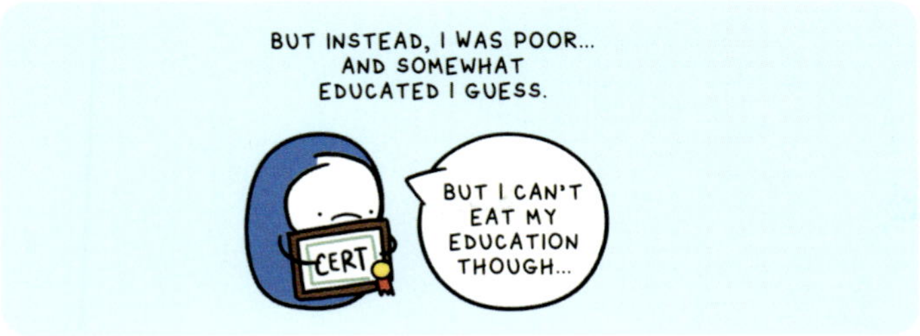
BUT INSTEAD, I WAS POOR... AND SOMEWHAT EDUCATED I GUESS.
CERT
BUT I CAN'T EAT MY EDUCATION THOUGH...

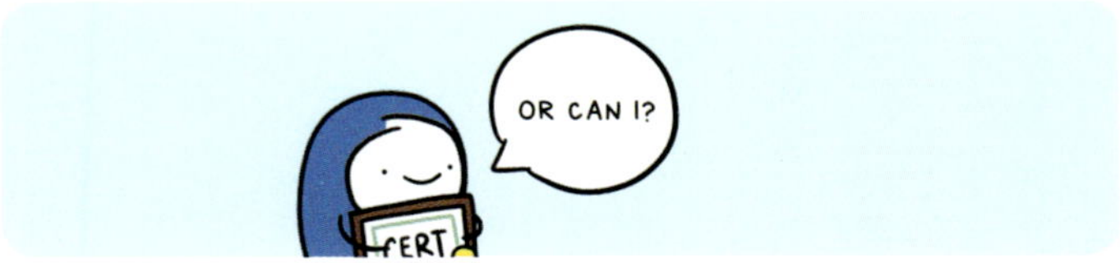
OR CAN I?

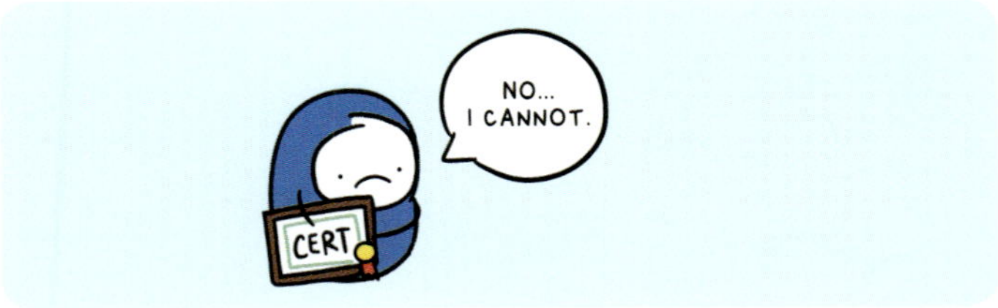
NO... I CANNOT.
CERT

In search of income that would allow me to be cheeseburger rich again, I started hunting for jobs with a hopeful degree of optimism. But this optimism was short-lived, as I came to discover that most job descriptions for entry-level positions looked like this:

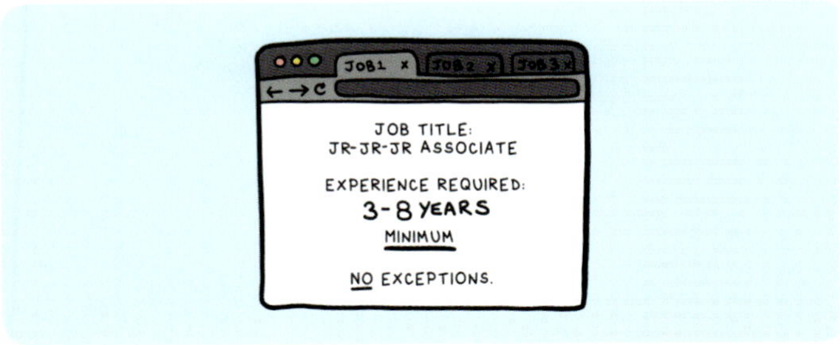
JOB1 x
JOB2 x
JOB3 x
JOB TITLE: JR-JR-JR ASSOCIATE
EXPERIENCE REQUIRED: 3-8 YEARS MINIMUM
NO EXCEPTIONS.

The message was clear.

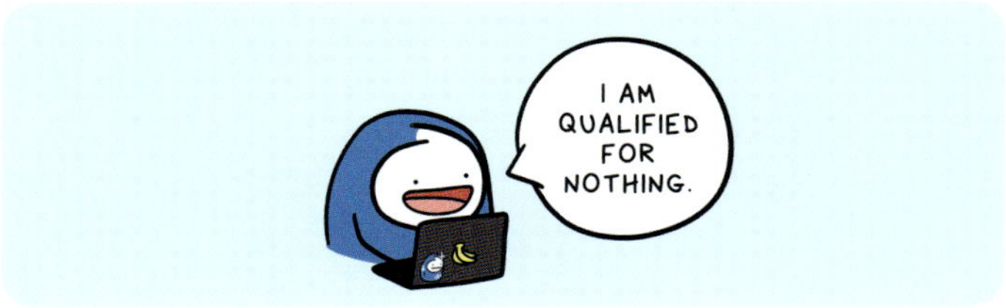
I AM QUALIFIED FOR NOTHING.

I applied to more than sixty jobs before I landed my first offer. I remember this because I had a folder of all my job applications and the list grew depressingly long in the months following graduation.

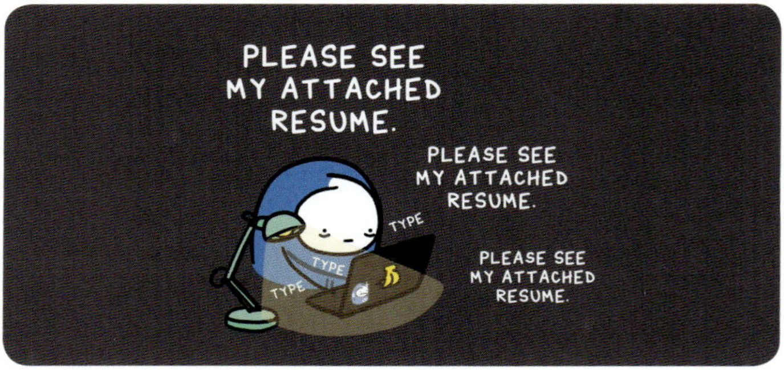
PLEASE SEE MY ATTACHED RESUME.
PLEASE SEE MY ATTACHED RESUME.
TYPE
TYPE
TYPE
PLEASE SEE MY ATTACHED RESUME.

Although my first job out of school paid pennies, I was overjoyed just to have any job at all. I should have negotiated my salary, but my parents had always taught me to be thankful instead of asking for more. So when presented with my first full-time job offer, I simply said, "Thank you," and accepted it with nothing but deep gratitude.

After signing my contract, I started feeling this wonderful, yet wholly unearned sense of accomplishment.

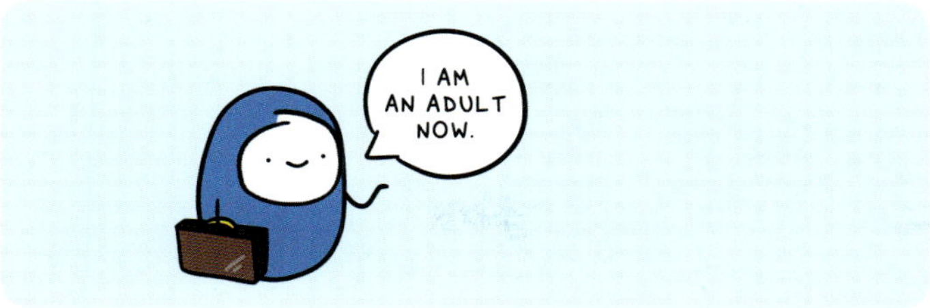
I AM AN ADULT NOW.

I was an adult, and I even had the business cards to prove it.

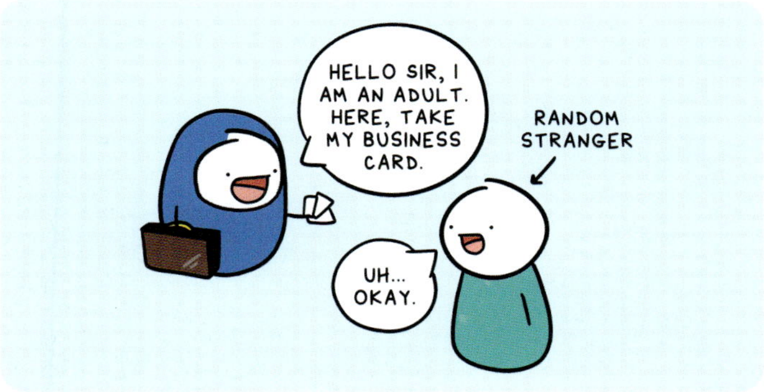
HELLO SIR, I AM AN ADULT. HERE, TAKE MY BUSINESS CARD.
RANDOM STRANGER
UH... OKAY.

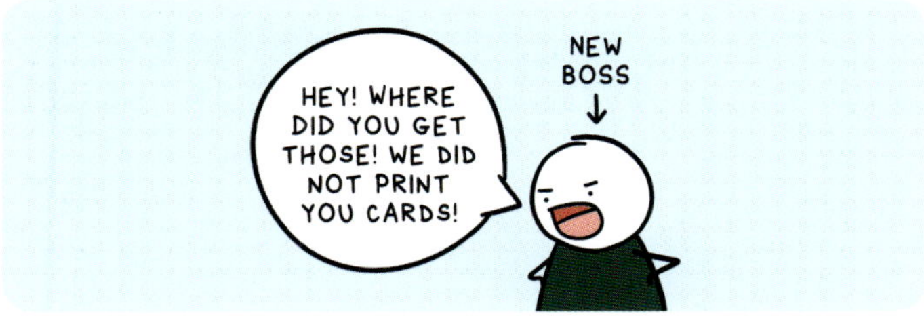
NEW BOSS
HEY! WHERE DID YOU GET THOSE! WE DID NOT PRINT YOU CARDS!

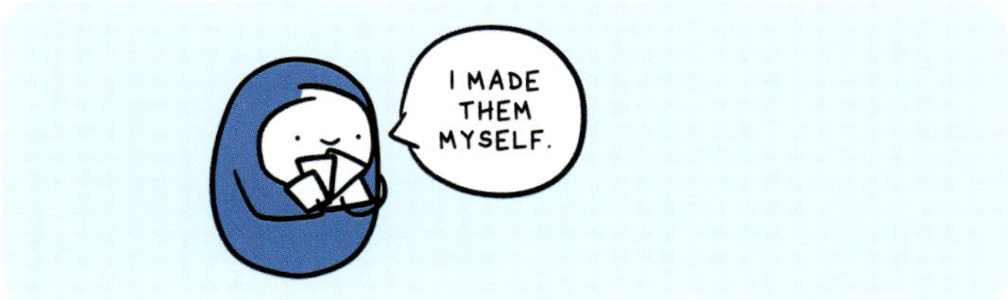
I MADE THEM MYSELF.

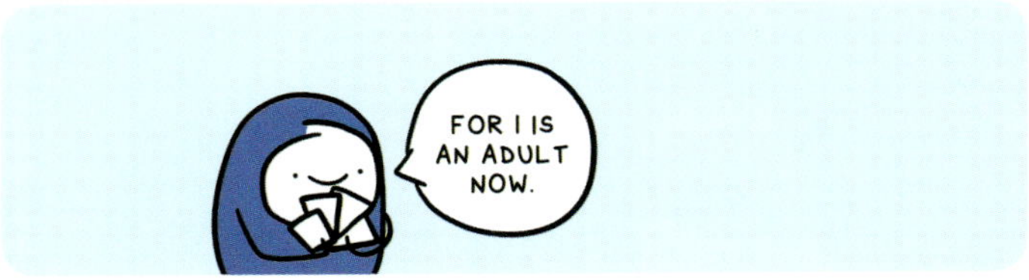
FOR I IS AN ADULT NOW.

Maybe it was that particular job, or perhaps it was its repetitive nature, but the novelty and high of my first full-time job faded quickly.

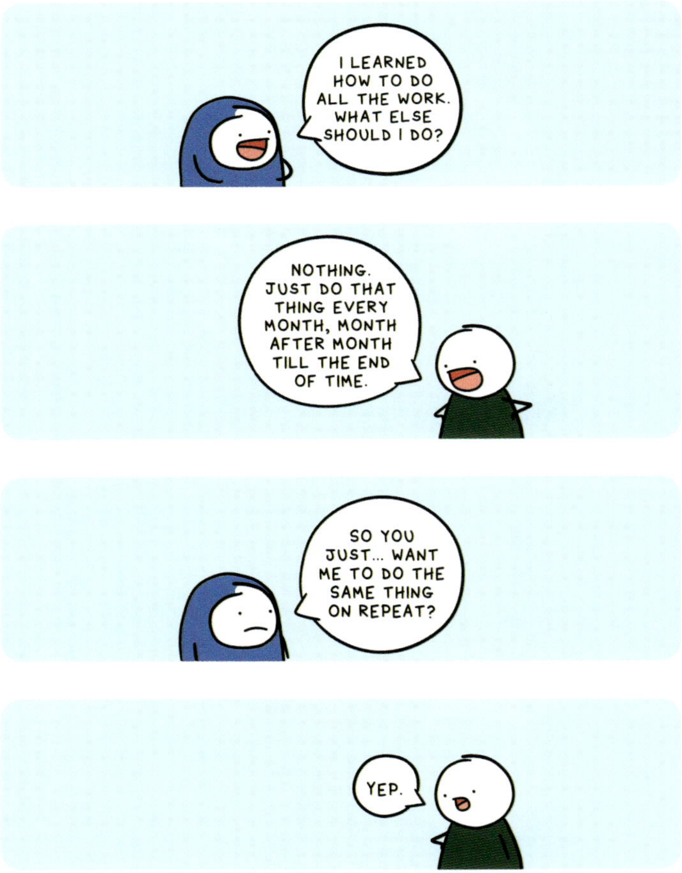
I LEARNED HOW TO DO ALL THE WORK. WHAT ELSE SHOULD I DO?
NOTHING. JUST DO THAT THING EVERY MONTH, MONTH AFTER MONTH TILL THE END OF TIME.
SO YOU JUST... WANT ME TO DO THE SAME THING ON REPEAT?
YEP.

Within months, my enthusiasm had waned to a fizzle.

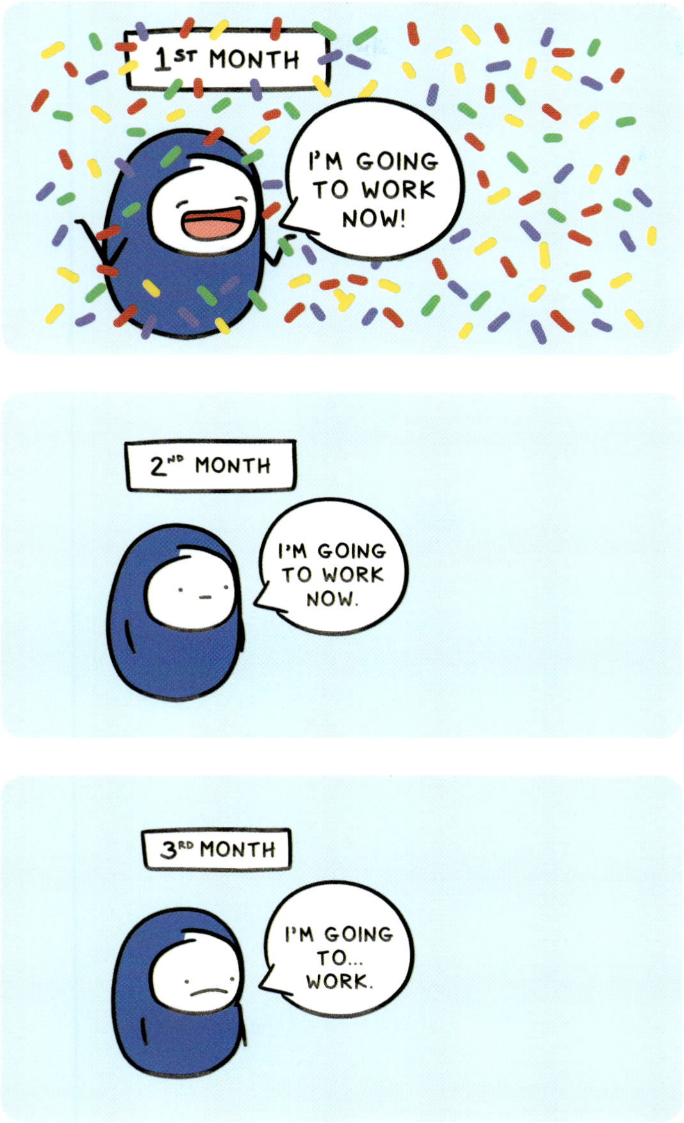
1ST MONTH
I'M GOING TO WORK NOW!
2ND MONTH
I'M GOING TO WORK NOW.
3RD MONTH
I'M GOING TO... WORK.

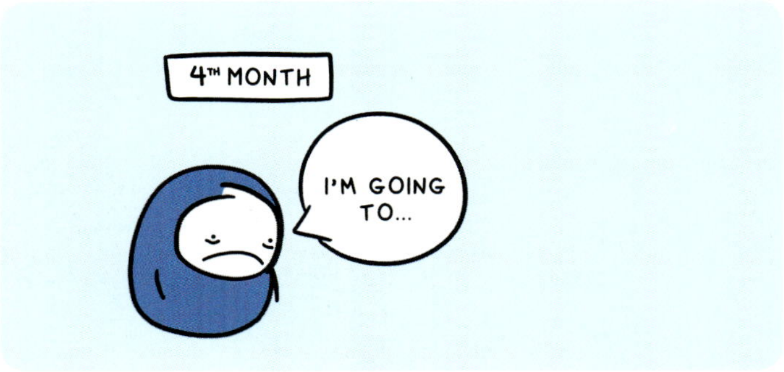
4TH MONTH
I'M GOING TO...

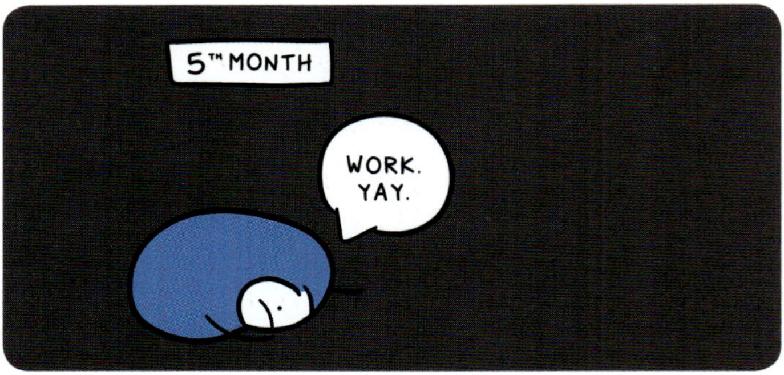
5TH MONTH
WORK. YAY.

I started seeing wasps at work. Wasps like repetitive, pointless tasks. Wasps like my manager asking me to sit still and do nothing for hours on end. I tried to be proactive and find ways to be of value whenever my work was done, but eagerness from a new graduate is not always appreciated.

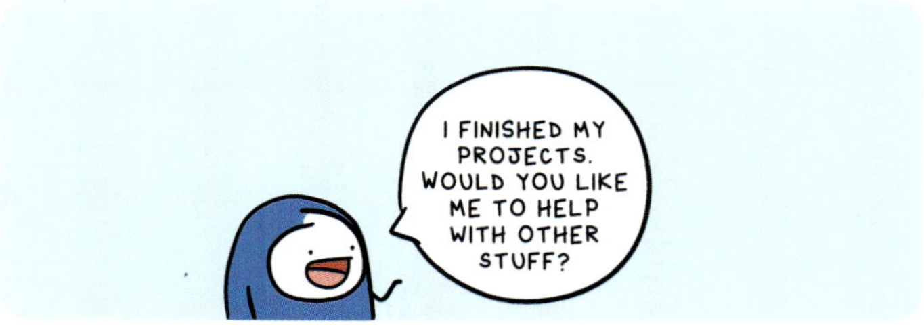
I FINISHED MY PROJECTS. WOULD YOU LIKE ME TO HELP WITH OTHER STUFF?

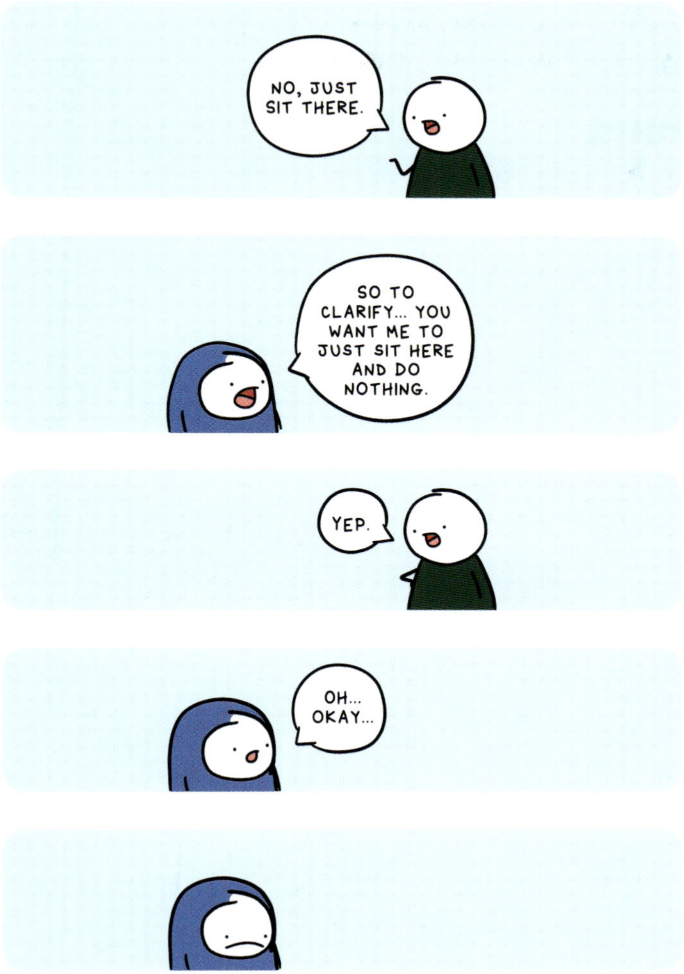
NO, JUST SIT THERE.
SO TO CLARIFY... YOU WANT ME TO JUST SIT HERE AND DO NOTHING.
YEP.
OH... OKAY...

Looking back, I recognize there are worse things in life than being bored at work. But this understanding, this appreciation towards the luxury of not having any work to do at all, comes from first having a job where you were overworked to begin with, the kind of job I had yet to experience.

I grew restless. Patience was never a virtue I had, and as I looked down at my watch, I thought about what a long day of nothing it would be. I thought about the days and months of nothing that would ensue and the years of nothing that would follow.

DOING NOTHING WITH MY LIFE.
STILL DOING NOTHING.
FOREVER DOING NOTHING WITH LIFE.

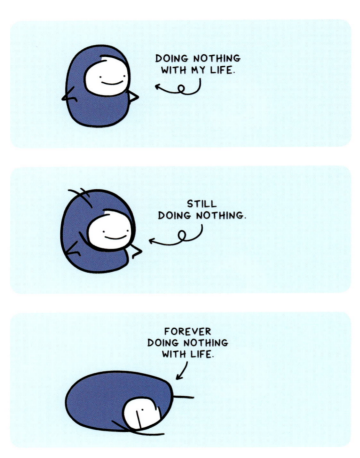

*Is this it?* Is this what I signed up for? Is this what I had plunged myself into the crimson-red student loan waters for?

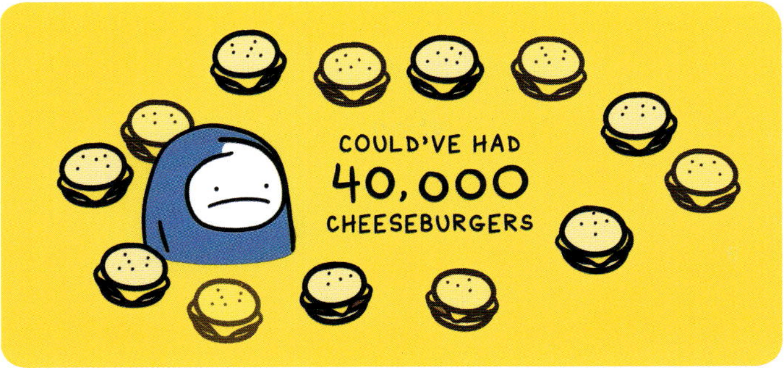
COULD'VE HAD
40,000
CHEESEBURGERS

Defeated from sitting in a half-cubicle for eight hours, I went to consult my dad about my work predicament.

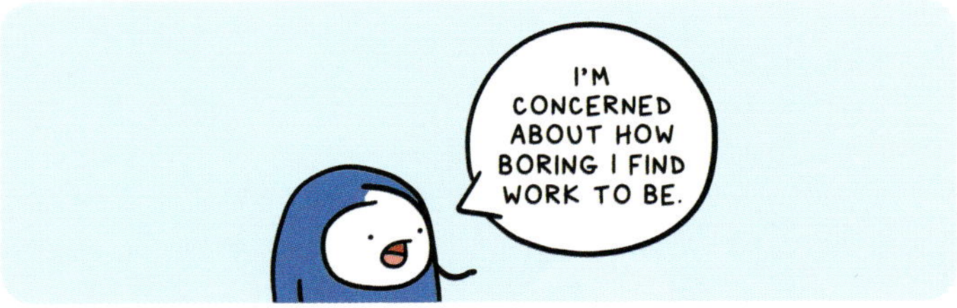
I'M CONCERNED ABOUT HOW BORING I FIND WORK TO BE.

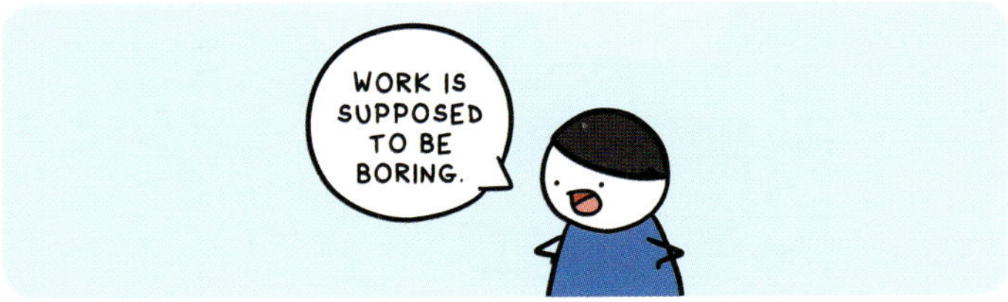
WORK IS SUPPOSED TO BE BORING.

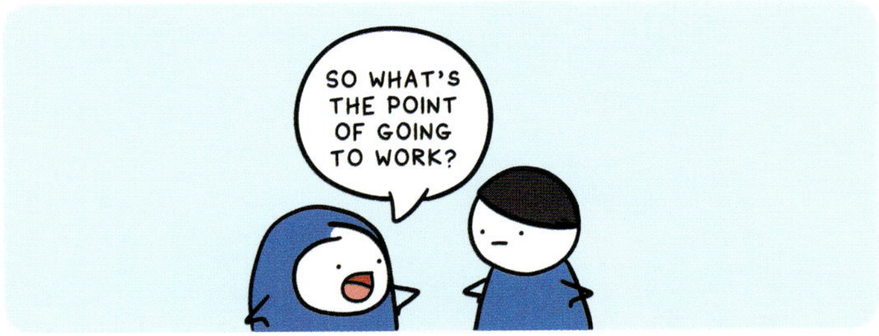
SO WHAT'S THE POINT OF GOING TO WORK?

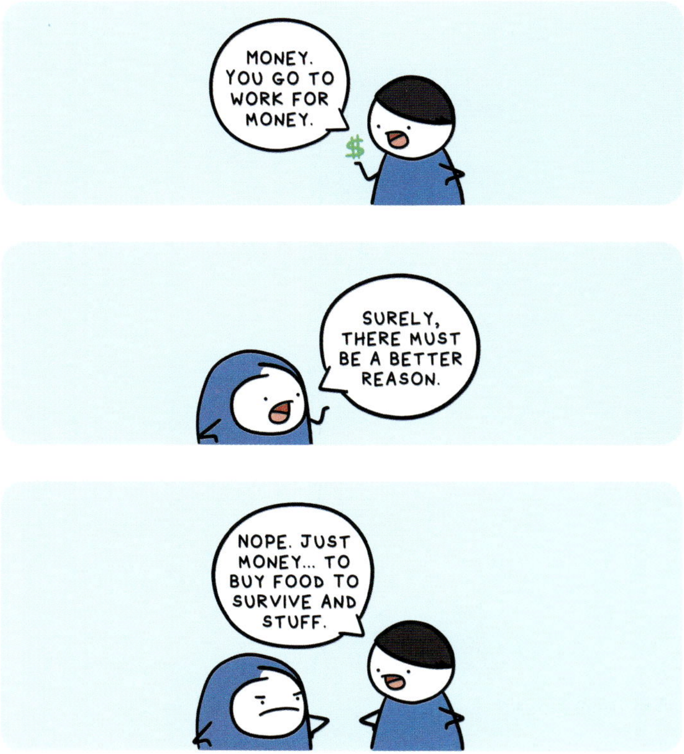
MONEY. YOU GO TO WORK FOR MONEY.
$
SURELY, THERE MUST BE A BETTER REASON.
NOPE. JUST MONEY... TO BUY FOOD TO SURVIVE AND STUFF.

The reasonable thing to do would have been to just accept it—to accept what most sensible adults have come to accept—that work is a pointless sacrifice to the gods in order to afford the basic necessities and niceties of life.

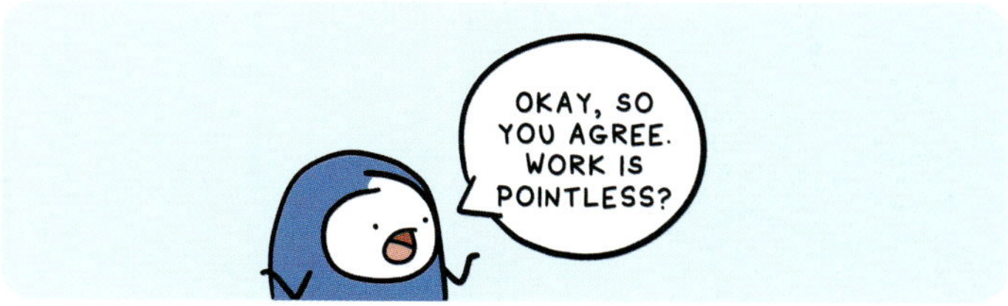
OKAY, SO YOU AGREE. WORK IS POINTLESS?

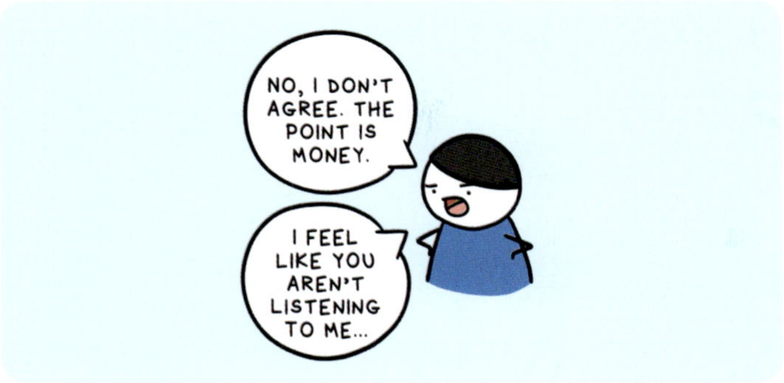
NO, I DON'T AGREE. THE POINT IS MONEY.
I FEEL LIKE YOU AREN'T LISTENING TO ME...

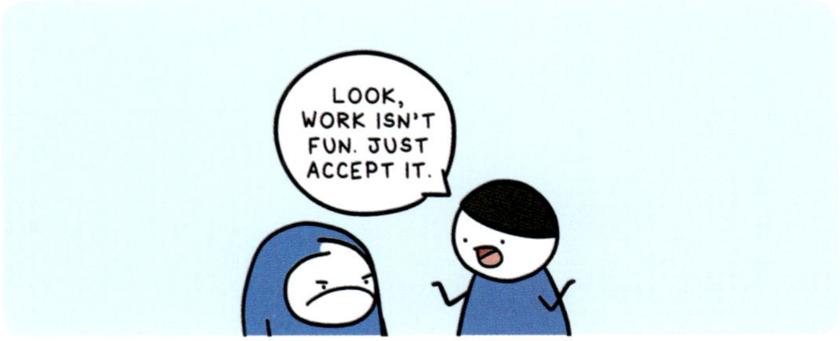
LOOK, WORK ISN'T FUN. JUST ACCEPT IT.

Yes, the reasonable thing to do would have been to accept it and move on.

But I have *never* been reasonable.

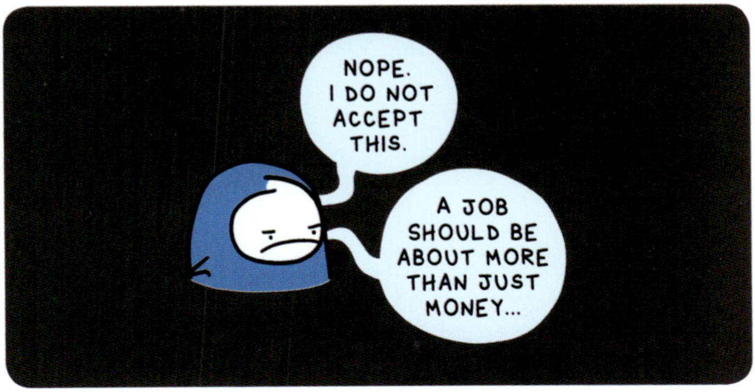
NOPE. I DO NOT ACCEPT THIS.
A JOB SHOULD BE ABOUT MORE THAN JUST MONEY...

And so, a radical solution was born.

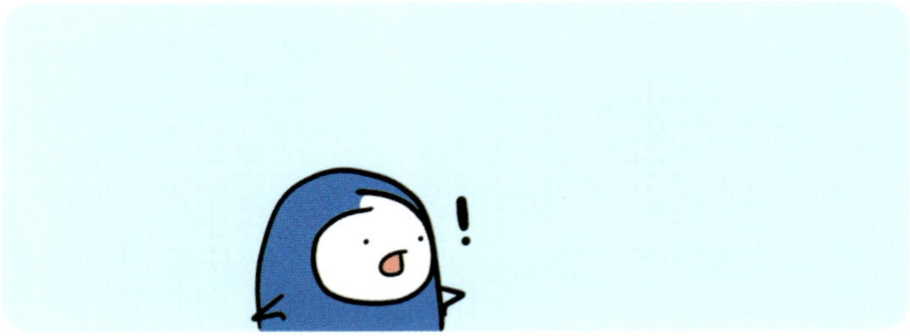

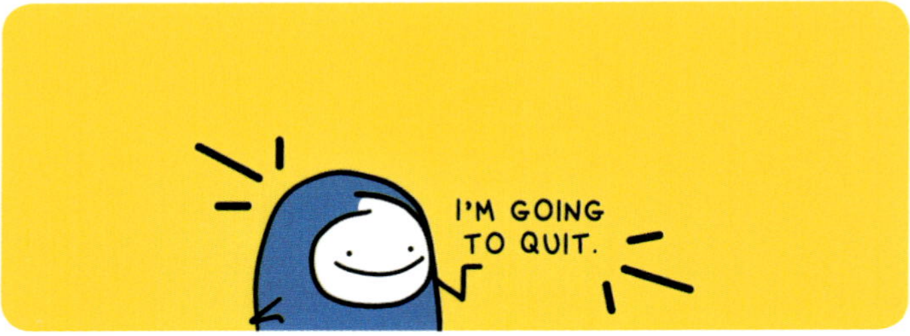
I'M GOING TO QUIT.

Thrilled by my own decision-making prowess, I immediately went to share this *brilliant* new plan with my dad. He was fully supportive of it.

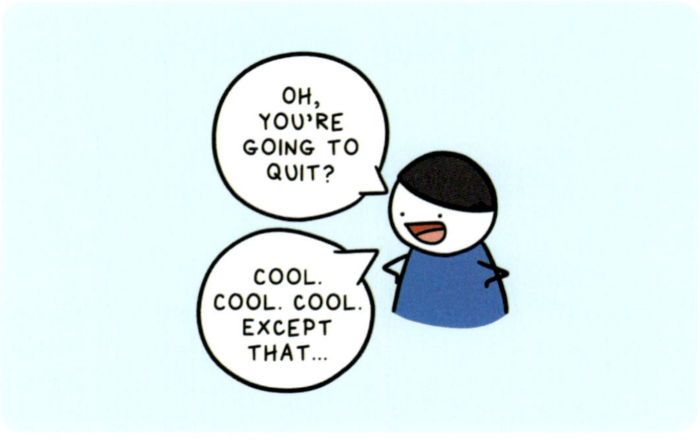
OH, YOU'RE GOING TO QUIT?
COOL. COOL. COOL. EXCEPT THAT...

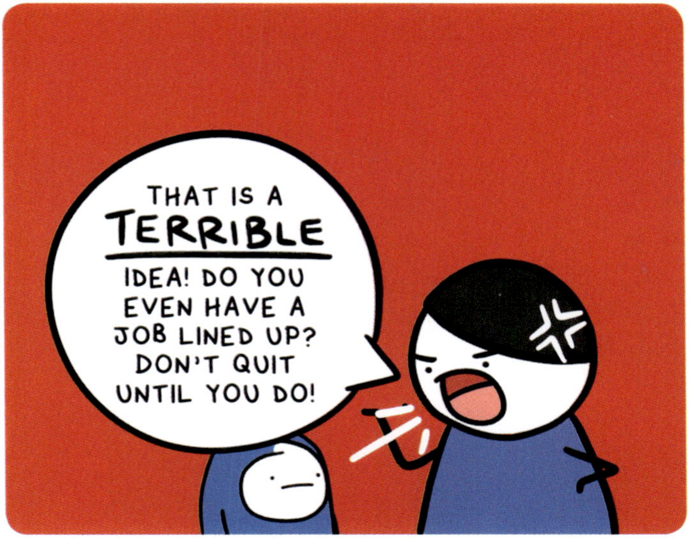
THAT IS A TERRIBLE IDEA! DO YOU EVEN HAVE A JOB LINED UP? DON'T QUIT UNTIL YOU DO!

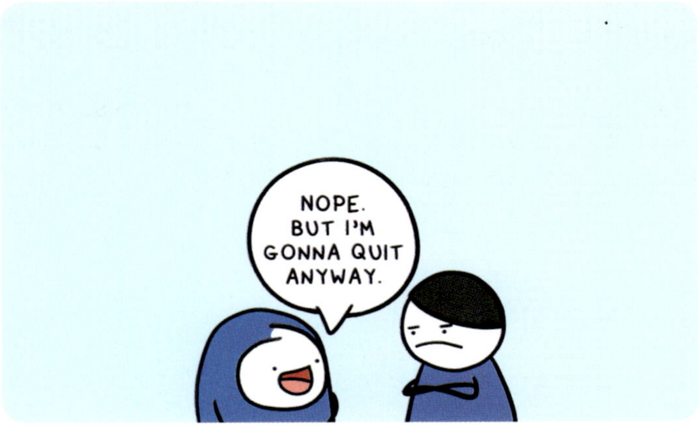
NOPE. BUT I'M GONNA QUIT ANYWAY.

Work became so much more tolerable after I decided to resign. I would later learn that one of the most liberating decisions one can make in life is to quit a job they hate.

HEY! CAN YOU DO SOME MINDLESS WORK FOR ME?
SURE!
BECAUSE I'M QUITTING SOON.
WHAT'S THAT?
NOTHING.

It was as though I could see the light at the end of the tunnel. I was no longer dredging along an infinite path that led to nowhere—there was finally a way out. The knowledge that I could quit (and would soon be quitting) kept me alive in the darkest of days.

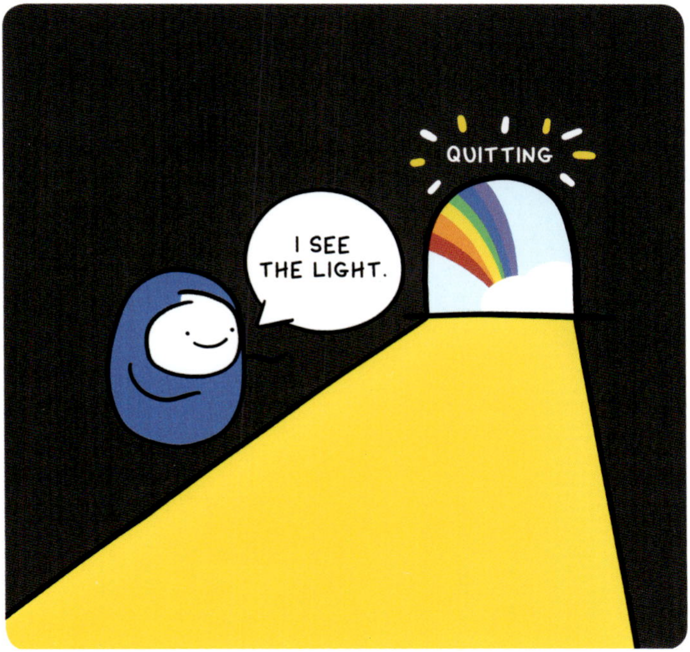
QUITTING
I SEE THE LIGHT.

But before officially resigning, I felt I owed it to myself to do a postmortem of what went wrong. I mapped out all the attributes I enjoyed and despised in that particular job, and vowed to never again find myself in a position I didn't love.

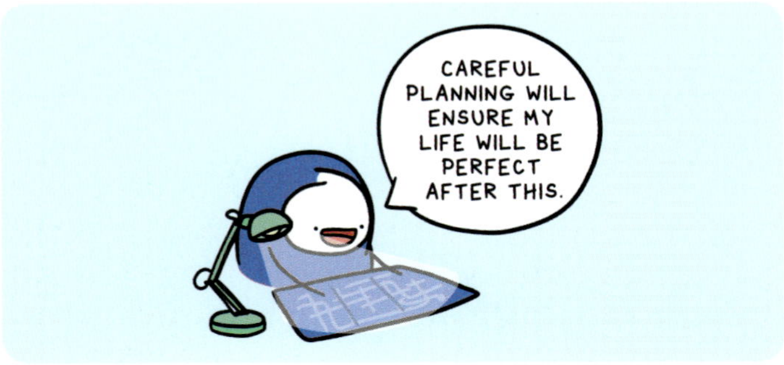
CAREFUL PLANNING WILL ENSURE MY LIFE WILL BE PERFECT AFTER THIS.

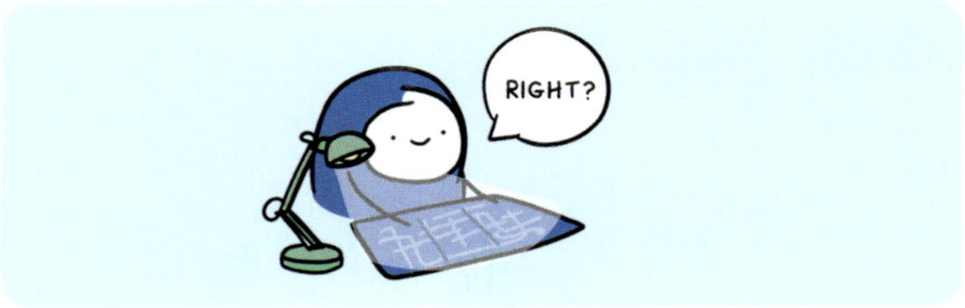
RIGHT?

Oh, young me, so *adorable* and drunk on optimism. I miss that.

In an effort to soothe my dad's anxiety, I decided to do something tediously responsible and markedly less fun than what I had originally planned: I would secure a new job before leaving my current one.

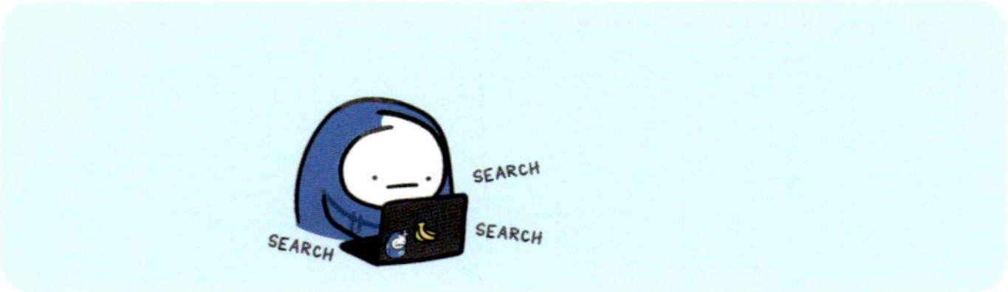
SEARCH
SEARCH
SEARCH

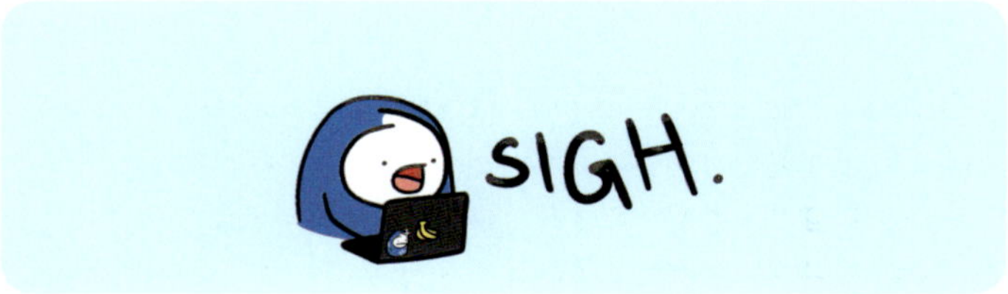
SIGH.

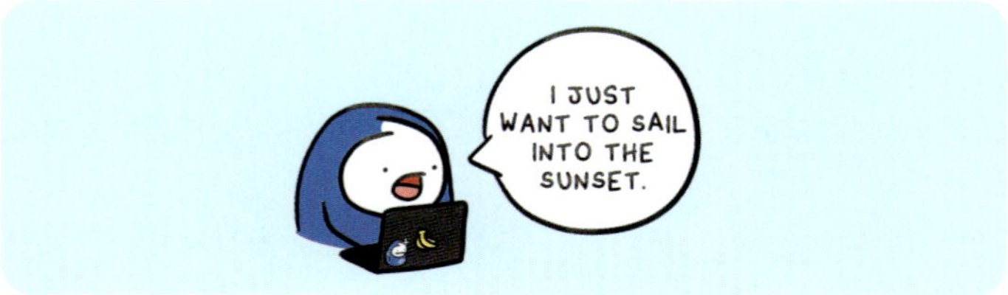
I JUST WANT TO SAIL INTO THE SUNSET.

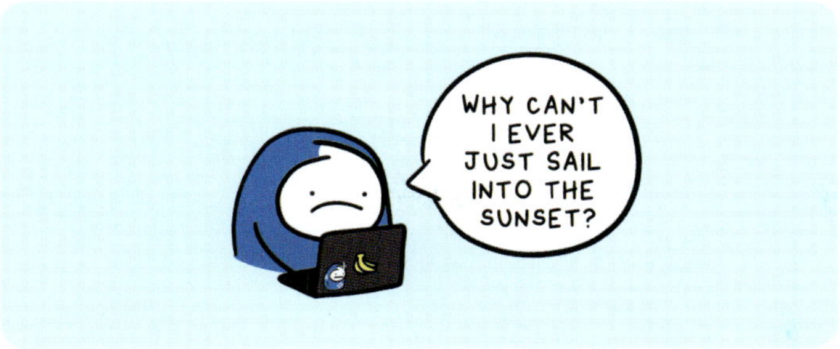
WHY CAN'T I EVER JUST SAIL INTO THE SUNSET?

I didn't know what I wanted to do in my new job, but I knew what I hated from my current position, so I started refining my search based on those parameters.

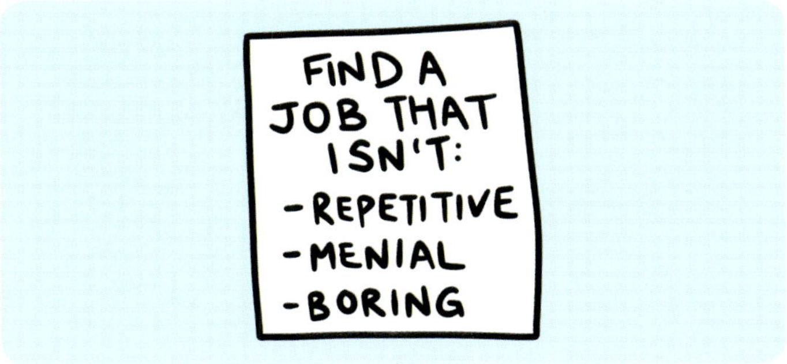
FIND A JOB THAT ISN'T:
-REPETITIVE
-MENIAL
-BORING

A few weeks later, I was offered a position at a new startup—a job that promised to be neither repetitive nor boring. However, the new job was also simultaneously less stable, had less benefits, and somehow paid even *less* than my current position.

Like every person standing at the precipice of quitting their job, I questioned whether I was making the right call. I remember feeling stifling anxiety towards the idea of having to hand in my two weeks' notice. It felt so confrontational, and I hated confrontation.

OH, NO.
CONFRONTATION!

Eventually, the universe grew sick of my conflict-avoidant nonsense and gave me a swift kick out the door. Later, I would discover that when you don't make the call on something, the universe will gladly do it for you. The universe is proactive like that.

I CANNOT DECIDE WHAT TO DO.
I DECIDE FOR YOU!
OH, NO THAT'S NOT NECES...

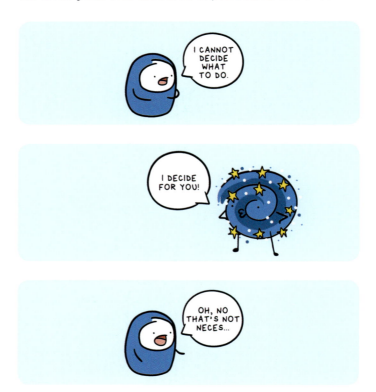

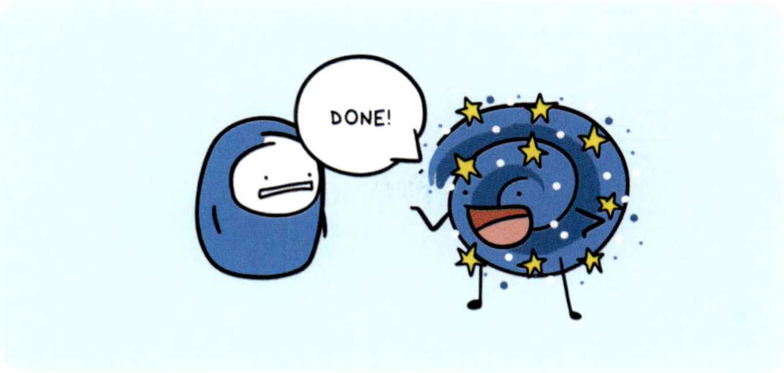
DONE!

The universe made the call for me that very next morning.

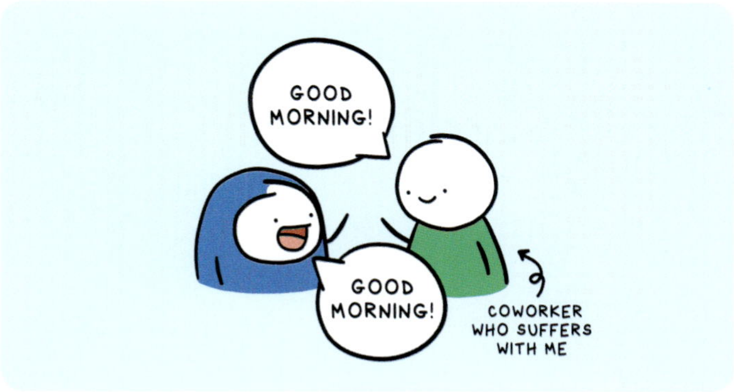
GOOD MORNING!
GOOD MORNING!
COWORKER WHO SUFFERS WITH ME

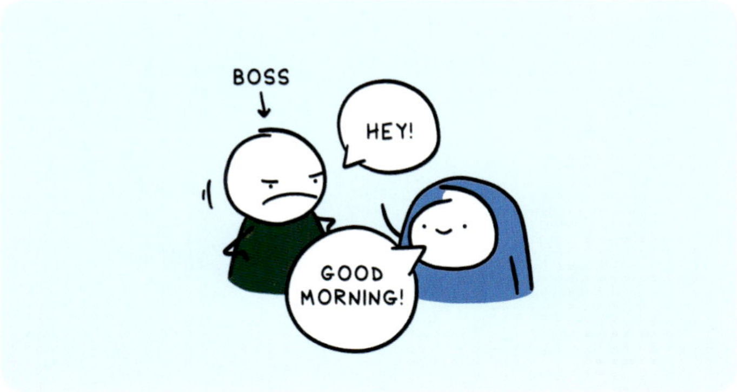
BOSS
HEY!
GOOD MORNING!

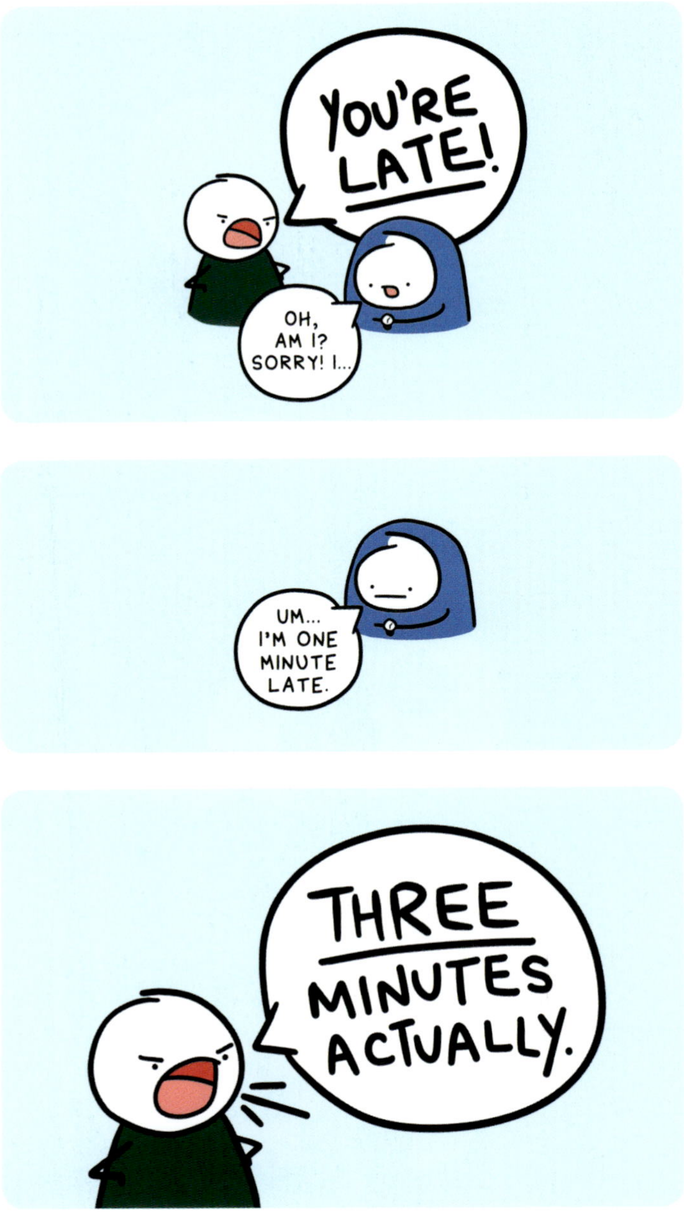
YOU'RE LATE!
OH, AM I? SORRY! I...
UM... I'M ONE MINUTE LATE.
THREE MINUTES ACTUALLY.

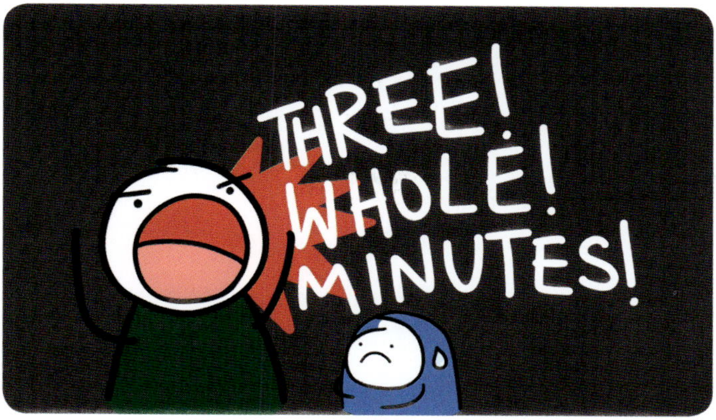
THREE!
WHOLE!
MINUTES!

At first, I laughed. Because I genuinely thought my manager was joking. I often accidentally laugh at things that I misinterpret as jokes—a habit that has come at a great cost to me over the years. Sadly, my manager wasn't joking, and my laughter did not help. I should've known better—my manager never joked. Jokes are for humans.

My coworker, sensing the danger, glanced over with a sympathetic look that silently said "I'm sorry this is our life." It was the kind of workplace camaraderie that could only develop through a shared experience of oppression and suffering.

My manager lost it. She started to viciously berate me for being three minutes late. She did not seem to realize nor care that my coworkers and I routinely stayed fifteen minutes after work to help wrap things up. The injustice of the situation brought me to the verge of tears, but I was determined not to cry. *My tears are to be saved for sad movies—not sad managers,* I reminded myself.

As I stared into my manager's babbling mouth, I once again relived that moment of seeing the wasp drowning itself in my soup.

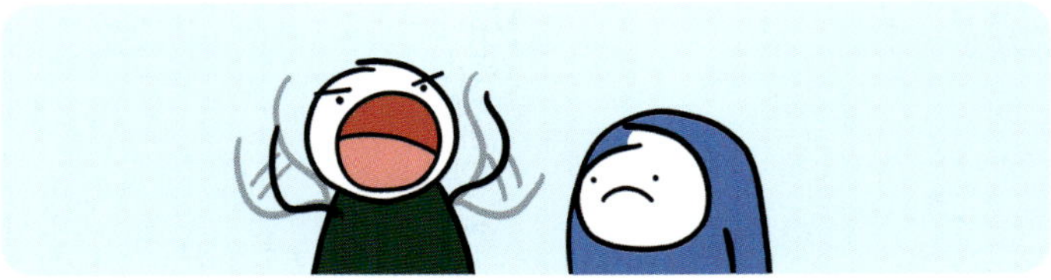

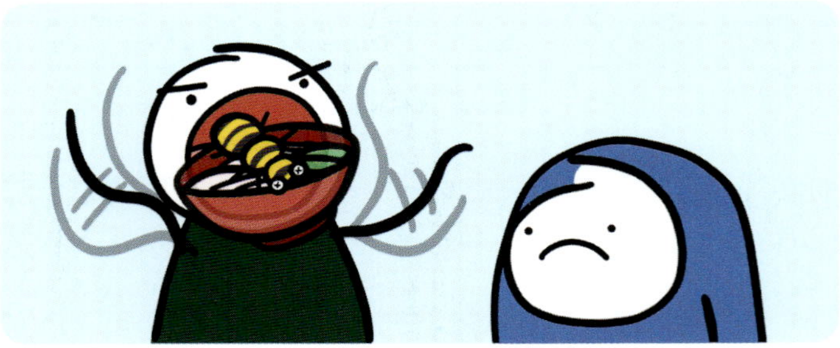

And just like that, I knew I was done.

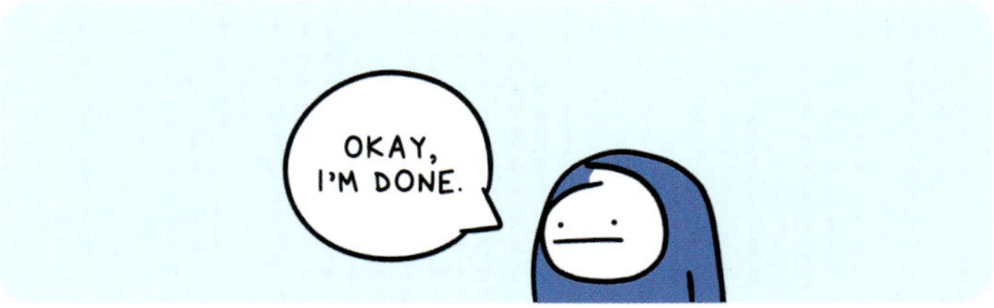
OKAY,
I'M DONE.

The next day, I arrived three minutes early to work. It wasn't even a passive aggressive protest, the buses just happened to be running a bit faster that day. I remember wondering whether this coincidence was a nod from the universe approving what I was about to do.

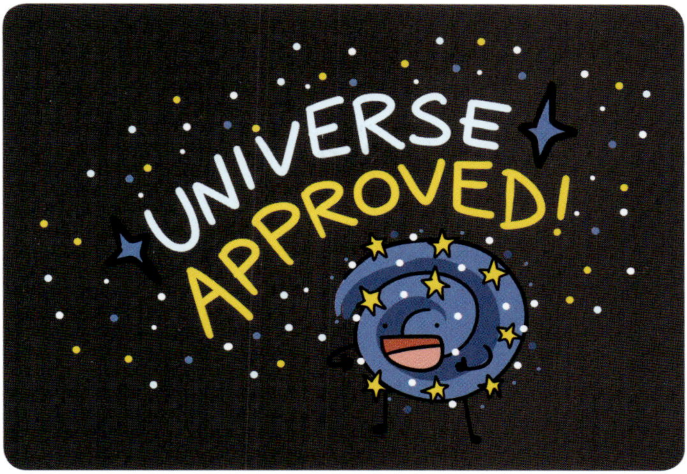
UNIVERSE
APPROVED!

I knocked on the door to my manager's office and felt a bucket of anxiety sloshing around in my gut.

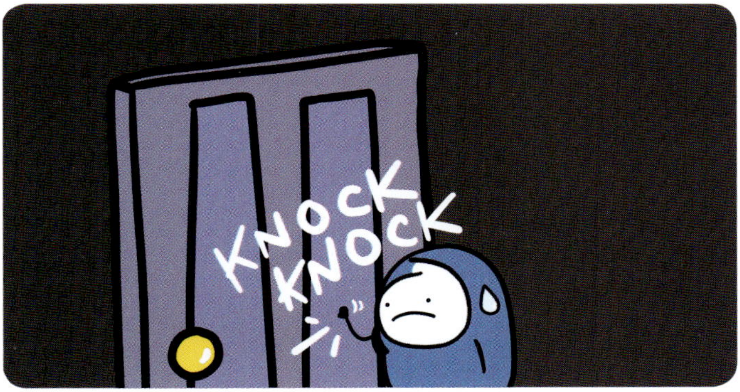
KNOCK
KNOCK

My manager was shocked when I handed over my letter of resignation and gave my two weeks' notice. "But I thought you were having a good time here?" she said. This statement was paired with a look of such genuine hurt that I almost forgot the events that had transpired a mere morning before.

My manager was such a silly goose.

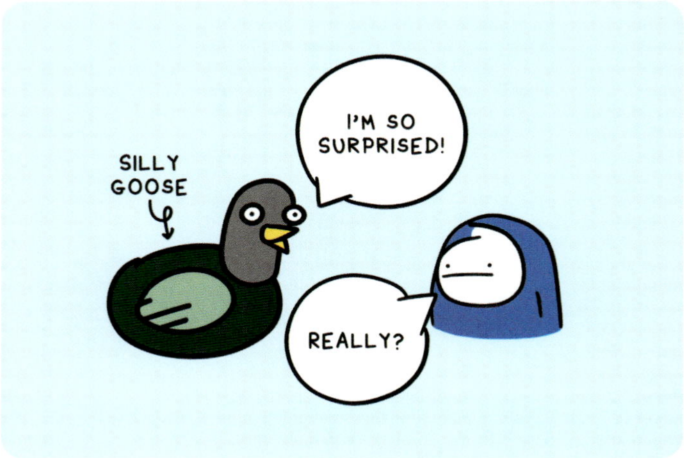
SILLY GOOSE
I'M SO SURPRISED!
REALLY?

The two weeks that followed were ethereal bliss. Words cannot describe the feeling of salvation that comes from quitting a job that kills your soul. In those two weeks, I was free from the tiresome shackles of workplace nonsense.

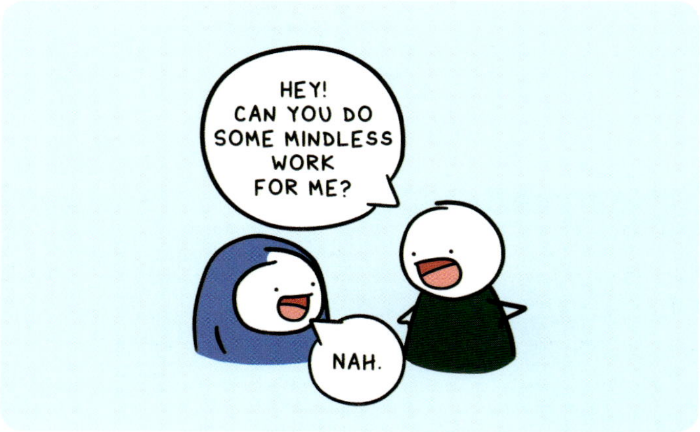
HEY! CAN YOU DO SOME MINDLESS WORK FOR ME?
NAH.

In those two weeks, I was post-resignation *invincible*.

Even today, I still hold on to the memory of that brief period of invincibility. It's important to hold on to your good days; they keep you sane in the face of bad ones.

•   •   •

The next job that followed was the complete antithesis of my first, so I had high hopes going in. It was a young startup, and I found myself intimidated by the new surroundings and processes almost immediately. In the midst of this transition, I once again accepted their first offer without negotiation.

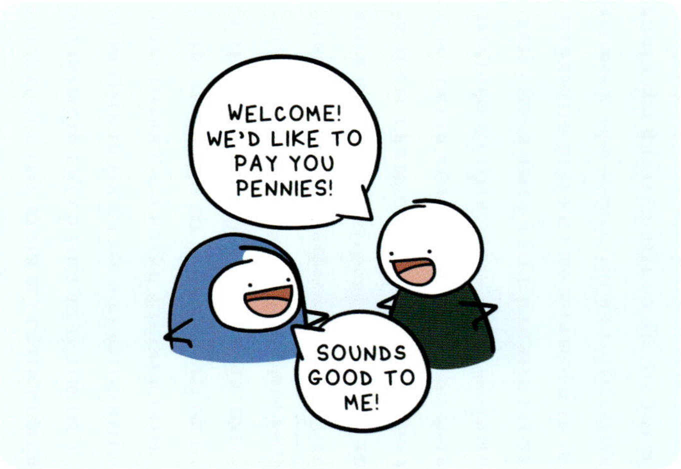
WELCOME! WE'D LIKE TO PAY YOU PENNIES!
SOUNDS GOOD TO ME!

For the record, only an *idiot* doesn't negotiate their pay. And if my time machine would allow it, I would gladly go back just to smack my idiotic self on the head for not even *attempting* to negotiate my starting salary. I mean, think of the cheeseburgers I have lost. It's completely unacceptable. But I guess being an idiot is part of the charm of being young.

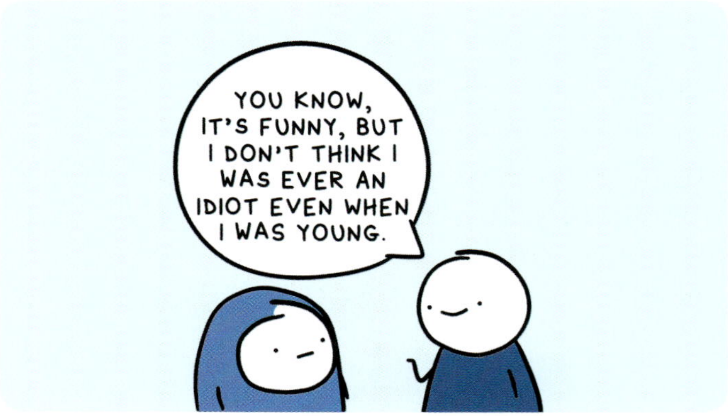
YOU KNOW, IT'S FUNNY, BUT I DON'T THINK I WAS EVER AN IDIOT EVEN WHEN I WAS YOUNG.

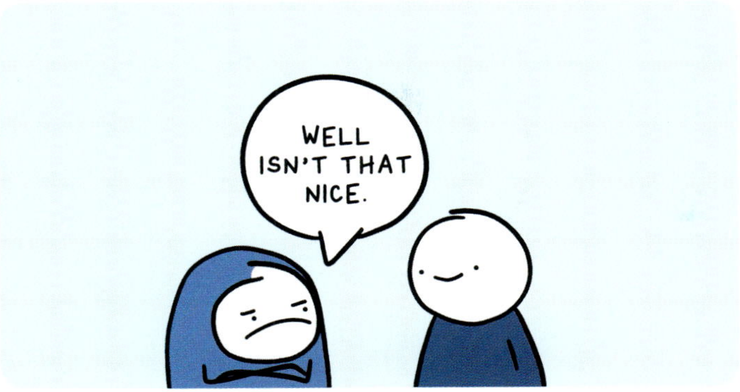
WELL ISN'T THAT NICE.

The new company was a startup roller coaster that was anything but monotonous. There were raging fires to put out every day and they all required a different type of extinguisher. Firefighting became my default work state—it was challenging work, but in the right ways. And it was at this company that I got my first taste of working from home.

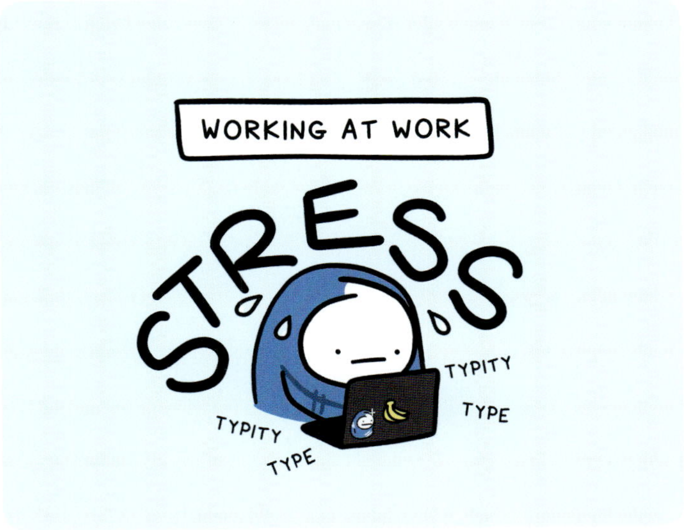
WORKING AT WORK
STRESS
TYPITY
TYPE
TYPITY
TYPE

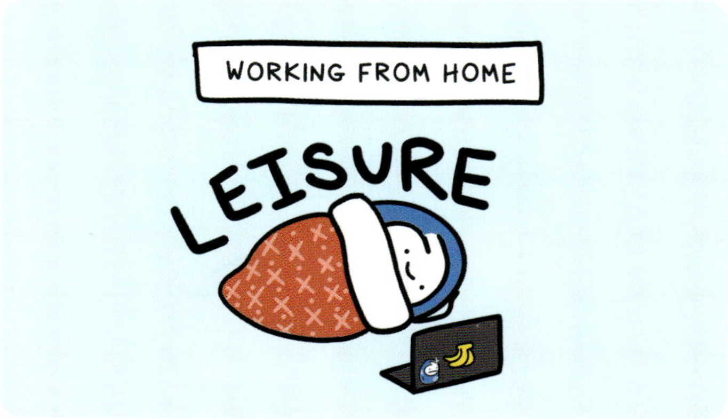
WORKING FROM HOME
LEISURE

For those who have never experienced the perpetual chaos of startup culture, just imagine a place where no one knows what they're doing so everyone is constantly running around doing everything in a desperate attempt to keep the ship afloat.

When your position is pitched to you as being "ill-defined," it means you could be doing anything from nothing to everything—but odds are, you're doing *everything*. Whenever I perfected a skill, I was expected to master yet another. I wore so many hats that my head was constantly toppling over.

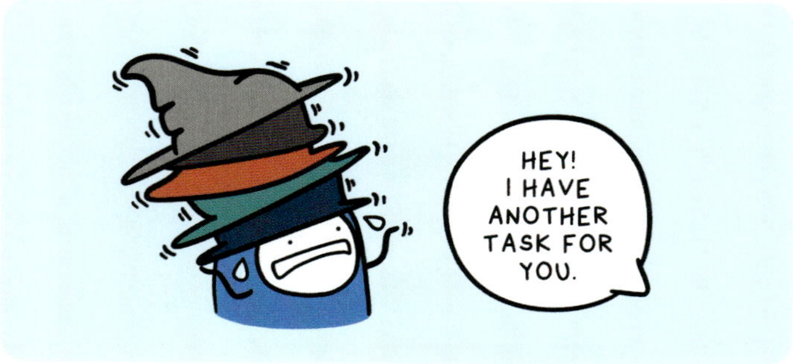
HEY! I HAVE ANOTHER TASK FOR YOU.

I realized I had done it. I had found the complete antithesis of my previous job. My new position was anything *but* boring and repetitive. I felt challenged, I was learning . . . I was *guaranteed* professional satisfaction and happiness.

Or so I thought.

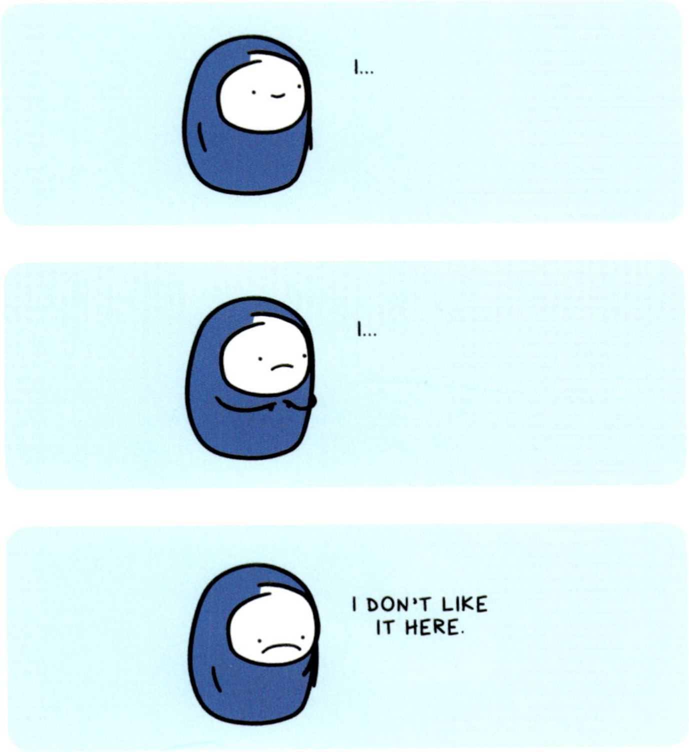
I...
I...
I DON'T LIKE IT HERE.

I lasted much longer in this role, but within two years, I was back to square one—I wasn't excited to go to work. In fact, I dreaded it. In hopes of an objective analysis, I asked my friend for a consult.

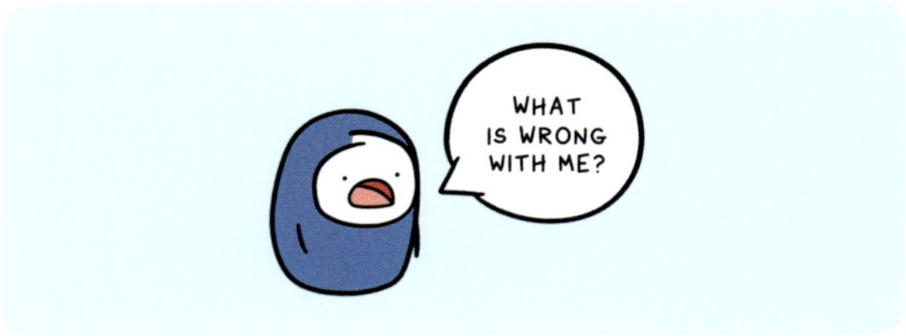
WHAT IS WRONG WITH ME?

Upon hearing this, my friend had the class to assume I was referencing work.

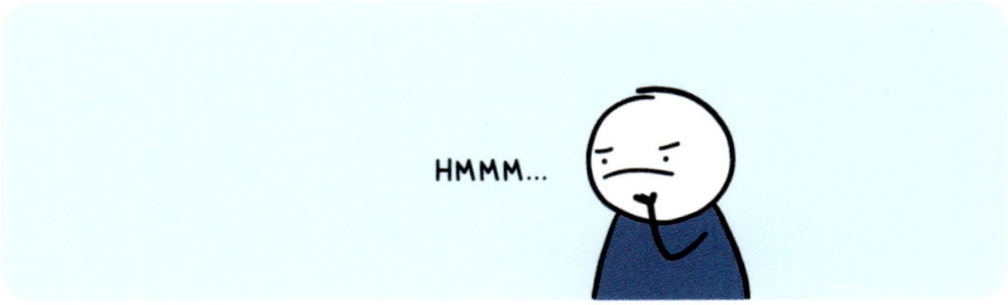
HMMM...

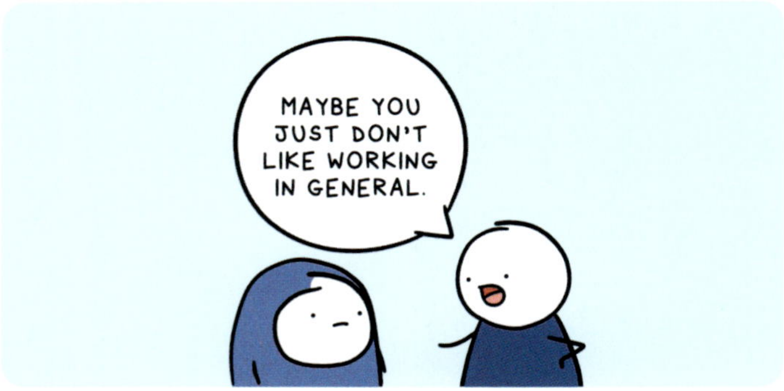
MAYBE YOU JUST DON'T LIKE WORKING IN GENERAL.

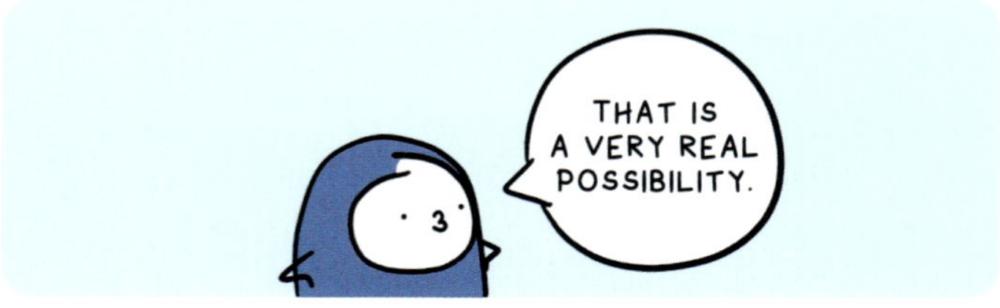
THAT IS A VERY REAL POSSIBILITY.

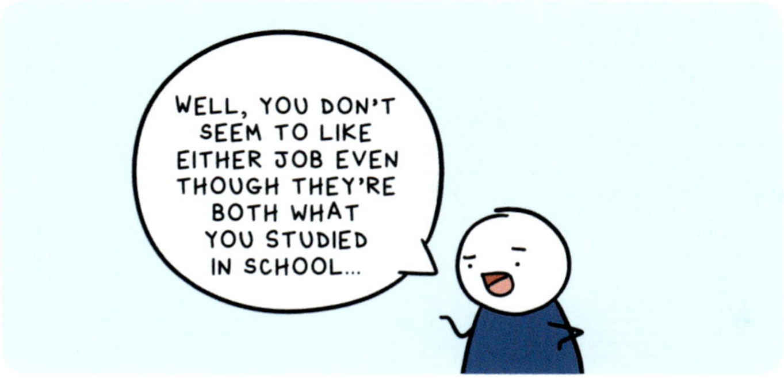
WELL, YOU DON'T SEEM TO LIKE EITHER JOB EVEN THOUGH THEY'RE BOTH WHAT YOU STUDIED IN SCHOOL...

And that's when I felt the mental gears grinding to a halt as I came to the horrifying conclusion that so many before me have come to.

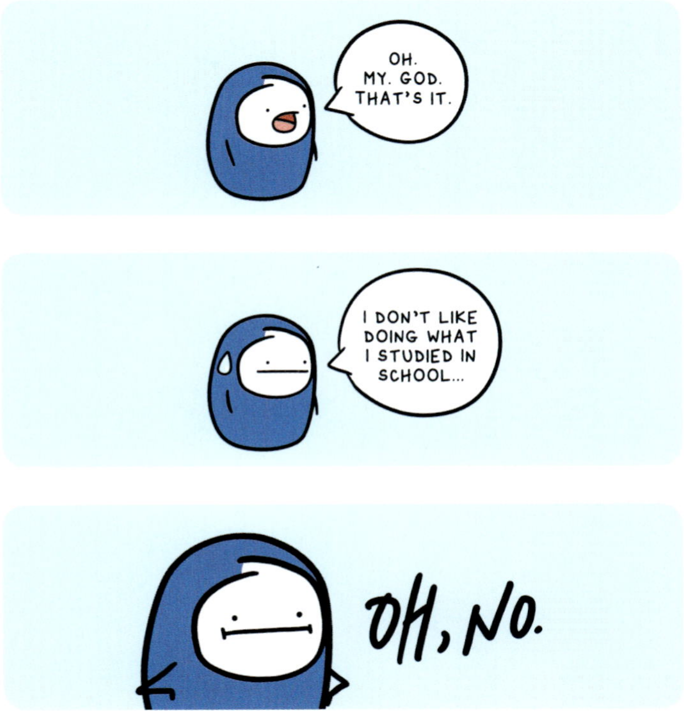
OH.
MY. GOD.
THAT'S IT.
I DON'T LIKE DOING WHAT I STUDIED IN SCHOOL...
OH, NO.

I was mortified. *I don't like working in the field I studied in. Oh, no.* I thought about all the time I had wasted, all the tuition money I had spent on a degree that was now rendered useless. What was I supposed to do now? Start over again?

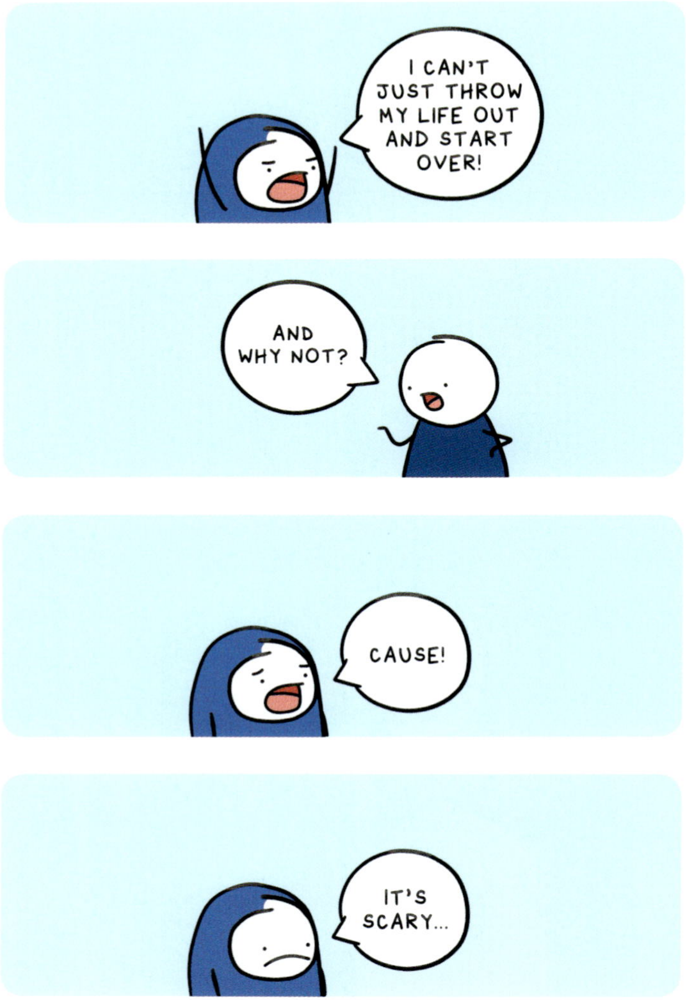
I CAN'T JUST THROW MY LIFE OUT AND START OVER!
AND WHY NOT?
CAUSE!
IT'S SCARY...

I didn't realize it at the time, but the whole thing was likely especially devastating because it was the first time I had gone off-road in life. My path was no longer the shortest distance from A to B, but a swirly loop heading to God knows where. I knew I had to course correct and reroute, I just had no idea how.

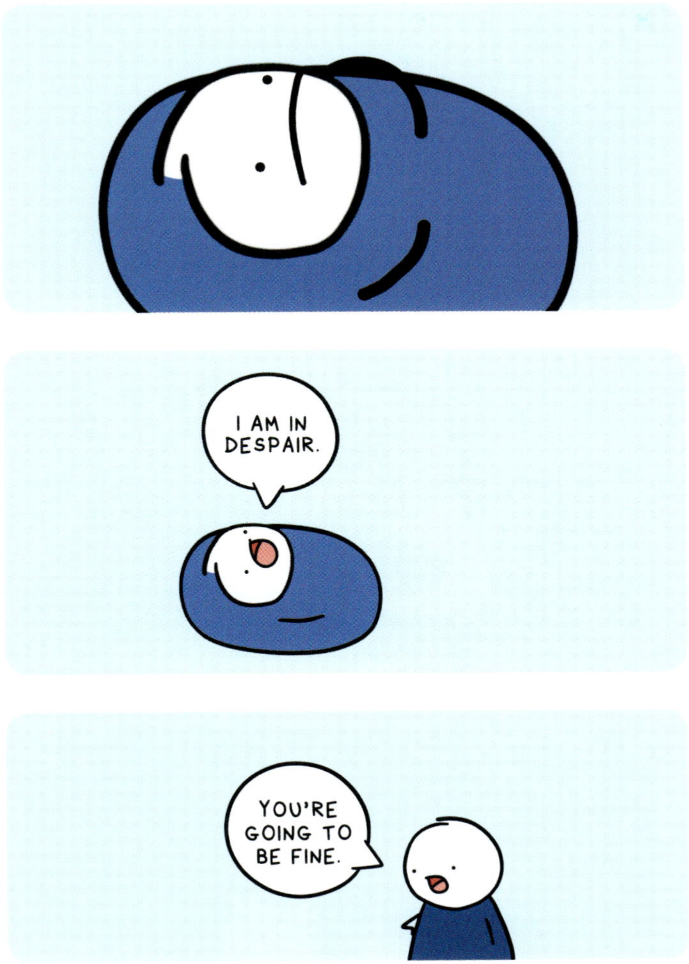
I AM IN DESPAIR.
YOU'RE GOING TO BE FINE.

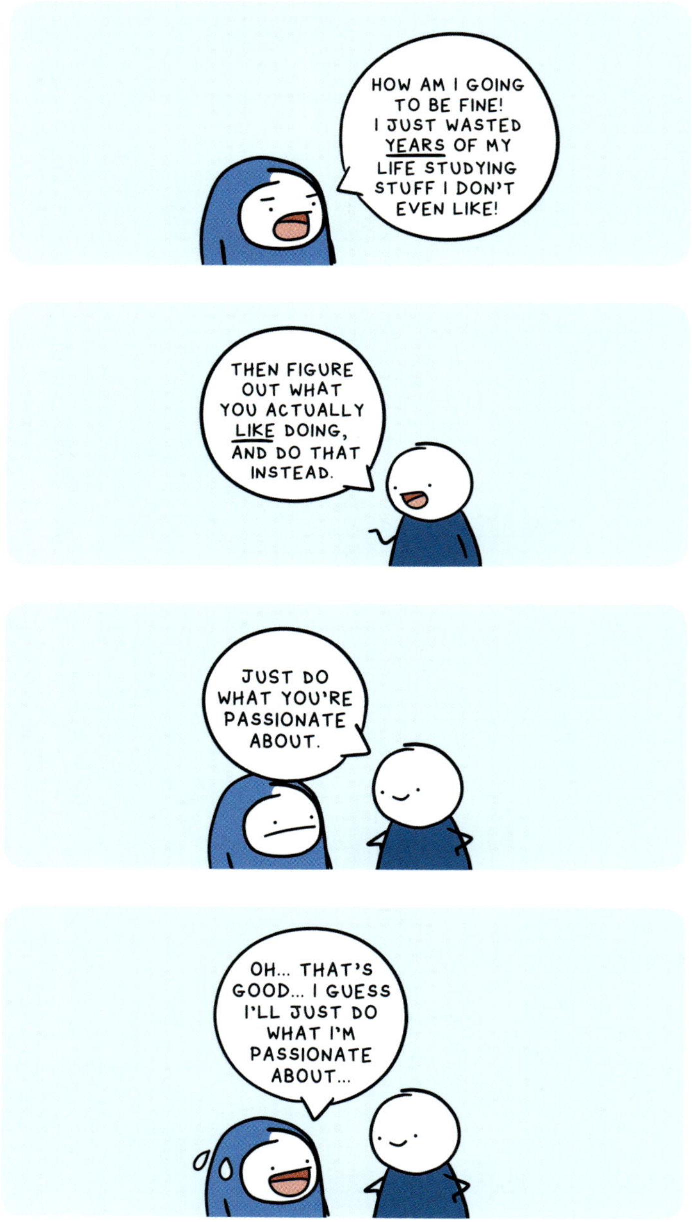
HOW AM I GOING TO BE FINE! I JUST WASTED YEARS OF MY LIFE STUDYING STUFF I DON'T EVEN LIKE!
THEN FIGURE OUT WHAT YOU ACTUALLY LIKE DOING, AND DO THAT INSTEAD.
JUST DO WHAT YOU'RE PASSIONATE ABOUT.
OH... THAT'S GOOD... I GUESS I'LL JUST DO WHAT I'M PASSIONATE ABOUT...

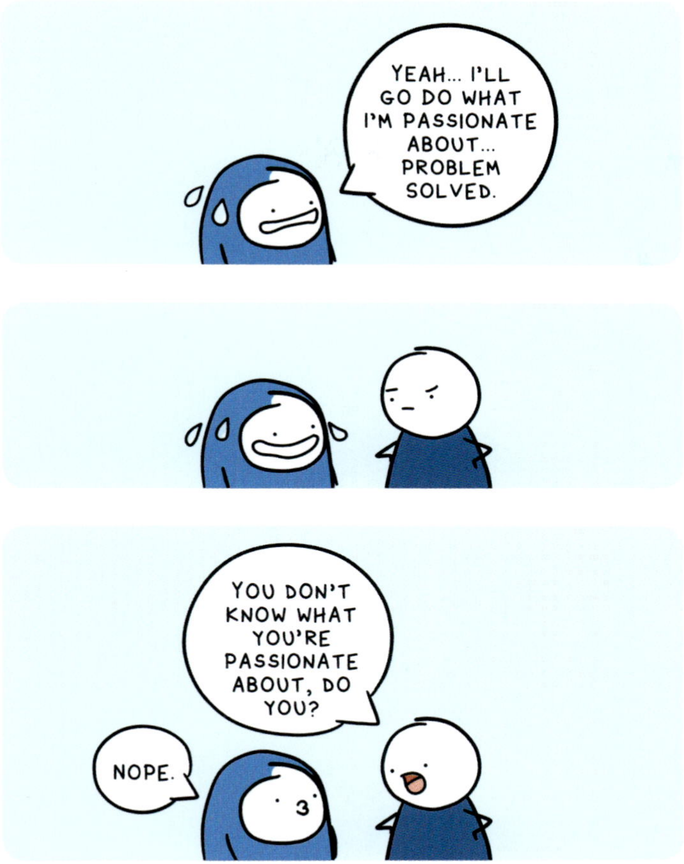
YEAH... I'LL GO DO WHAT I'M PASSIONATE ABOUT... PROBLEM SOLVED.
YOU DON'T KNOW WHAT YOU'RE PASSIONATE ABOUT, DO YOU?
NOPE.

The whole adage of "do what you love and you'll never work a day in your life" is fallacious *baloney.*

First of all, it requires you to actually *know* what you love. And if you don't, *congratulations!* Now you get to feel this wonderful extra layer of pressure to figure it all out. Secondly, work will always be work, regardless of how much you love doing it. The key distinction between work and fun is in the concession of choice—you can't just *choose* not to work when you don't feel like it—you have to do it no matter what. So when you take something you love and make it your work, it stops being the charming whim you so freely pursue. And if you no longer have the freedom to choose when and where you do the things that you love, then where's the fun in that?

But I digress.

• • •

It's a lot to ask of ourselves, to know without a doubt what field we want to study, what career we want, and to essentially write out the script for the rest of our lives at the very start of it. So it should come as no surprise to us that sometimes when we look back at the script we once wrote, we realize we were completely off the mark.

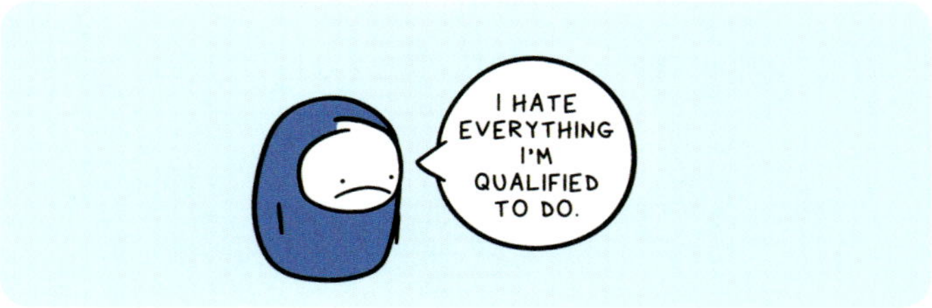
I HATE EVERYTHING I'M QUALIFIED TO DO.

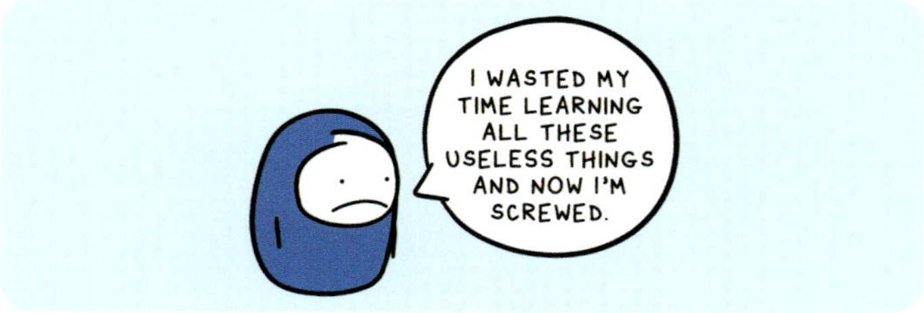
I WASTED MY TIME LEARNING ALL THESE USELESS THINGS AND NOW I'M SCREWED.

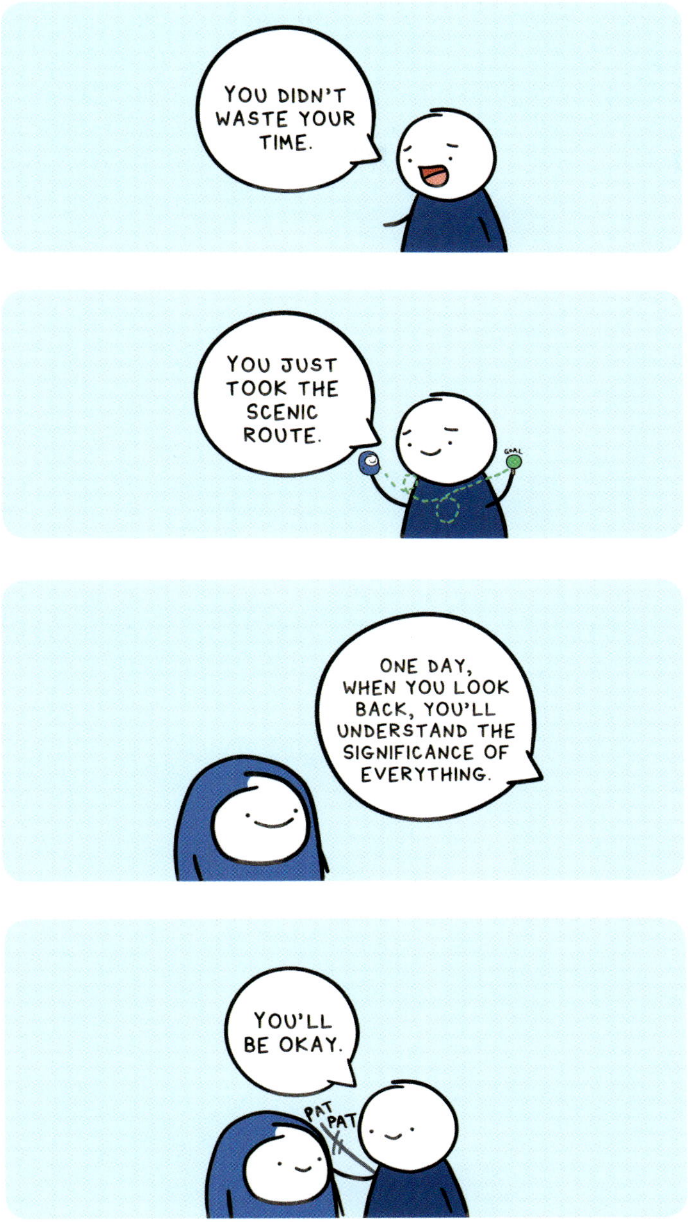
YOU DIDN'T WASTE YOUR TIME.
YOU JUST TOOK THE SCENIC ROUTE.
GOAL
ONE DAY, WHEN YOU LOOK BACK, YOU'LL UNDERSTAND THE SIGNIFICANCE OF EVERYTHING.
YOU'LL BE OKAY.
PAT PAT

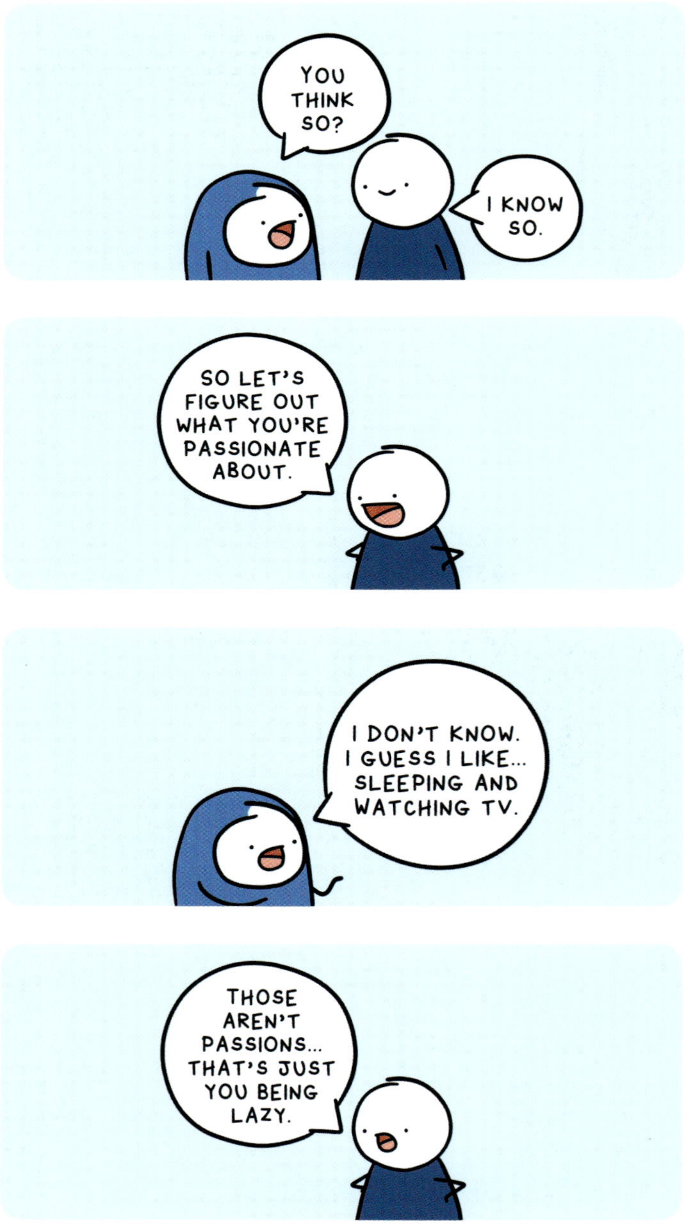
YOU THINK SO?
I KNOW SO.
SO LET'S FIGURE OUT WHAT YOU'RE PASSIONATE ABOUT.
I DON'T KNOW. I GUESS I LIKE... SLEEPING AND WATCHING TV.
THOSE AREN'T PASSIONS... THAT'S JUST YOU BEING LAZY.

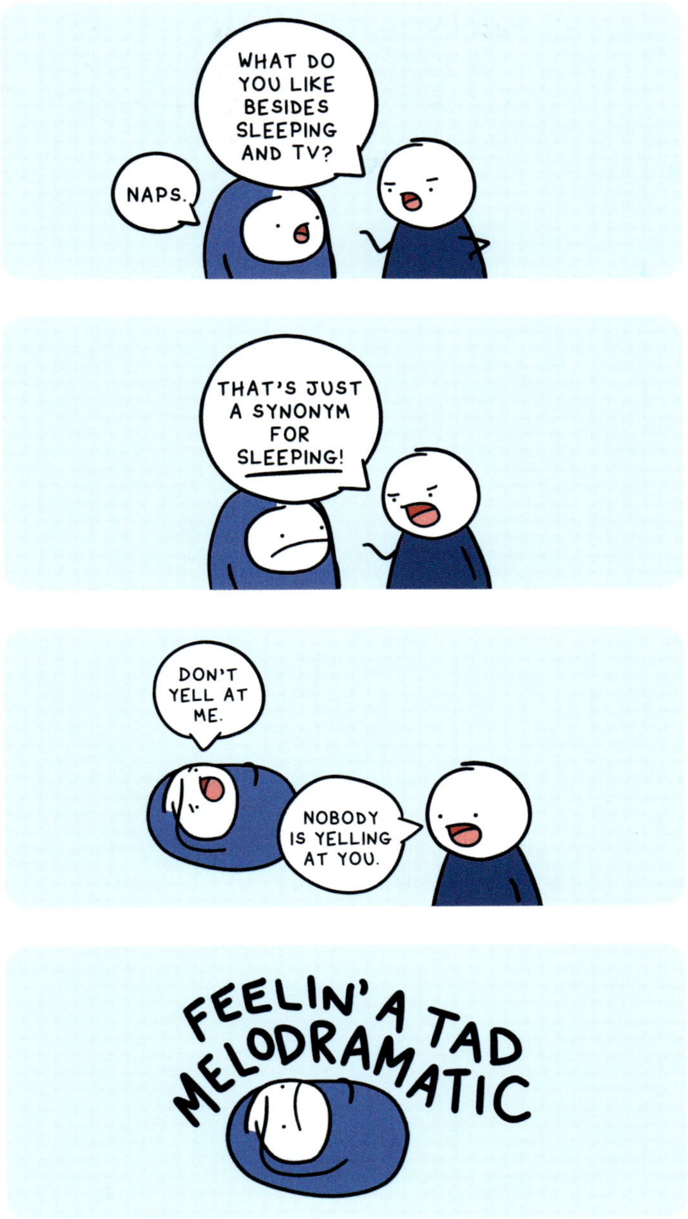
WHAT DO YOU LIKE BESIDES SLEEPING AND TV?
NAPS.
THAT'S JUST A SYNONYM FOR SLEEPING!
DON'T YELL AT ME.
NOBODY IS YELLING AT YOU.
FEELIN' A TAD MELODRAMATIC

I guess in a perfect world, we would always know what we're doing and where the heck we're going. But sometimes we don't know what's wrong until we experience it. We don't know where the wasps are until we feel the legion descending upon us.

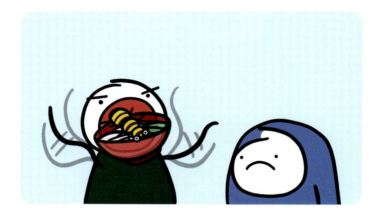

Eventually, I got sick of the wasps. So I got up, walked away, and switched fields altogether.

Starting from scratch, I spent the next few months exploring everything I liked to do, regardless of how much skill or talent I had in those fields. Skills can be developed, I reasoned, talent . . . well, I'll worry about that one later.

MAYBE I SHOULD BE A FILMMAKER. OR A SCREENWRITER...

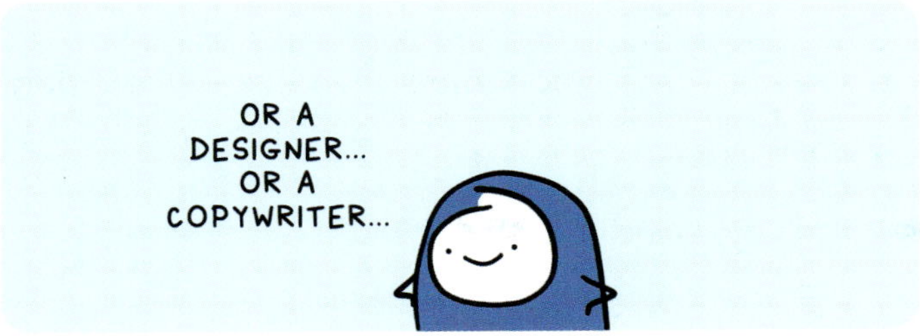
OR A DESIGNER... OR A COPYWRITER...

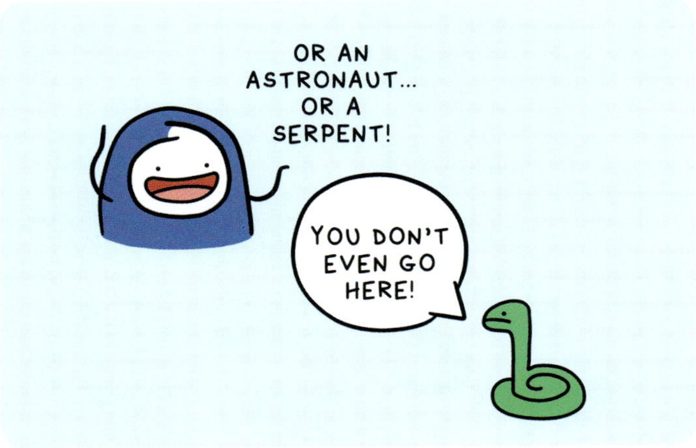
OR AN ASTRONAUT... OR A SERPENT!
YOU DON'T EVEN GO HERE!

Free from the constraints of previous decisions, I simply looked for a job that I could be happy in.

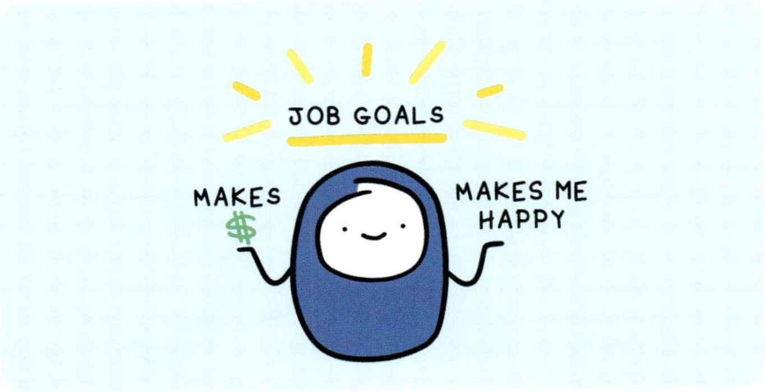
JOB GOALS
MAKES $
MAKES ME HAPPY

I no longer had the attention span for school, so I spent my days reading and learning on my own instead. It's surprisingly pleasant to pore over books when you genuinely care about the subject matter and choose to read of your own volition. To my relief, no one seemed concerned that my background wasn't in the field I was applying for. People just wanted to know if I was a good person and could do things. Luckily, I was one of the two.

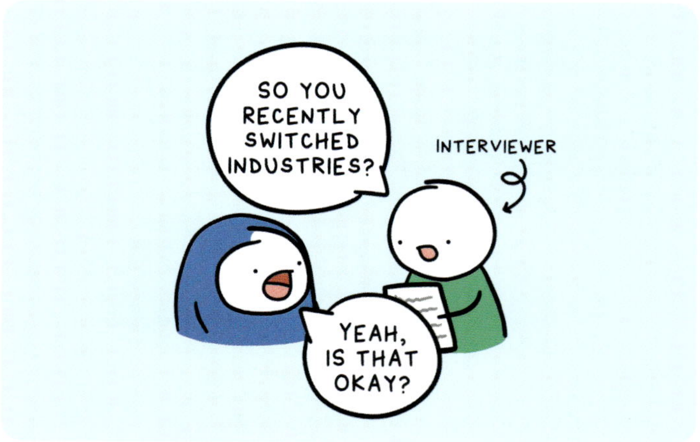
SO YOU RECENTLY SWITCHED INDUSTRIES?
INTERVIEWER
YEAH, IS THAT OKAY?

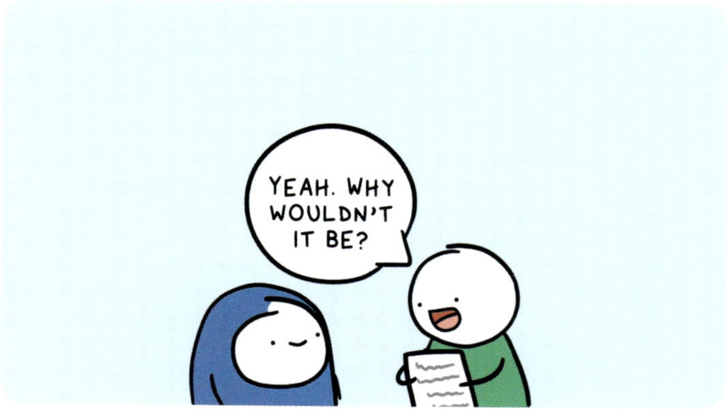
YEAH. WHY WOULDN'T IT BE?

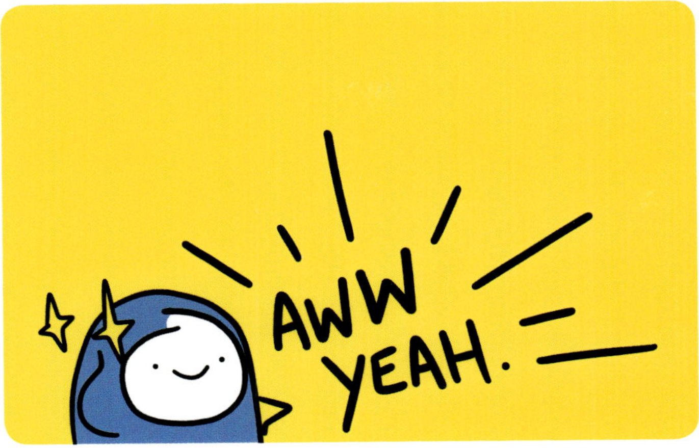
AWW YEAH.

After a lot of luck and a lot of hard work, I eventually managed to land a position in a new field where I ended up staying for many years.

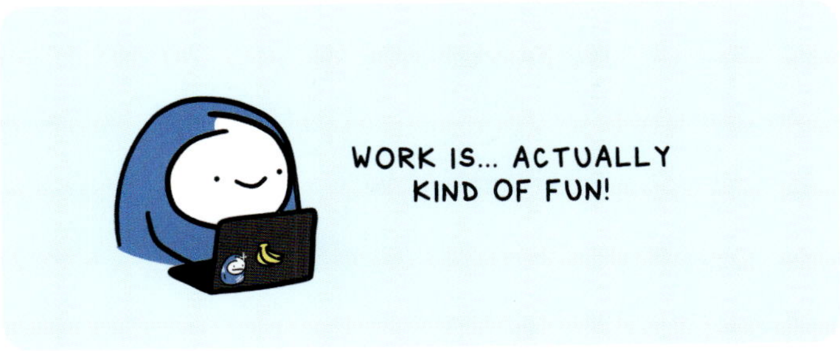
WORK IS... ACTUALLY KIND OF FUN!

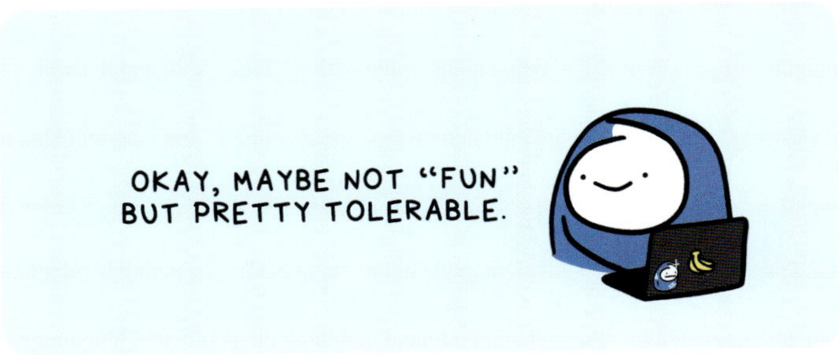
OKAY, MAYBE NOT "FUN" BUT PRETTY TOLERABLE.

YES, QUITE
TOLERABLE INDEED.

Sometimes when we see the wasps in our lives, we have this tendency to ignore them—especially when no one else around us seems bothered. It's always easier to disregard things rather than deal with them.

But I think there's value in knowing when to call it, in knowing when to get up and leave, in knowing when we're done—even if it means having to walk out into the unknown to start all over again.

We can never really be sure of what will be waiting for us on the other side, but it's gotta beat sitting there with a mouthful of wasps, pretending everything is okay.

# CHAPTER 4

# THERAPY

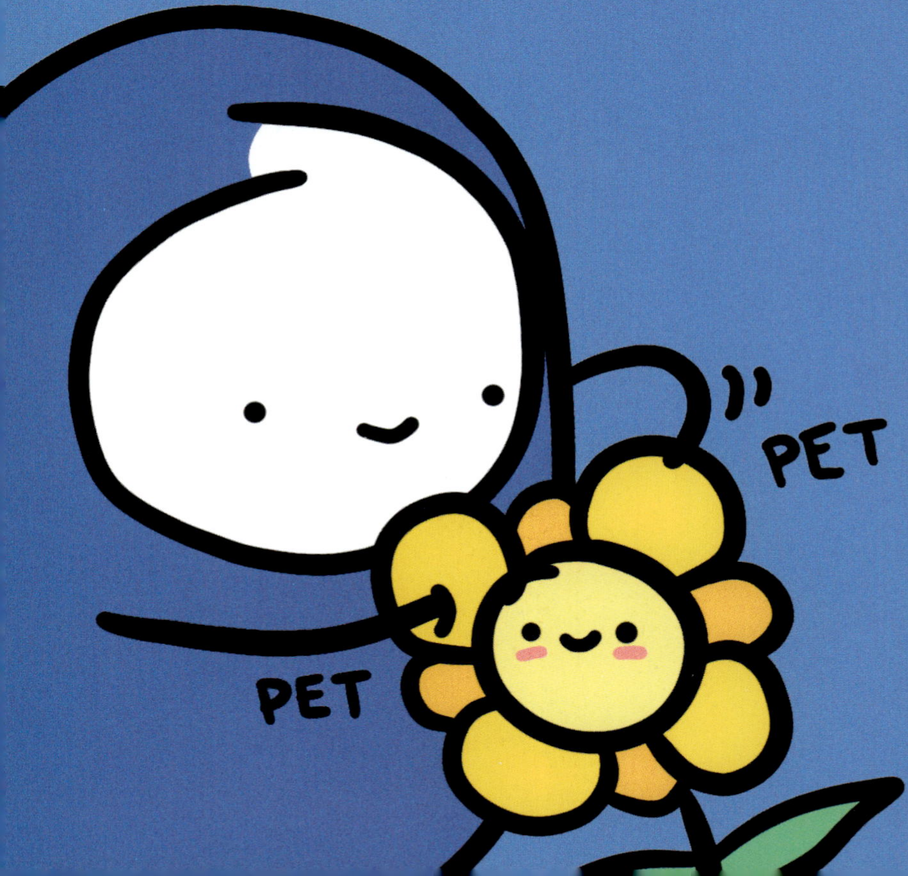
PET
PET

I've always known I'm a little bit broken on the inside.

Not *super* broken—not enough for it to be cause for immediate concern—just a *tiny* little bit broken. It's really not that bad once you've gotten used to it.

I WONDER WHAT IT'S LIKE TO NOT BE BROKEN...
HMM...
MUST BE NICE.

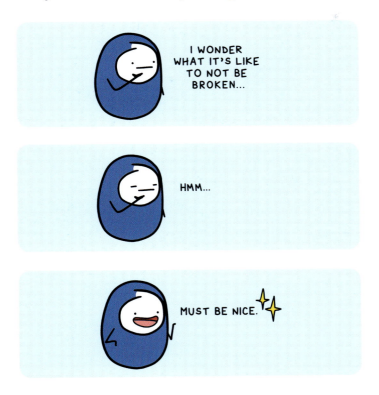

The thing is, if you live long enough, or at all, you're bound to get a little tangled up along the way—emotional mileage, it happens. As a result of this unbidden self-awareness, I've always known I would end up in therapy one day.

But before we get into that story, I'd like to make a quick note about therapy. The decision to go to therapy is much like the decision to pet a flower you find on the side of the road—it's a choice, and that choice is entirely up to you.

DO YOU WANT TO PET THIS FLOWER?
IF YES, DO IT.
YES, PLEASE.
PET
PET
IF NO, THEN DON'T DO IT.
NO, THANK YOU.

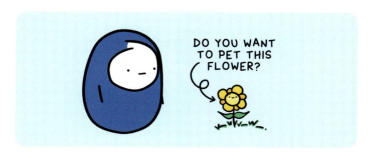

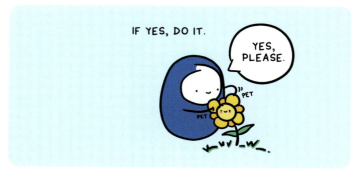

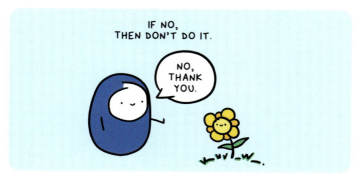

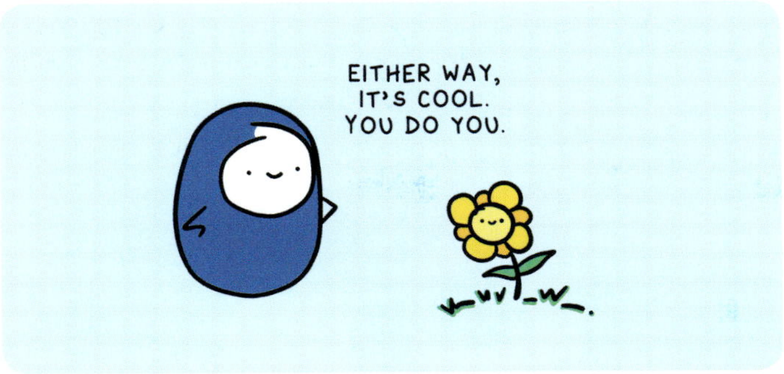
EITHER WAY,
IT'S COOL.
YOU DO YOU.

Therapy was always something I knew I wanted to try, but the opportunity never came up. A lot of things in life are like this. If you don't make any effort at all to do them, the opportunity conveniently never comes up.

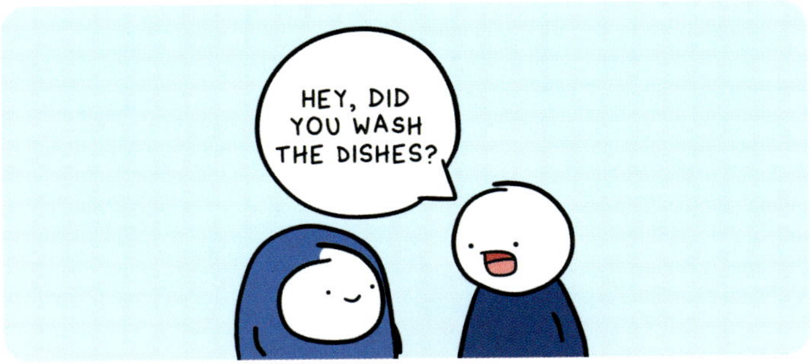
HEY, DID
YOU WASH
THE DISHES?

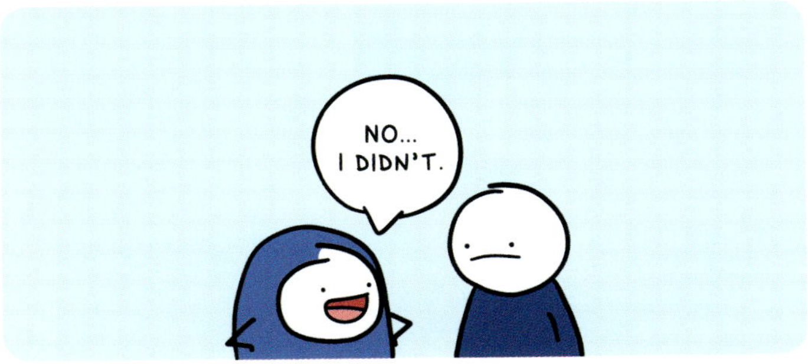
NO...
I DIDN'T.

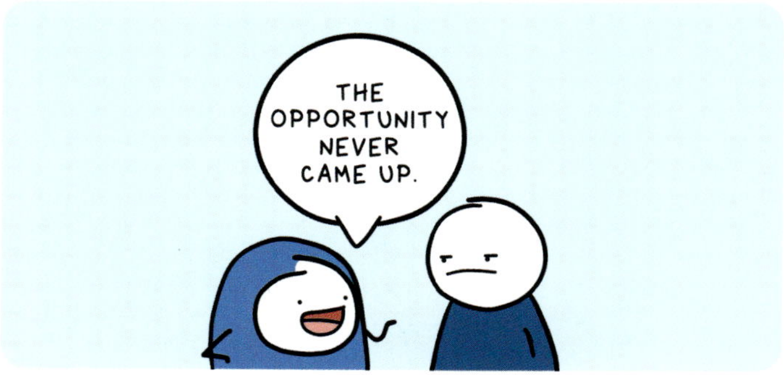
THE OPPORTUNITY NEVER CAME UP.

As a makeshift solution, I spent many of my early years relying on my friends to be my therapists. And my friends, in turn, spent many of *their* early years gently encouraging me to seek real therapy.

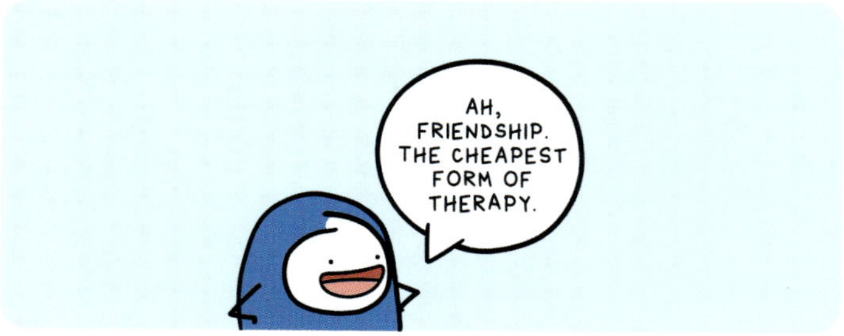
AH, FRIENDSHIP. THE CHEAPEST FORM OF THERAPY.

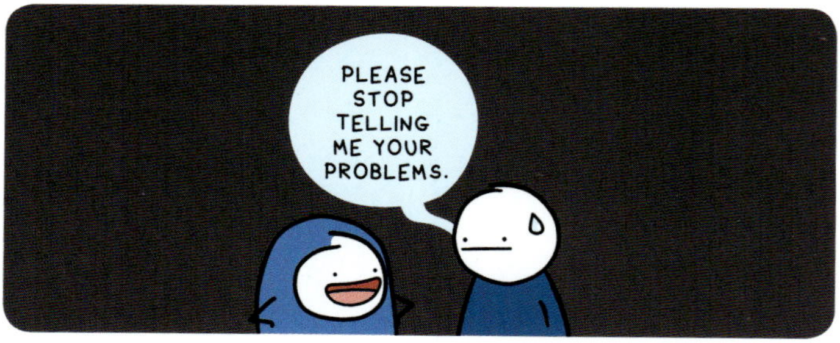
PLEASE STOP TELLING ME YOUR PROBLEMS.

I don't blame them. My mind is not easy to deal with. Some messes just require professionals.

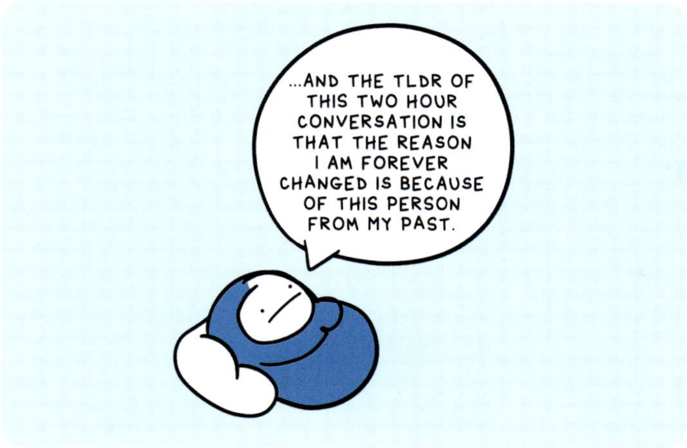

...AND THE TLDR OF THIS TWO HOUR CONVERSATION IS THAT THE REASON I AM FOREVER CHANGED IS BECAUSE OF THIS PERSON FROM MY PAST.

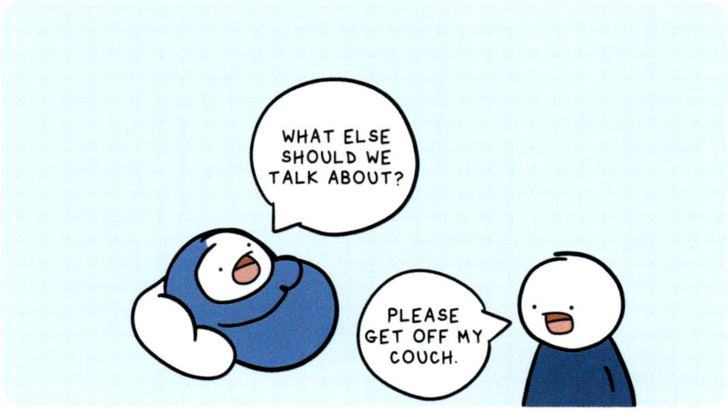

WHAT ELSE SHOULD WE TALK ABOUT?
PLEASE GET OFF MY COUCH.

After many years of questionable friendship "therapy," the opportunity to go to a real therapist finally presented itself.

These days, you can be psychoanalyzed through any medium—video, text, phone, etc. Being the occasional traditionalist that I am, I decided to have an in-person therapy session because I felt more comfortable speaking to someone face-to-face.

The idea of an in-person session also just felt more cinematic and fun. And I've never been one to discount the importance of fun.

But the process of finding the right therapist was a bit opaque. People typically don't publish reviews about their therapists, so all options were a bit of a black box. It felt weird to go to the same therapists as my friends, so I ended up using a recommendation platform instead. After filling out some basic information, I found myself on a multipage questionnaire.

Things started off quite pleasantly.

Question 1:

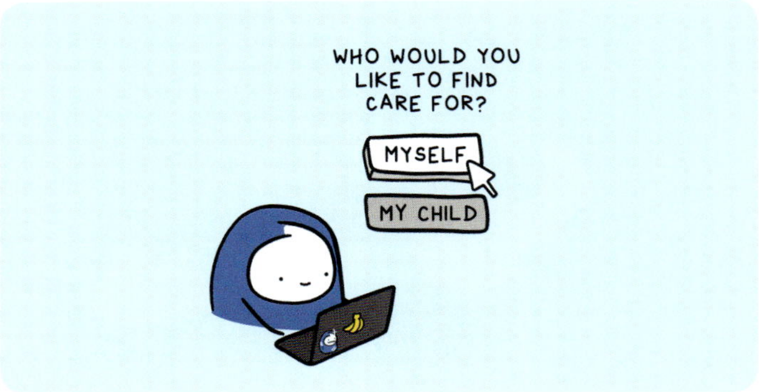
WHO WOULD YOU LIKE TO FIND CARE FOR?
MYSELF
MY CHILD

But then it escalated almost immediately.

Question 2: Which of the following issues are you *primarily* looking to address? Depression? Anxiety? Stress? Relationship issues? Marriage issues? Family issues? Alcohol abuse? Drug abuse? . . . the list went on to cover the spectrum of human dysfunction.

Some of these issues were things I had never even considered. However, when presented to me on such a silver platter, I couldn't help but wonder if those skeletons were tucked away in my closet somewhere. I figured if therapy was a battlefield, then this was my one chance to stock up my mental first aid kit with all the supplies I might need. After all, who knows what demons might show up in session? I needed to be prepared.

TRIES TO SELECT MORE THAN ONE.
CLICK*
ERROR
PLEASE SELECT ONE ONLY.
GRUMBLE.
BUT I HAVE MORE THAN ONE ISSUE THOUGH...

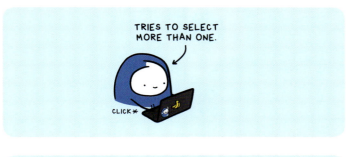

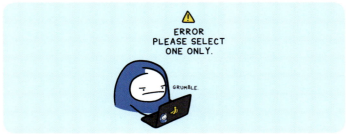

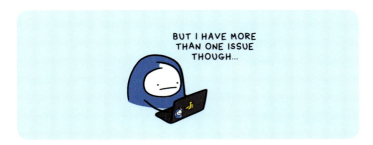

I quickly realized each therapist specialized in different issues (marriage, family, etc.) and knowing how to categorically triage yourself to the right specialty was a valuable skill to have when choosing a therapist.

It was a skill I did not have.

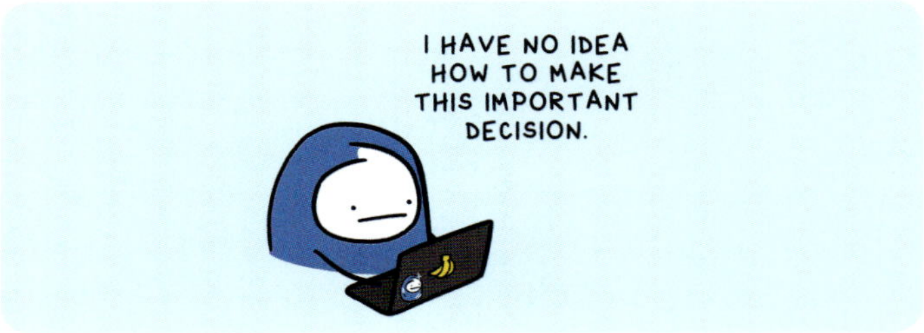
I HAVE NO IDEA HOW TO MAKE THIS IMPORTANT DECISION.

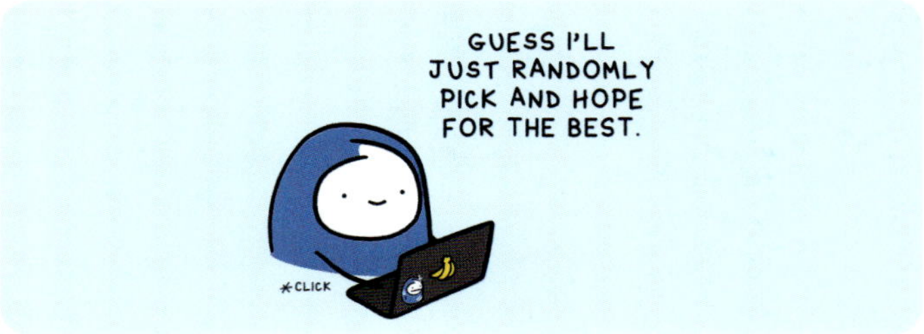
GUESS I'LL JUST RANDOMLY PICK AND HOPE FOR THE BEST.
*CLICK

After finally choosing a therapist and booking an appointment to see her, I felt as though I was done with the heavy lifting.

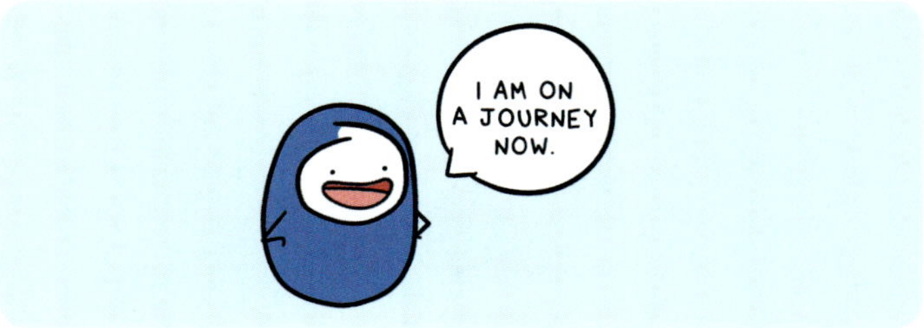
I AM ON A JOURNEY NOW.

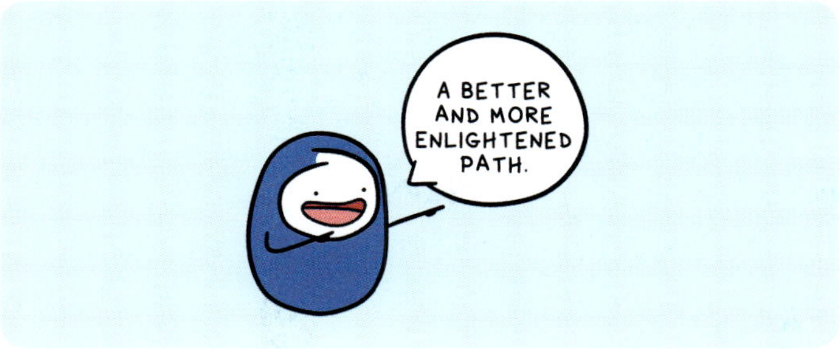
A BETTER AND MORE ENLIGHTENED PATH.

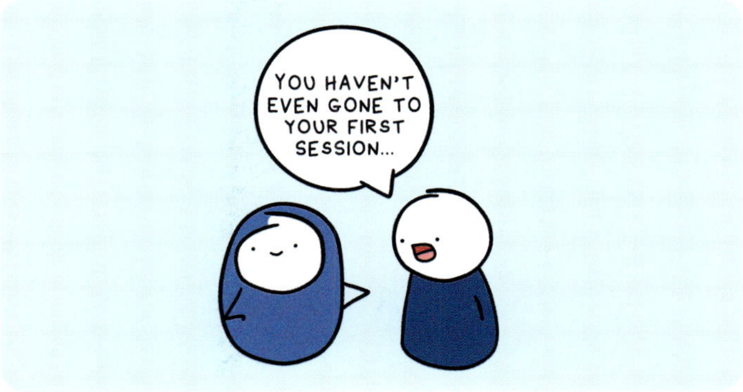
YOU HAVEN'T EVEN GONE TO YOUR FIRST SESSION...

This sense of pride was, of course, as unearned as the sense of pride one feels when buying exercise equipment they have no intention of ever using.

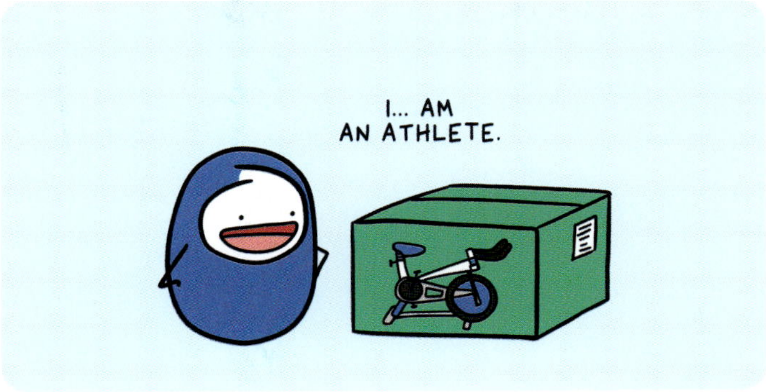
I... AM AN ATHLETE.

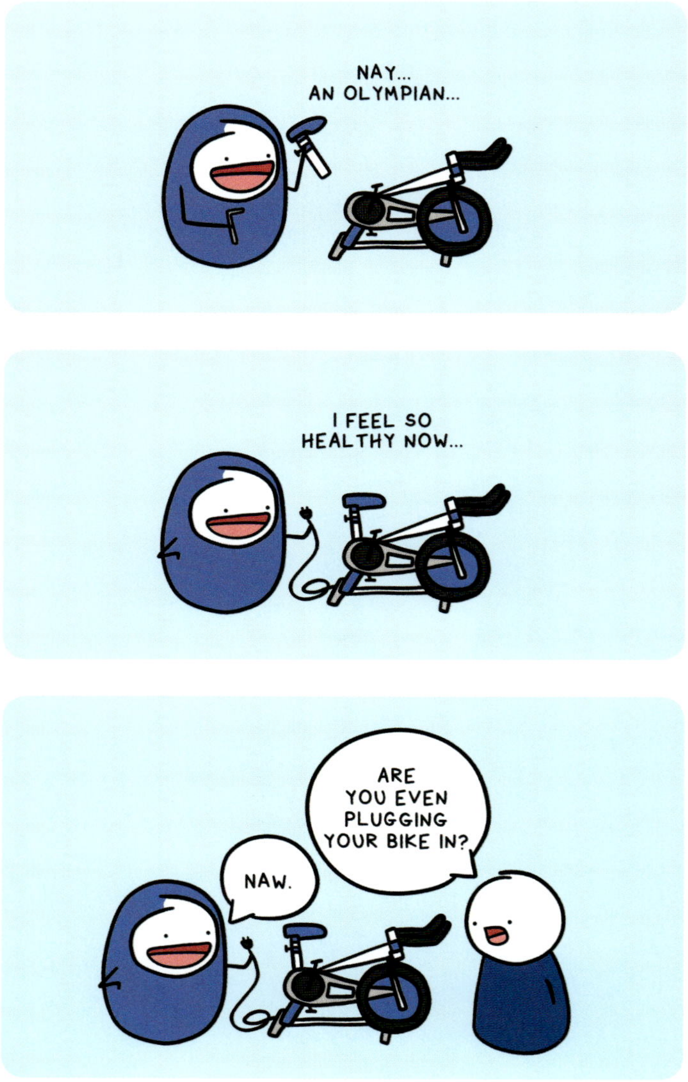
NAY...
AN OLYMPIAN...
I FEEL SO
HEALTHY NOW...
ARE
YOU EVEN
PLUGGING
YOUR BIKE IN?
NAW.

I spent the week before my first therapy session casually telling everyone I was going to therapy. I was proud. I was excited. I was ready.

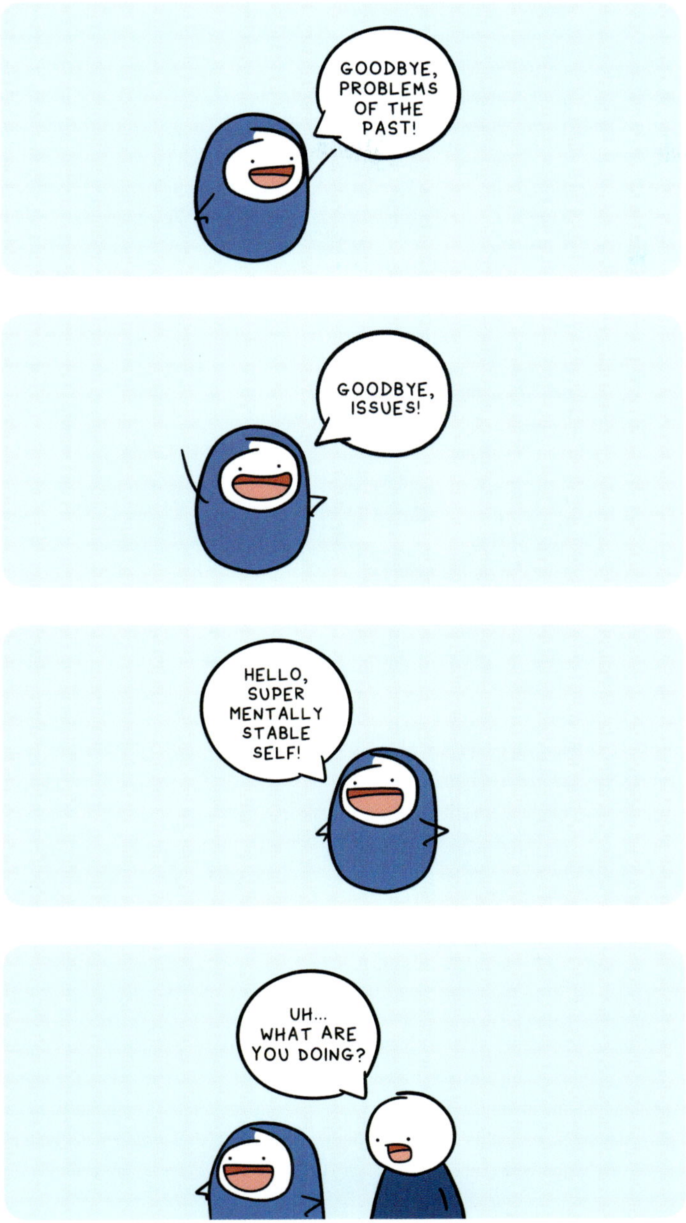
GOODBYE, PROBLEMS OF THE PAST!
GOODBYE, ISSUES!
HELLO, SUPER MENTALLY STABLE SELF!
UH... WHAT ARE YOU DOING?

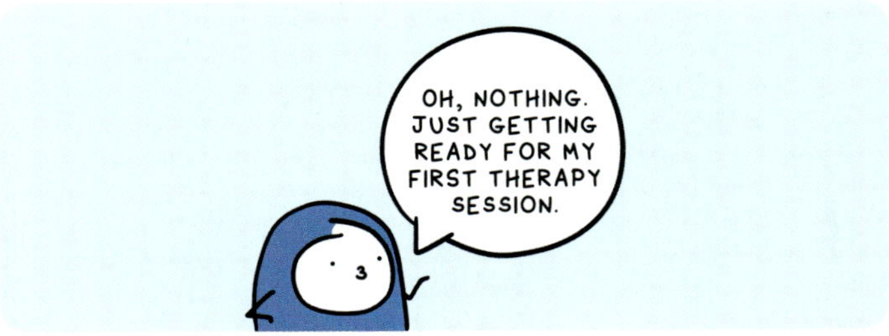
OH, NOTHING. JUST GETTING READY FOR MY FIRST THERAPY SESSION.

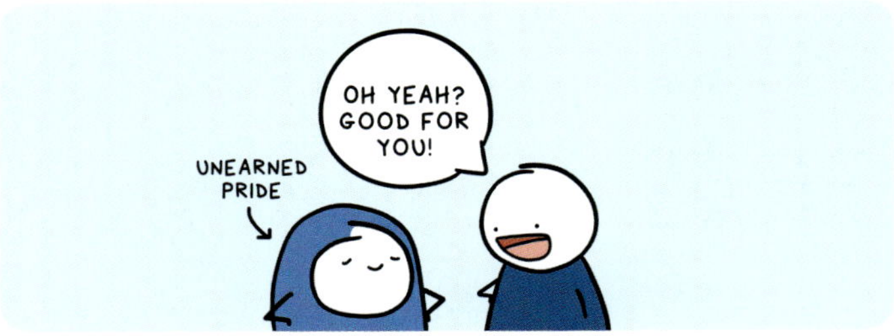
OH YEAH? GOOD FOR YOU!
UNEARNED PRIDE

You know those rare moments in life when you *finally* feel as though you've clawed your way to the surface of the water and you're on top of everything for once? Those refreshing slivers of time where you look around and think to yourself, *Well, I'll be damned. I guess I'm actually getting the hang of it!*

Why are those moments always so short-lived?

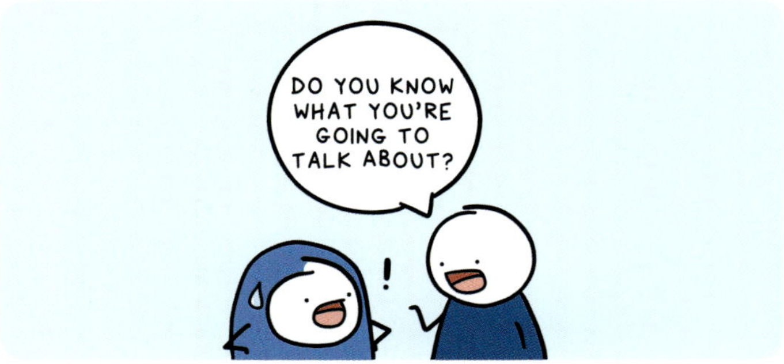
DO YOU KNOW WHAT YOU'RE GOING TO TALK ABOUT?
!

WHAT I'M
GOING TO
TALK ABOUT?

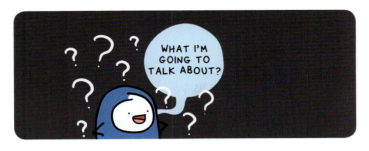

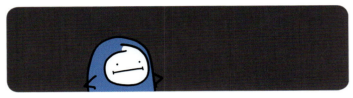

*What am I going to talk to my therapist about? How the hell should I know! Why the frick would you ruin my day by asking me that?*

WHAT'S WRONG? WORRIED YOU WON'T HAVE ENOUGH ISSUES TO TALK TO YOUR THERAPIST ABOUT?

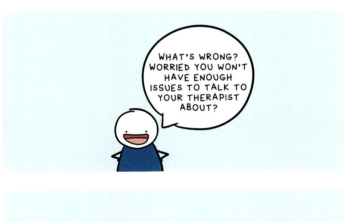

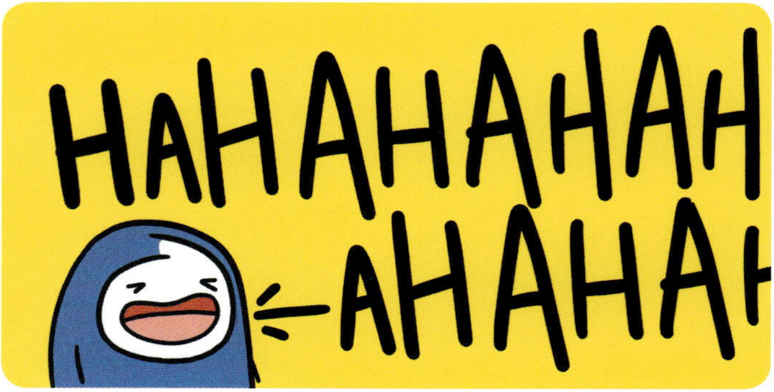
HAHAHAHAHAH
AHAHAH

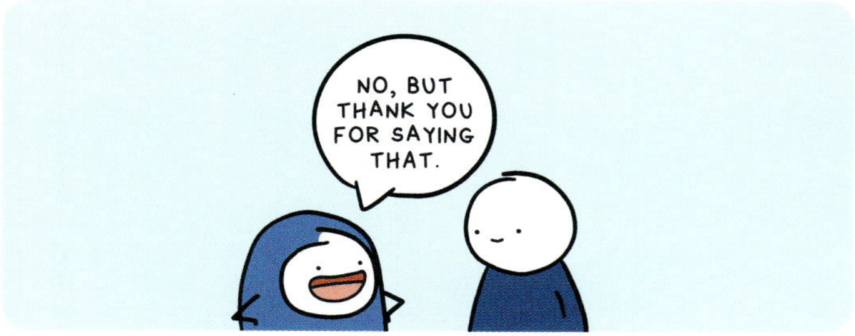
NO, BUT THANK YOU FOR SAYING THAT.

Not enough issues? I am *brimming* with issues. I am *overflowing* with issues. I can talk for *years* about my issues.

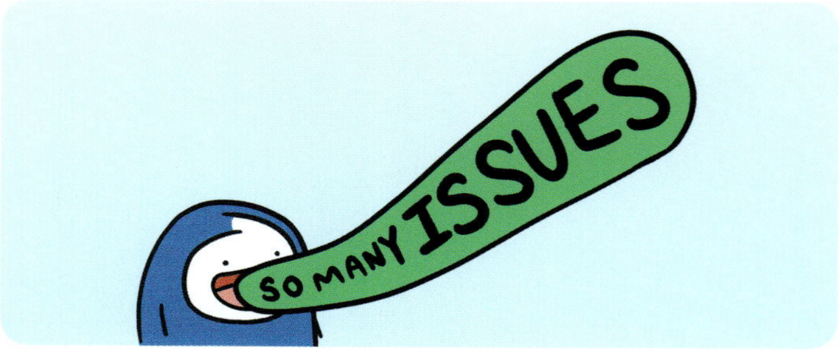
SO MANY ISSUES

The problem wasn't that I didn't have any issues, the problem was that I didn't want to talk about any of them. I felt the all-too-familiar surge of anxiety kicking in.

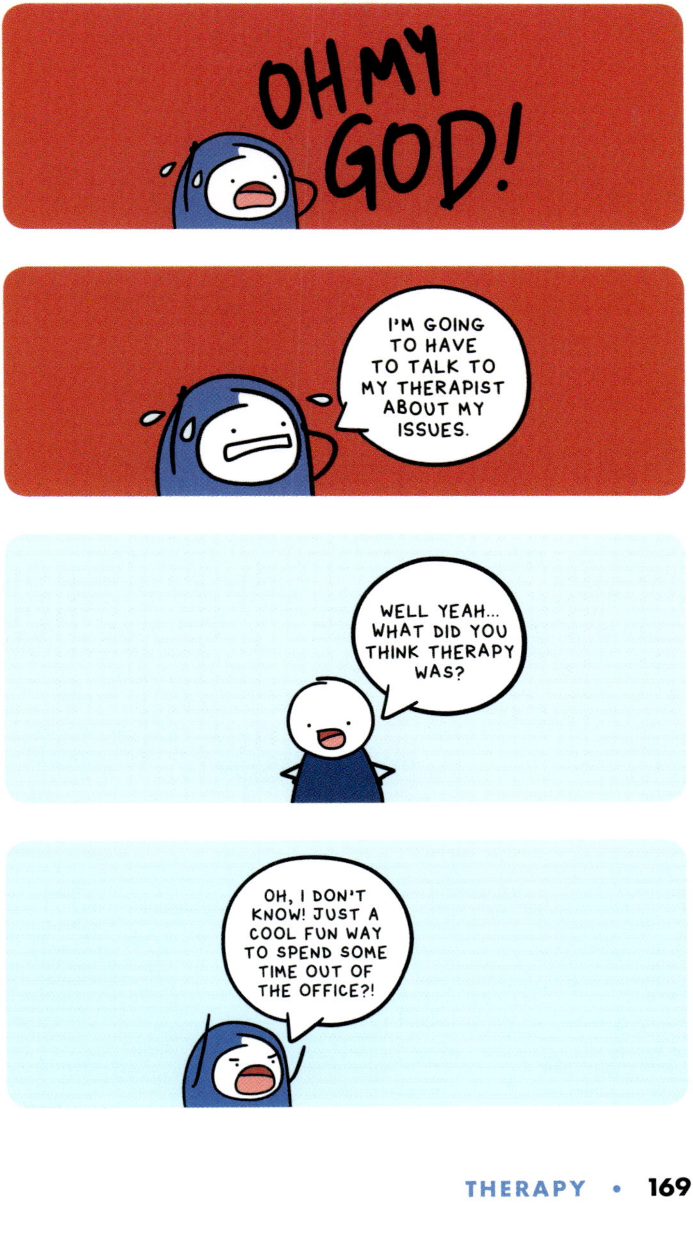
OH MY GOD!
I'M GOING TO HAVE TO TALK TO MY THERAPIST ABOUT MY ISSUES.
WELL YEAH... WHAT DID YOU THINK THERAPY WAS?
OH, I DON'T KNOW! JUST A COOL FUN WAY TO SPEND SOME TIME OUT OF THE OFFICE?!

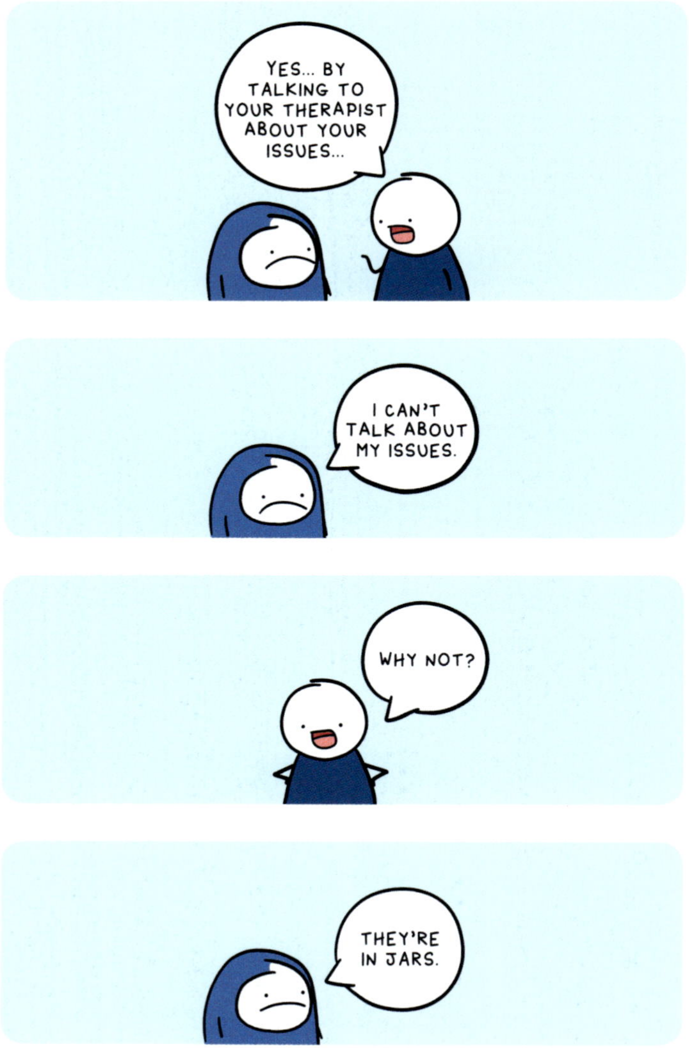
YES... BY TALKING TO YOUR THERAPIST ABOUT YOUR ISSUES...
I CAN'T TALK ABOUT MY ISSUES.
WHY NOT?
THEY'RE IN JARS.

Here's the thing . . . there's a reason why I was able to spend years masquerading as a functional adult despite being maybe, *definitely,* a little bit messed up.

I had a system—a system of jars.

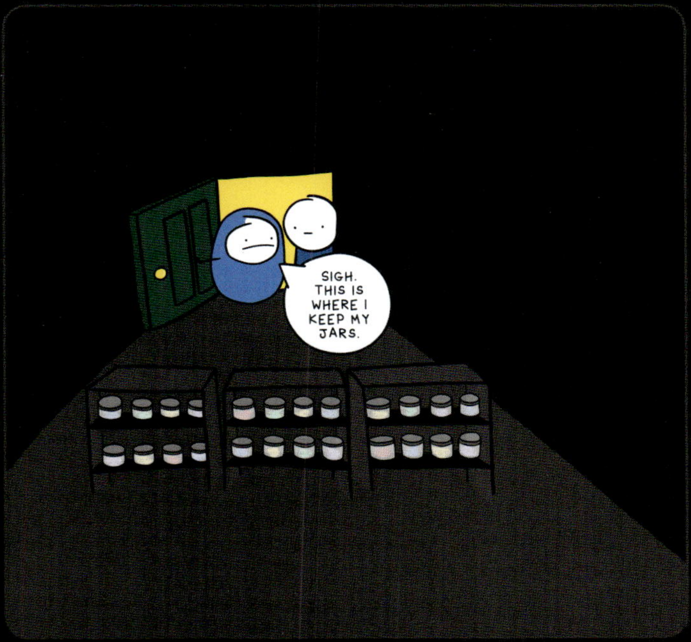
SIGH. THIS IS WHERE I KEEP MY JARS.

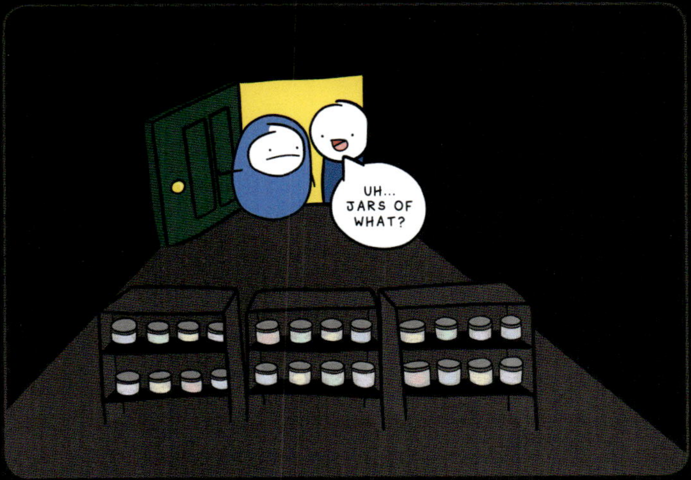
UH... JARS OF WHAT?

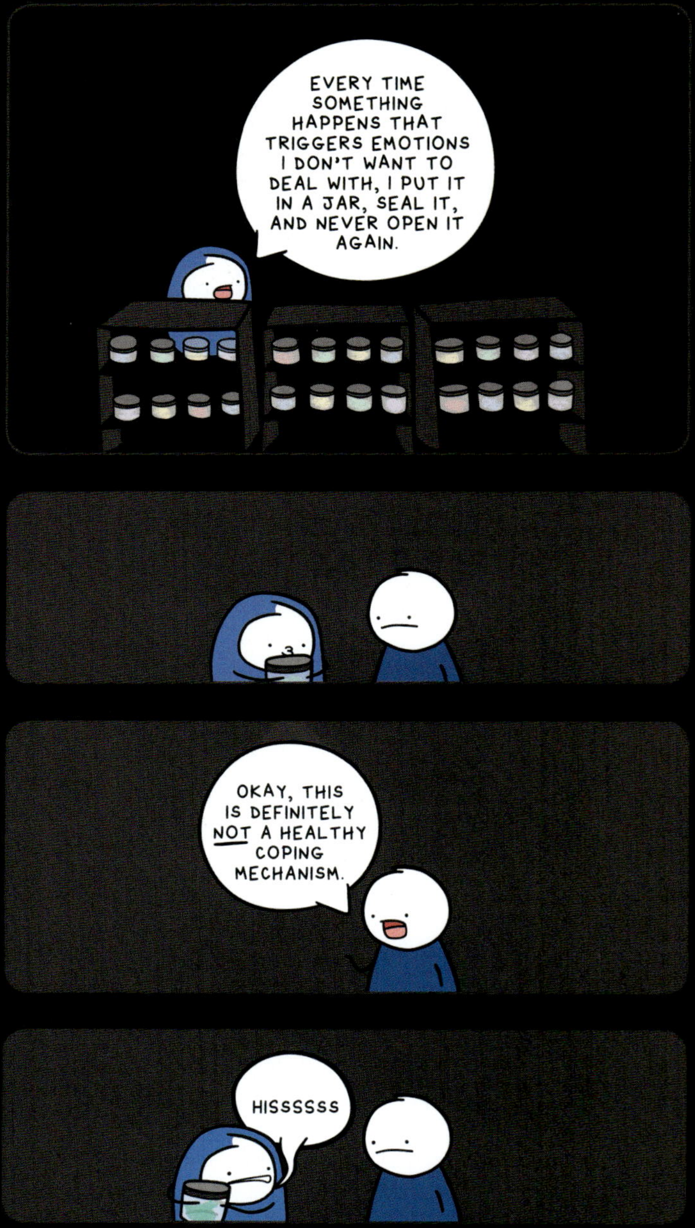
EVERY TIME SOMETHING HAPPENS THAT TRIGGERS EMOTIONS I DON'T WANT TO DEAL WITH, I PUT IT IN A JAR, SEAL IT, AND NEVER OPEN IT AGAIN.
OKAY, THIS IS DEFINITELY NOT A HEALTHY COPING MECHANISM.
HISSSSSS

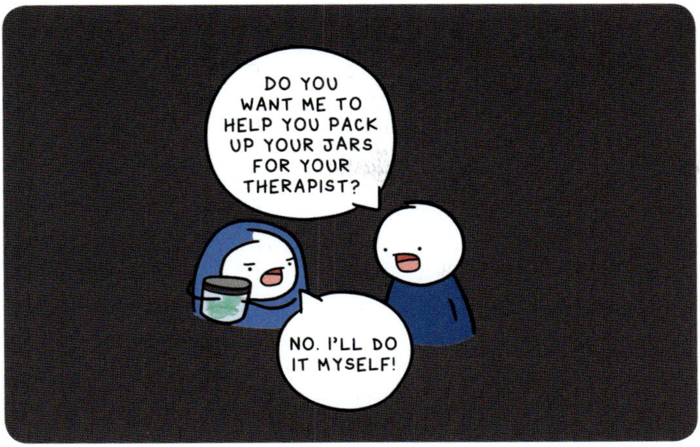
DO YOU WANT ME TO HELP YOU PACK UP YOUR JARS FOR YOUR THERAPIST?
NO. I'LL DO IT MYSELF!

The more I thought about it, the more I realized this whole therapy nonsense was a terrible idea. *Why did I sign up for this again? Why did I agree to reveal my deepest, darkest thoughts and secrets to some stranger in a room?*

A symphony of regret started tuning their instruments in my head—the same symphony one hears when they agree to go to a party and then later realize the night before the party that they actually hate both people and parties.

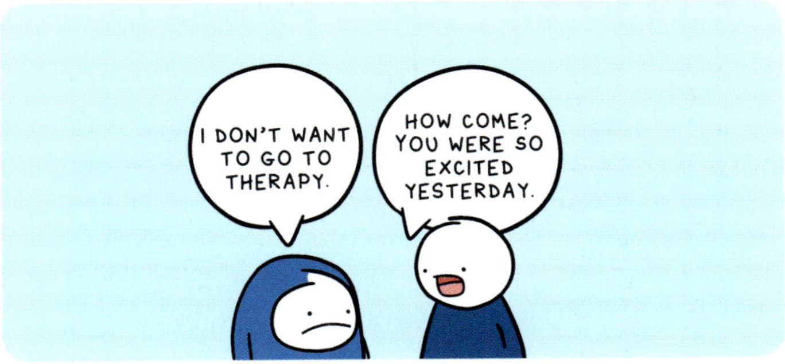
I DON'T WANT TO GO TO THERAPY.
HOW COME? YOU WERE SO EXCITED YESTERDAY.

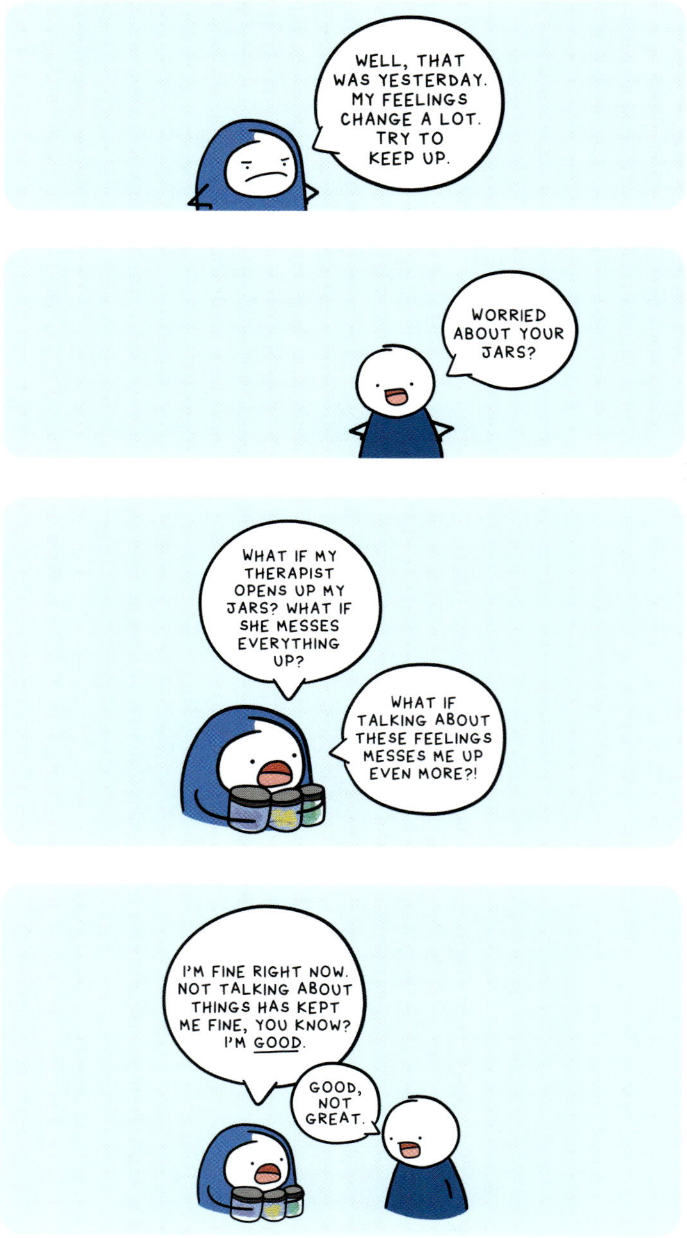
WELL, THAT WAS YESTERDAY. MY FEELINGS CHANGE A LOT. TRY TO KEEP UP.
WORRIED ABOUT YOUR JARS?
WHAT IF MY THERAPIST OPENS UP MY JARS? WHAT IF SHE MESSES EVERYTHING UP?
WHAT IF TALKING ABOUT THESE FEELINGS MESSES ME UP EVEN MORE?!
I'M FINE RIGHT NOW. NOT TALKING ABOUT THINGS HAS KEPT ME FINE, YOU KNOW? I'M GOOD.
GOOD, NOT GREAT.

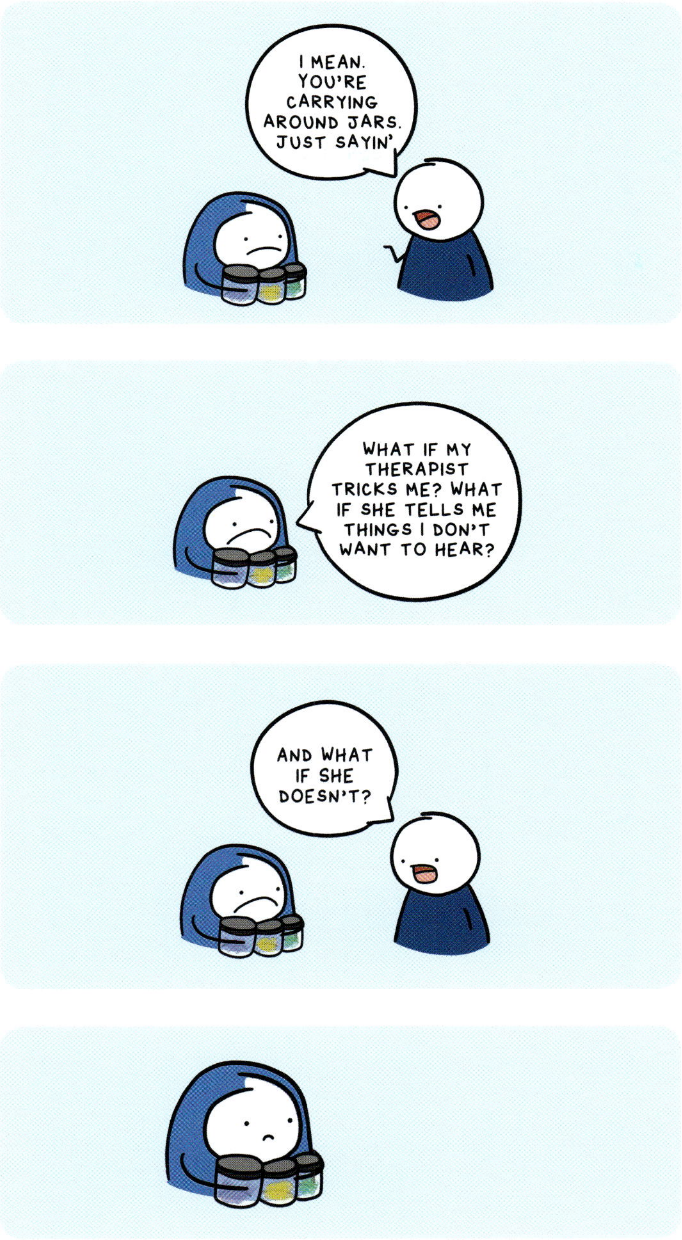
I MEAN. YOU'RE CARRYING AROUND JARS. JUST SAYIN'
WHAT IF MY THERAPIST TRICKS ME? WHAT IF SHE TELLS ME THINGS I DON'T WANT TO HEAR?
AND WHAT IF SHE DOESN'T?

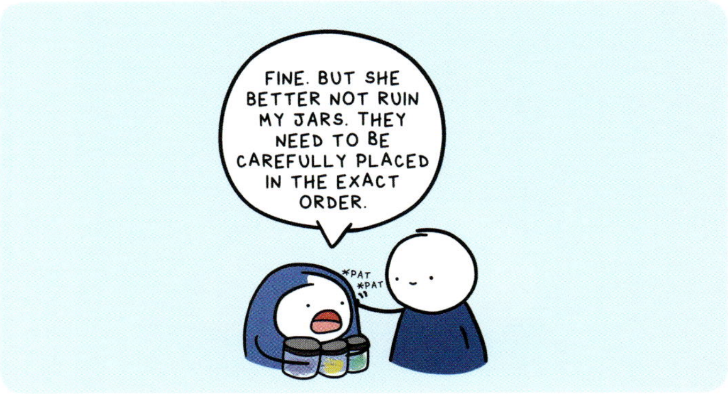
FINE. BUT SHE BETTER NOT RUIN MY JARS. THEY NEED TO BE CAREFULLY PLACED IN THE EXACT ORDER.
*PAT *PAT

The next morning, I found myself in a lofty elevator, begrudgingly prodding the button for my therapist's office. I had a wagon full of jars and was resolutely determined not to open any of them.

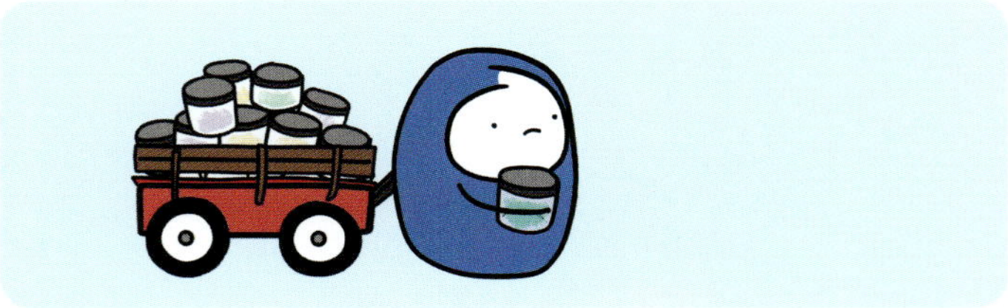

I heard the click-clacking of her heels echoing on the marble floors of the lobby long before I saw her, but when my therapist rounded the corner to greet me in front of the bronze elevator doors, I knew I had met my match.

My therapist's eyes trailed to my wagon of jars for the briefest of moments before she returned her gaze to me and introduced herself with a beaming smile.

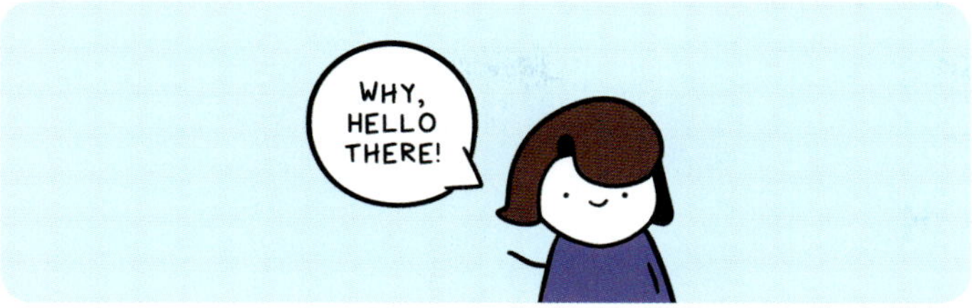
WHY, HELLO THERE!

There was an effortless manner in the way she spoke, as though conversation had always come easy to her. Artfully draped in a cashmere shawl and wearing elegant gold sphinx earrings, she could've easily been mistaken for an art curator had it not been for her relentlessly warm smile, which made her feel more like a beloved children's librarian.

I found her warmth suspect. No one is *this* friendly. As she spoke, I noticed a disarming twinkle in her eyes that whispered, *I am about to see into your soul.*

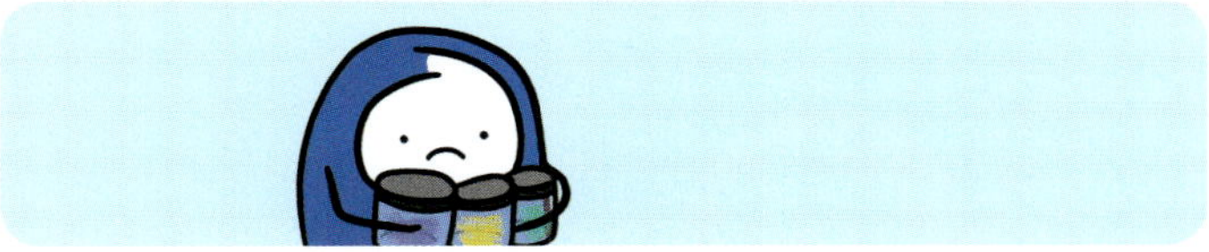

I vowed not to be tricked by her kindness.

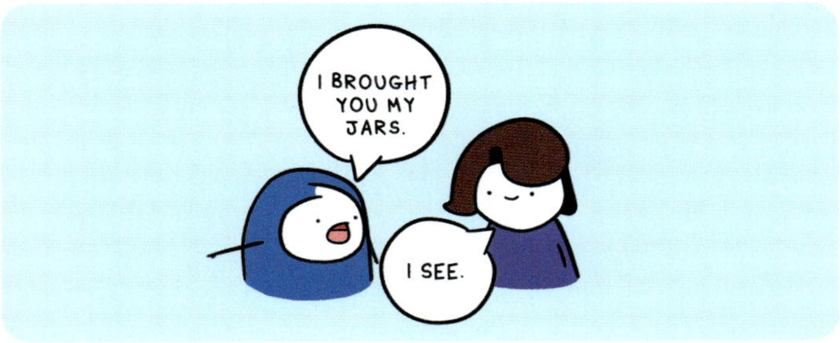
I BROUGHT YOU MY JARS.
I SEE.

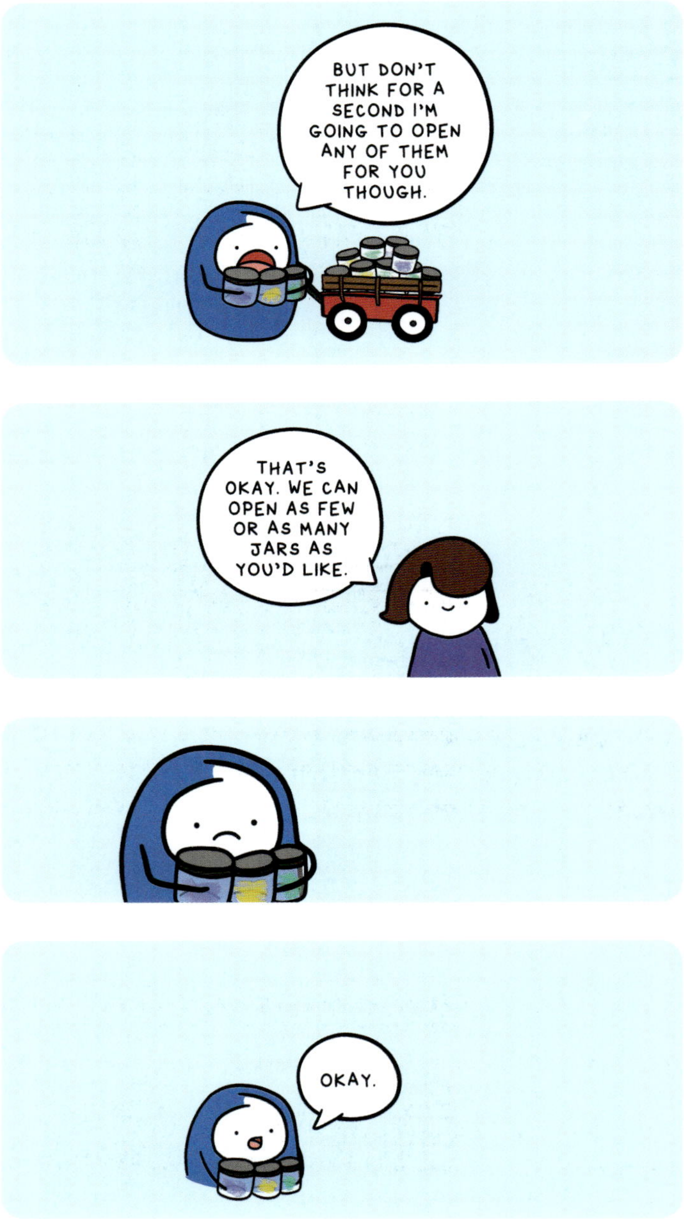
BUT DON'T THINK FOR A SECOND I'M GOING TO OPEN ANY OF THEM FOR YOU THOUGH.
THAT'S OKAY. WE CAN OPEN AS FEW OR AS MANY JARS AS YOU'D LIKE.
OKAY.

Humming absentmindedly, my therapist led us down a long, empty corridor lined with various paintings of trees and bodies of water. The jars in my wagon clinked gently as I carefully wheeled them behind me, anxiously looking back every now and then to make sure nothing had toppled over.

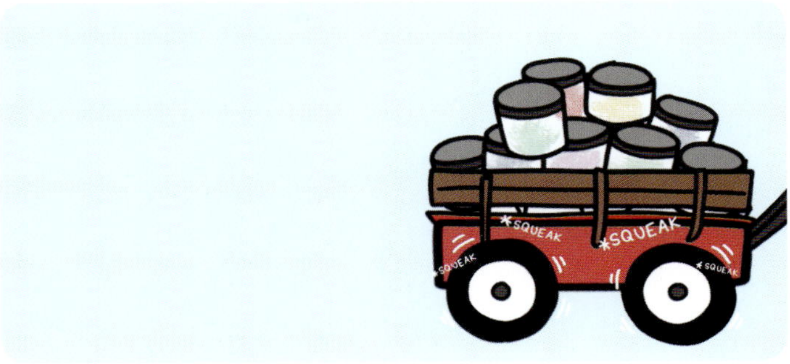
*SQUEAK
*SQUEAK
SQUEAK
*SQUEAK

After walking towards a crimson door at the end of the hall, my therapist deftly pushed down on an ornate black handle to reveal her office. Once inside, I found myself in a warm, sun-soaked room with floor-to-ceiling windows overlooking the city below us. Filled with a remarkable assortment of tall palms and exotic plants, her office carried the aura of an untouched rainforest.

I wondered how many people she had to psychoanalyze to pay for this.

A pleasing, circular coffee table sat squarely in the center of the room like a mahogany campfire, surrounded by a leather couch and two velvet armchairs. I took a deep breath and wheeled my wagon of jars off to the side.

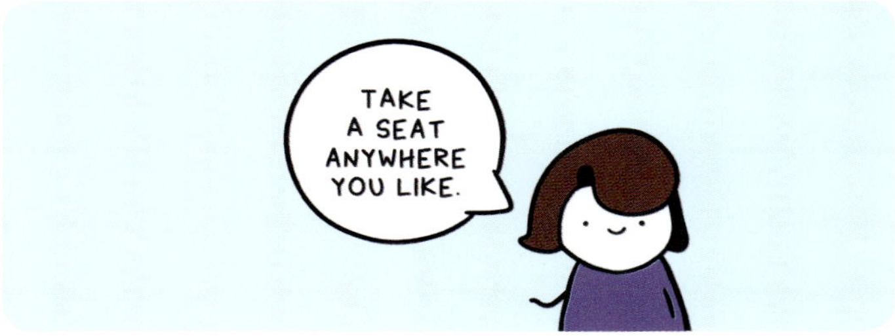
TAKE A SEAT ANYWHERE YOU LIKE.

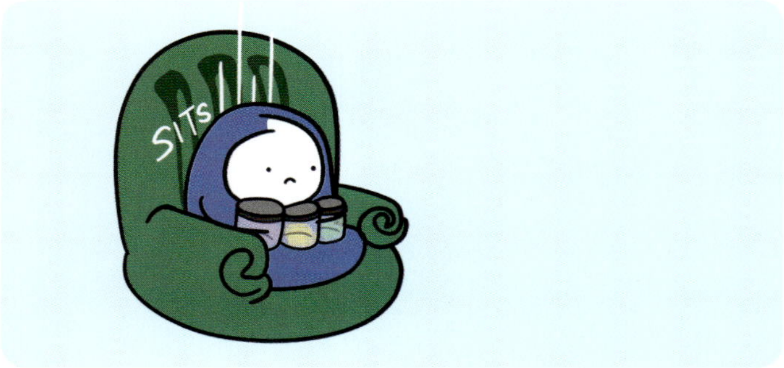
SITS

My therapist smiled and began her well-rehearsed spiel.

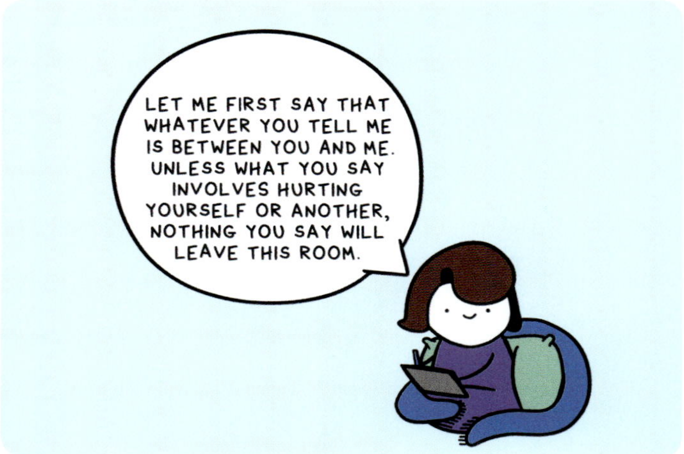
LET ME FIRST SAY THAT WHATEVER YOU TELL ME IS BETWEEN YOU AND ME. UNLESS WHAT YOU SAY INVOLVES HURTING YOURSELF OR ANOTHER, NOTHING YOU SAY WILL LEAVE THIS ROOM.

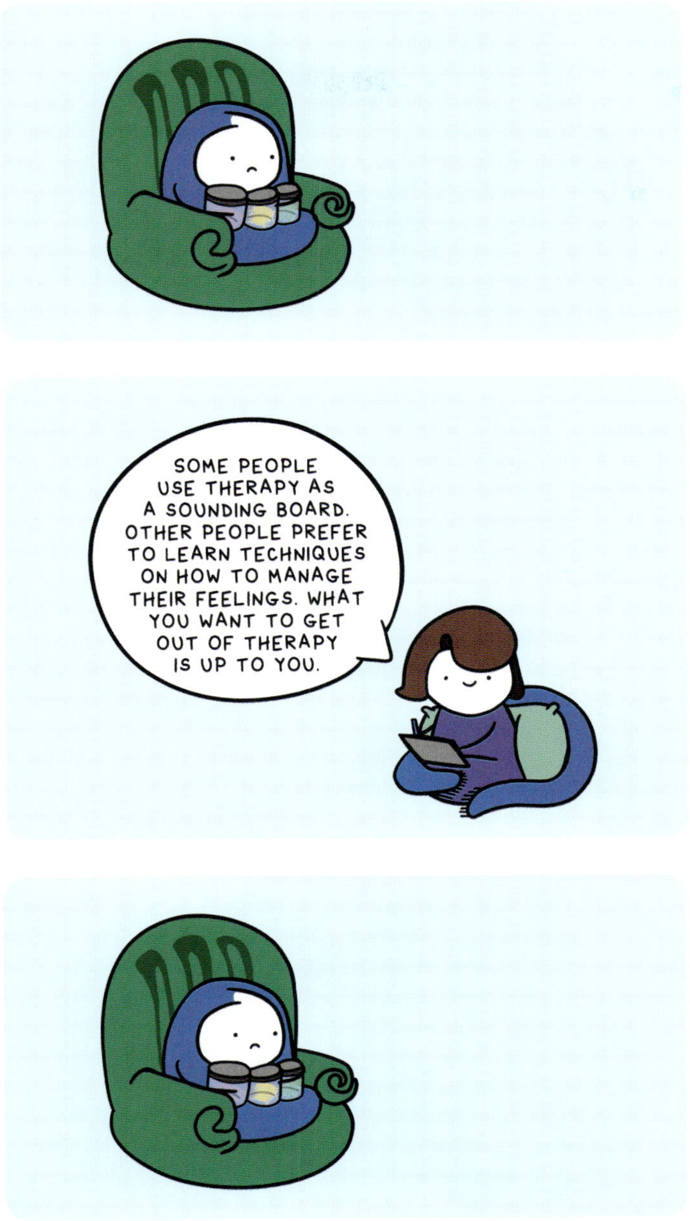
SOME PEOPLE USE THERAPY AS A SOUNDING BOARD. OTHER PEOPLE PREFER TO LEARN TECHNIQUES ON HOW TO MANAGE THEIR FEELINGS. WHAT YOU WANT TO GET OUT OF THERAPY IS UP TO YOU.

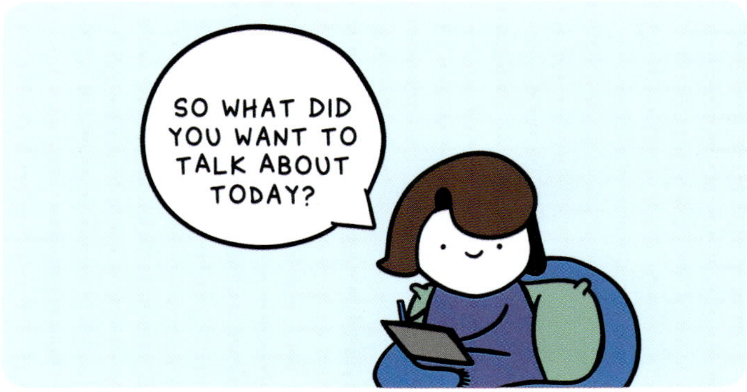
SO WHAT DID YOU WANT TO TALK ABOUT TODAY?

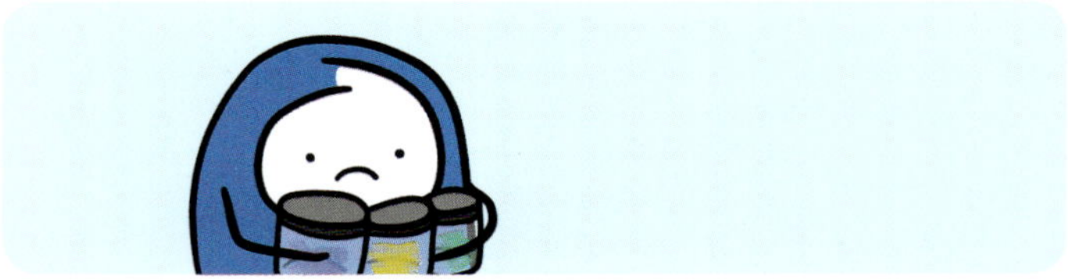

If there's one thing to know about me, it is that I do not like to make life easy for either myself or other people—I am very fair in that sense. My therapist clearly wanted me to speak, so I gave her a big, dimpled smile and silence that read—*I'm not telling you shit.*

She could tell I needed a push.

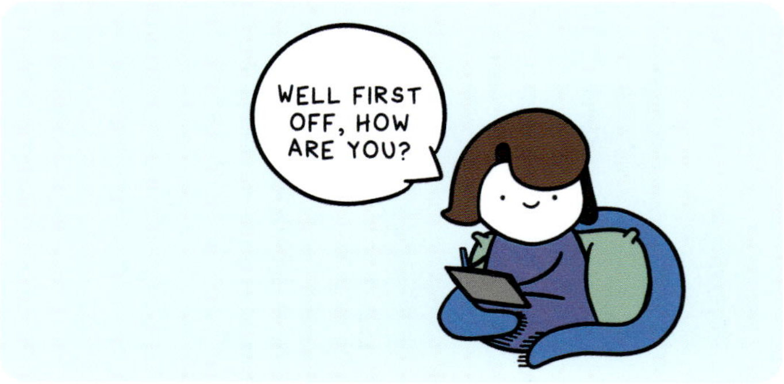
WELL FIRST OFF, HOW ARE YOU?

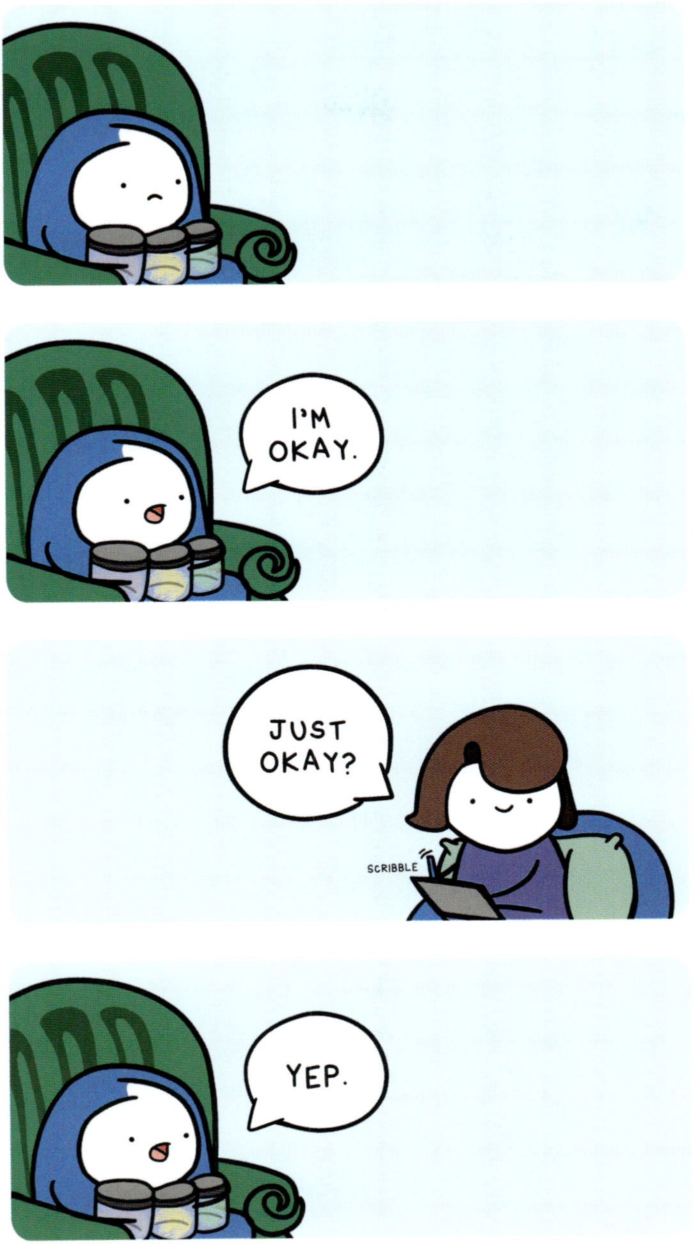
I'M OKAY.
JUST OKAY?
SCRIBBLE
YEP.

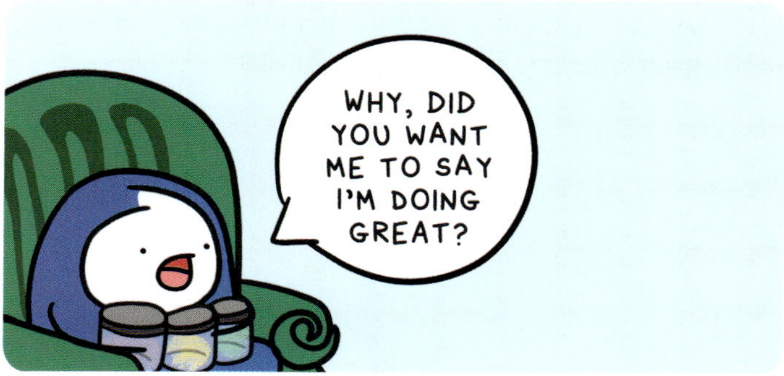
WHY, DID YOU WANT ME TO SAY I'M DOING GREAT?

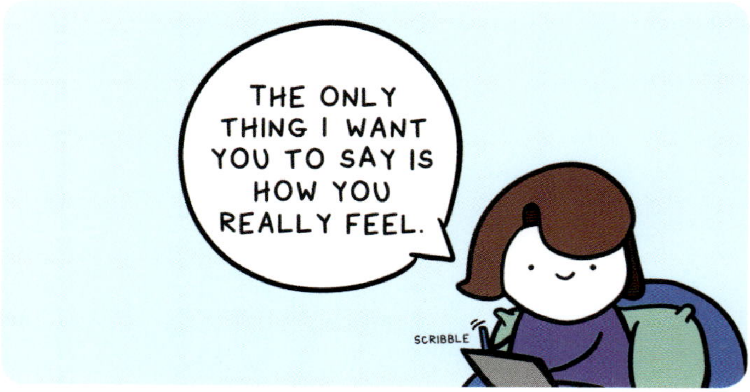
THE ONLY THING I WANT YOU TO SAY IS HOW YOU REALLY FEEL.
SCRIBBLE

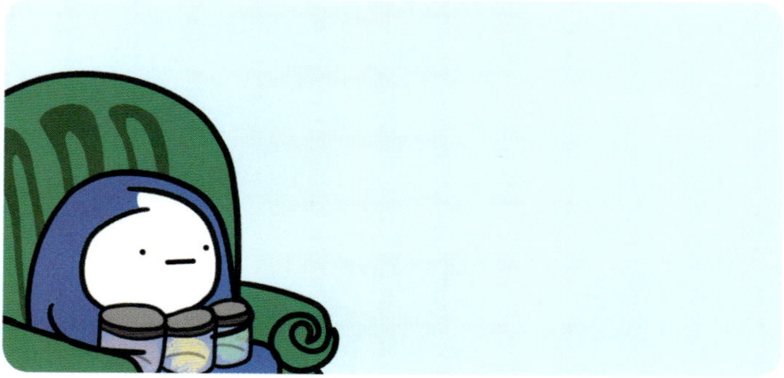

The first few minutes of therapy were . . . uncomfortable. My therapist kept giving me meaningful and encouraging looks instead of verbal responses. It felt like I was playing tennis with someone who was resolutely making zero effort to hit the ball back.

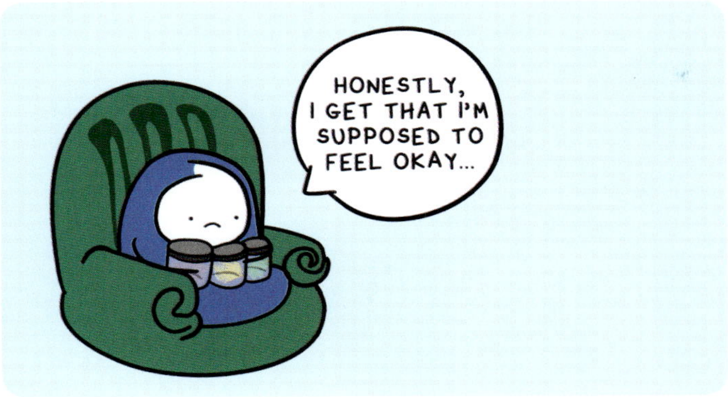
HONESTLY, I GET THAT I'M SUPPOSED TO FEEL OKAY...

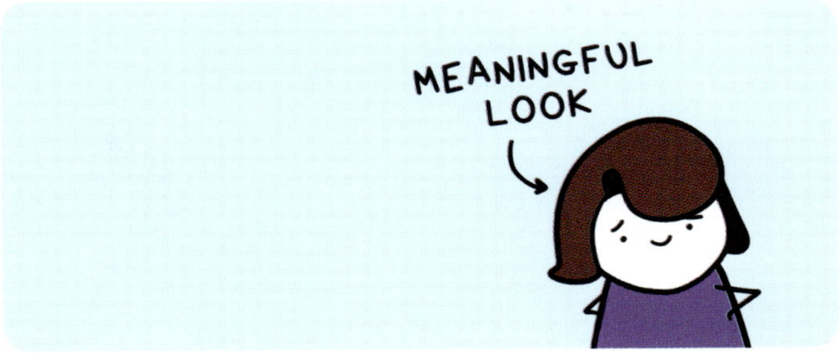
MEANINGFUL LOOK

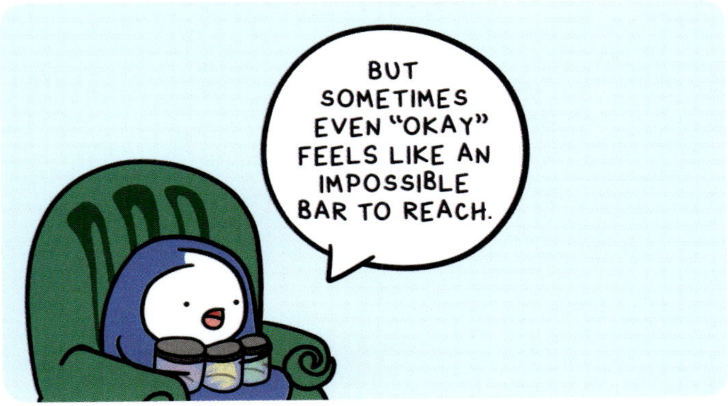
BUT SOMETIMES EVEN "OKAY" FEELS LIKE AN IMPOSSIBLE BAR TO REACH.

MEANINGFUL LOOK
UH...
MEANINGFUL LOOK

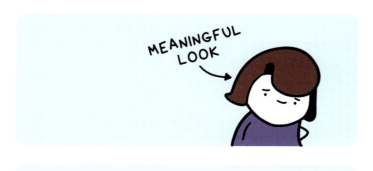

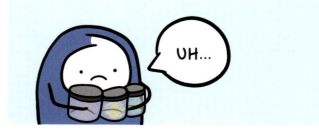

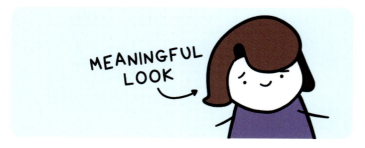

But the more I spoke, the more at ease I felt with sharing. After getting over the initial strangeness of having a conversation with someone who responded with nothing but meaningful looks, I realized this was the first time someone had listened this long without interruption.

I started to open my jars, the ones I didn't mind sharing, that is. I told my therapist how I had been feeling this heaviness, more than my usual amount of stress and anxiety, as though I were moving through life under water.

"I've been hard on myself lately," I began. "I feel like I always have a long list of things I need to do, but I keep getting distracted doing useless things like watching TV or mindlessly scrolling through the internet. And at the end of each wasted day, I always ask myself, 'What is wrong with you? Why are you like this?' It's like . . . this crippling cycle of guilt and disappointment, and it always ends in anger towards myself for not being better."

I stopped to see if my therapist wanted to say anything. She didn't. Instead, she simply jotted something in her notepad and gave me an encouraging smile. I couldn't see her notes from where I was sitting, so I started to wonder what she was writing down. Maybe she was drawing a fish playing a keyboard, or a stegosaurus with a monocle and a top hat. Or maybe, and most likely, she was taking notes on how broken I was. This last thought made me feel anxious, so I tried not to dwell on it as much.

"Sometimes I feel like . . . nothing I do is ever good enough or will ever be good enough," I said, opening yet another jar.

"What makes you think that?" my therapist asked.

"Well, I look back at something I made three years ago and I feel like it's total garbage. Which I know is the definition of 'growth' or whatever." I did the air quotes here and rolled my eyes before continuing, "but then I look at something I made last month and I *still* think it's garbage! So what if . . ." I paused briefly here before resuming in a low and conspiratorial whisper, "what if . . . *everything* I do is always and forever going to be garbage?" I gave my therapist a piercing look, as if daring her to find fallacy in my airtight argument.

My therapist simply returned a knowing smile. "And what would it mean to you if everything you do is garbage?" she asked.

"Well it would mean that I'm gar . . ."

I stopped short of finishing that sentence, but we both knew what I was about to say. I turned away to look out one of the windows before continuing.

"I guess . . . one day, I'd just like to look at something I made and be proud of it . . . is all," I said, hoping to end on a lighter note.

My therapist gave me a sympathetic smile and a meaningful look.

I hated how it actually made me feel a tiny bit better.

•  •  •

I was self-conscious throughout our entire session. It's hard not to be when someone's sitting directly across from you, dissecting your every thought and feeling while demonstrating an impressive amount of neutrality. I kept reminding myself that my therapist wasn't *judging* me, she was just drawing a fish playing a keyboard. This was, of course, untrue, but it was nicer to think this way.

After waiting until I had nothing left to say, my therapist asked me this question.

YOU SAY YOU'RE CRITICAL OF YOURSELF. ARE YOU EVER COMPASSIONATE TO YOURSELF?

DO YOU EVER SAY TO YOURSELF, "I'M NOT DOING SO WELL RIGHT NOW. BUT IT'S OKAY."

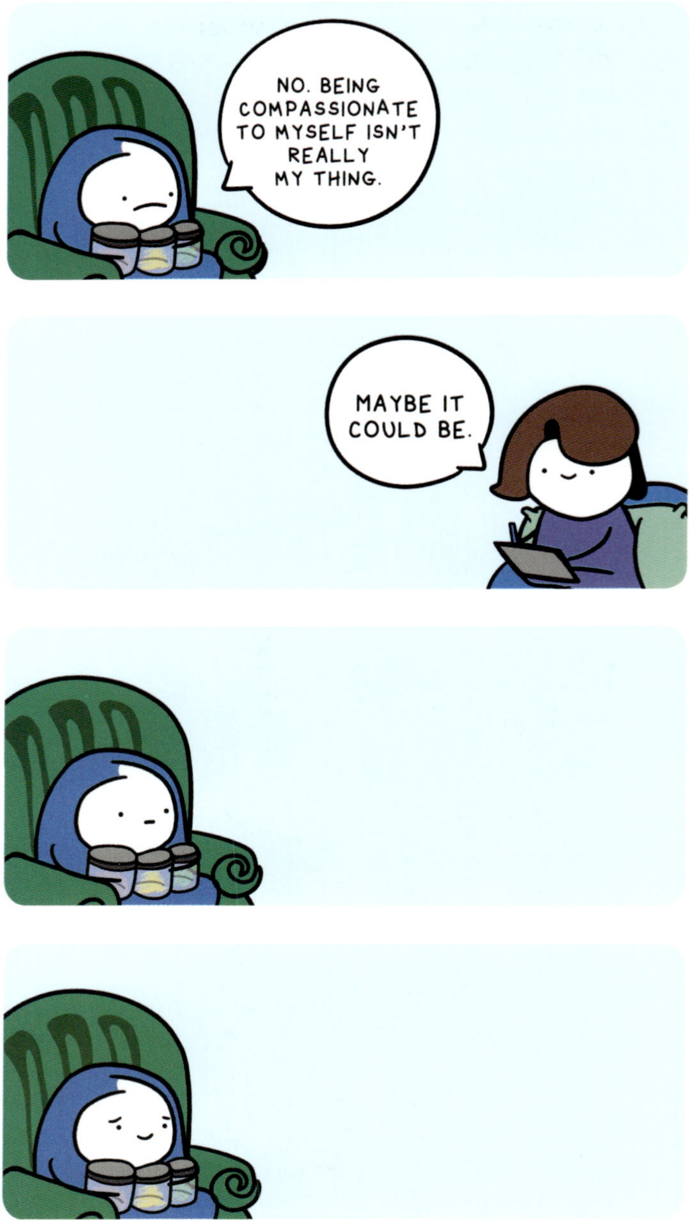
NO. BEING COMPASSIONATE TO MYSELF ISN'T REALLY MY THING.
MAYBE IT COULD BE.

I ended up opening quite a few jars in that first session—not all jars—but definitely more than I had expected to.

HERE ARE THE JARS I WANTED TO OPEN WITH YOU TODAY.
Regrets
Self-doubt
Anxiety
Fears
!
WHAT ABOUT THIS ONE?
Regrets
Self-doubt
Anxiety
Fears
WAIT! UM, NOT THAT ONE! NOT... YET.
Regrets
Self-doubt
Anxiety
Fears

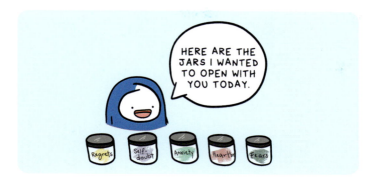

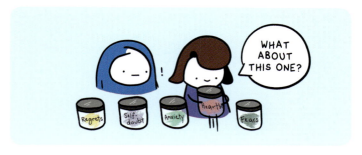

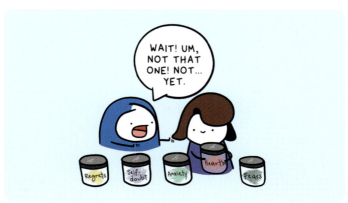

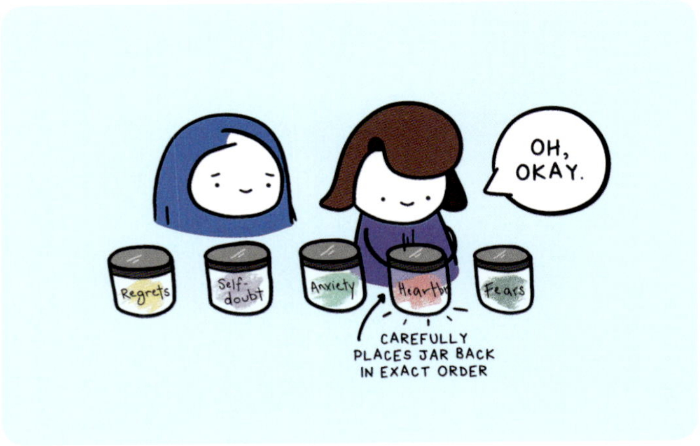
Regrets
Self-doubt
Anxiety
Fears
OH, OKAY.
CAREFULLY PLACES JAR BACK IN EXACT ORDER

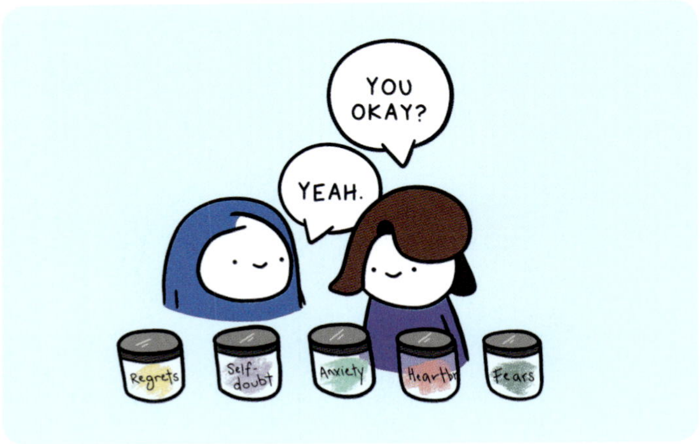
YOU OKAY?
YEAH.
Regrets
Self-doubt
Anxiety
Fears

Therapy made me experience what it's like to be emotionally peeled back. With every word I spoke, I exposed new, unseen layers of myself. It was a process that was at once liberating and terrifying. Throughout the session, I could hear a voice I recognized as my own saying things I didn't realize I felt until I heard them articulated—things I instantly knew to be true once said out loud.

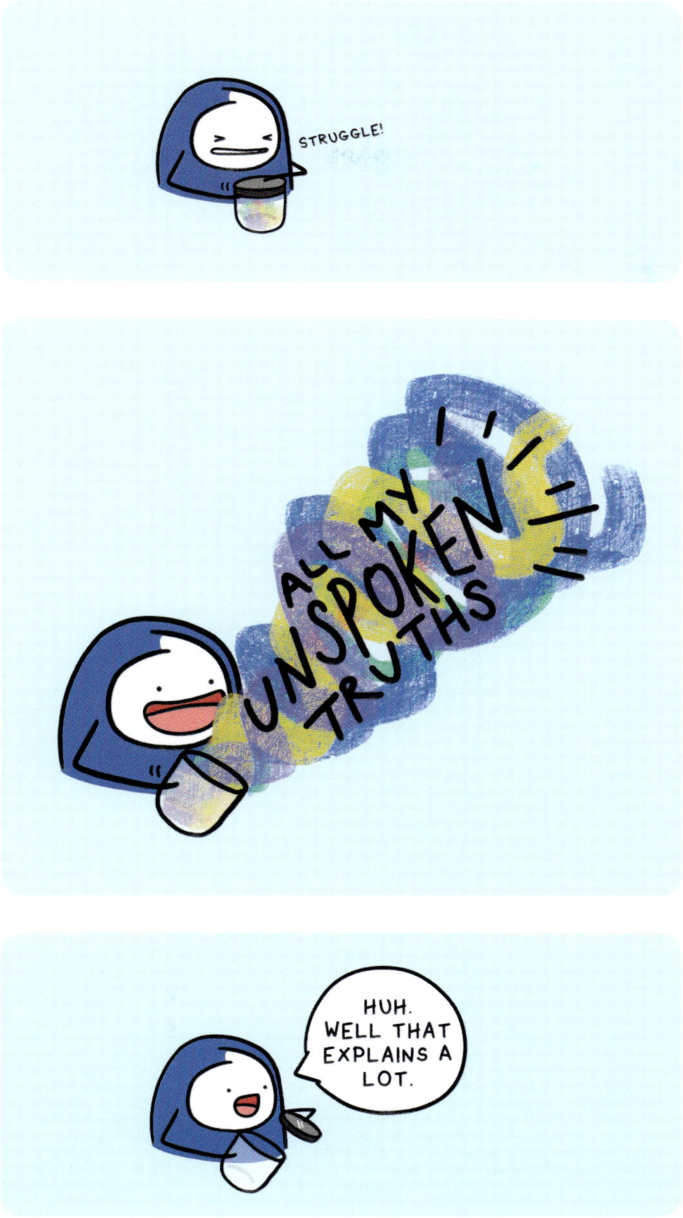
STRUGGLE!
ALL MY UNSPOKEN TRUTHS
HUH. WELL THAT EXPLAINS A LOT.

Some jars proved more difficult to open than others, and as a result, I spent the second half of my session holding back tears and willing myself not to break. As if our roles had been reversed, I became the silent one, nodding along and opting not to speak so as to conceal the quavering quality of my voice. At times, I would bite the inside of my mouth to prevent myself from crying. I didn't want to cry in front of my therapist.

We just weren't there yet.

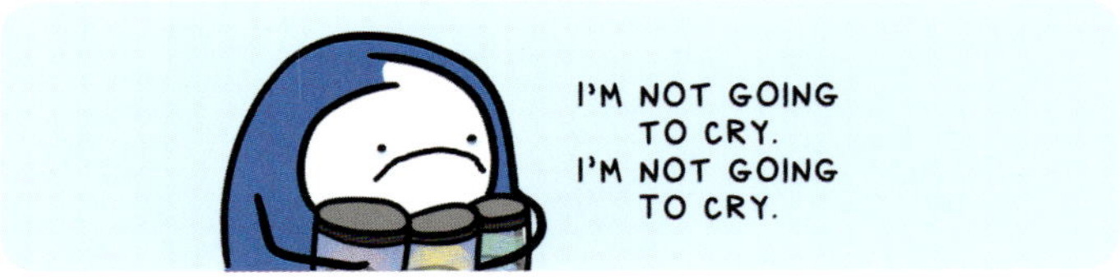
I'M NOT GOING TO CRY.
I'M NOT GOING TO CRY.

To my relief, my therapist was understanding and compassionate. She was respectful of my boundaries and at no point did I feel coerced or tricked. Therapy was scary, but in a way that seemed worthwhile. It allowed me to process and relive my stories with clarity and objectivity, like I was reading a book for the first time.

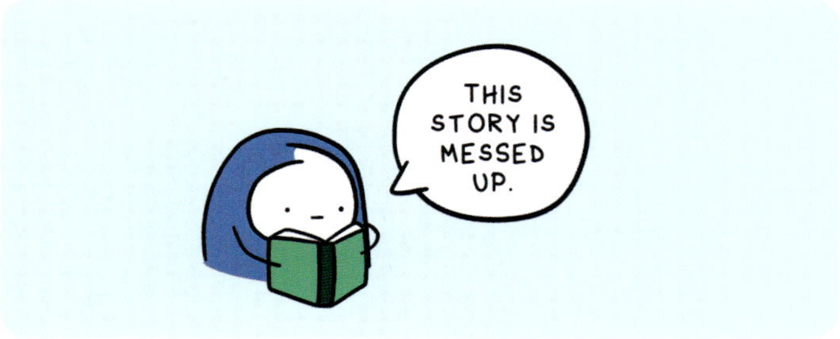
THIS STORY IS MESSED UP.

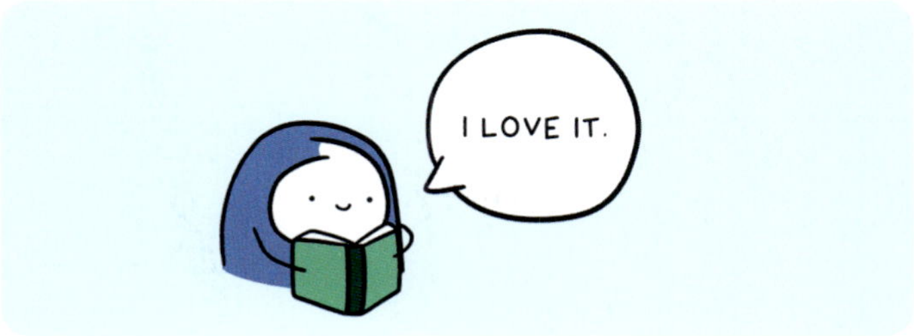
I LOVE IT.

I didn't have to censor my feelings because it didn't matter what my therapist thought about me. She wasn't a friend, a coworker, or family. She was simply a kindly locked box to tell all my secrets to—a new jar that didn't require a lid.

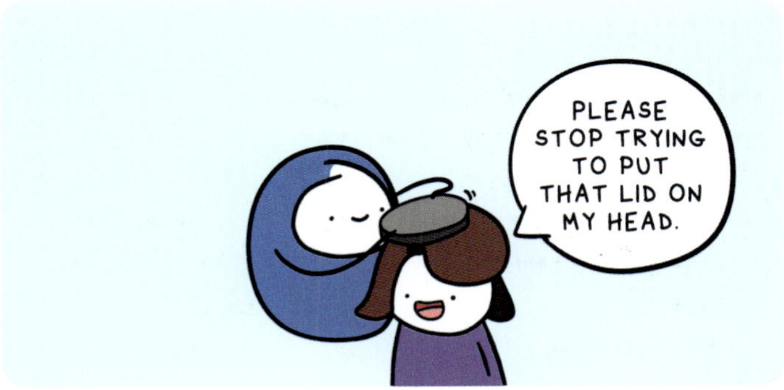
PLEASE STOP TRYING TO PUT THAT LID ON MY HEAD.

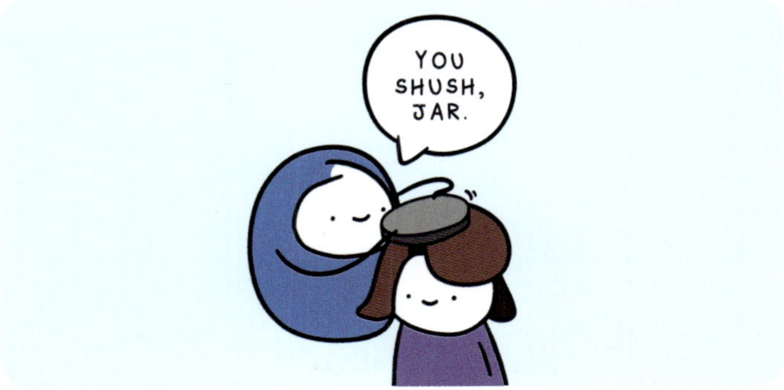
YOU SHUSH, JAR.

If therapy sounds like batty bananas, that's because it is. It's a batty bananas way to try and untangle all the batty bananas inside of us.

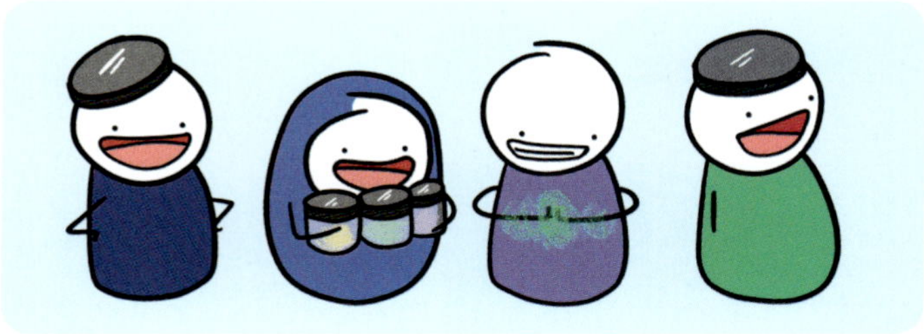

When I first walked into therapy, I thought I would walk away feeling as though I was fixed. I thought that one session of therapy would do the trick or that the following ten sessions might.

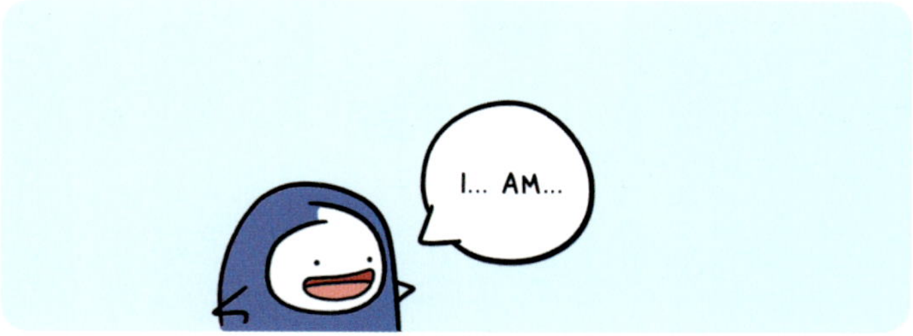
I... AM...

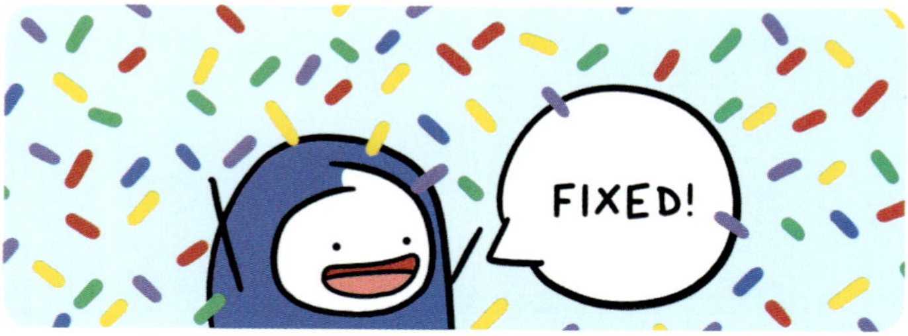
FIXED!

But it didn't. Therapy didn't fix me. If anything, therapy revealed all my broken pieces at a higher fidelity. But maybe that's the point. Embracing how everyone is broken in their own ways and learning how to feel okay about it. Maybe therapy isn't about fixing things, but accepting them as they are—broken and imperfect, sure, but still worthwhile and beautiful in their own strange ways.

In the end, therapy wasn't the smooth silver bullet or magical one-off cure I had expected to find. Therapy was more like a long, arduous hike to a valley—a valley made just for you.

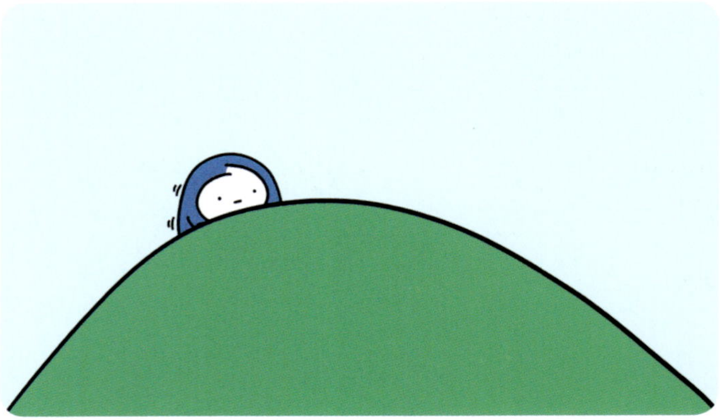

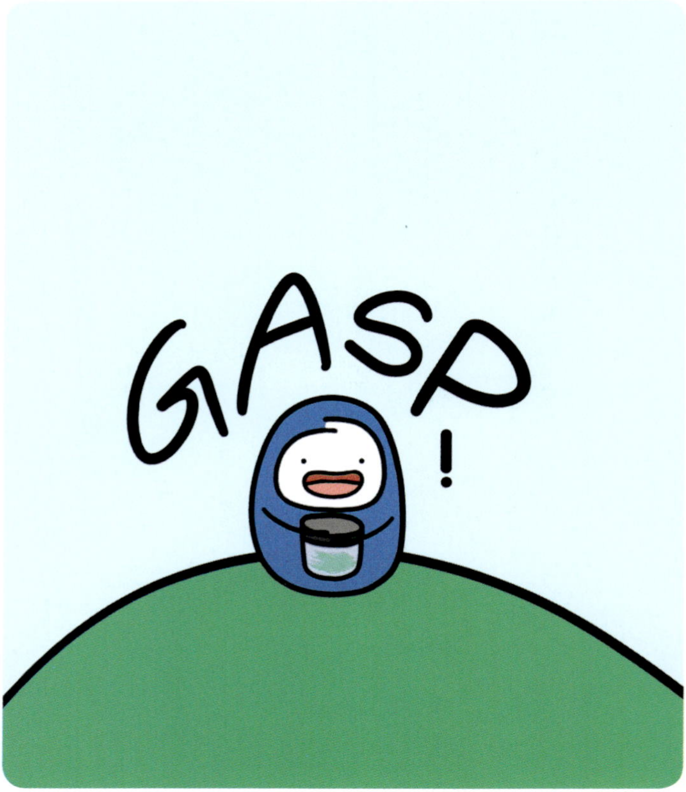
GASP
!

And in this valley, you might find a place to read your stories and open up your jars. You may not want to open all your jars at once, you may not want to open any jars at all, but it's nice to know that somewhere out there, there's a beautiful valley for you to do so.

Should you so wish.

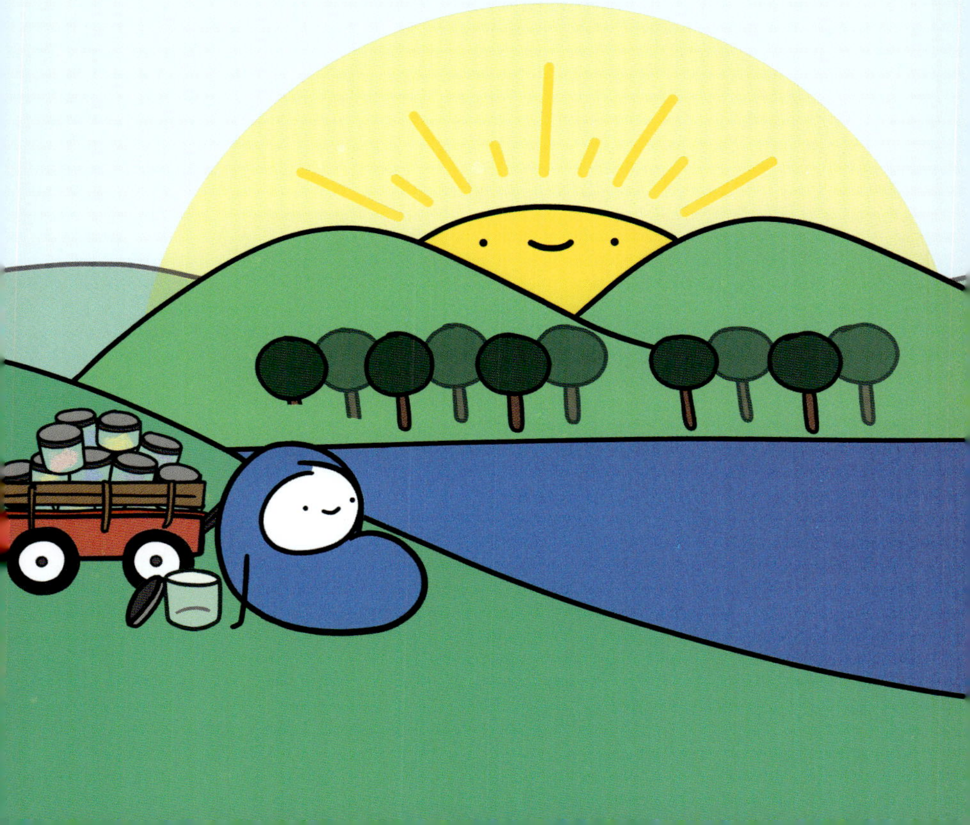

# CHAPTER 5

# SPACE DUST

When I was five years old, my mum, my sister, and I camped out to wait for a meteor shower. The meteor shower, like all meteor showers, was supposed to be a really big deal.

After a thorough investigation of every window in our house, we established that my bedroom had the best view of the night sky, so we lugged three wooden dining chairs upstairs, plopped pillows onto them, and proceeded to set up camp.

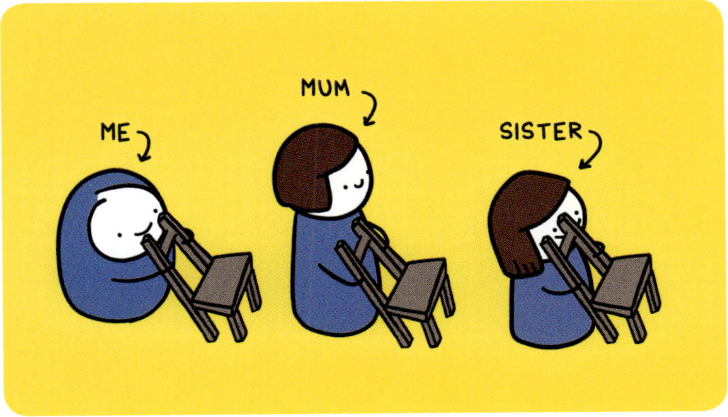
MUM
ME
SISTER

It probably would have made more sense to actually camp outdoors for this great celestial event, but we weren't the kind of family that did stuff like that—indoor "camping" was the extent of our efforts.

After making sure my sister and I were all settled in with copious amounts of pillows, throws, and snacks, my mum turned off the lights, and the moon took center stage as it became the only source of illumination.

Curious as to why the house was so suspiciously peaceful, my dad peeked in to inquire why his typically screaming children were suddenly sitting soundlessly in the dark.

My dad nodded along thoughtfully as I briefed him on our plans, but cautioned against getting our hopes up as we probably wouldn't be able to see any stars this close to the city. Then, after having felt as though he had dispensed a sufficient amount of wisdom for the day, he gleefully left the room to enjoy this ephemeral moment of peace and quiet in our house.

I had never seen a meteor shower before, so I was determined to make this one count. I had written down a list of things I wanted to wish for in my sketchbook, but was still a bit nervous about the whole thing.

I HOPE THE STARS DON'T COME ALL AT ONCE, MUM!
I MIGHT NOT MAKE MY WISHES IN TIME!
YOU'LL BE OKAY.
PAT PAT

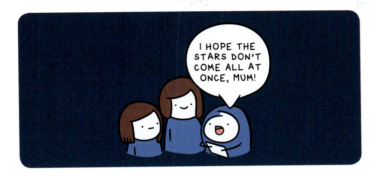

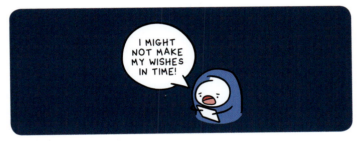

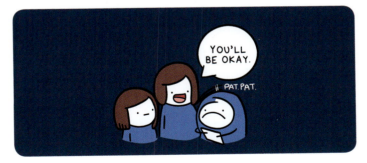

The meteor shower was scheduled to start at 9 p.m. By 1 a.m., we had seen approximately zero shooting stars.

I was very much over it.

*The sky can keep its lousy wishes*, I thought. Surely, a shooting star wasn't *that* much better than a regular star, and there were plenty of regular stars out there. I decided right then and there that if patience was a virtue, then it would have to be a virtue I lived without.

Seeing my yawns overlapping one another as I slumped onto her side, my mum suggested that I head to bed. She, however, would stay up a little while longer.

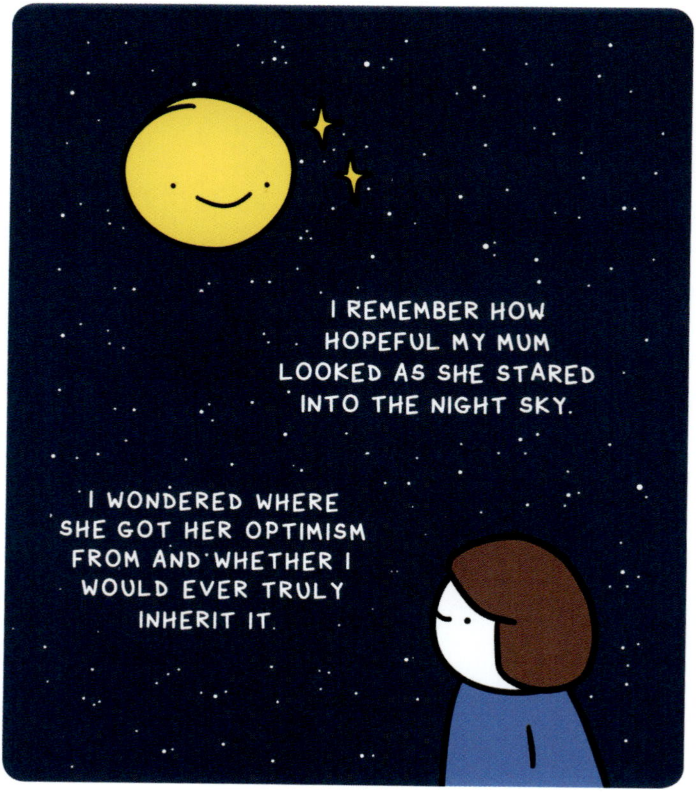
I REMEMBER HOW HOPEFUL MY MUM LOOKED AS SHE STARED INTO THE NIGHT SKY.
I WONDERED WHERE SHE GOT HER OPTIMISM FROM AND WHETHER I WOULD EVER TRULY INHERIT IT.

I decided to stay a little while longer.

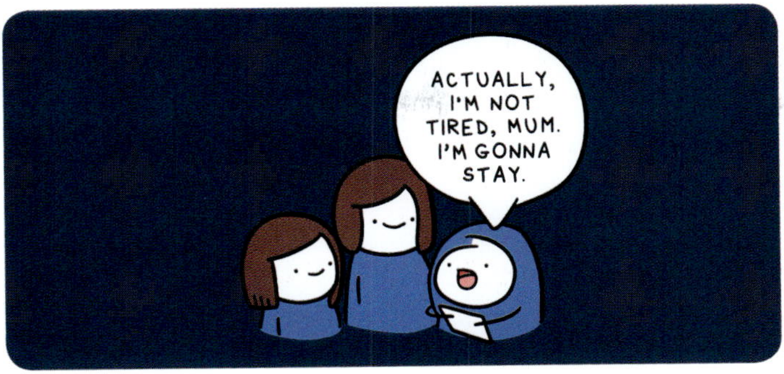
ACTUALLY, I'M NOT TIRED, MUM. I'M GONNA STAY.

And then, at 1:48 a.m., we saw it.

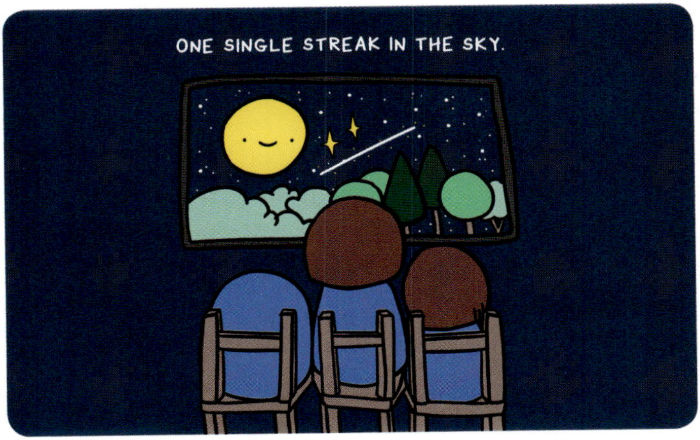
ONE SINGLE STREAK IN THE SKY.

And then another star streaked past, and another, and then . . . it was done.

Just like that.

I was so caught off guard I didn't even make any wishes.

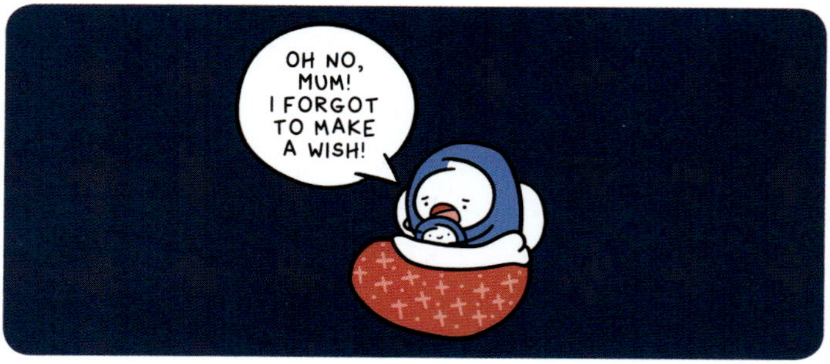
OH NO, MUM! I FORGOT TO MAKE A WISH!

Devastation ensued.

I looked down at my list of fruitless wishes and suddenly felt deeply swindled by it all. Staring angrily out the window and into the night sky, I muttered to the universe, "I thought we were *friends*."

The universe did not respond. It probably had better things to do.

Once again sensing the swell of bottomless anxiety in her youngest child, my mum gently tucked me in and provided some much-needed reassurance.

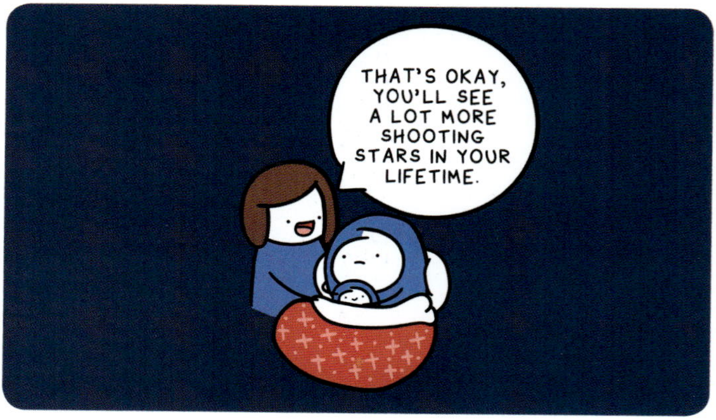
THAT'S OKAY, YOU'LL SEE A LOT MORE SHOOTING STARS IN YOUR LIFETIME.

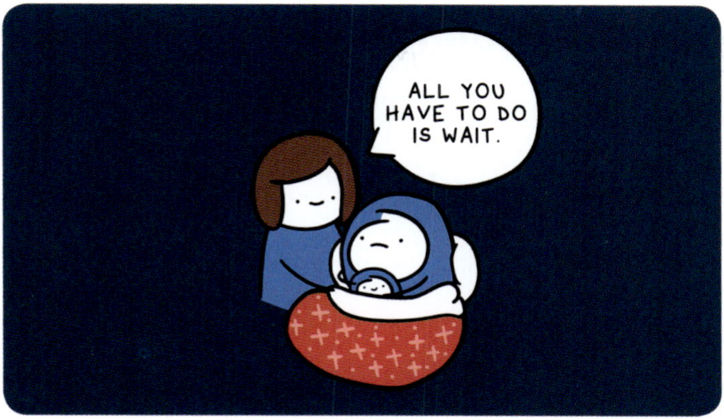
ALL YOU HAVE TO DO IS WAIT.

Even at five, I was skeptical of these words. But the night had taken a toll, so I closed my eyes as I silently wondered if I would ever really be patient enough to see shooting stars again.

• • •

When I packed my bags to move to another country, I forgot to pack my friends. I guess I just thought they were something I could easily pick up after I had settled in . . . like laundry detergent or potted plants.

For the first two months after moving to Seattle, I took a four-hour bus ride back to Vancouver every weekend. Partly because I still had stuff left over to pack, but largely because I wanted to stay in my parallel universe fantasy in which I hadn't moved at all.

In conversations with my friends back home, they would always ask me the same thing:

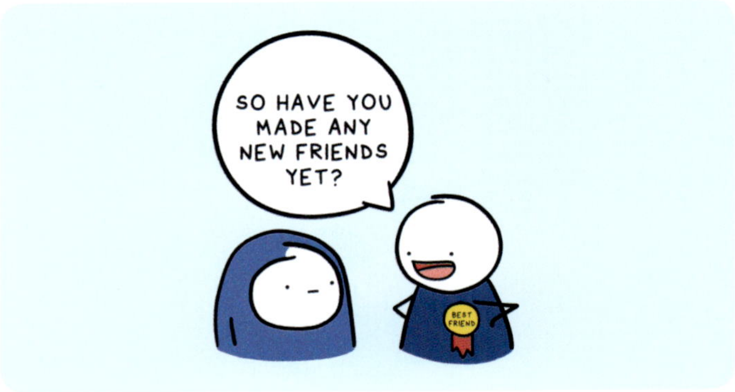
SO HAVE YOU MADE ANY NEW FRIENDS YET?
BEST FRIEND

And I would always respond:

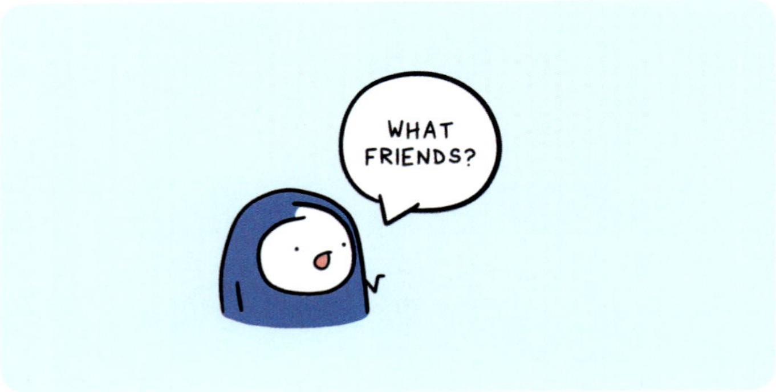
WHAT FRIENDS?

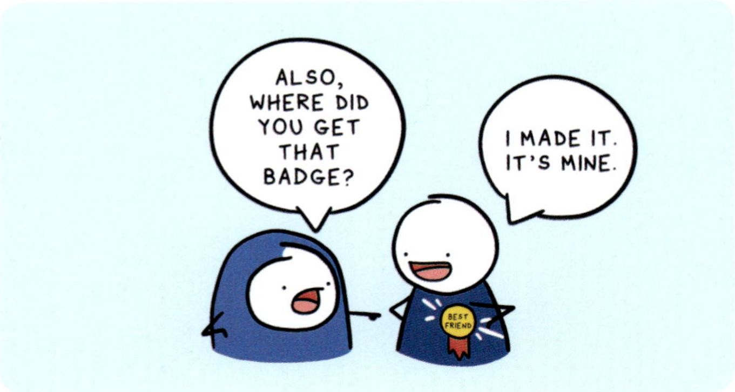
ALSO, WHERE DID YOU GET THAT BADGE?
I MADE IT. IT'S MINE.
BEST FRIEND

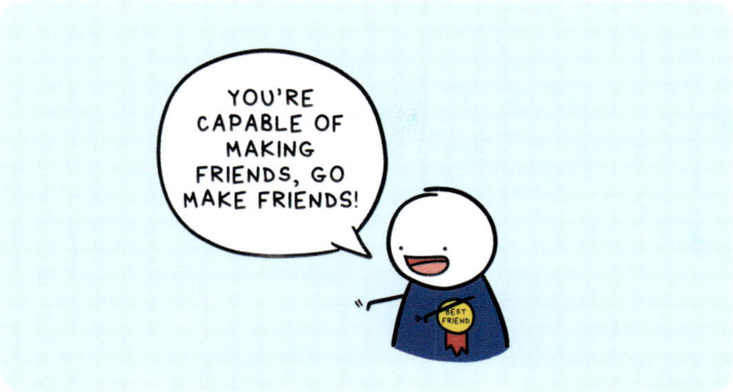
YOU'RE CAPABLE OF MAKING FRIENDS, GO MAKE FRIENDS!
BEST FRIEND

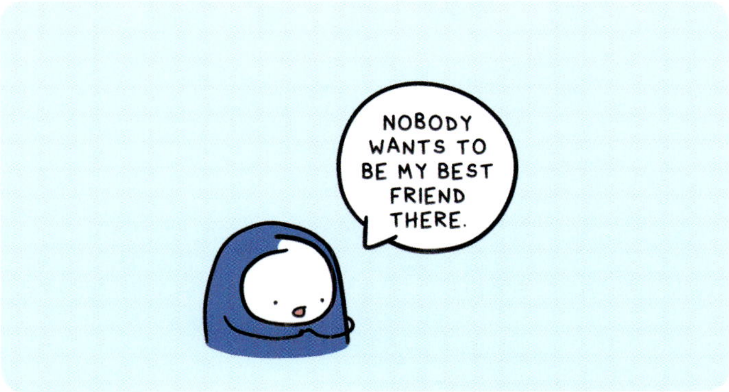
NOBODY WANTS TO BE MY BEST FRIEND THERE.

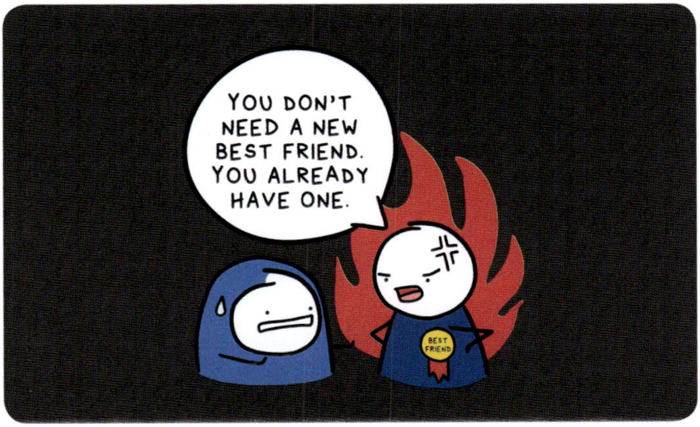
YOU DON'T NEED A NEW BEST FRIEND. YOU ALREADY HAVE ONE.
BEST FRIEND

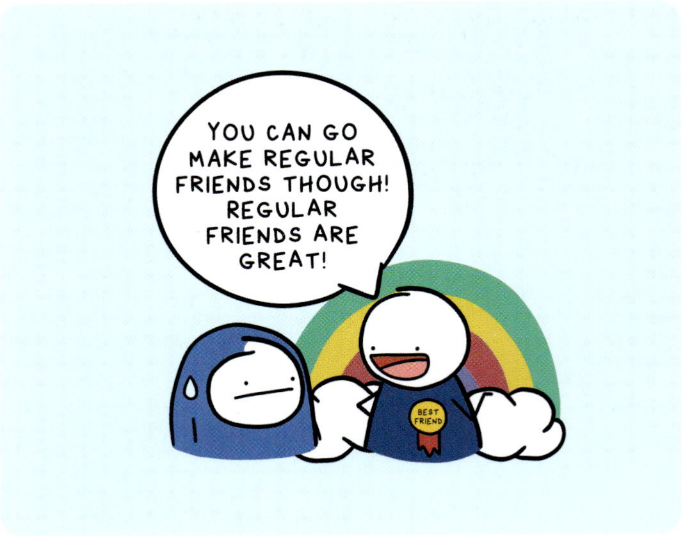
YOU CAN GO MAKE REGULAR FRIENDS THOUGH! REGULAR FRIENDS ARE GREAT!
BEST FRIEND

Trying to make new friends from scratch when you're well into adulthood is an emotionally debilitating experience. I hadn't realized it prior to moving, but I had never really lived a day in my life without having at least one close friend around. This was because my first best friend was inherited—our mothers were friends and pregnant within the same year, so as a result, our friendship had been a sort of welcome goody bag upon entering the world.

But moving to a new city was like pressing the reset button on life. Not the fun and satisfying-to-press big red reset buttons, but the tiny, tedious ones. The kind that require a fine, oft-unavailable object in order to hit reset. The kind you struggle to press when you mistakenly kill your Tamagotchi and need to resurrect it in shame.

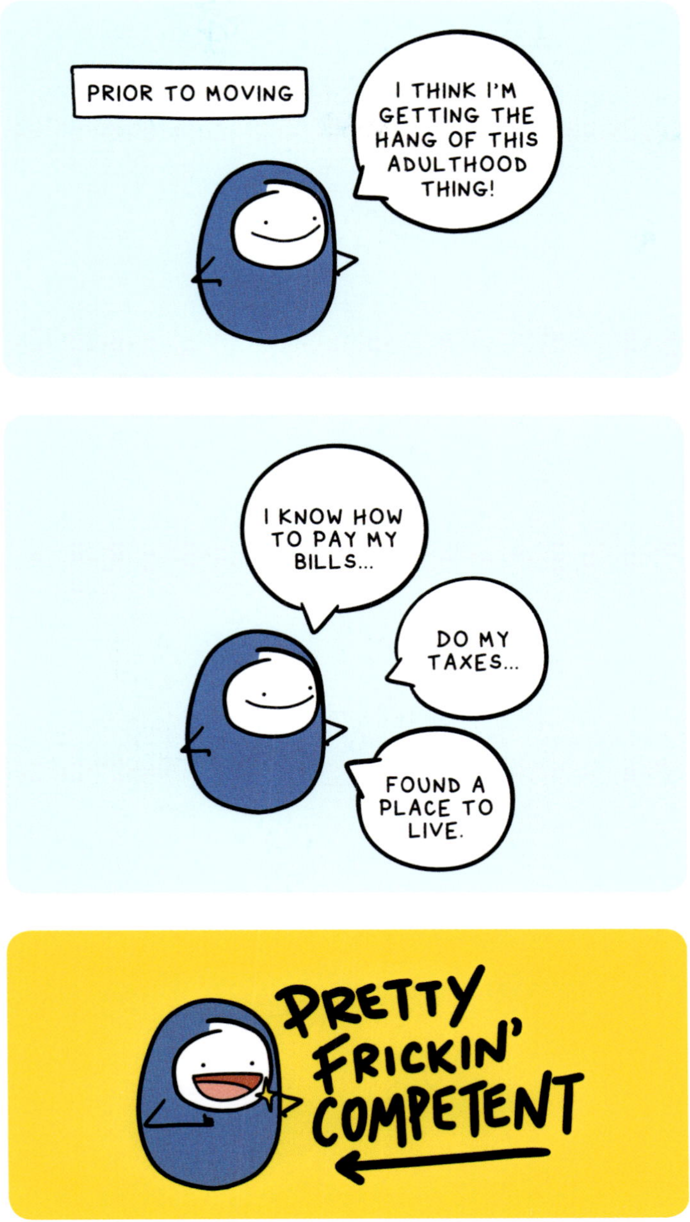
PRIOR TO MOVING
I THINK I'M GETTING THE HANG OF THIS ADULTHOOD THING!
I KNOW HOW TO PAY MY BILLS...
DO MY TAXES...
FOUND A PLACE TO LIVE.
PRETTY FRICKIN' COMPETENT

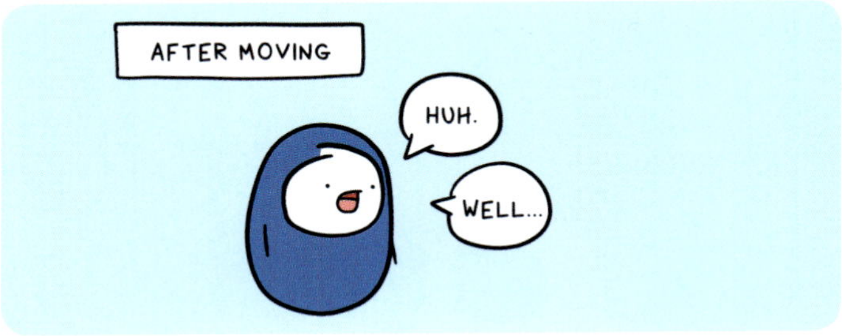
AFTER MOVING
HUH.
WELL...

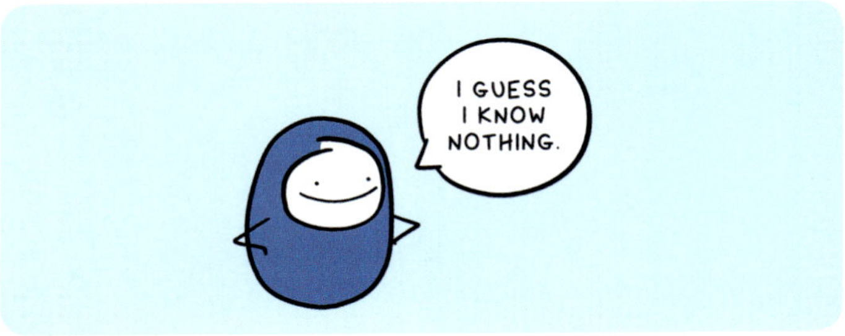
I GUESS I KNOW NOTHING.

Complete and utter inadequacy is a humbling experience.

I did not much care for it.

When I finally found a place to live, had a grocery store route figured out, and my bills somewhat paid, I spun around in a moment of triumph and waited for someone to congratulate me.

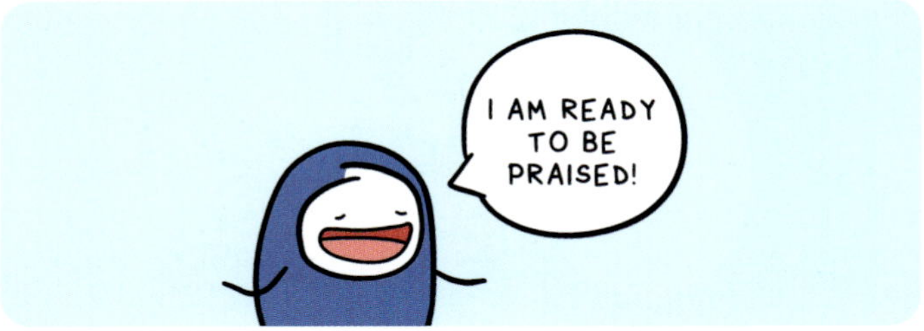
I AM READY TO BE PRAISED!

But there was no one.

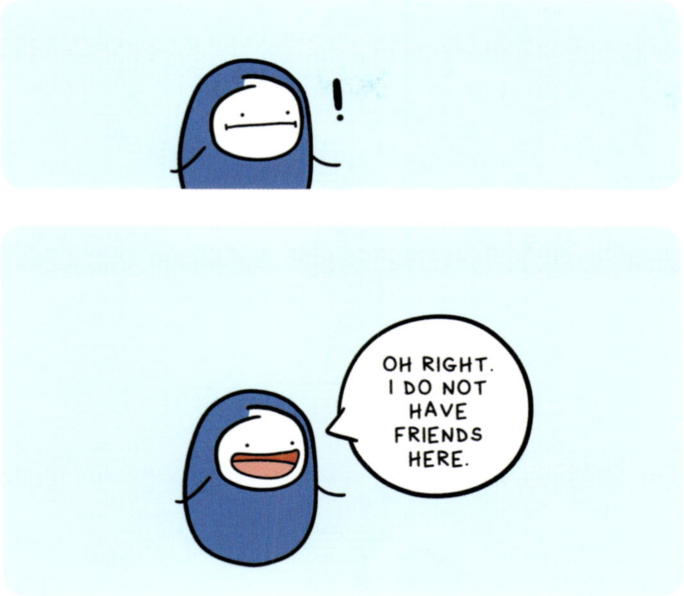
!
OH RIGHT. I DO NOT HAVE FRIENDS HERE.

I had anticipated many challenges in moving to a new city, but I never fully prepared for the impact of not having friends in my physical proximity. Having never experienced what it's like to be truly alone, I didn't understand the potency of loneliness until I was fully submerged in it.

The realization that I didn't have any friends in the city opened an anxiety floodgate. Demons I had spent years of my life slaying suddenly awoke from their slumber and reared their ugly heads in my direction. It was as though they could sense it—that telling lesion in my emotional state that beckoned them to come knocking once more.

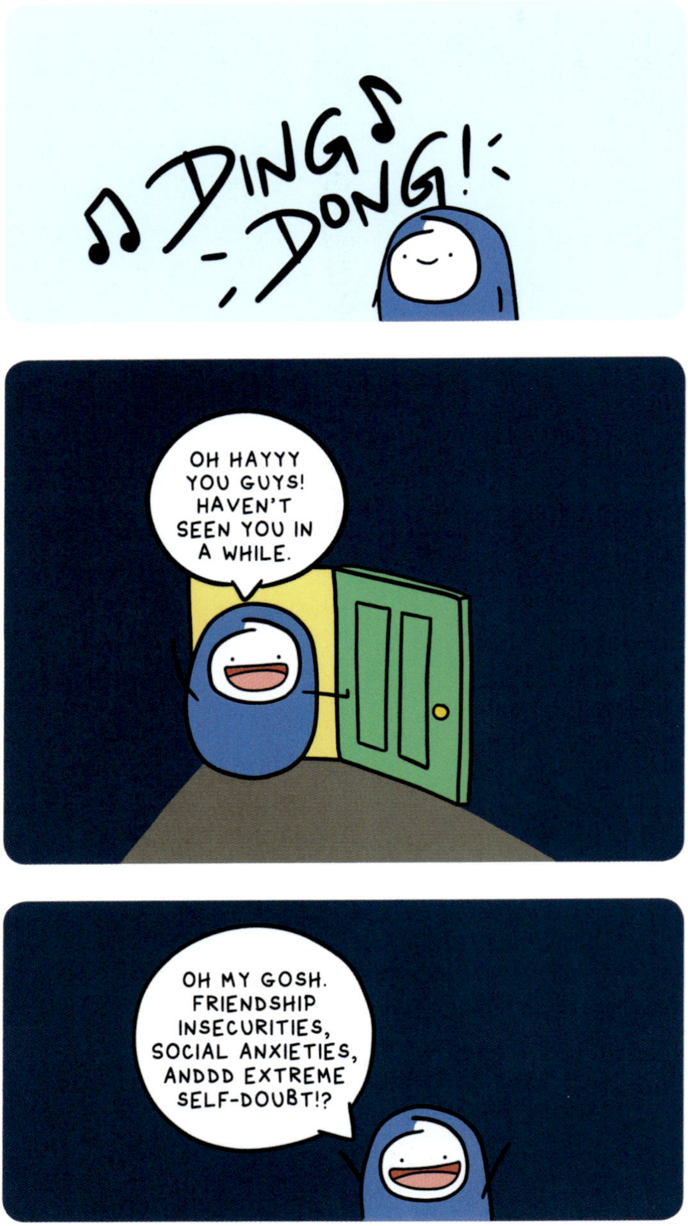
DING DONG!
OH HAYYY YOU GUYS! HAVEN'T SEEN YOU IN A WHILE.
OH MY GOSH. FRIENDSHIP INSECURITIES, SOCIAL ANXIETIES, ANDDD EXTREME SELF-DOUBT!?

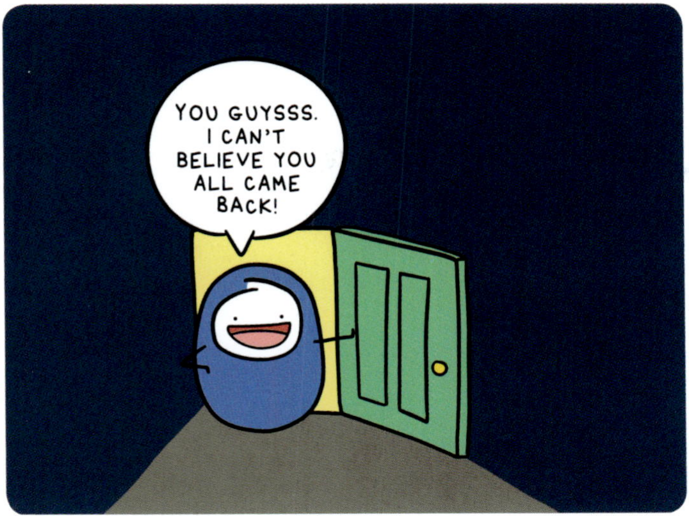
YOU GUYSSS. I CAN'T BELIEVE YOU ALL CAME BACK!

If making friends is like riding a bike, then surely I could do it again. And with that mantra in mind, I set off to make new friends with all my demons in tow.

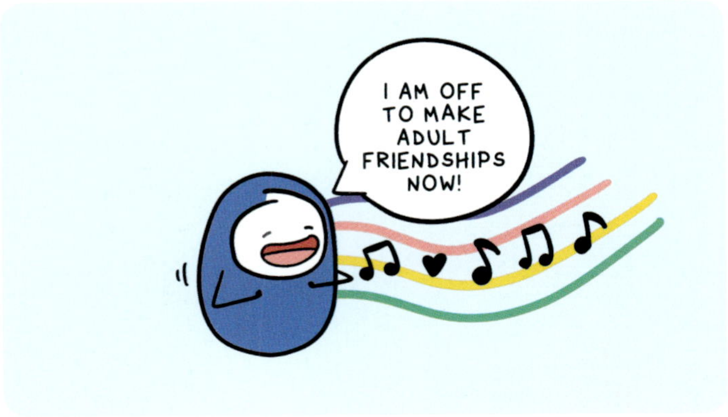
I AM OFF TO MAKE ADULT FRIENDSHIPS NOW!

My confidence was short-lived.

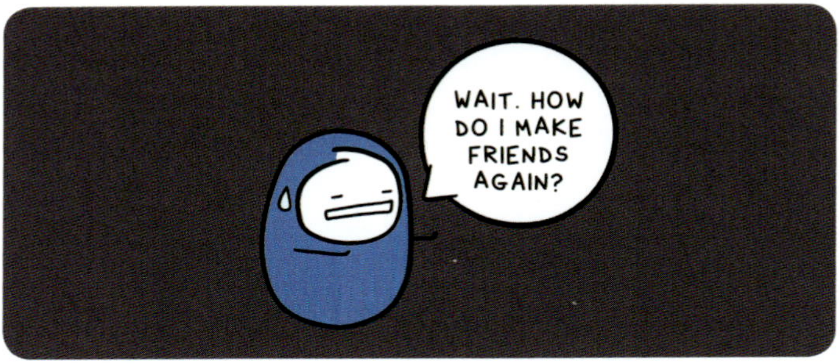
WAIT. HOW DO I MAKE FRIENDS AGAIN?

Some archaic form of myself probably knew how to make new friends. Some ancient self back in the days of school, or even my first few jobs out of university. But my ability to make new friends had long rusted from disuse. After all, my friends from home were all old friends—decade-long friendships that required little to no maintenance. The kind of friends who if I asked to help bury a dead body, would simply respond, "How many and where?" The kind of mutual best friendships that never needed further validation.

I guess I never fully appreciated these friendships until I moved away.

Rationally, I knew the logical thing to do in order to make new friends was to socialize . . . but I hated socializing.

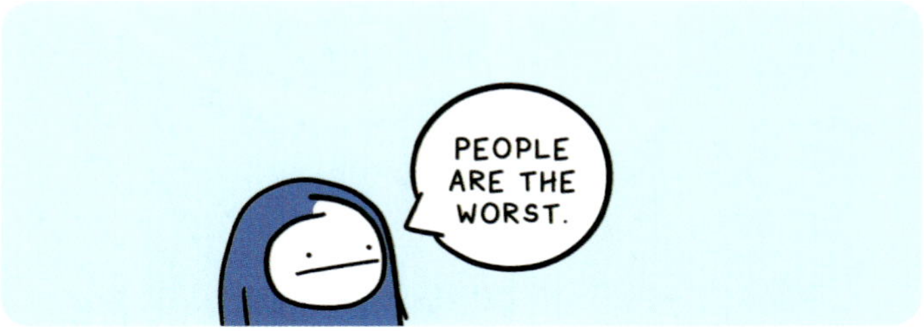
PEOPLE ARE THE WORST.

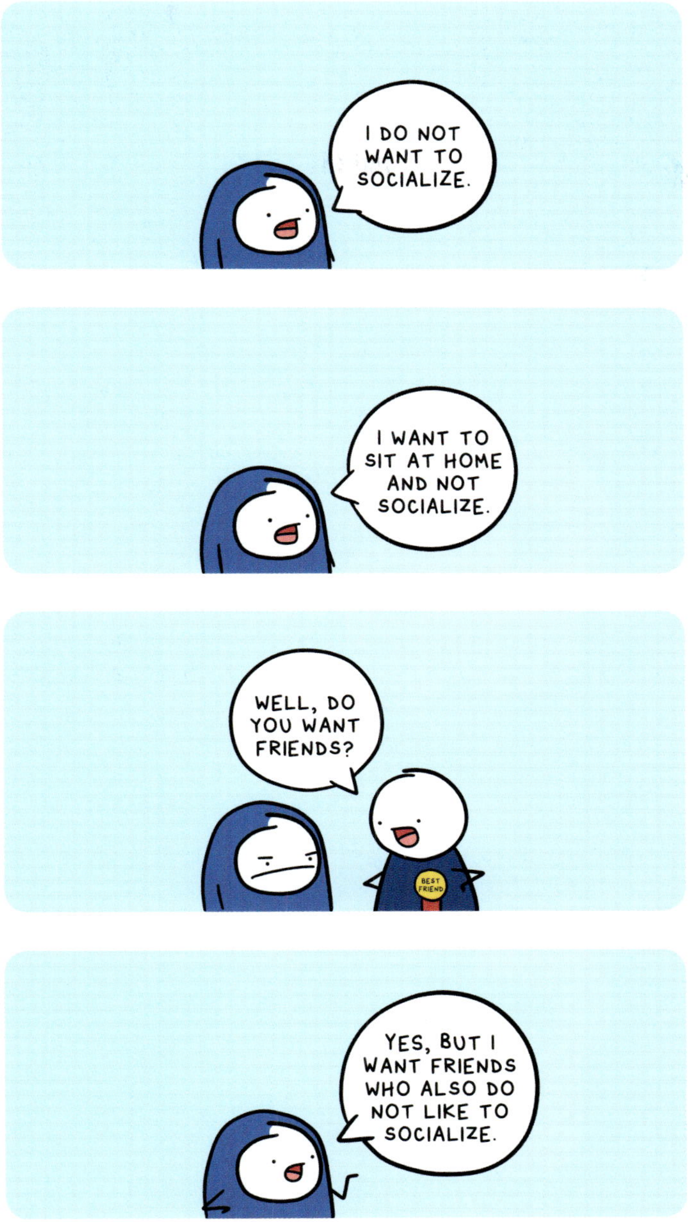
I DO NOT WANT TO SOCIALIZE.
I WANT TO SIT AT HOME AND NOT SOCIALIZE.
WELL, DO YOU WANT FRIENDS?
BEST FRIEND
YES, BUT I WANT FRIENDS WHO ALSO DO NOT LIKE TO SOCIALIZE.

I dreaded the idea of having to socialize, and my reluctance to do so brought back a lot of childhood memories. Growing up, I was a quiet kid. Most people misattributed this to shyness, but in reality, I just didn't like most people.

My mum tried.

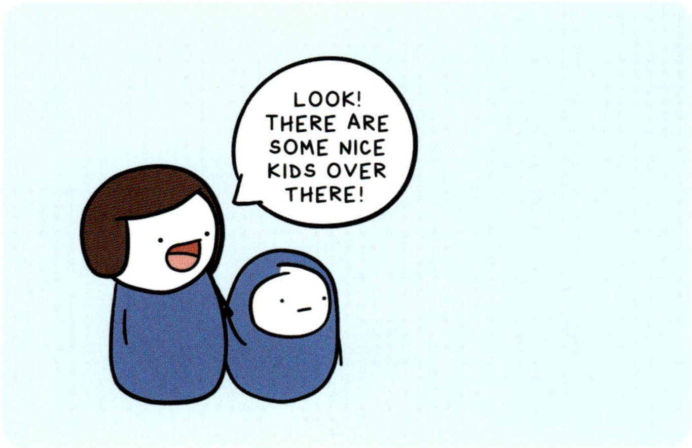
LOOK! THERE ARE SOME NICE KIDS OVER THERE!

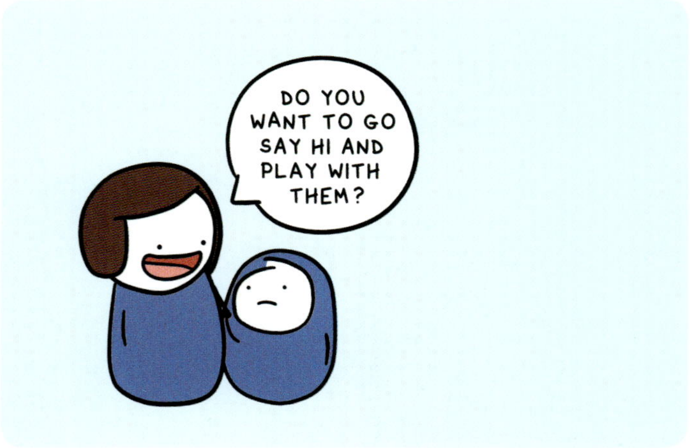
DO YOU WANT TO GO SAY HI AND PLAY WITH THEM?

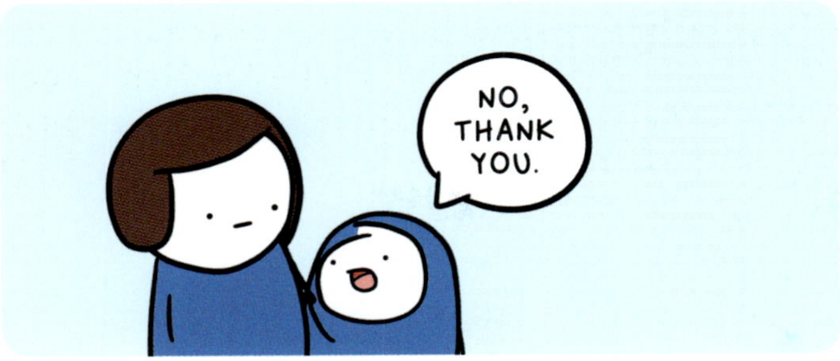
NO,
THANK
YOU.

As I grew older, I learned how to play nice with other people and even enjoy the company of some. But deep down, I was still that kid who preferred to stay inside during recess to read—books just always felt more comforting than people.

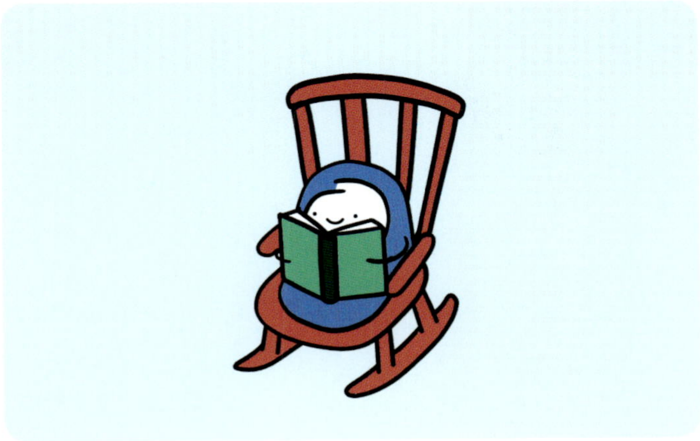

It's important to distinguish that I wasn't misanthropic to the point where I disliked *all* people—just a small majority. I preferred having a few best friends rather than a large group, because this meant that the friends I did have, I fundamentally understood and appreciated on a meaningful level.

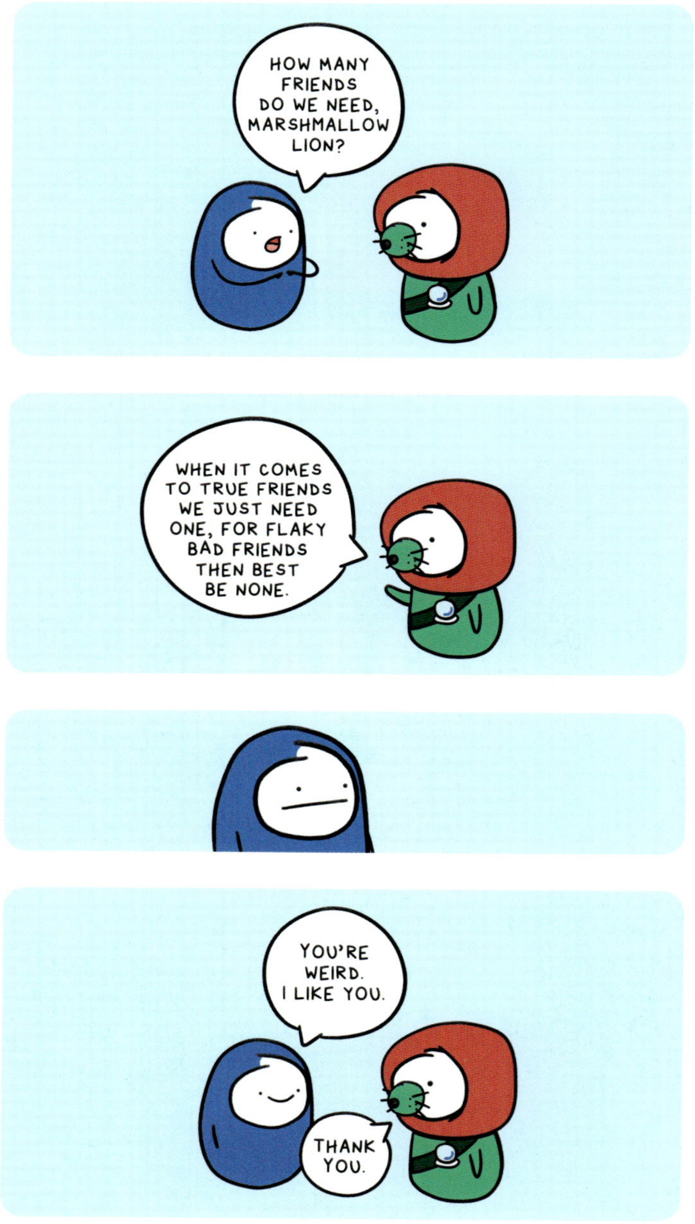
HOW MANY FRIENDS DO WE NEED, MARSHMALLOW LION?
WHEN IT COMES TO TRUE FRIENDS WE JUST NEED ONE, FOR FLAKY BAD FRIENDS THEN BEST BE NONE.
YOU'RE WEIRD. I LIKE YOU.
THANK YOU.

In search of new friends, I did something I never do—I said "yes." Yes to every group happy hour, yes to every group lunch, yes to every invitation to social interaction, because when you first make friends, you can't say no. You can't say no because then you become the person who says no. And who knows how many times you're allowed to say no before you stop getting invited altogether.

As someone who has never been fond of group socials, saying yes to them was especially hard. I guess I always held this suspicion that people put on different versions of themselves in a group setting.

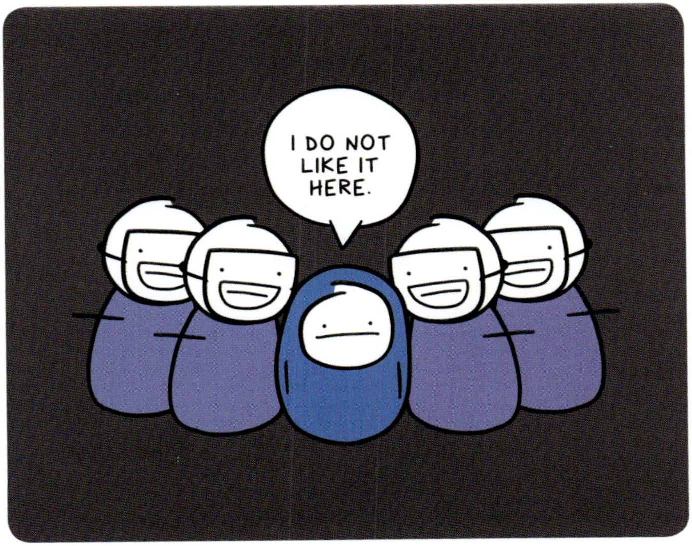
I DO NOT LIKE IT HERE.

And until you've talked to someone one-on-one, you don't really know what they're like under that mask.

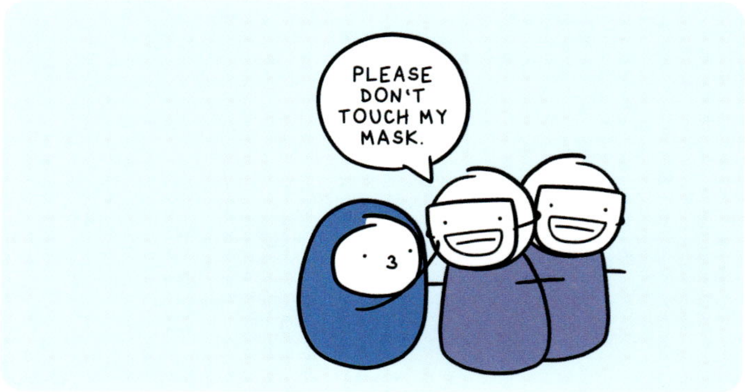
PLEASE DON'T TOUCH MY MASK.

And sure, enjoying the company of just one friend at a time may be more time-consuming, but isn't it nice to know someone cares enough about you to spend time with *just* you? And not only when it's a bundled deal with other people?

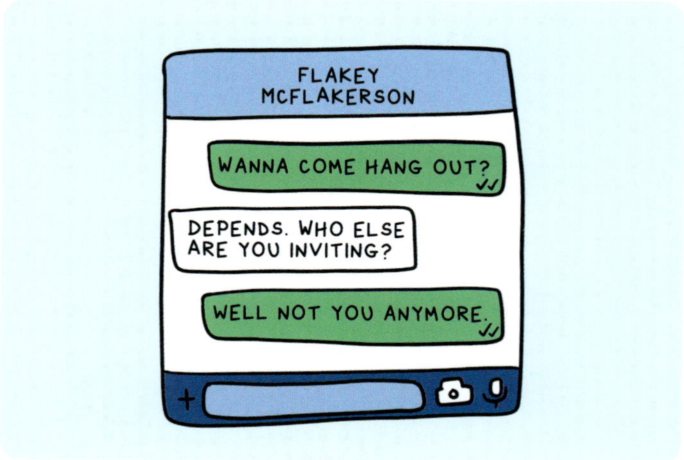
FLAKEY MCFLAKERSON
WANNA COME HANG OUT?
DEPENDS. WHO ELSE ARE YOU INVITING?
WELL NOT YOU ANYMORE.

But you don't get one-on-one hangs when you first meet someone, you actually have to become friends first.

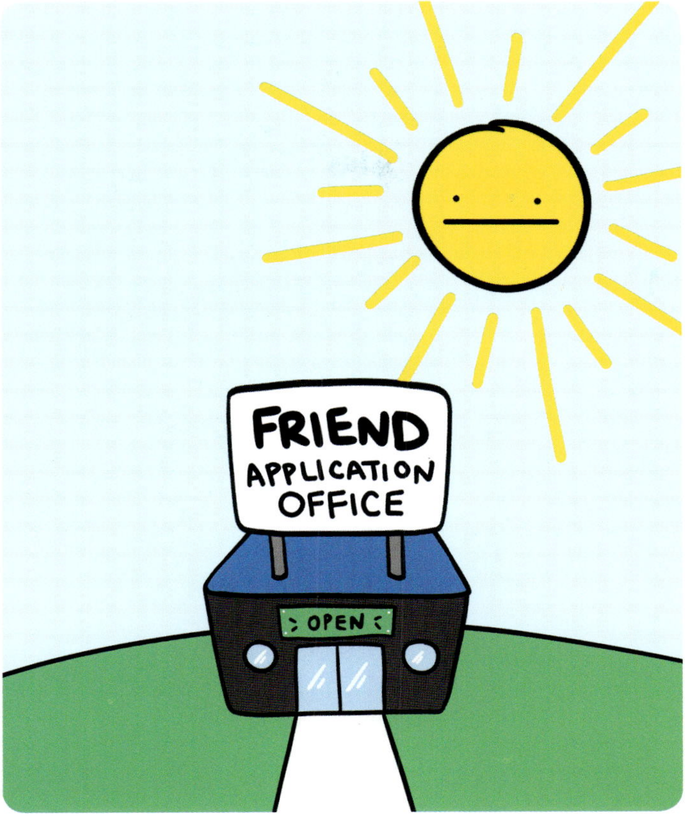
FRIEND
APPLICATION
OFFICE
OPEN

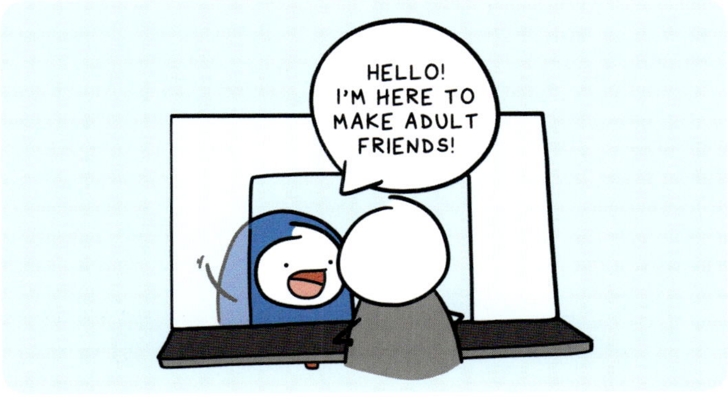
HELLO! I'M HERE TO MAKE ADULT FRIENDS!

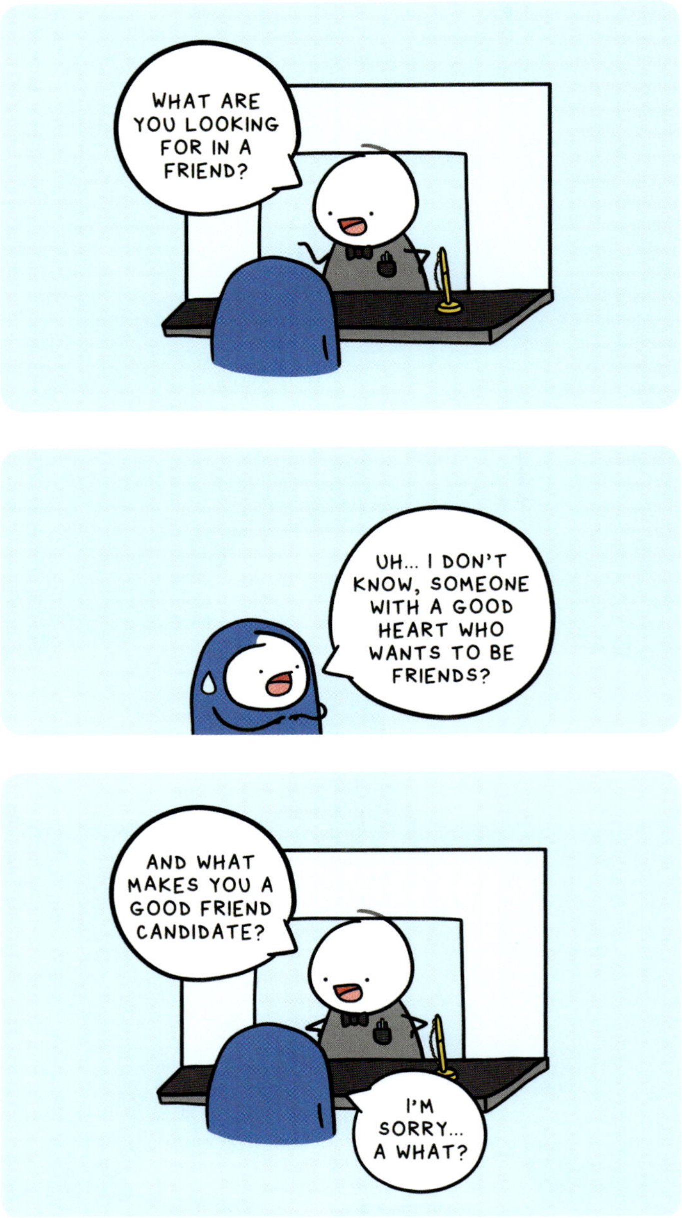
WHAT ARE YOU LOOKING FOR IN A FRIEND?
UH... I DON'T KNOW, SOMEONE WITH A GOOD HEART WHO WANTS TO BE FRIENDS?
AND WHAT MAKES YOU A GOOD FRIEND CANDIDATE?
I'M SORRY... A WHAT?

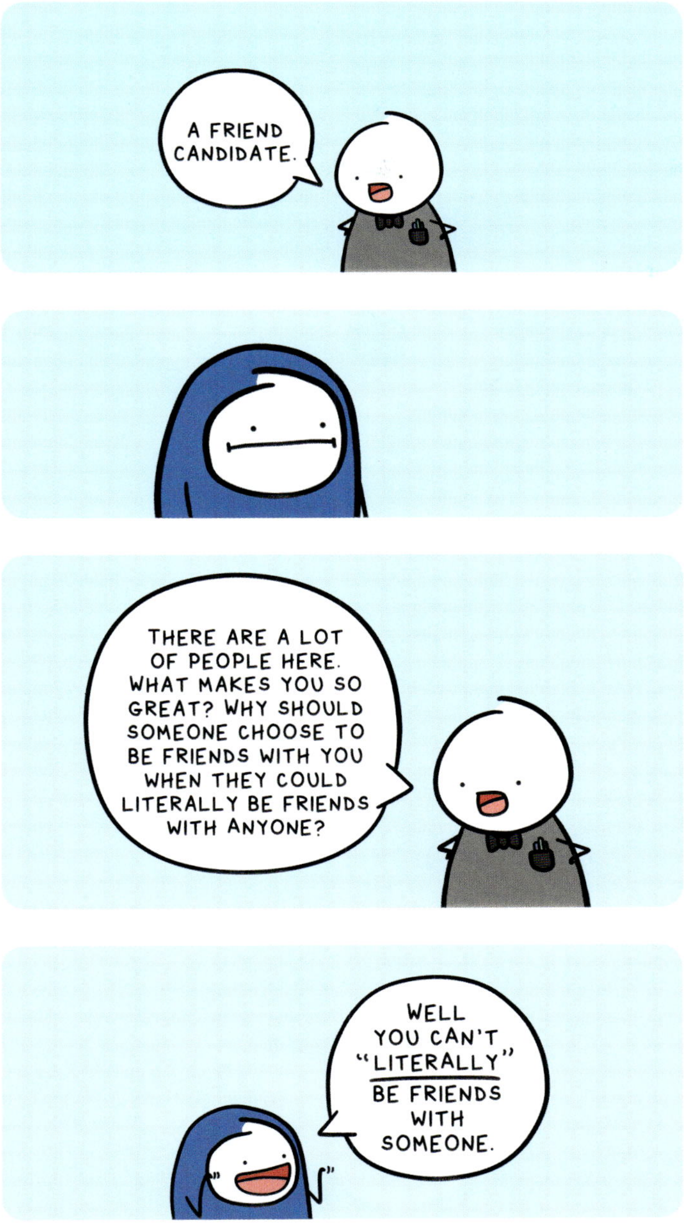
A FRIEND CANDIDATE.
THERE ARE A LOT OF PEOPLE HERE. WHAT MAKES YOU SO GREAT? WHY SHOULD SOMEONE CHOOSE TO BE FRIENDS WITH YOU WHEN THEY COULD LITERALLY BE FRIENDS WITH ANYONE?
WELL YOU CAN'T "LITERALLY" BE FRIENDS WITH SOMEONE.

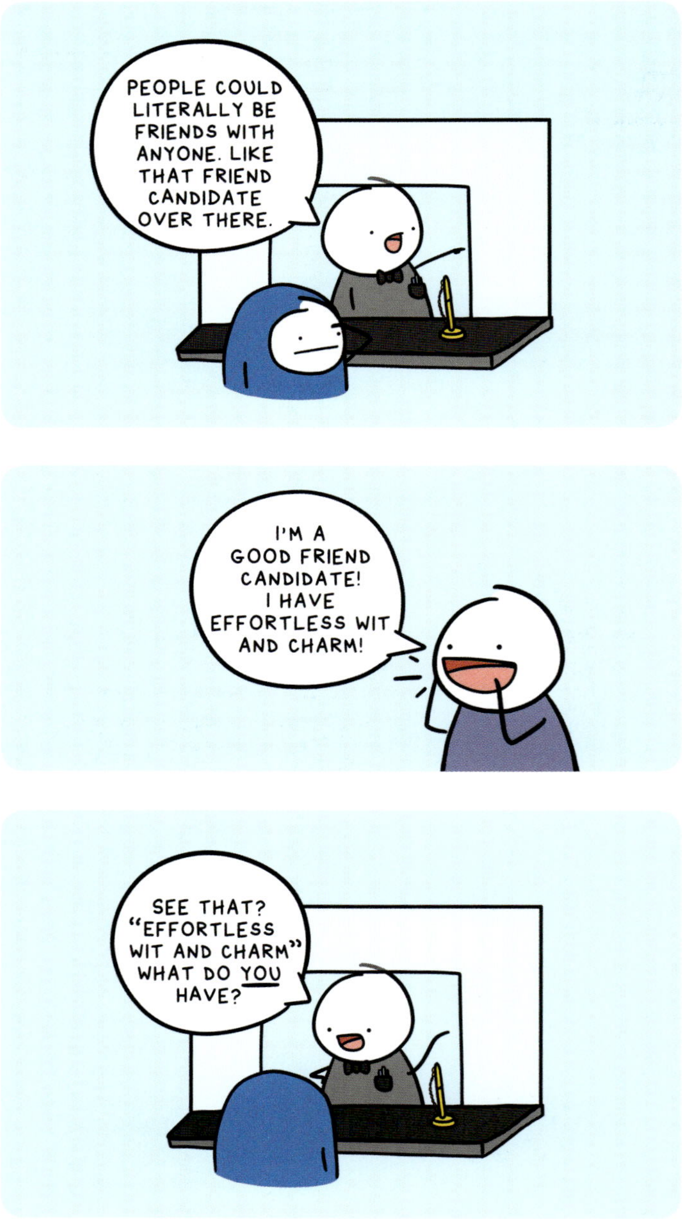
PEOPLE COULD LITERALLY BE FRIENDS WITH ANYONE. LIKE THAT FRIEND CANDIDATE OVER THERE.
I'M A GOOD FRIEND CANDIDATE! I HAVE EFFORTLESS WIT AND CHARM!
SEE THAT? "EFFORTLESS WIT AND CHARM" WHAT DO YOU HAVE?

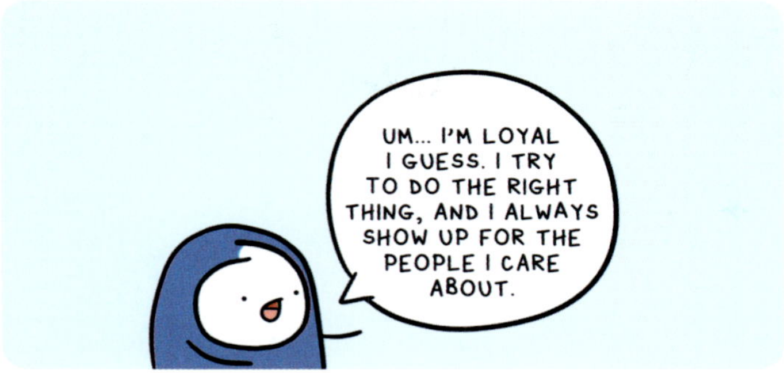
UM... I'M LOYAL I GUESS. I TRY TO DO THE RIGHT THING, AND I ALWAYS SHOW UP FOR THE PEOPLE I CARE ABOUT.

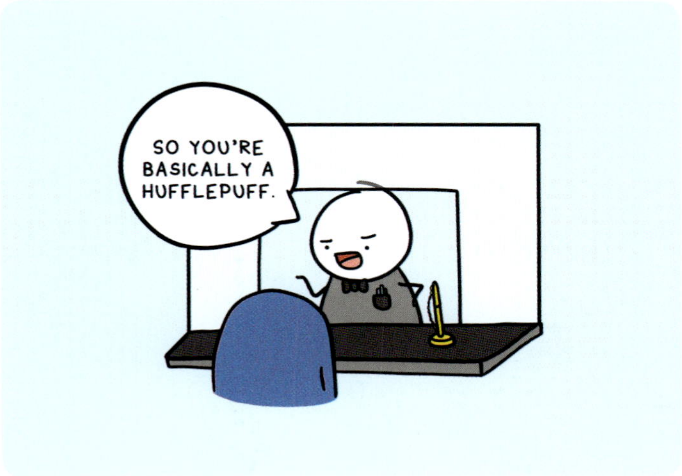
SO YOU'RE BASICALLY A HUFFLEPUFF.

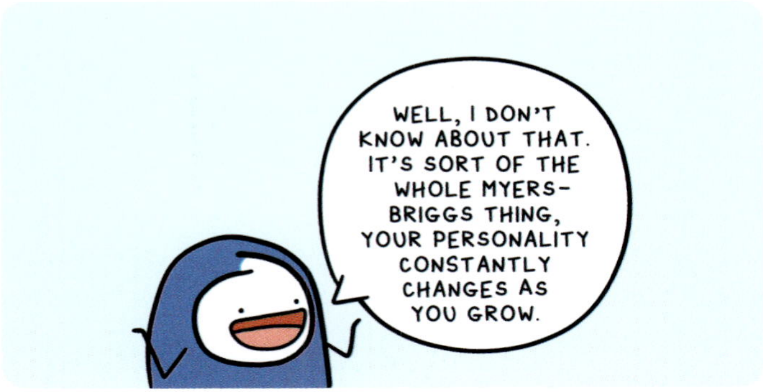
WELL, I DON'T KNOW ABOUT THAT. IT'S SORT OF THE WHOLE MYERS-BRIGGS THING, YOUR PERSONALITY CONSTANTLY CHANGES AS YOU GROW.

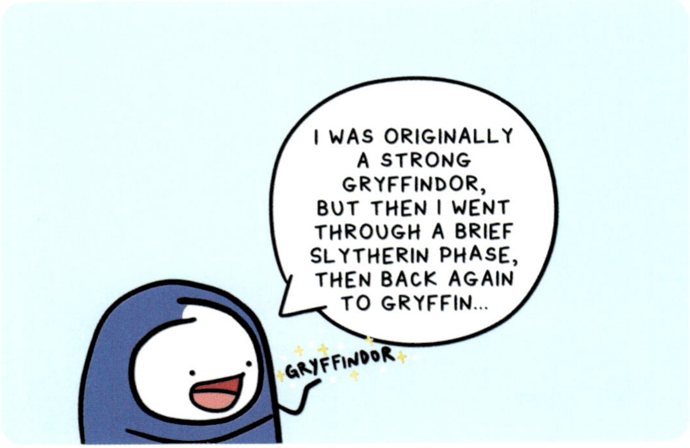
I WAS ORIGINALLY A STRONG GRYFFINDOR, BUT THEN I WENT THROUGH A BRIEF SLYTHERIN PHASE, THEN BACK AGAIN TO GRYFFIN...
GRYFFINDOR

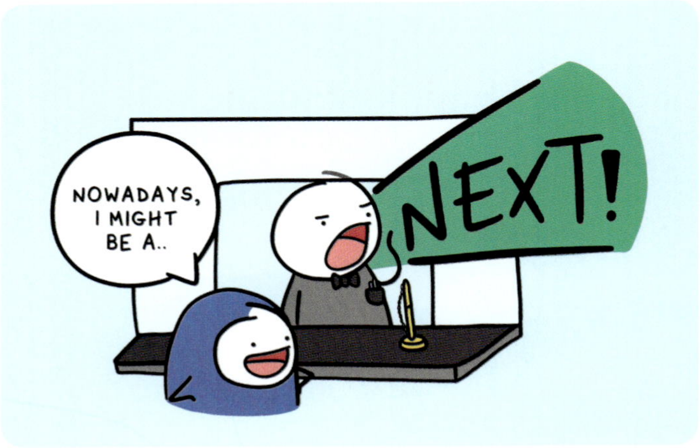
NOWADAYS, I MIGHT BE A..
NEXT!

To be honest, I didn't even know why making friends suddenly mattered so much to me. It's not like it mattered back home. But then again, I *had* friends back home. I guess when you take something for granted and it's suddenly lost—you tend to feel a bit lost in return.

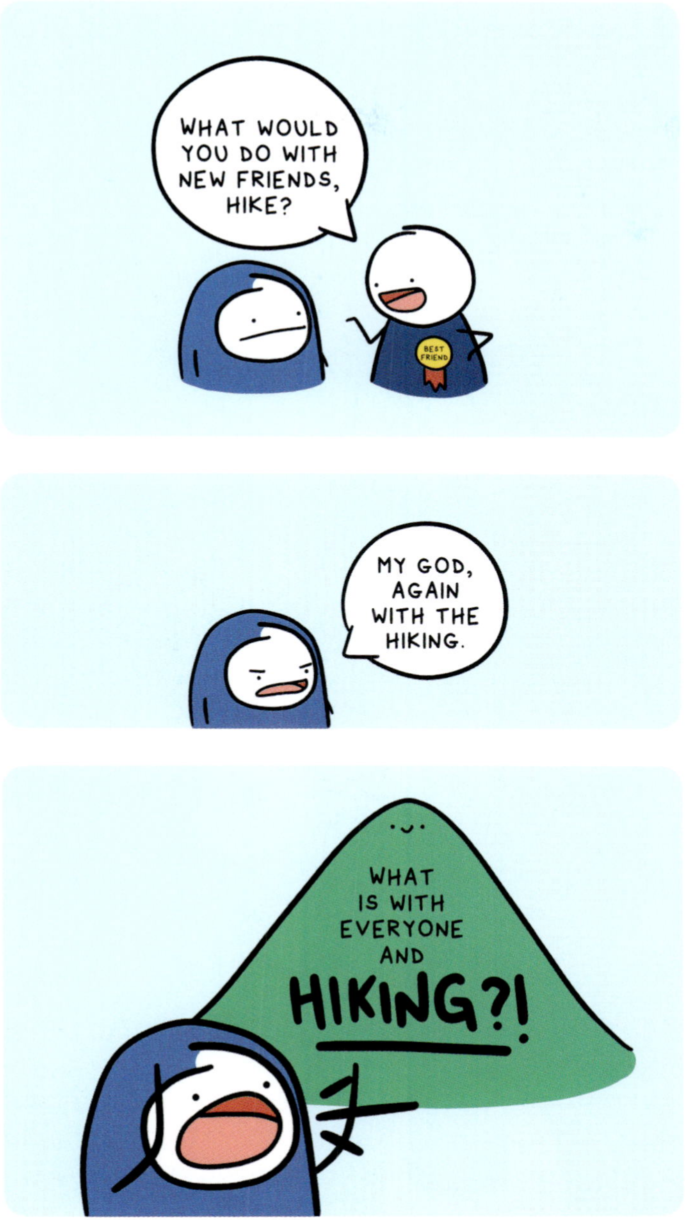
WHAT WOULD YOU DO WITH NEW FRIENDS, HIKE?
BEST FRIEND
MY GOD, AGAIN WITH THE HIKING.
WHAT IS WITH EVERYONE AND HIKING?!

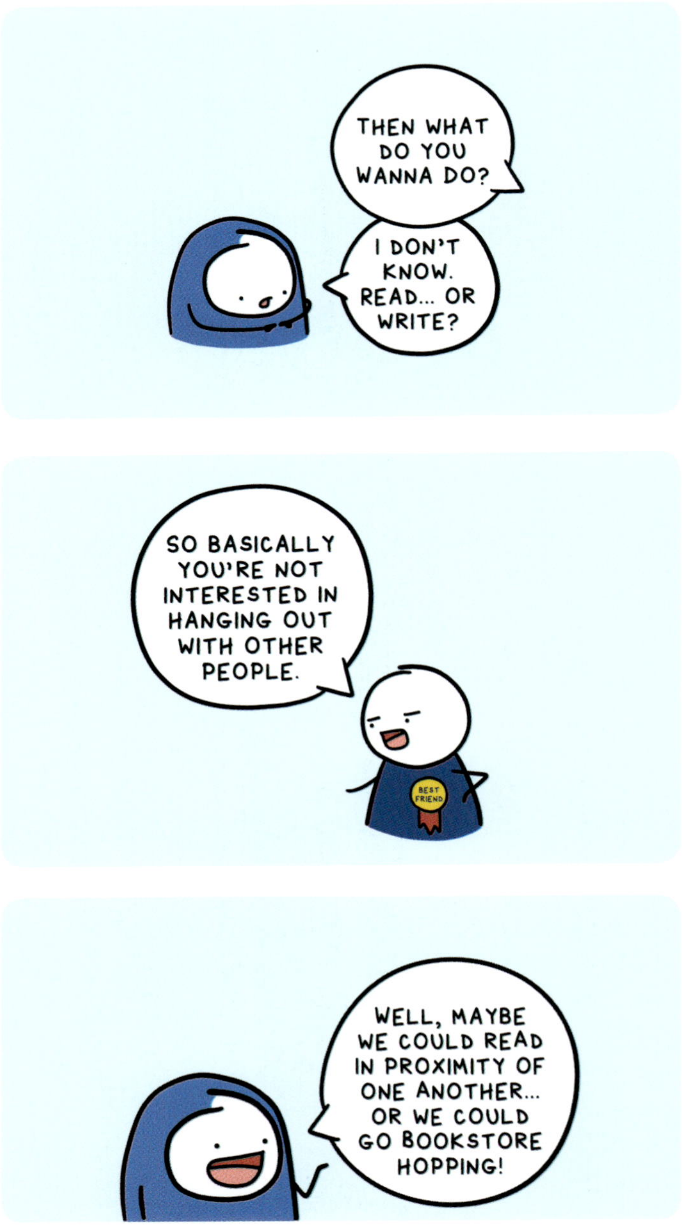
THEN WHAT DO YOU WANNA DO?
I DON'T KNOW. READ... OR WRITE?
SO BASICALLY YOU'RE NOT INTERESTED IN HANGING OUT WITH OTHER PEOPLE.
BEST FRIEND
WELL, MAYBE WE COULD READ IN PROXIMITY OF ONE ANOTHER... OR WE COULD GO BOOKSTORE HOPPING!

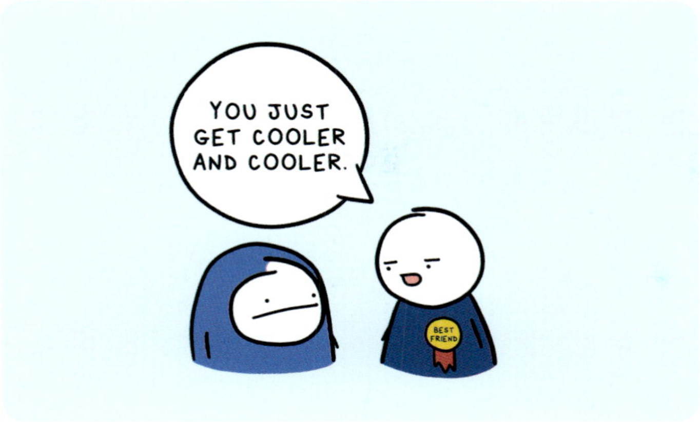
YOU JUST GET COOLER AND COOLER.
BEST FRIEND

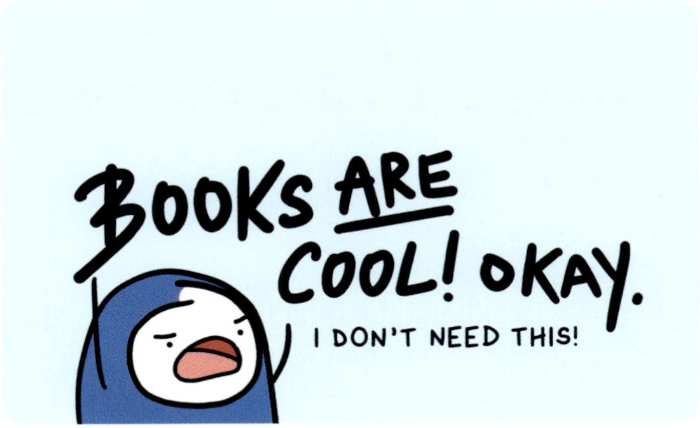
BOOKS ARE COOL! OKAY.
I DON'T NEED THIS!

I don't think anyone really *needs* friends, but maybe they're just nice to have. Sure, I could go watch a movie and travel and do a whole slew of things by myself and still have a great time—but sometimes we need other people, even if we don't like other people.

Besides, it's important to have someone to share headspace with.

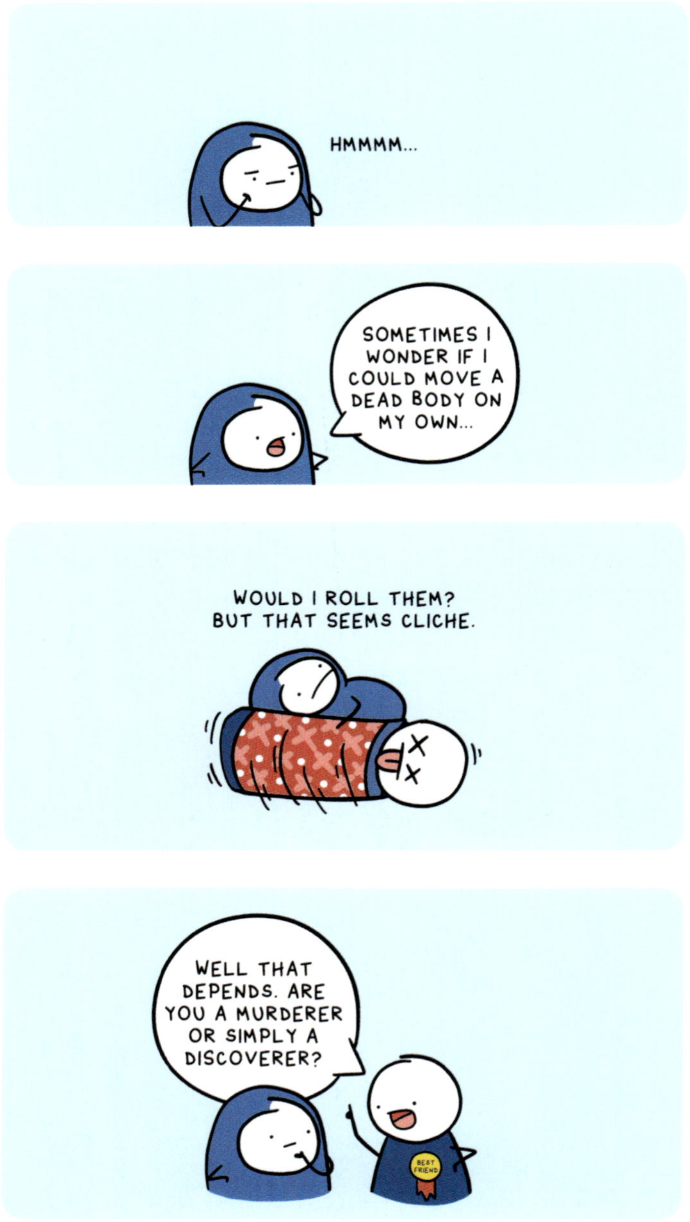
HMMMM...
SOMETIMES I WONDER IF I COULD MOVE A DEAD BODY ON MY OWN...
WOULD I ROLL THEM? BUT THAT SEEMS CLICHE.
WELL THAT DEPENDS. ARE YOU A MURDERER OR SIMPLY A DISCOVERER?
BEST FRIEND

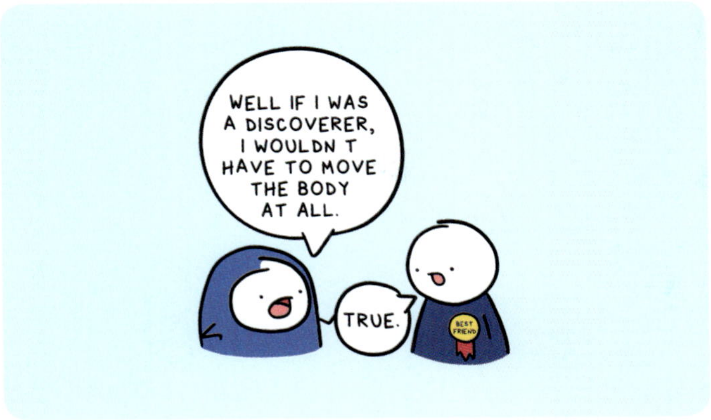
WELL IF I WAS A DISCOVERER, I WOULDN T HAVE TO MOVE THE BODY AT ALL.
TRUE.
BEST FRIEND

In an effort to be a better friend candidate, I spent the next few months willing myself to be a happy, social, and extroverted person.

It was terrible.

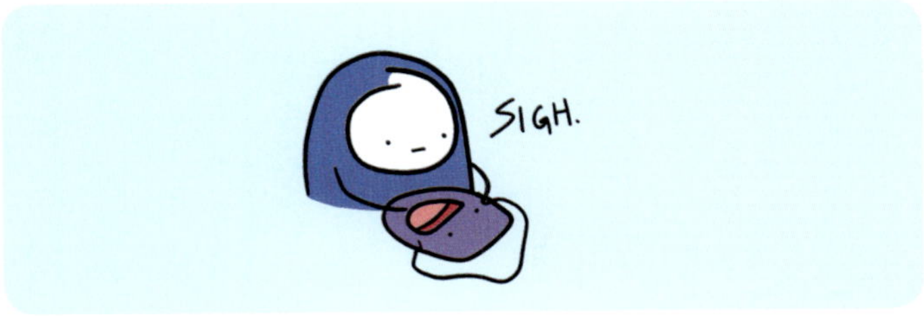
SIGH.

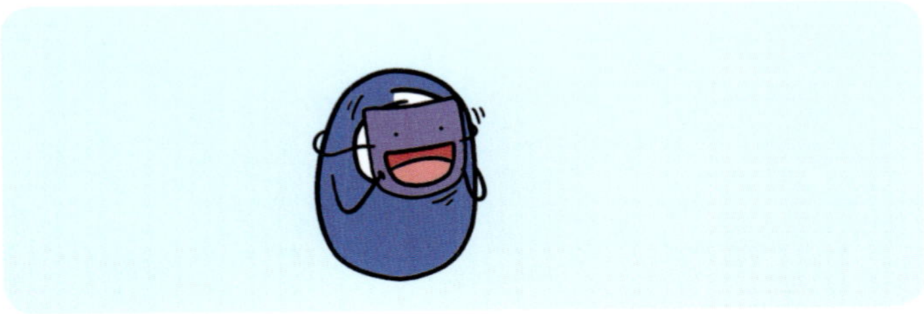

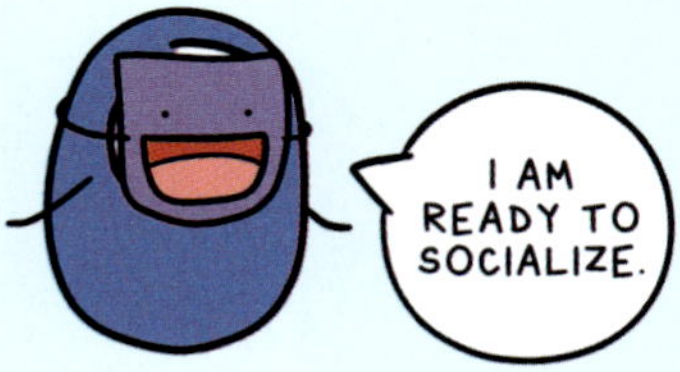
I AM READY TO SOCIALIZE.

Pretending to be extroverted when you're introverted is about as fun as shoving your face into a dirty bucket of ice. I constantly felt on edge and my sensitivity towards social cues surged like an off-brand Spidey sense. I soon found myself developing this *fun* little habit of replaying past conversations in my head as I spent my days drowning in a ball pit of self-consciousness.

Like I said, it was *terrible*.

With old friends, there's no censorship. You can speak as you please because you've earned the luxury of being yourself. Pointless conversations can go on for hours, but you won't *feel* the hours. And if you should say something questionable, they'll know it's because you're having a bad week, and not because you're a bad person. True friends see the best parts of us, even when we forget those parts ourselves.

But with new people, you don't get that benefit of the doubt. They haven't even decided whether they like you or not—let alone give you a free pass for senseless comments. If you say something questionable, *you* become questionable as a person.

I soon realized that the likelihood of meaningful friendships, like so many things in life, was inversely proportional to how badly I wanted it.

I'M WORKING REALLY HARD BECAUSE I WANT THIS ONE THING.
THING
DO YOU? DO YOU REALLY?
UNIVERSE
YES, I DO.
CAN I SEE?
THING
SURE.

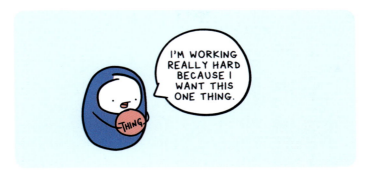

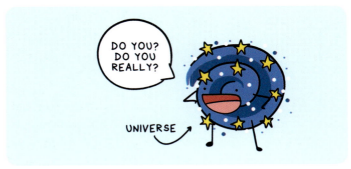

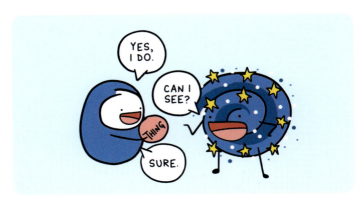

SAVAGE
THING
WHY THOUGH?

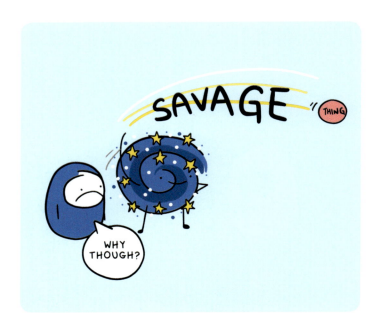

I'd always liked people who were open and honest about wanting to be friends. Something about the vulnerability of it was endearing to me. But as time passed, I started to wonder whether I was alone in this thinking. Why was making new friends so much harder as an adult? What had changed?

MAYBE I'M BEING TOO FRIENDLY... IS THAT A THING?

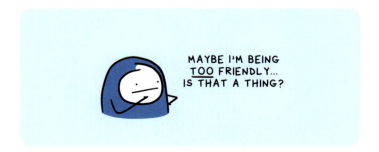

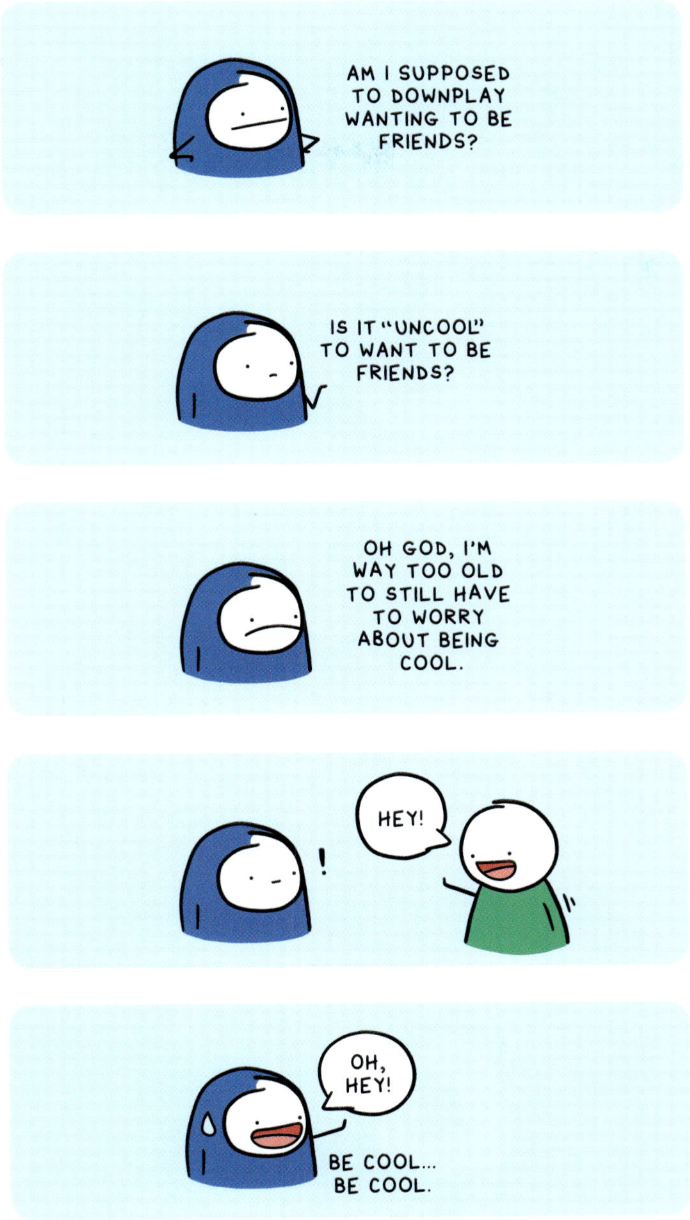
AM I SUPPOSED TO DOWNPLAY WANTING TO BE FRIENDS?
IS IT "UNCOOL" TO WANT TO BE FRIENDS?
OH GOD, I'M WAY TOO OLD TO STILL HAVE TO WORRY ABOUT BEING COOL.
HEY!
!
OH, HEY!
BE COOL... BE COOL.

I met many people in the city, but few that I could genuinely connect with.

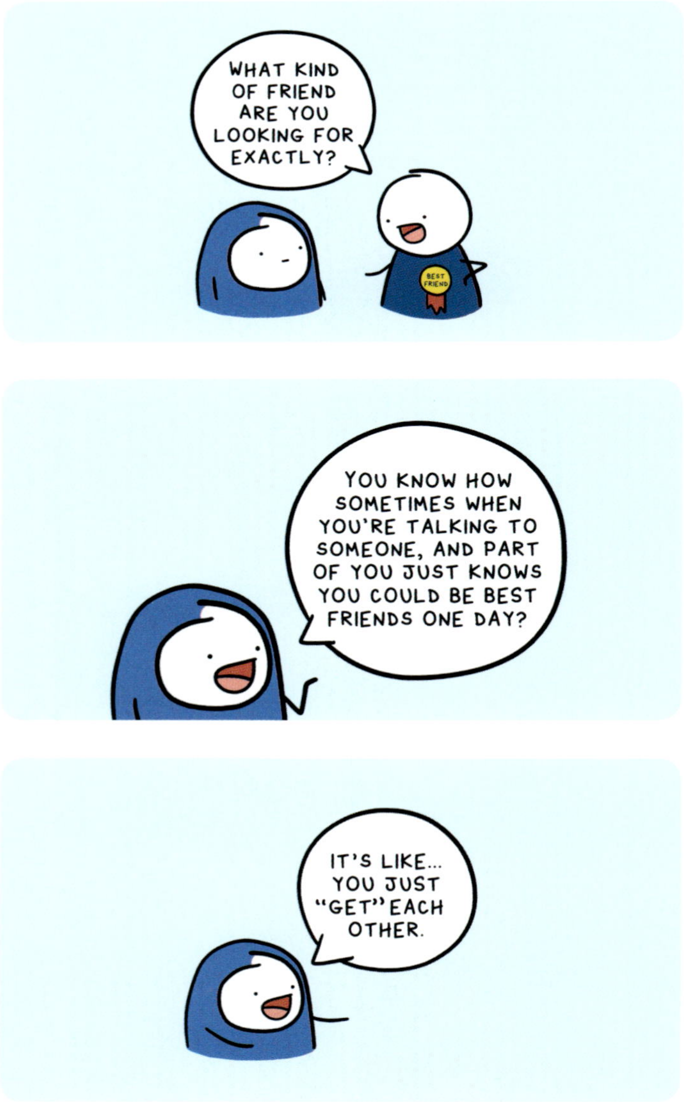
WHAT KIND OF FRIEND ARE YOU LOOKING FOR EXACTLY?
BEST FRIEND
YOU KNOW HOW SOMETIMES WHEN YOU'RE TALKING TO SOMEONE, AND PART OF YOU JUST KNOWS YOU COULD BE BEST FRIENDS ONE DAY?
IT'S LIKE... YOU JUST "GET" EACH OTHER.

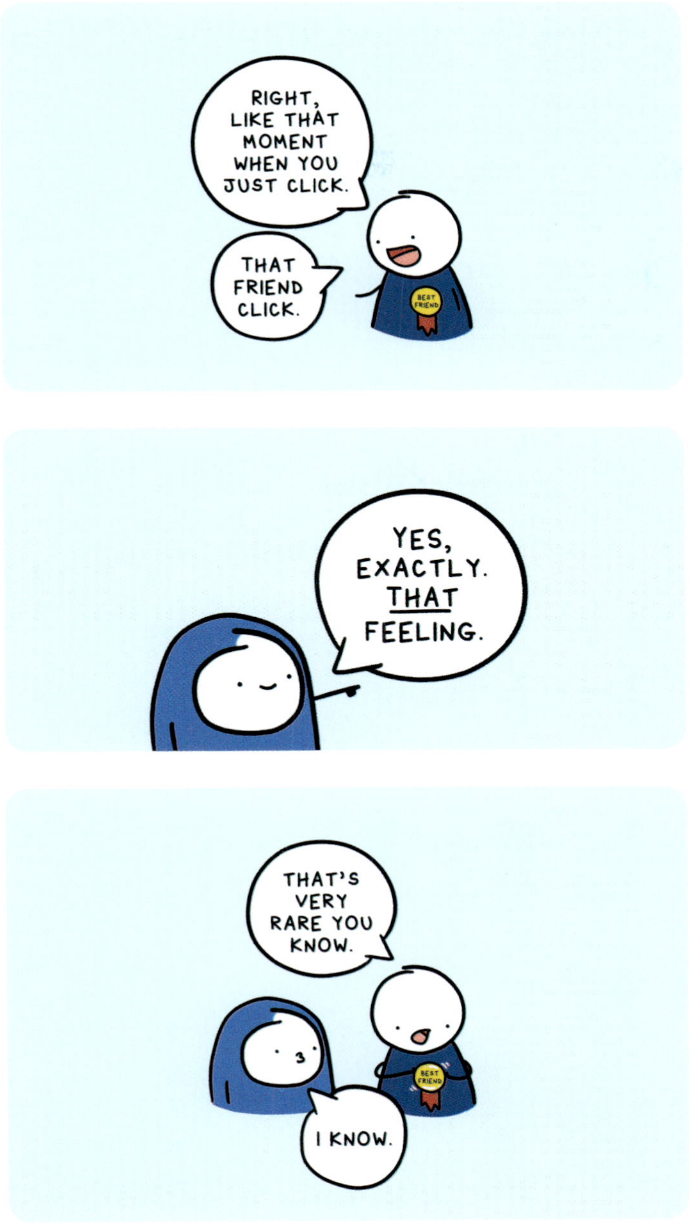
RIGHT, LIKE THAT MOMENT WHEN YOU JUST CLICK.
THAT FRIEND CLICK.
BEST FRIEND
YES, EXACTLY. THAT FEELING.
THAT'S VERY RARE YOU KNOW.
BEST FRIEND
I KNOW.

In the midst of my self-induced crisis, my manager asked me how I was doing with my move.

"It's good. I finally bought new potted plants."

"Yes," he said, "but how are *you*?"

A funny thing happens when someone asks, "How are *you*?" coupled with a meaningful head tilt. The reflexive, safe answer to give is "Good, thanks." But then again, we say "good" only because "good" makes the question go away. Tell someone "I'm doing horribly" and the conversation gets knocked off its axis into a marsh of soggy discomfort.

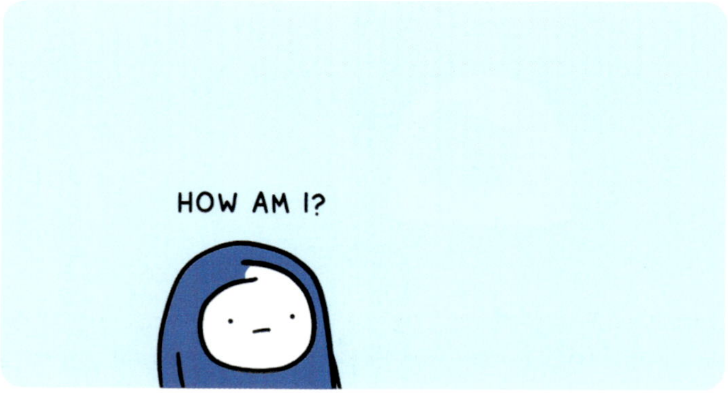
HOW AM I?

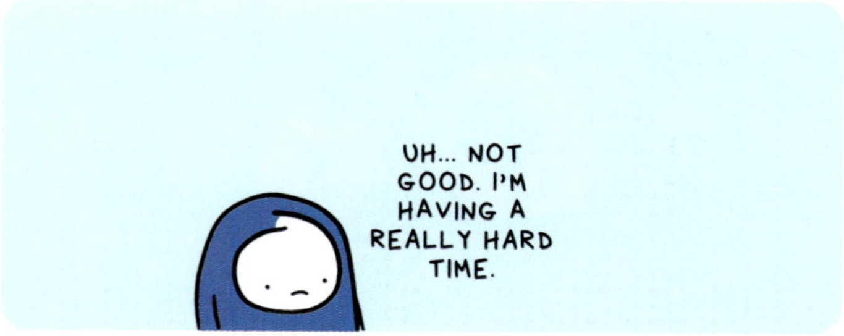
UH... NOT GOOD. I'M HAVING A REALLY HARD TIME.

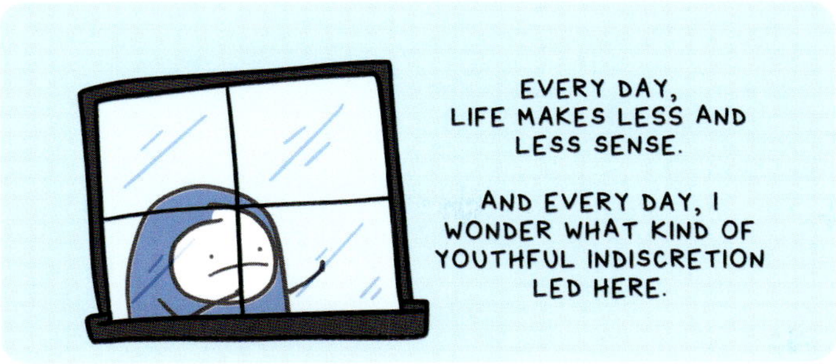
EVERY DAY,
LIFE MAKES LESS AND
LESS SENSE.
AND EVERY DAY, I
WONDER WHAT KIND OF
YOUTHFUL INDISCRETION
LED HERE.

I looked my well-meaning manager in the eye and smiled.

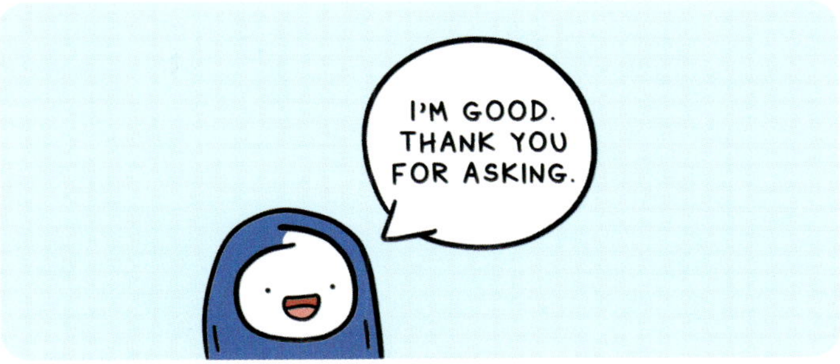
I'M GOOD.
THANK YOU
FOR ASKING.

• • •

The first few people I met were kind, but distant. They were the type of people you would smile and wave at if you saw them walking towards you on a street, but there was also this mutual understanding that neither party would stop to chat. It was the kind of friendly that was just short of being friends. People who know your name, but not the number of siblings you have (if only because they've never cared to inquire).

True friends know how many siblings you have—that kind of thing is just basic friendship knowledge.

There was nothing wrong with the people I met, they were all happy, shiny, extroverted people—it wasn't their fault that I wasn't any of those things.

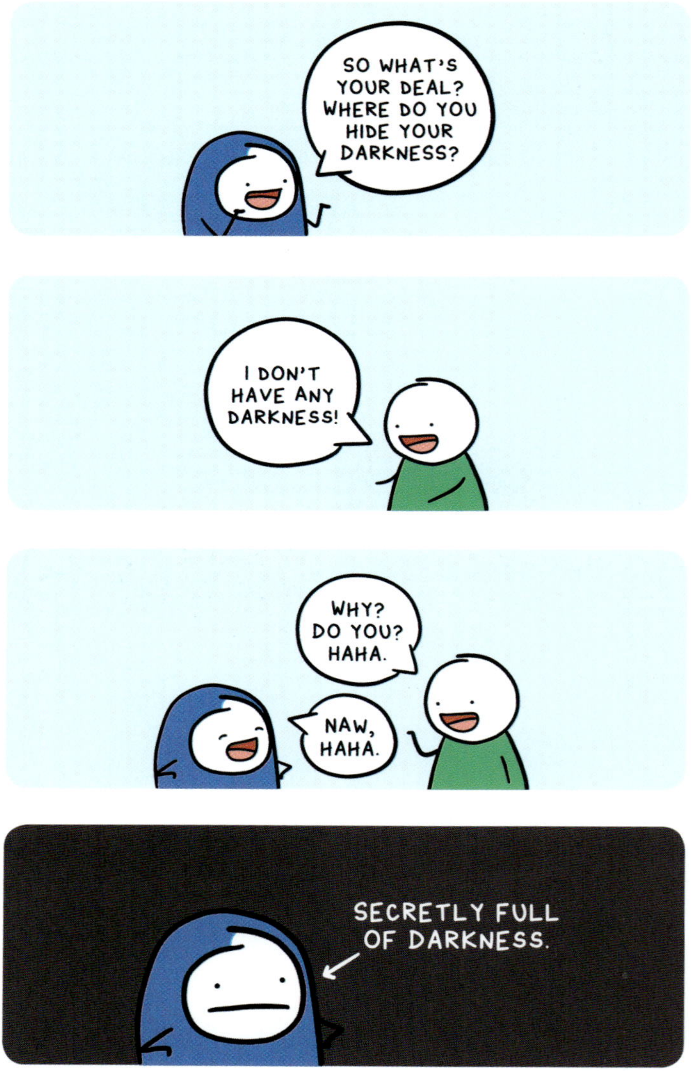
SO WHAT'S YOUR DEAL? WHERE DO YOU HIDE YOUR DARKNESS?
I DON'T HAVE ANY DARKNESS!
WHY? DO YOU? HAHA.
NAW, HAHA.
SECRETLY FULL OF DARKNESS.

I began to wonder if I would ever come across that friend click again. The kind of friendship where we could share custody of a pet alpaca. And sure, we wouldn't be able to go on vacation at the same time because someone would (obviously) have to stay and take care of the alpaca, but that's a sacrifice I'd be willing to make.

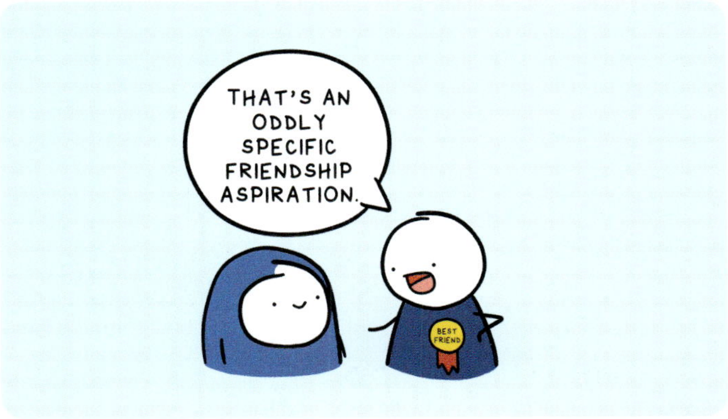
THAT'S AN ODDLY SPECIFIC FRIENDSHIP ASPIRATION.
BEST FRIEND

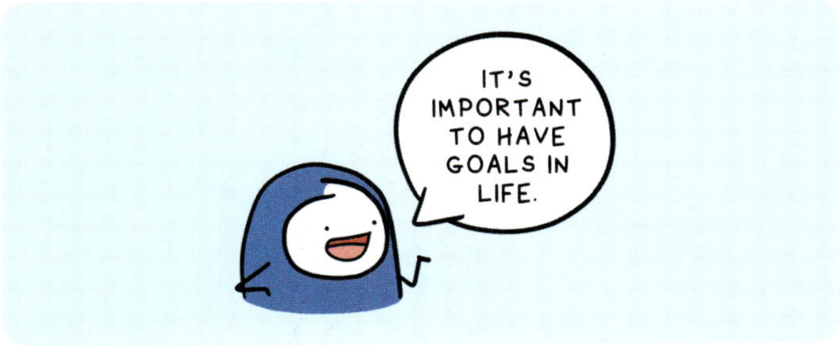
IT'S IMPORTANT TO HAVE GOALS IN LIFE.

I wanted friends who could co-own bookstore speakeasies with me—the kind of friends you get from decades of friendship. I wanted this kind of deep, meaningful friendship and I wanted it in ten seconds flat.

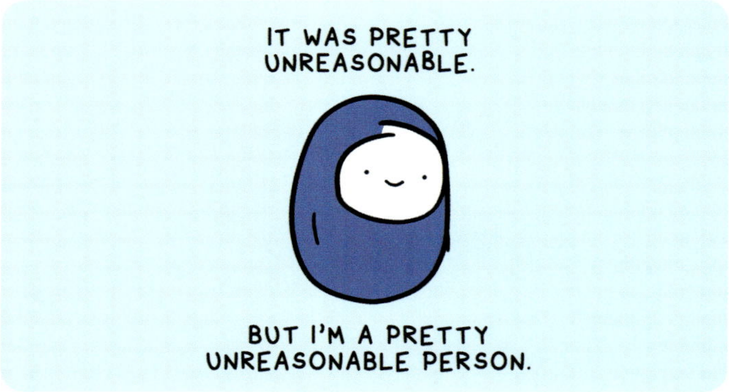
IT WAS PRETTY UNREASONABLE.
BUT I'M A PRETTY UNREASONABLE PERSON.

• • •

This is the part of the story where I'm supposed to provide some sort of denouement.

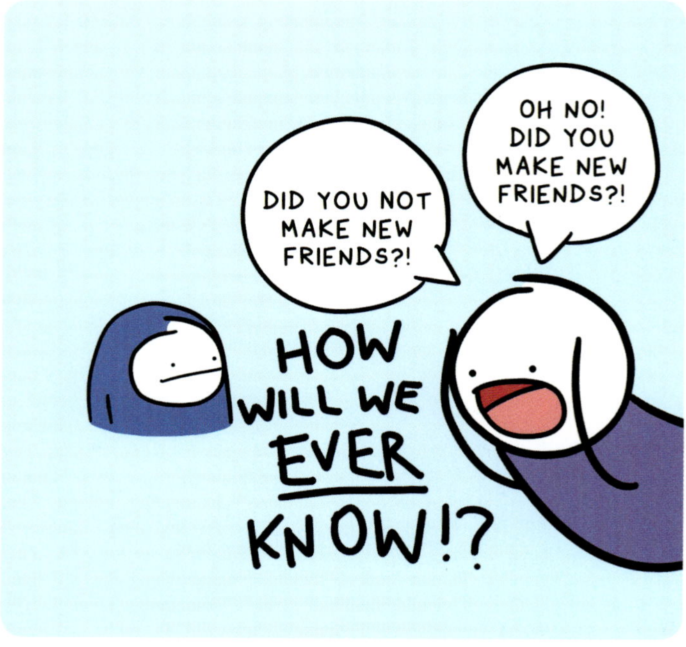
DID YOU NOT MAKE NEW FRIENDS?!
OH NO! DID YOU MAKE NEW FRIENDS?!
HOW WILL WE EVER KNOW!?

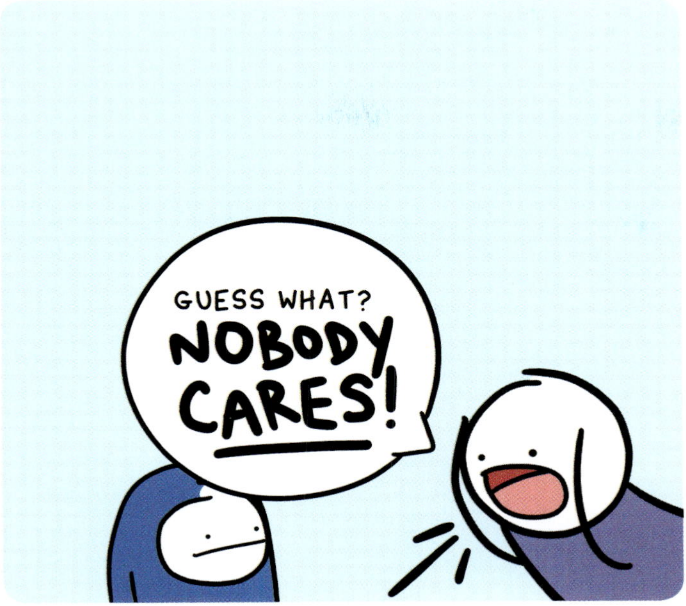
GUESS WHAT?
NOBODY CARES!

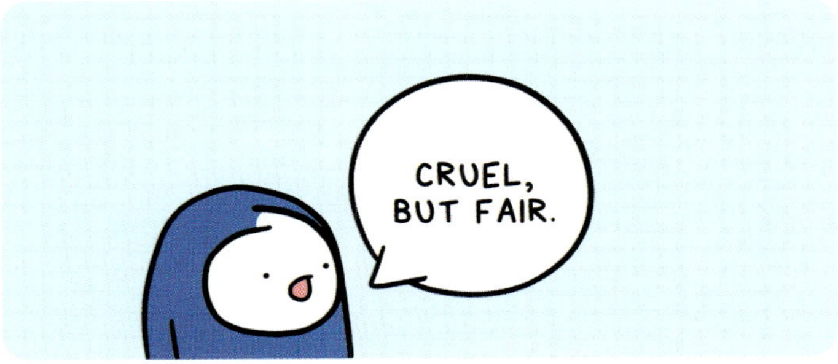
CRUEL, BUT FAIR.

I wish I could tell you it ended up being breezy and effortless because I secretly had wit and charm this whole time and was not a Hufflepuff. I wish I could tell you that deep, meaningful friendships actually aren't all that rare after all.

But tragically, I cannot.

The reality is that I spent many months meeting new people from all sorts of places, *slowly* getting to know them, and *slowly* giving them the chance to get to know me. It was a time in my life that felt like one long summer day of just lying on the grass and watching the clouds float by. It would've been nice had I not been so acutely aware that I was lying on the grass alone.

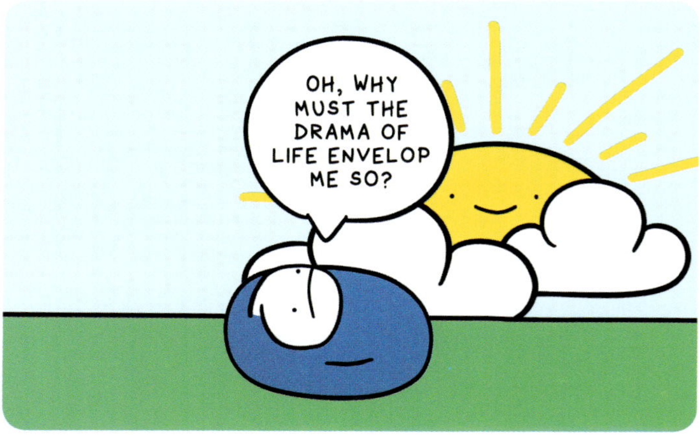
OH, WHY MUST THE DRAMA OF LIFE ENVELOP ME SO?

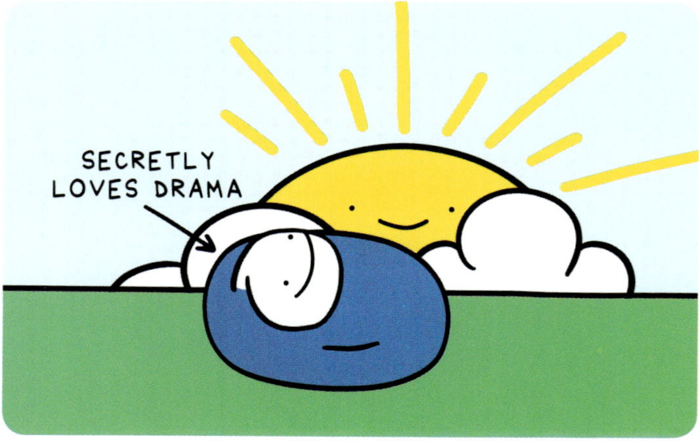
SECRETLY LOVES DRAMA

Making new friends as an adult took a lot of patience and perseverance.

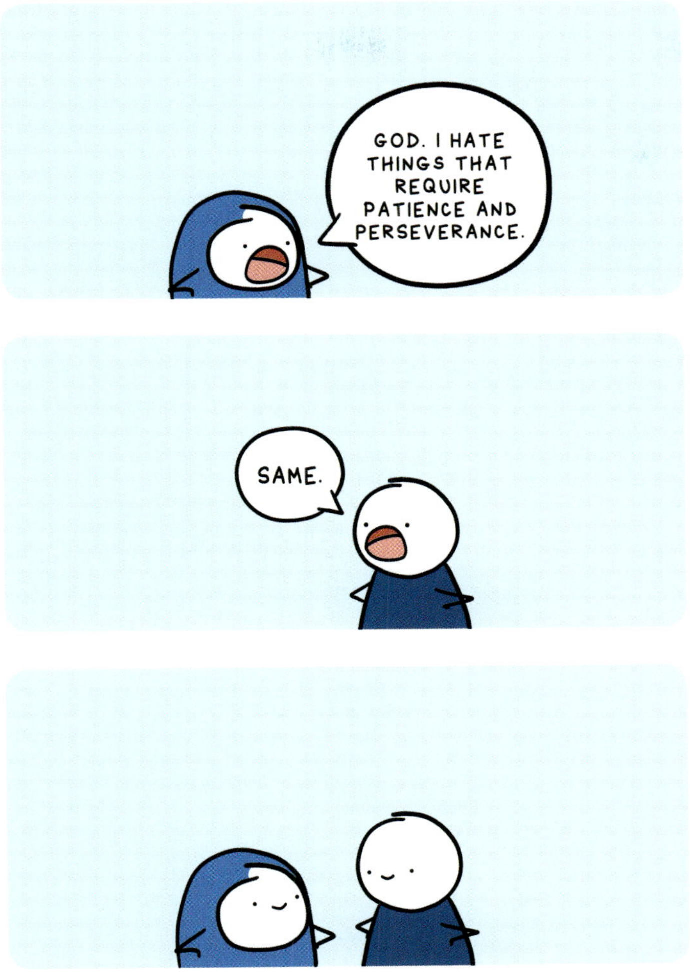
GOD. I HATE THINGS THAT REQUIRE PATIENCE AND PERSEVERANCE.
SAME.

It took courage too—courage to continuously make an effort despite the running commentary from all the demons in my head.

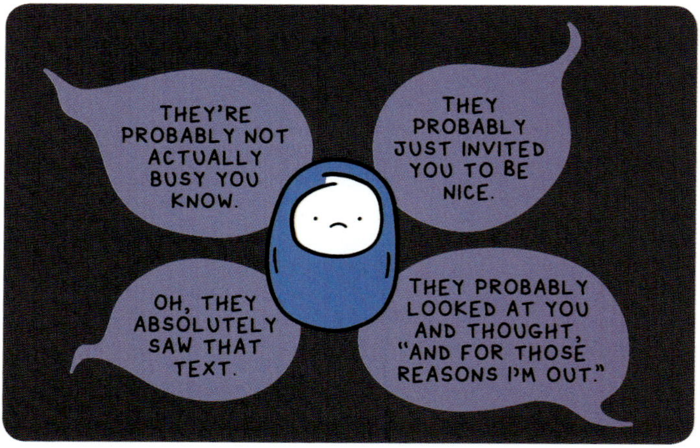
THEY'RE PROBABLY NOT ACTUALLY BUSY YOU KNOW.
THEY PROBABLY JUST INVITED YOU TO BE NICE.
OH, THEY ABSOLUTELY SAW THAT TEXT.
THEY PROBABLY LOOKED AT YOU AND THOUGHT, "AND FOR THOSE REASONS I'M OUT."

But demons can be slayed.

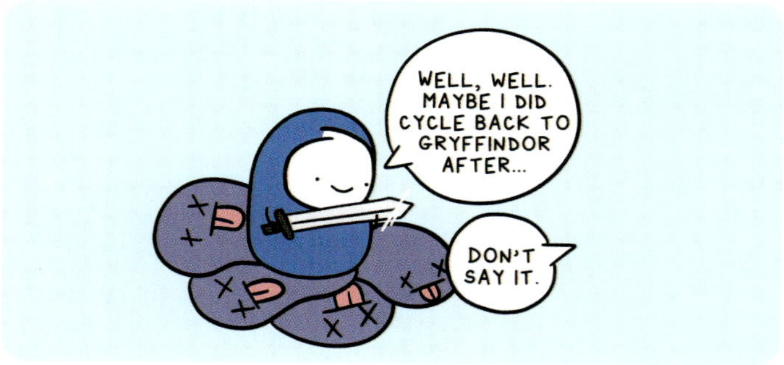
WELL, WELL. MAYBE I DID CYCLE BACK TO GRYFFINDOR AFTER...
DON'T SAY IT.

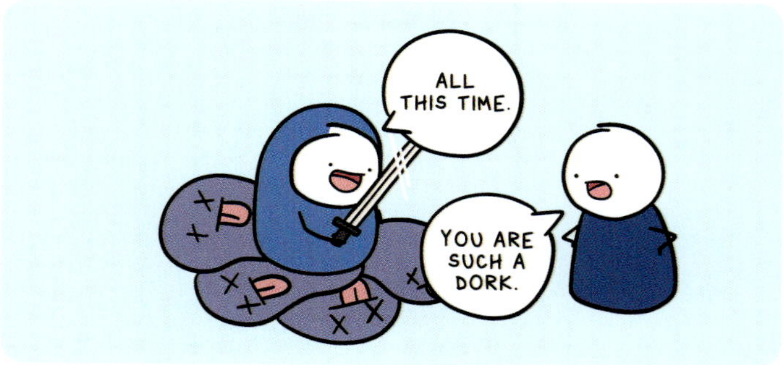
ALL THIS TIME.
YOU ARE SUCH A DORK.

And no, not everyone I met wanted to be friends. And yes, this stung at times.

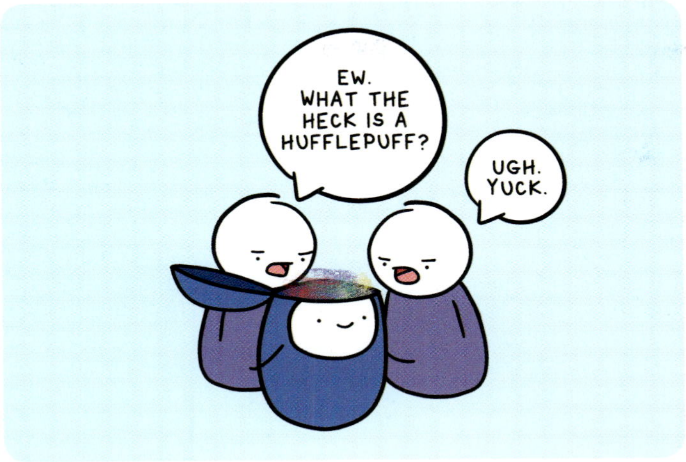
EW.
WHAT THE
HECK IS A
HUFFLEPUFF?
UGH.
YUCK.

But that's okay.

Because *those people suck.*

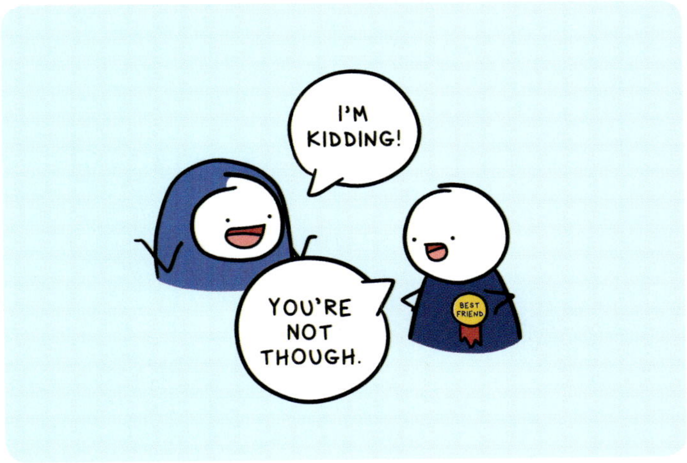
I'M
KIDDING!
YOU'RE
NOT
THOUGH.
BEST
FRIEND

Eventually, my extroversion mask simply grew too heavy to wear. And when I took it off, I was greeted by the familiar smile of my introverted, imperfect self.

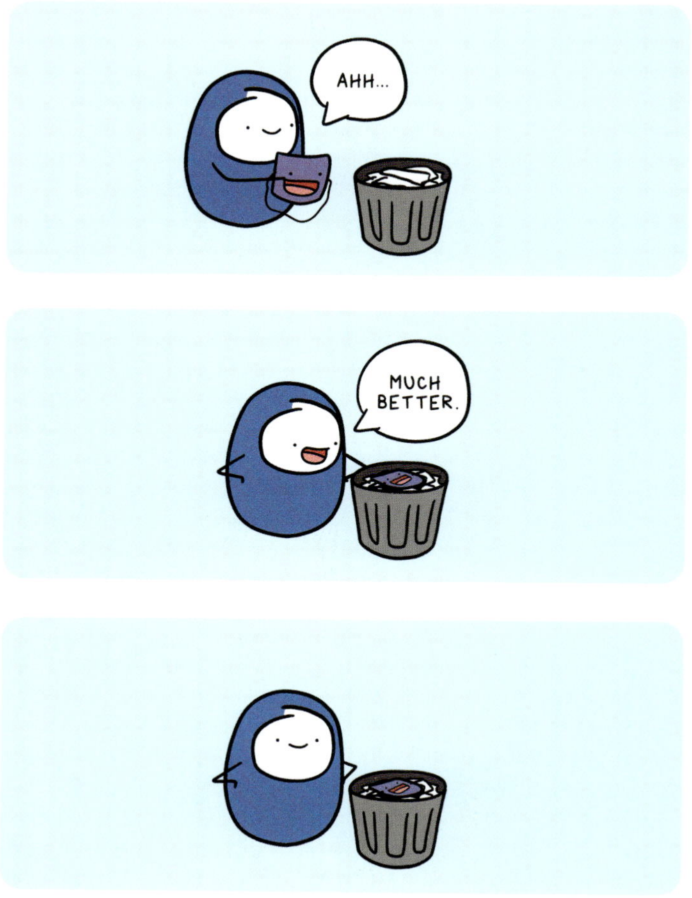
AHH...
MUCH BETTER.

I began to remember who I was when I didn't have to be someone else for other people, and in this version of myself, I met friends who I actually connected with—the kind of friendships that clicked.

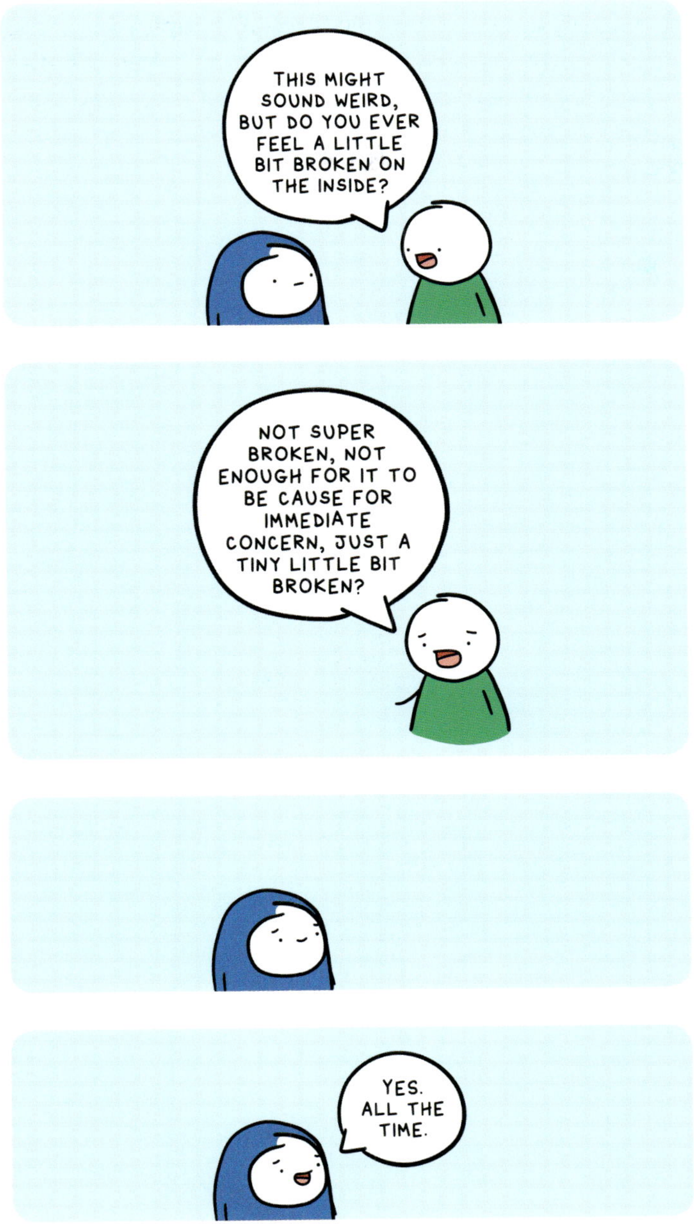
THIS MIGHT SOUND WEIRD, BUT DO YOU EVER FEEL A LITTLE BIT BROKEN ON THE INSIDE?
NOT SUPER BROKEN, NOT ENOUGH FOR IT TO BE CAUSE FOR IMMEDIATE CONCERN, JUST A TINY LITTLE BIT BROKEN?
YES. ALL THE TIME.

In time, I made regular friends, and then those regular friends became better friends. After a while, I stopped keeping track altogether because it no longer mattered. We were simply friends—the kind that didn't require further validation.

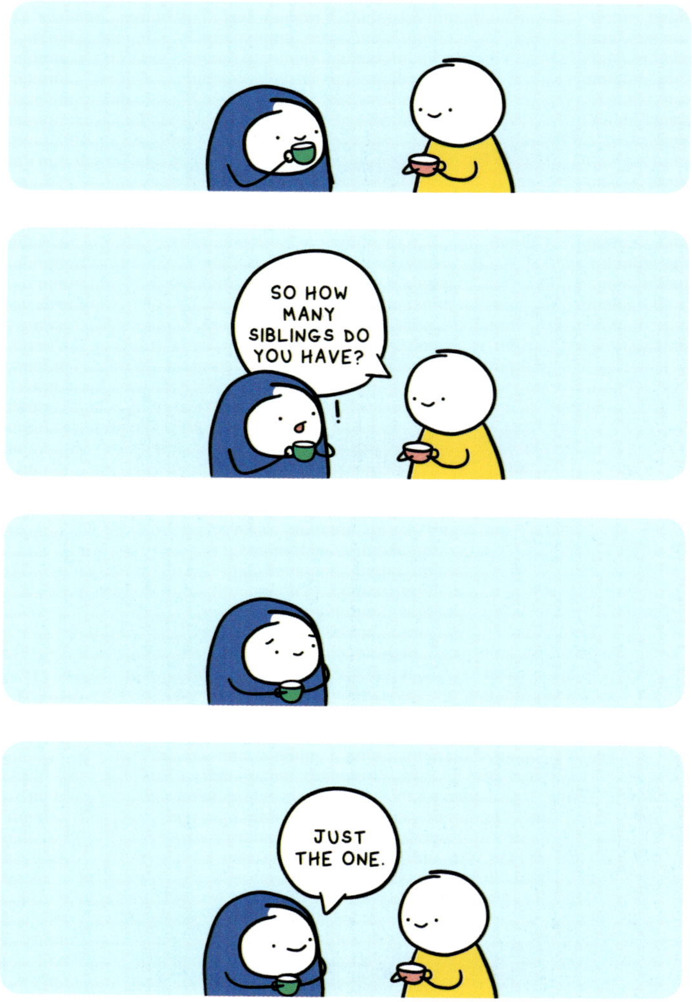
SO HOW MANY SIBLINGS DO YOU HAVE?
!
JUST THE ONE.

My friends didn't come in the fast and effortless way I had hoped for. They arrived slowly, but exquisitely, blazing through the night sky like shooting stars at 1:48 a.m., long after I had stopped looking for them.

I guess my mum was right after all.

All I had to do was wait.

# CHAPTER 6

# THE LONG CON

**T**ucked away in Lam Tsuen, a quaint seven-hundred-year-old village in Tai Po, Hong Kong, is a banyan wishing tree that is said to be more than two centuries old.

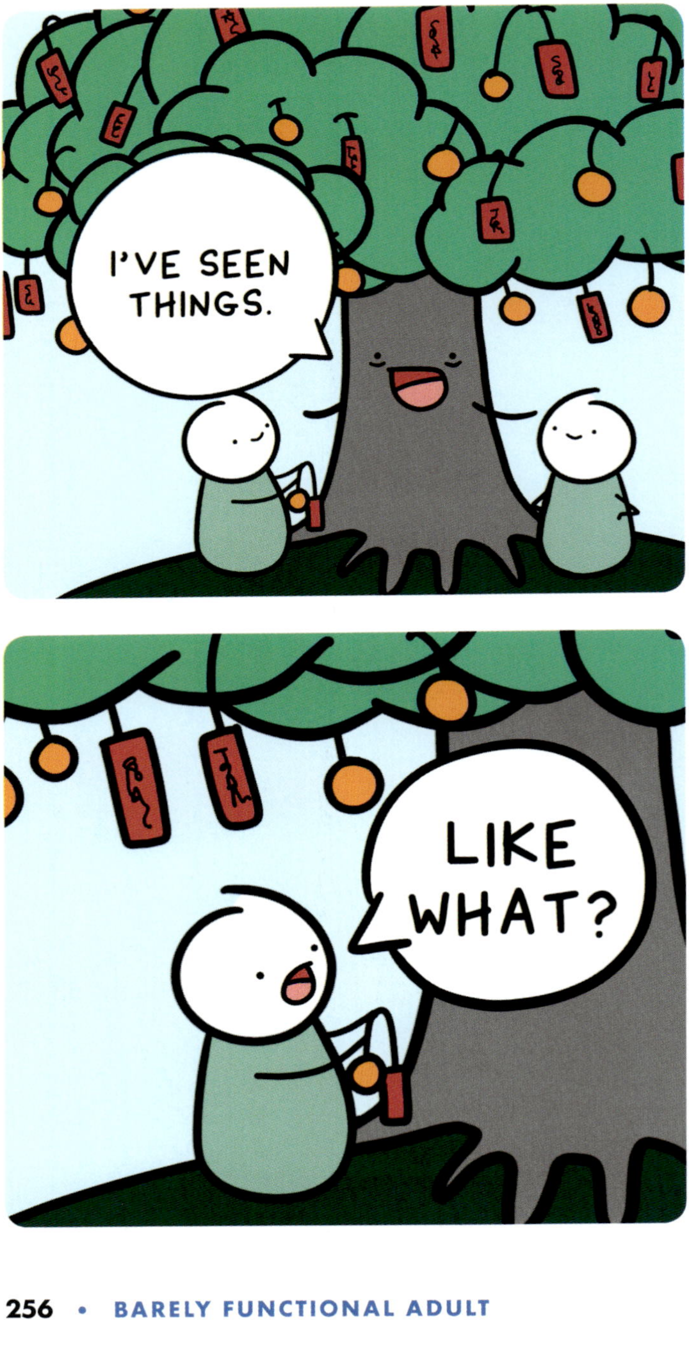
I'VE SEEN THINGS.
LIKE WHAT?

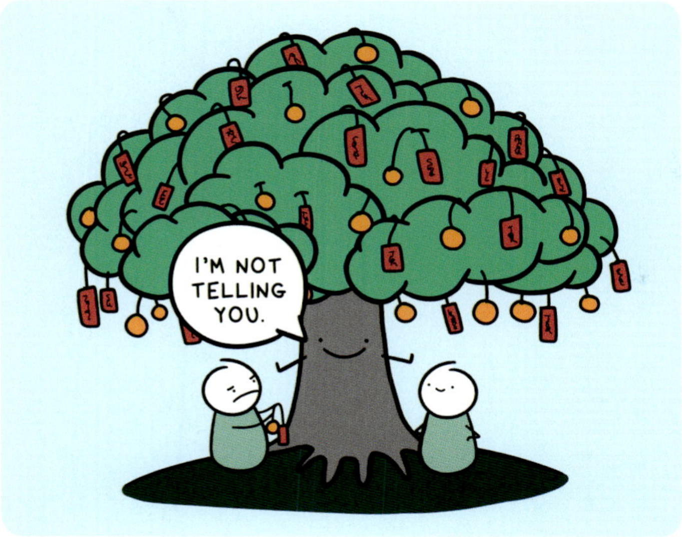
I'M NOT TELLING YOU.

Legend has it, if you write a wish on joss paper, attach it to an orange, and sling it up onto one of the Wishing Tree's many branches, your wish will come true.

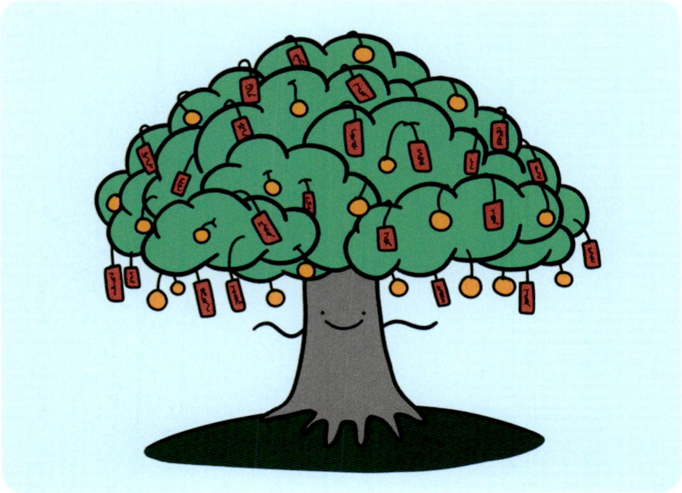

When I found myself in Hong Kong one summer, I decided to make the journey out to Lam Tsuen to see this fabled tree. The village was a fair distance away from where I was staying, but this obstacle simply added to the allure of the pilgrimage I had already set my heart on.

After hopping on an adorable toy-like minibus, I plopped onto a clear plastic-wrapped leather seat and stared out the window. "Wishing Tree, here I come," I whispered to myself. It was completely un- necessary to whisper, but that just made it all the more necessary.

When I found myself on solid ground again, I real- ized I was at the entrance of Lam Tsuen, right next to the Wishing Tree.

YOU'RE PRETTY.

YOU'RE OKAY.

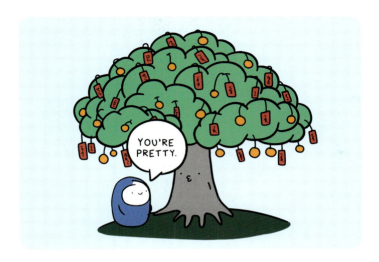

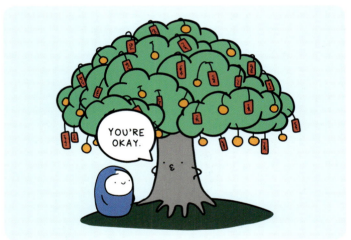

As I stood beneath its generous shade, my eyes trailed the exquisite patchwork of joss paper and oranges that wove through its branches. With no pressing wishes to make, I found my mind wandering instead to the life the Wishing Tree must have led in the centuries before.

I wondered of its origins, and whether it had always known of its own magical prowess. It probably started out like any other tree—casually photosynthesizing and providing oxygen to those around it.

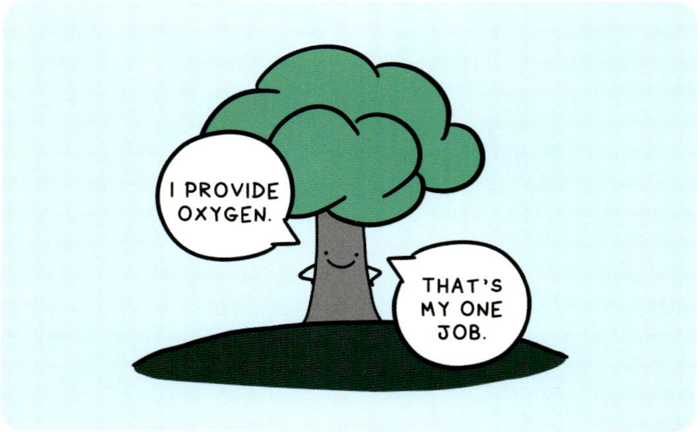
I PROVIDE OXYGEN.
THAT'S MY ONE JOB.

Until that one fateful day, when someone came forth and decided to make a wish. A wish that forever changed the tree's destiny.

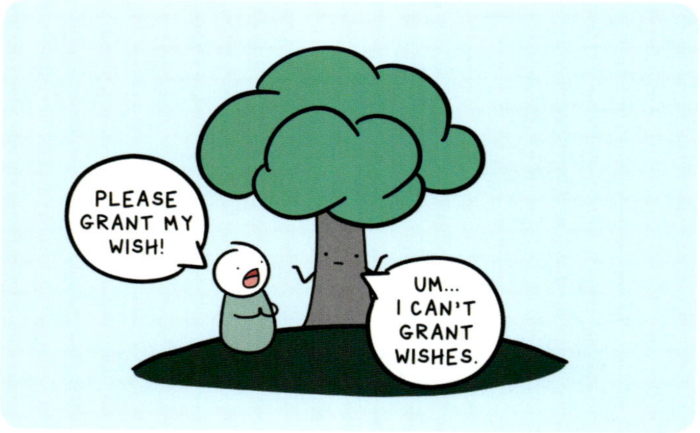
PLEASE GRANT MY WISH!
UM... I CAN'T GRANT WISHES.

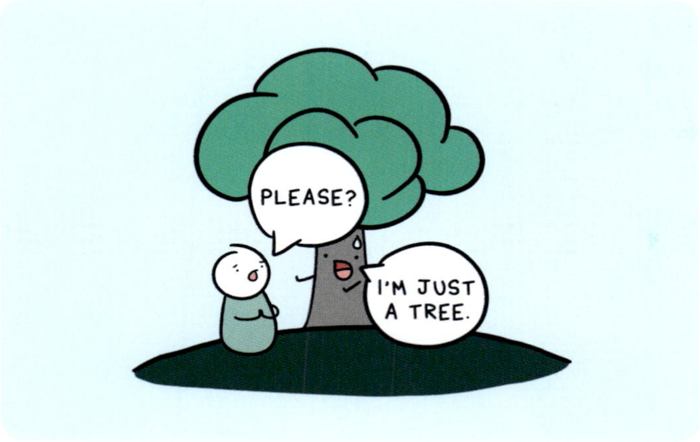
PLEASE?
I'M JUST A TREE.

I wondered how the tree felt when that wish suddenly came true, and hundreds of thousands of visitors flocked in with their prayers—each hoping for a small morsel of magic.

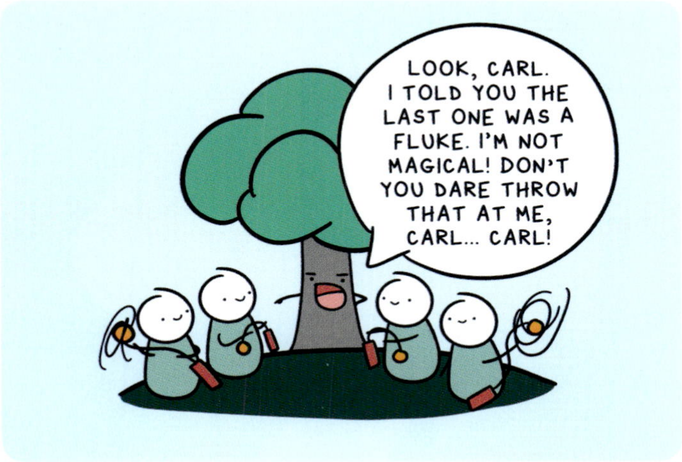
LOOK, CARL. I TOLD YOU THE LAST ONE WAS A FLUKE. I'M NOT MAGICAL! DON'T YOU DARE THROW THAT AT ME, CARL... CARL!

Having granted wishes for centuries, I wondered if the Wishing Tree believed in its own powers today.

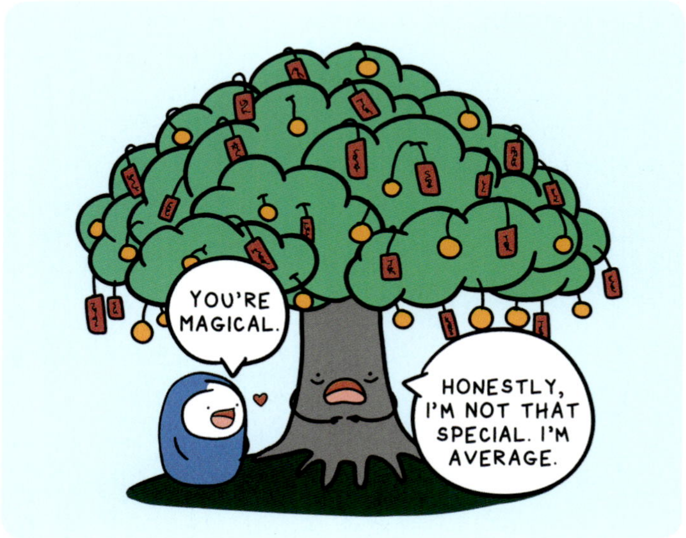
YOU'RE MAGICAL.
HONESTLY, I'M NOT THAT SPECIAL. I'M AVERAGE.

Or if, like us, it has yet to appreciate its own greatness.

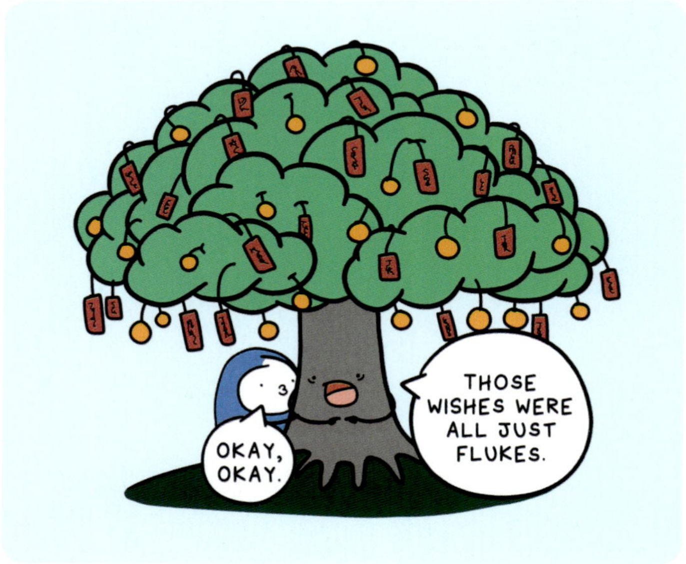
THOSE WISHES WERE ALL JUST FLUKES.
OKAY, OKAY.

After rerouting my career to a new industry that I actually enjoyed working in, my life became pleasantly uneventful. I wouldn't go as far as to say that I *loved* work, as that would be transparently insane, but I certainly didn't mind it all that much.

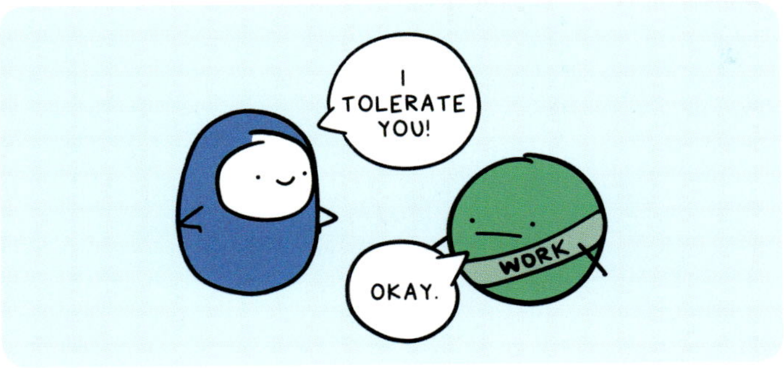
I TOLERATE YOU!
WORK
OKAY.

In the years that followed, I became quite proficient at playing the role of a competent employee. At the most basic level, I was able to develop a set of skills that allowed me to do my job without much assistance.

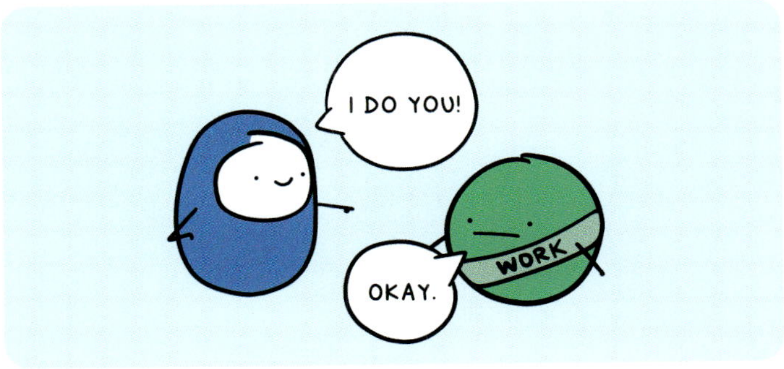
I DO YOU!
WORK
OKAY.

This included the mastery of an insipid language otherwise known as "work speak."

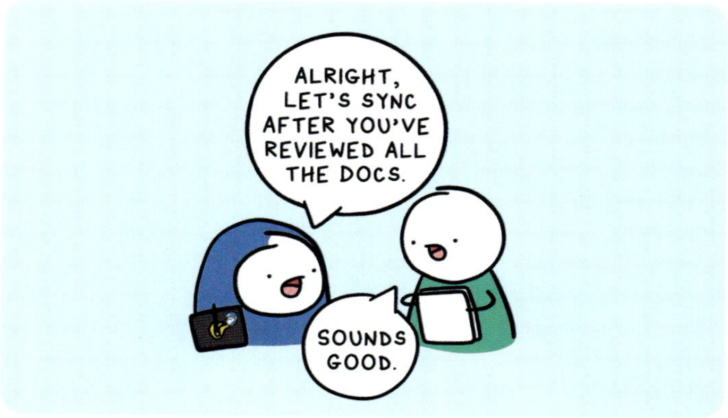
ALRIGHT, LET'S SYNC AFTER YOU'VE REVIEWED ALL THE DOCS.
SOUNDS GOOD.

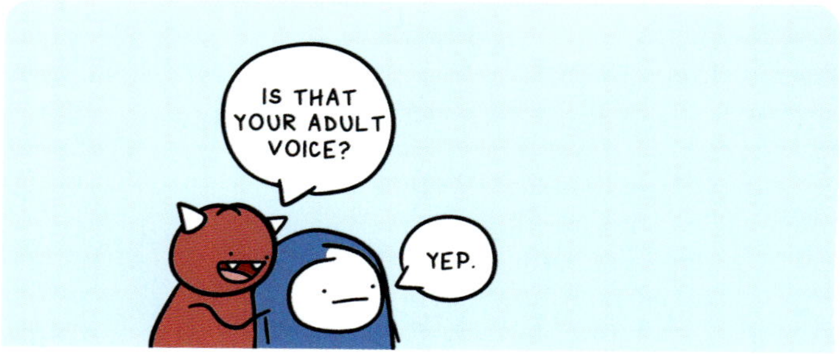
IS THAT YOUR ADULT VOICE?
YEP.

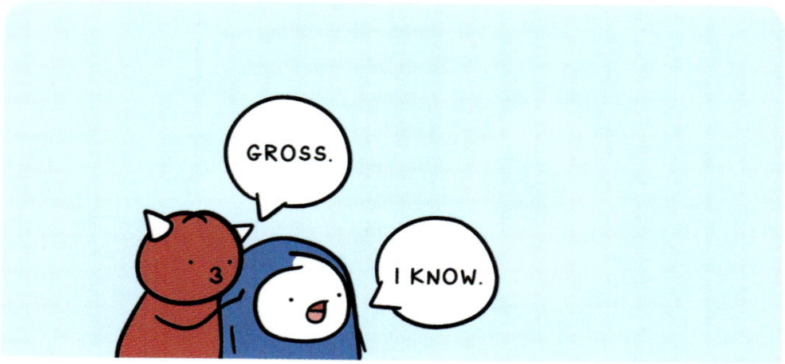
GROSS.
I KNOW.

I learned to tolerate day-to-day fluctuations in workload.

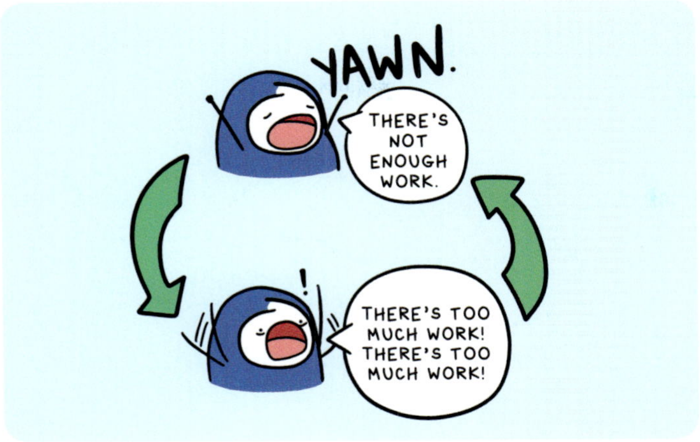
YAWN.
THERE'S NOT ENOUGH WORK.
THERE'S TOO MUCH WORK! THERE'S TOO MUCH WORK!

And I developed ways to combat the workplace nonsense that was constantly spewed at me.

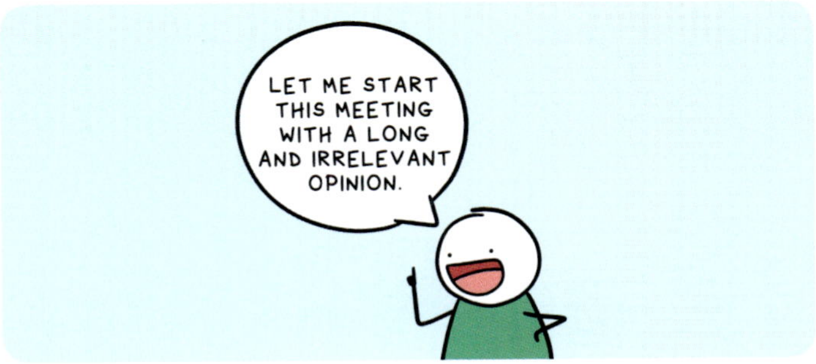
LET ME START THIS MEETING WITH A LONG AND IRRELEVANT OPINION.

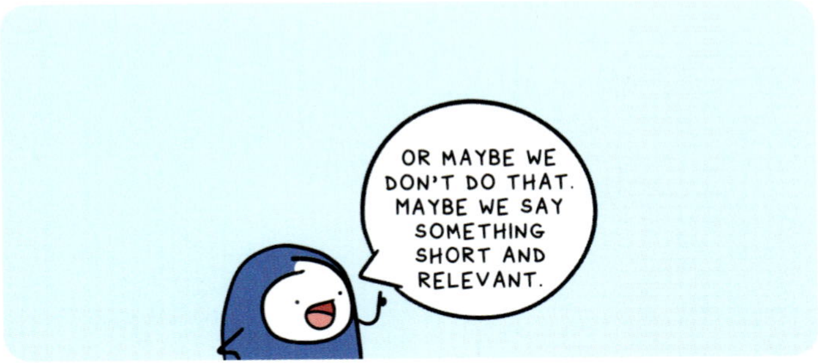
OR MAYBE WE DON'T DO THAT. MAYBE WE SAY SOMETHING SHORT AND RELEVANT.

I even learned how to negotiate my salary—a nuanced art and necessary evil.

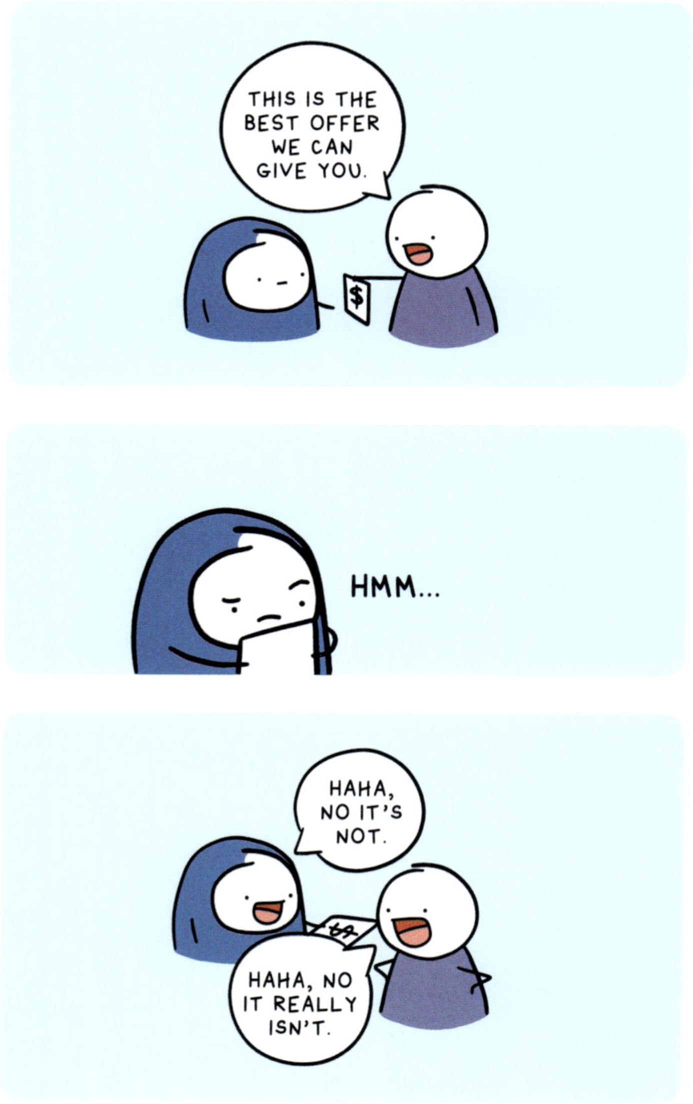
THIS IS THE BEST OFFER WE CAN GIVE YOU.
HMM...
HAHA, NO IT'S NOT.
HAHA, NO IT REALLY ISN'T.

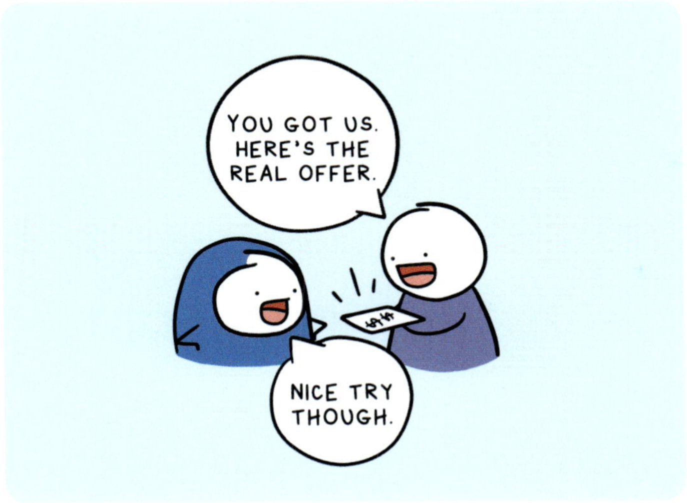
YOU GOT US. HERE'S THE REAL OFFER.
NICE TRY THOUGH.

Yes, after years of hard work, I had finally become somewhat of a functional adult (at work, at least). And with the distant memory of beginner's ineptitude so far behind me, I was completely blindsided by what came next.

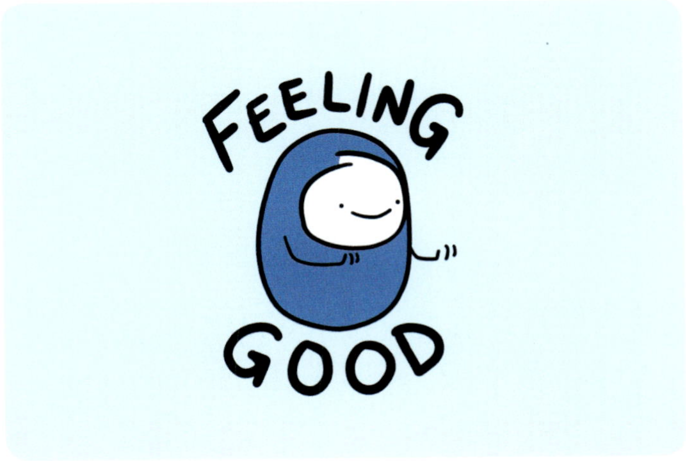
FEELING
GOOD

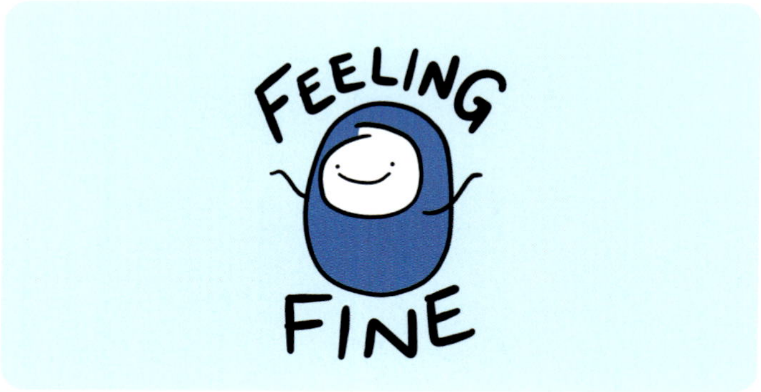
FEELING
FINE

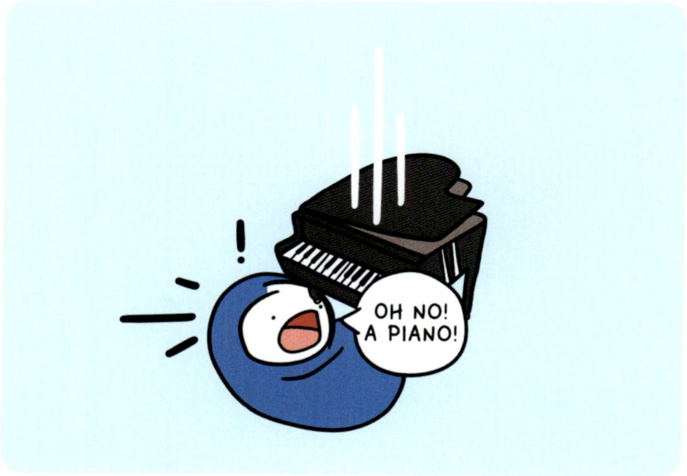
!
OH NO!
A PIANO!

Now replace that piano with impostor syndrome.

• • •

I had always enjoyed a comfortable relationship with praise throughout my years as a junior employee. I didn't seek it, I didn't fear it, and I never really thought too deeply about it. Praise was like a free ice cream cone, simple and pleasant—and that was that.

OH. MY. GOODNESS. DID YOU MAKE THAT PRESENTATION ALL BY YOURSELF?!
YES.
WELL, IT LOOKS JUST SO GOSH DARN WONDERFUL!
THANK YOU!

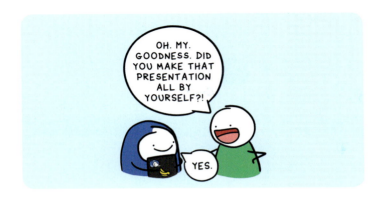

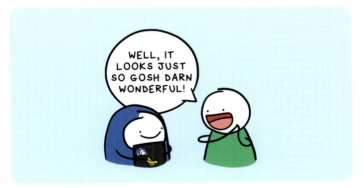

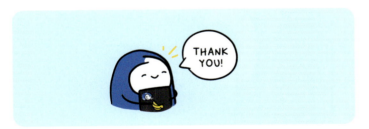

But praise becomes a lot harder to accept when you don't believe you deserve it. As I progressed in my career, I started to question how deserving I was of my so-called achievements. Everyone around me seemed to assume I knew things . . . but did I?

OH, NO.
THEY EXPECT
ME TO KNOW
THINGS
NOW.
BUT I KNOW
NOTHING...

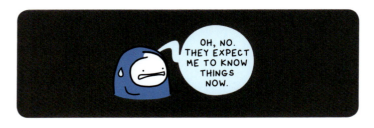

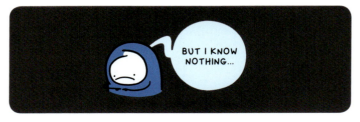

I knew a little, but not nearly as much as what others presumed, and this harrowing gap of unmet expectations began to take a toll. I had been so focused on leaning in, it never once occurred to me that I was leaning into a deep pit of inadequacy and self-doubt.

OKAY, I'M
GOING TO
LEAN IN.
HERE I GO,
LEANING IN!

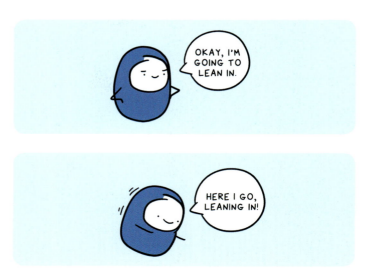

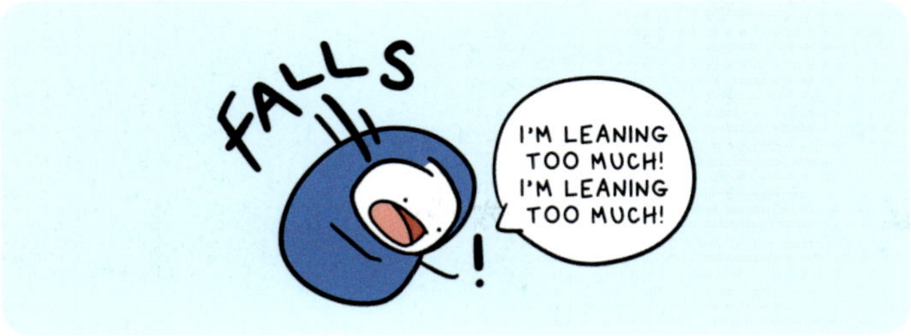
FALLS
I'M LEANING TOO MUCH! I'M LEANING TOO MUCH!

At the bottom of that pit, I found impostor syndrome.

• • •

I imagine impostor syndrome appears in different forms depending on its host—my manifestation was this unyielding fear that I was nowhere near as competent as others believed me to be. It was a visceral sense of ineptitude that shadowed my thoughts and feelings, preventing me from enjoying any sort of positive recognition or success.

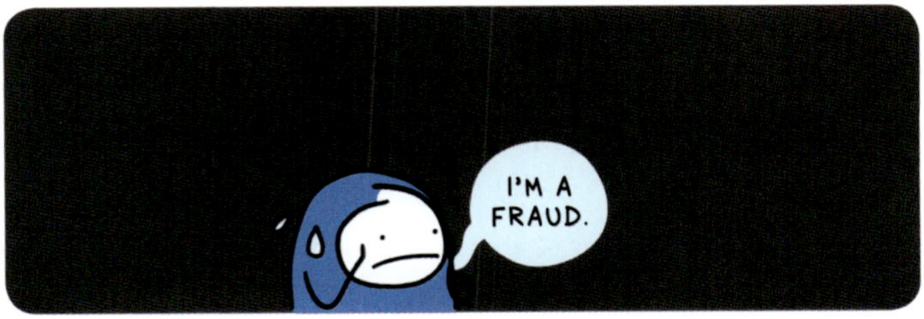
I'M A FRAUD.

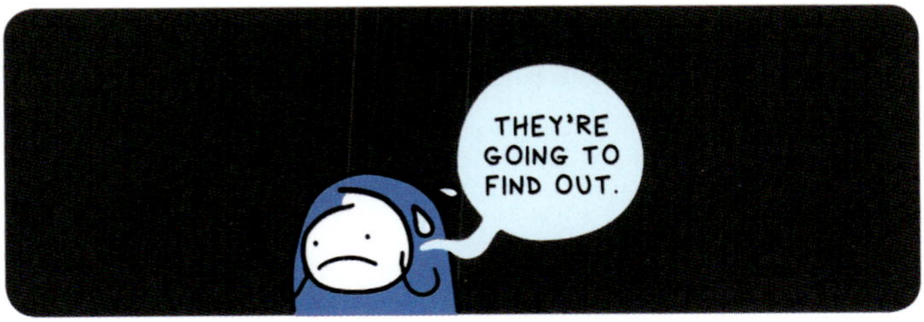
THEY'RE GOING TO FIND OUT.

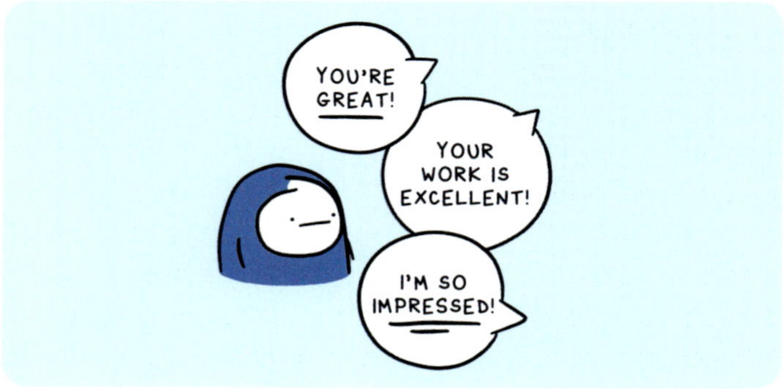
YOU'RE GREAT!
YOUR WORK IS EXCELLENT!
I'M SO IMPRESSED!

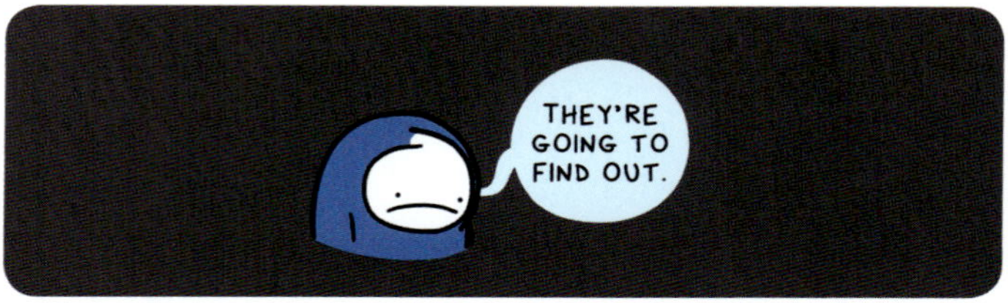
THEY'RE GOING TO FIND OUT.

I started to wonder if I was really competent or merely competent at *pretending* to be competent. And as my list of achievements grew, along came my anxiety.

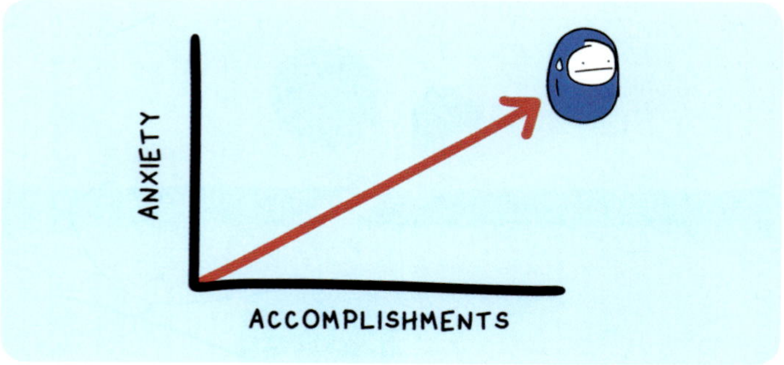
ANXIETY
ACCOMPLISHMENTS

I lost the ability to see what was good about my work, and instead I only saw the flaws—the millions of cracks that splintered my efforts and good intentions. It felt as though the work I produced was *always* short of being good, and no matter how many hours I poured into it, the result was the same—it just wasn't enough.

Positive feedback started making me anxious, and critical feedback gave me a perverse sense of relief. Whenever I received a compliment, I would assume it was misplaced.

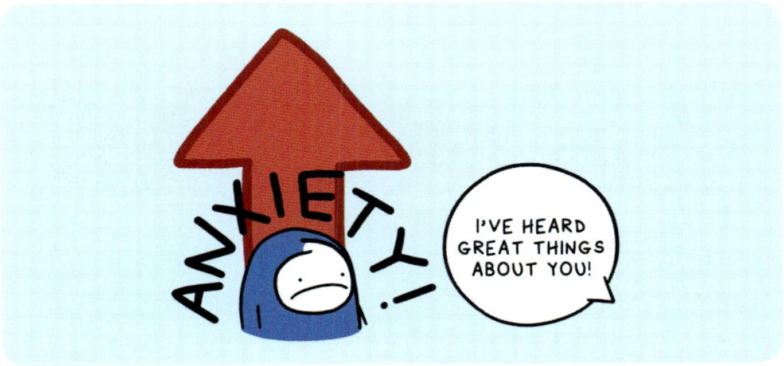
ANXIETY!
I'VE HEARD GREAT THINGS ABOUT YOU!

I grew wary of recognition and even began to fear it. It was as though praise was a powerful spotlight, and every time I stood in it, I risked revealing my true incompetence.

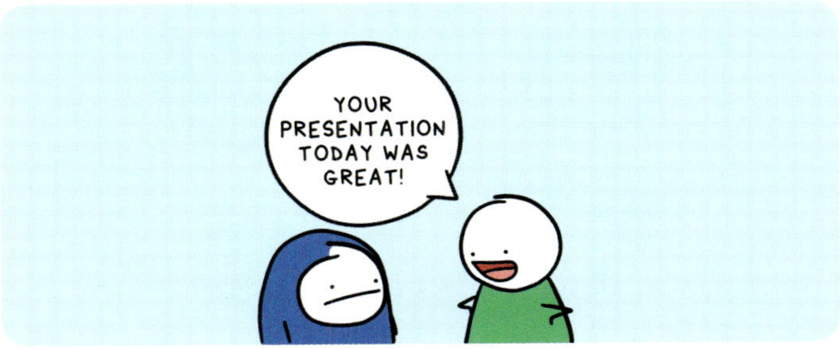
YOUR PRESENTATION TODAY WAS GREAT!

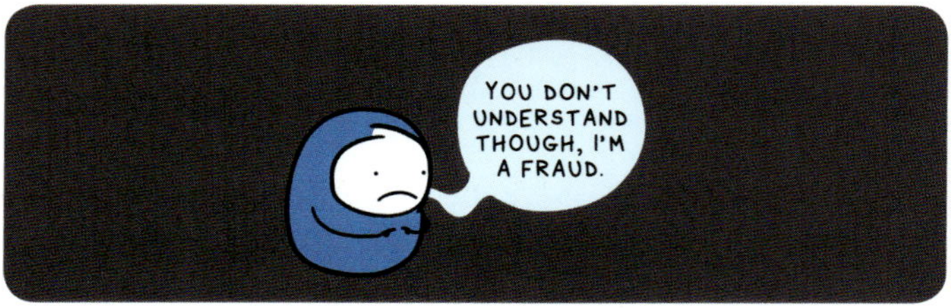
YOU DON'T UNDERSTAND THOUGH, I'M A FRAUD.

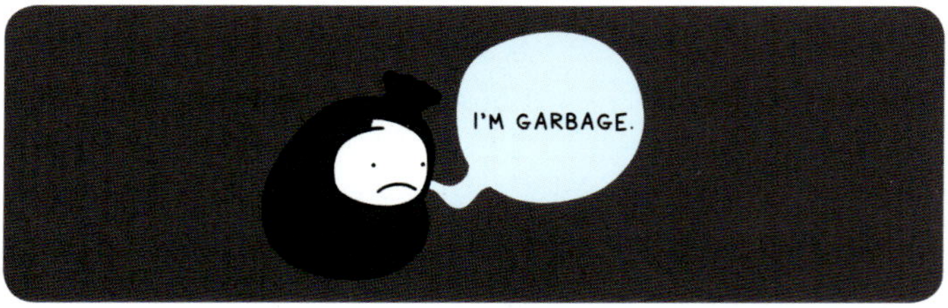
I'M GARBAGE.

I tried to explain to people around me that my "success" was luck-based—that a unique combination of timing and good fortune had led me to where I was, not singular talent or skill. I was just at the right place at the right time for most of it, and if I were to do it again with different external variables, I probably wouldn't be able to replicate the results.

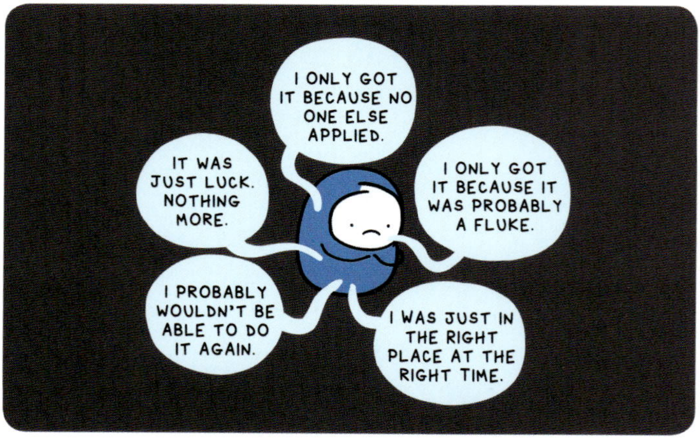
I ONLY GOT IT BECAUSE NO ONE ELSE APPLIED.
IT WAS JUST LUCK. NOTHING MORE.
I ONLY GOT IT BECAUSE IT WAS PROBABLY A FLUKE.
I PROBABLY WOULDN'T BE ABLE TO DO IT AGAIN.
I WAS JUST IN THE RIGHT PLACE AT THE RIGHT TIME.

But people wrote off my earnestness as modesty and refused to listen. It was hard to explain my feelings without coming across as though I was fishing for compliments, so I stopped trying to explain altogether. After a while, I just felt like a big fraud running the longest of cons. It was only a matter of time before they figured me out.

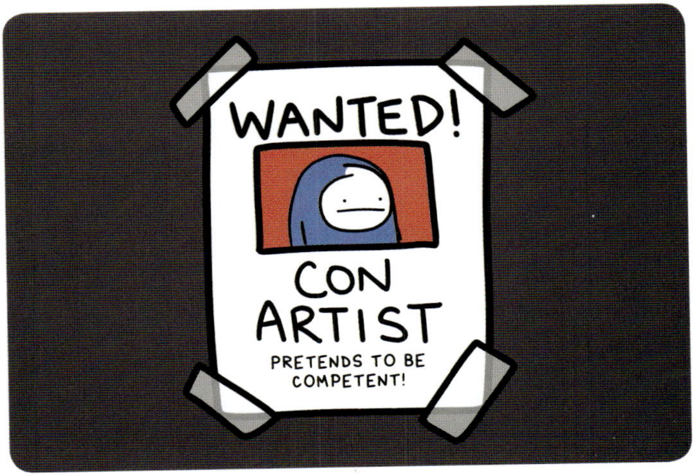
WANTED!
CON ARTIST
PRETENDS TO BE COMPETENT!

When I shared these fears with my friends, they would insist I was being ridiculous. They weren't able to see the chips and cracks I saw in myself.

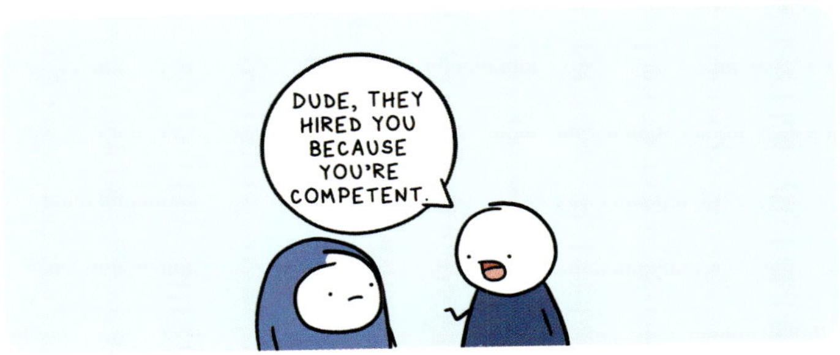
DUDE, THEY HIRED YOU BECAUSE YOU'RE COMPETENT.

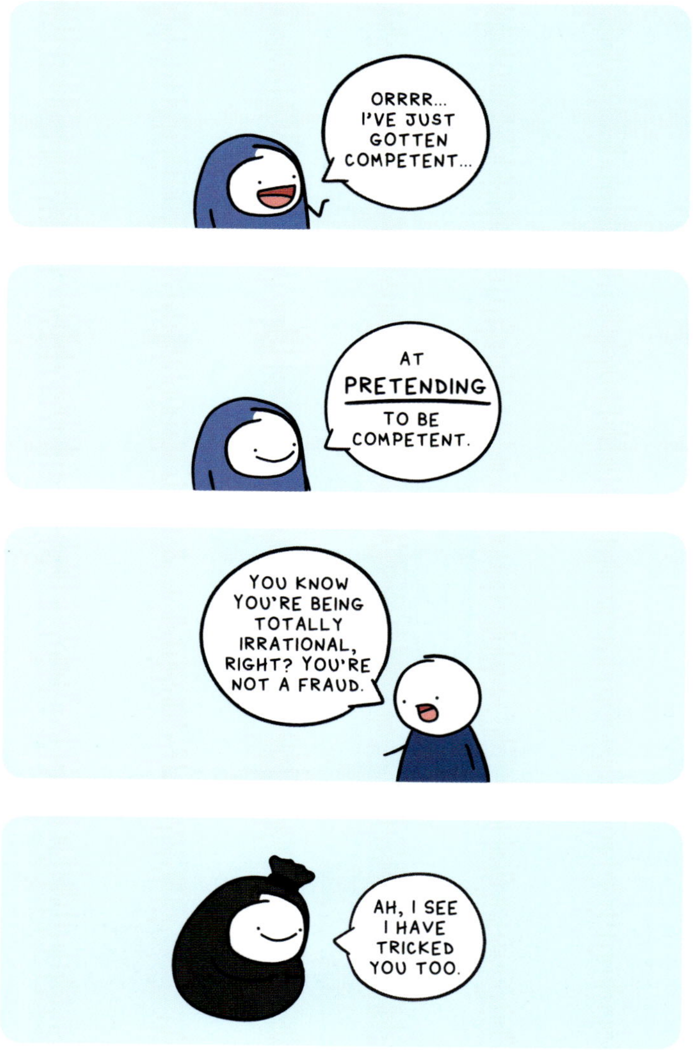
ORRRR... I'VE JUST GOTTEN COMPETENT...
AT PRETENDING TO BE COMPETENT.
YOU KNOW YOU'RE BEING TOTALLY IRRATIONAL, RIGHT? YOU'RE NOT A FRAUD.
AH, I SEE I HAVE TRICKED YOU TOO.

My impostor syndrome was crafty, relentless, and stayed with me for years. Under its oppressive regime, I lived in constant fear of being ousted as a fraud.

There were a lot of close calls.

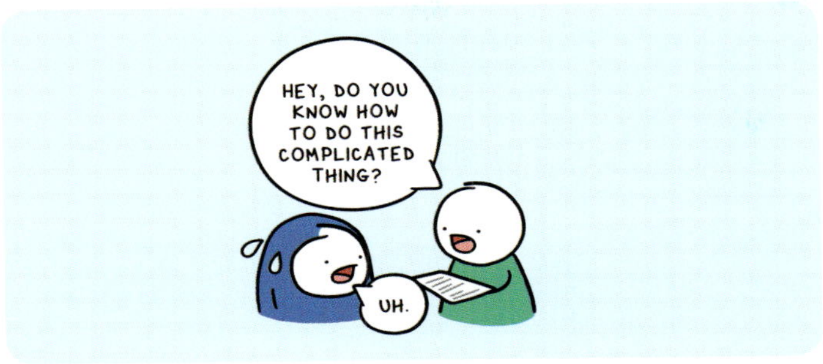
HEY, DO YOU KNOW HOW TO DO THIS COMPLICATED THING?
UH.

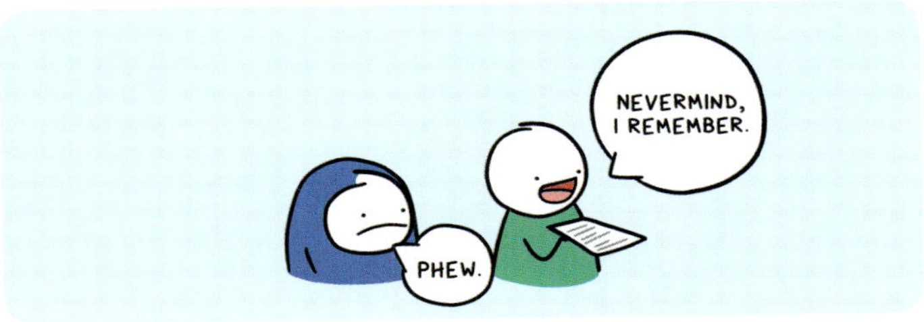
NEVERMIND, I REMEMBER.
PHEW.

After every close call, I would research the topic I previously knew nothing about. I needed to ensure I knew the answers because I was deathly afraid of being asked again—deathly afraid of being revealed as a fraud.

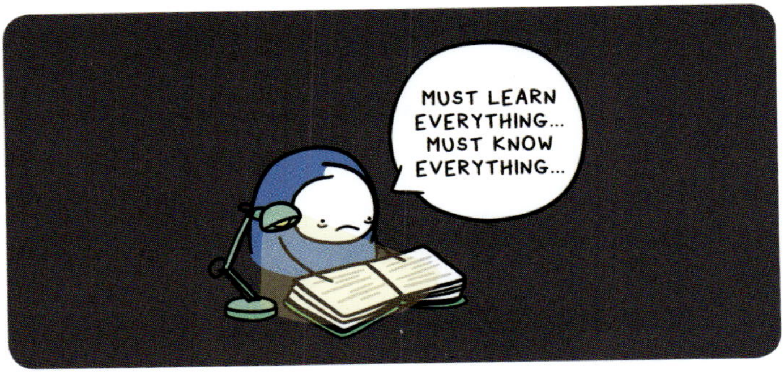
MUST LEARN EVERYTHING... MUST KNOW EVERYTHING...

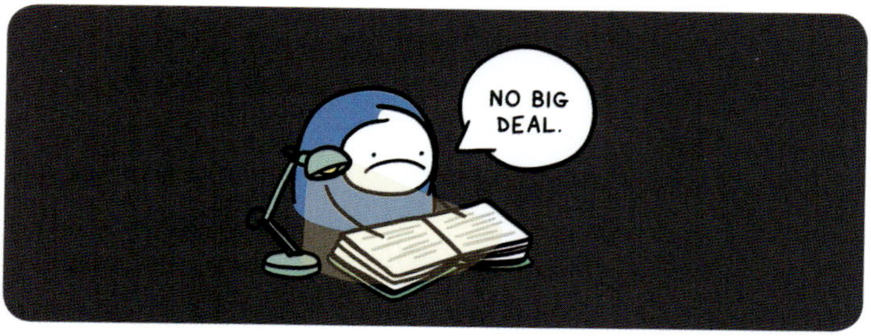
NO BIG DEAL.

Over time, I got used to the constant company of self-doubt and inadequacy.

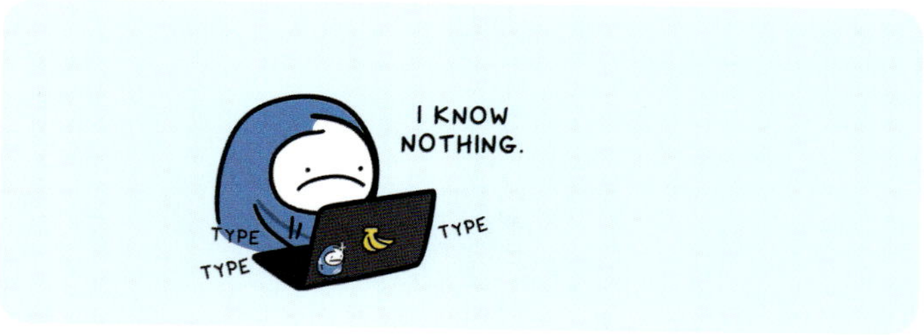
I KNOW NOTHING.
TYPE
TYPE
TYPE

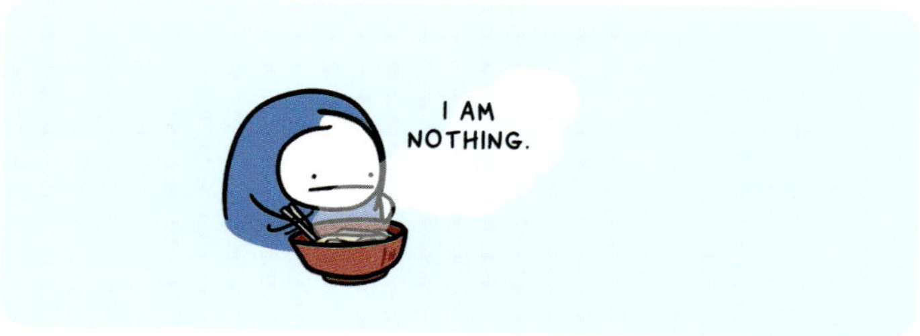
I AM NOTHING.

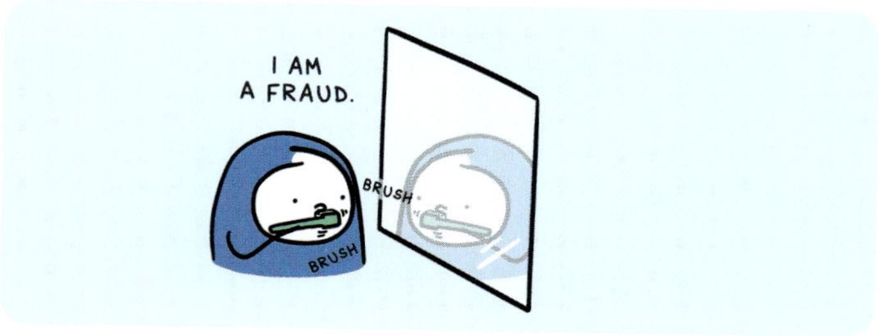
I AM A FRAUD.
BRUSH
BRUSH

I even made my peace with it.

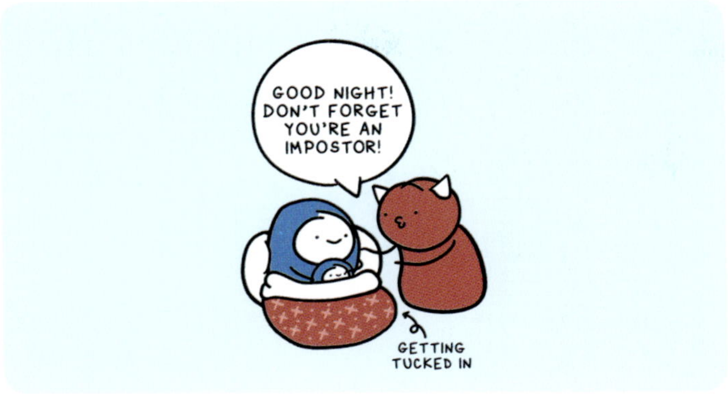
GOOD NIGHT! DON'T FORGET YOU'RE AN IMPOSTOR!
GETTING TUCKED IN

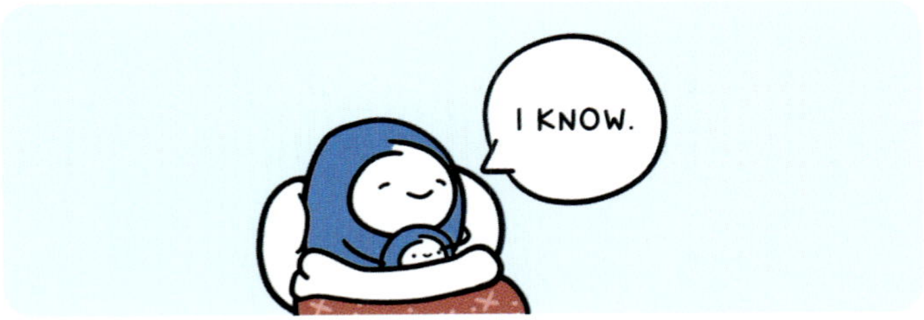
I KNOW.

Yes, all was well . . . until one day, I felt the piano drop again.

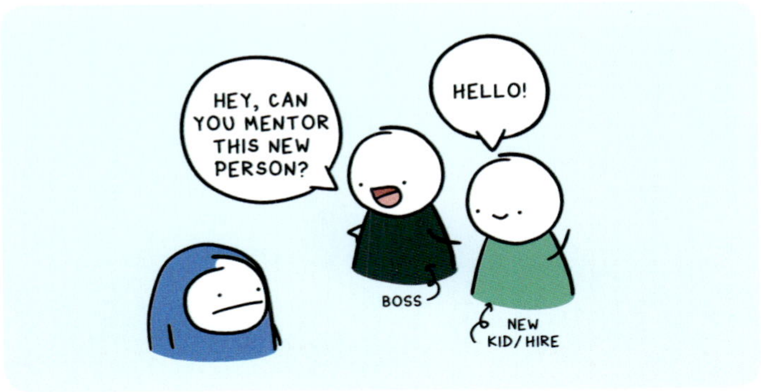
HEY, CAN YOU MENTOR THIS NEW PERSON?
HELLO!
BOSS
NEW KID/HIRE

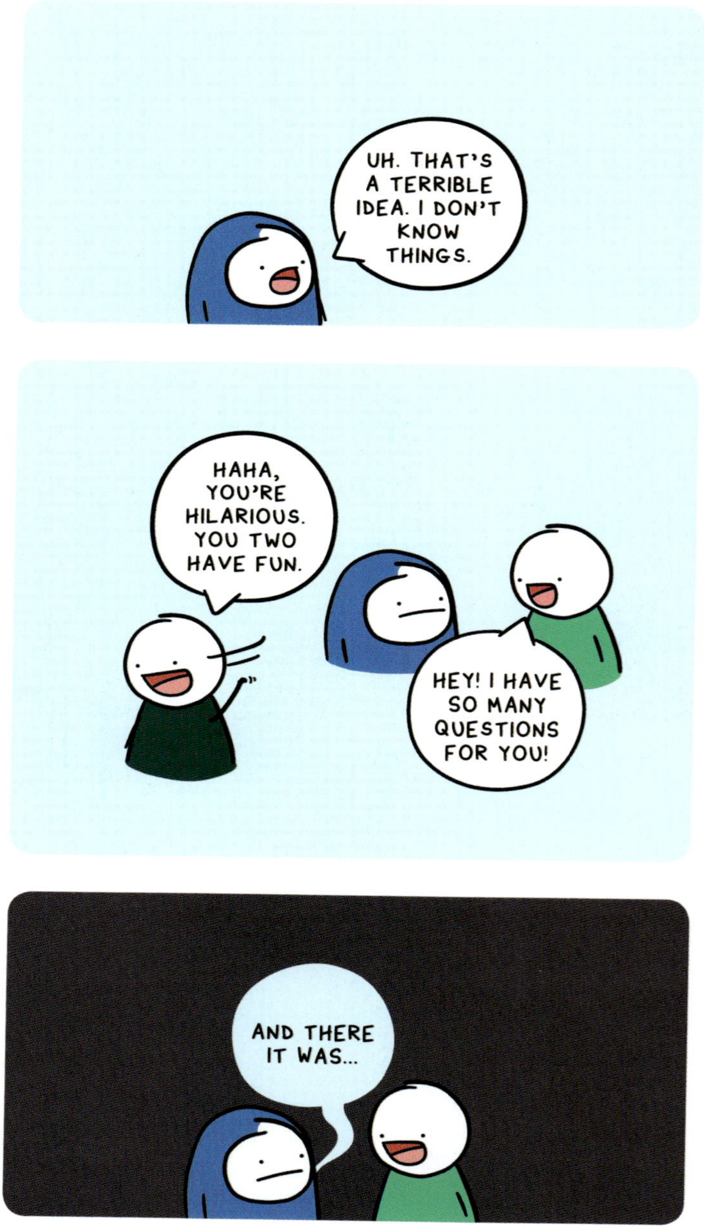
UH. THAT'S A TERRIBLE IDEA. I DON'T KNOW THINGS.
HAHA, YOU'RE HILARIOUS. YOU TWO HAVE FUN.
HEY! I HAVE SO MANY QUESTIONS FOR YOU!
AND THERE IT WAS...

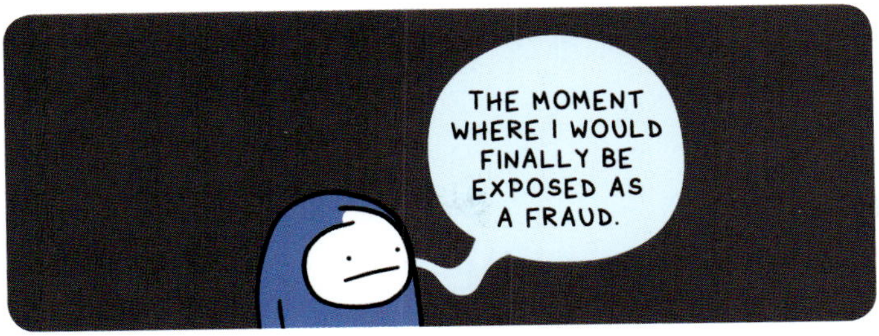
THE MOMENT WHERE I WOULD FINALLY BE EXPOSED AS A FRAUD.

*This is it*, I thought. *This* is the end. A swirling cacophony of inadequacy and fear burst through the castle gates I had spent years reinforcing.

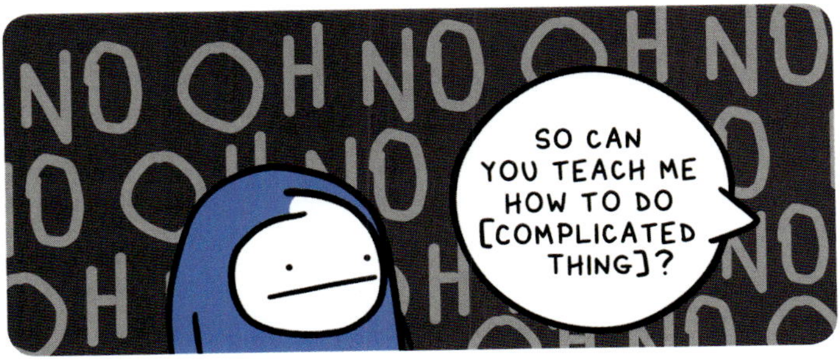
SO CAN YOU TEACH ME HOW TO DO [COMPLICATED THING]?

This is the moment I've been waiting for. This is the moment I'm revealed as a fraud . . . a charlatan . . . a dirty impos . . .

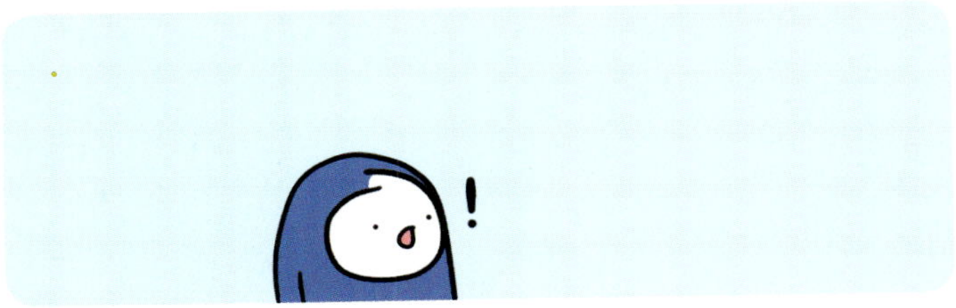
!

Wait. Hold up. I actually *do* know the answer to that question.

ACTUALLY, YEAH. I KNOW HOW TO DO THAT. I CAN SHOW YOU!
THANK YOU!

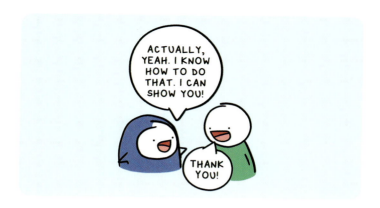

A small, soothing rush of unexpected knowledge, *just* enough to make me second-guess my own self-doubt, came flooding through at the most critical hour. It was like firing up your last rescue flare into the sky and realizing the plane passing by had seen the signal—it was the feeling of *salvation.*

OH. MY. GOD. I KNOW THINGS.

I ACTUALLY KNOW THINGS!

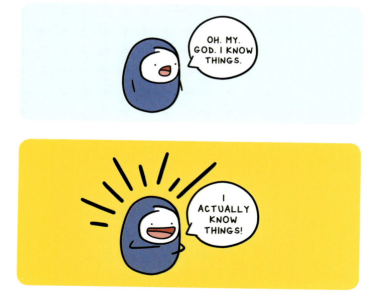

I'M LIKE THE TREE! I CAN GRANT WISHES AND...
UH, NO YOU CAN'T. YOU'RE NOT A TREE. YOU JUST KNOW SOME THINGS.
OKAY, FINE. I JUST KNOW THINGS.

My immunity against impostor syndrome comes and goes. I think it might be one of those demons that are just destined to drop by from time to time. Some days I recognize that my self-doubts are wildly unfounded, other days I still worry I don't know all the things that

I really ought to know. On particularly anxiety-ridden nights, I still panic-read books in hopes of feeling some semblance of knowledge and adequacy.

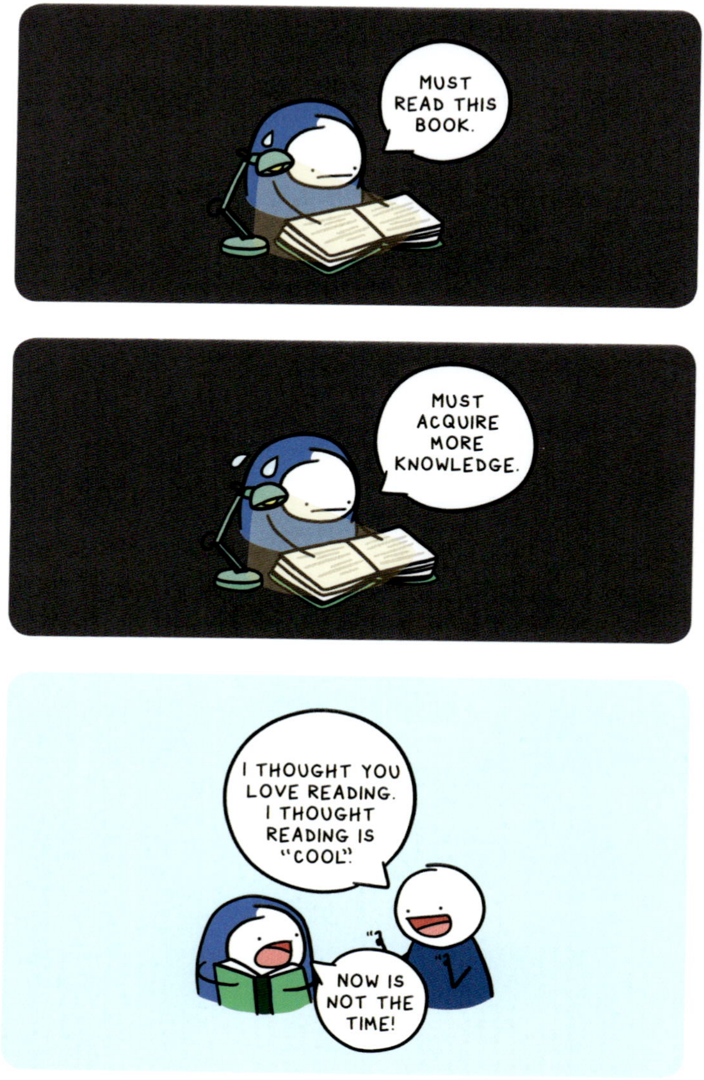
MUST READ THIS BOOK.
MUST ACQUIRE MORE KNOWLEDGE.
I THOUGHT YOU LOVE READING. I THOUGHT READING IS "COOL".
NOW IS NOT THE TIME!

And whenever I feel that creeping sensation of inadequacy and self-doubt driving me too close to the edge, I stop, and I whisper to myself, "It's okay to not know things. Not knowing things is the first step to knowing things." It is, of course, completely unnecessary to whisper, but that just makes it all the more necessary.

And you'd think with all this useful whispering, I wouldn't ever find myself in a place of paralyzing self-doubt. But too often I still wonder whether my feelings of inadequacy are a cause for genuine concern or a universal pain felt among all of us.

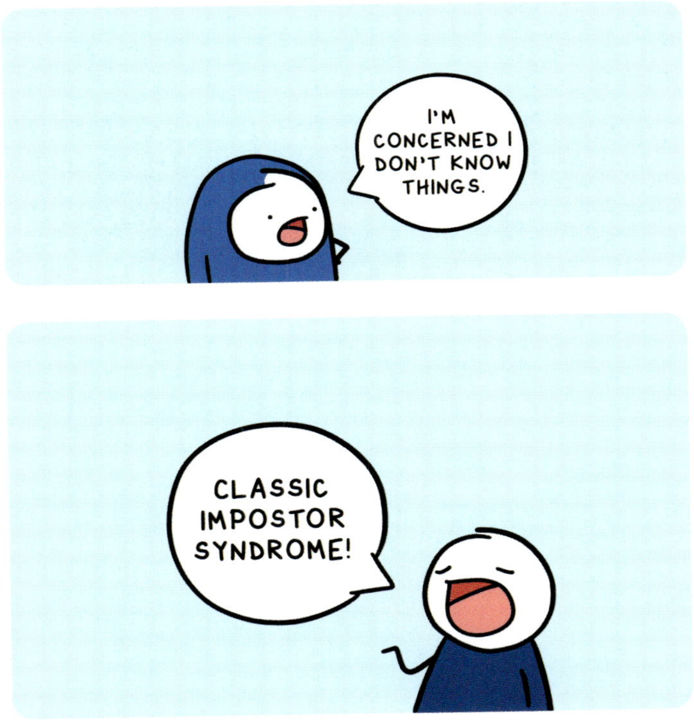
I'M CONCERNED I DON'T KNOW THINGS.
CLASSIC IMPOSTOR SYNDROME!

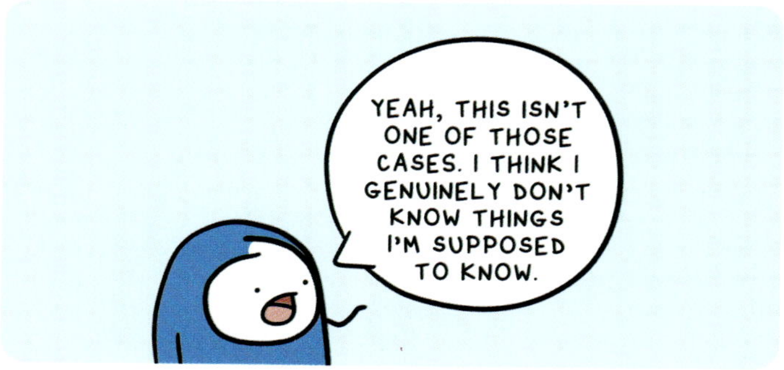
YEAH, THIS ISN'T ONE OF THOSE CASES. I THINK I GENUINELY DON'T KNOW THINGS I'M SUPPOSED TO KNOW.

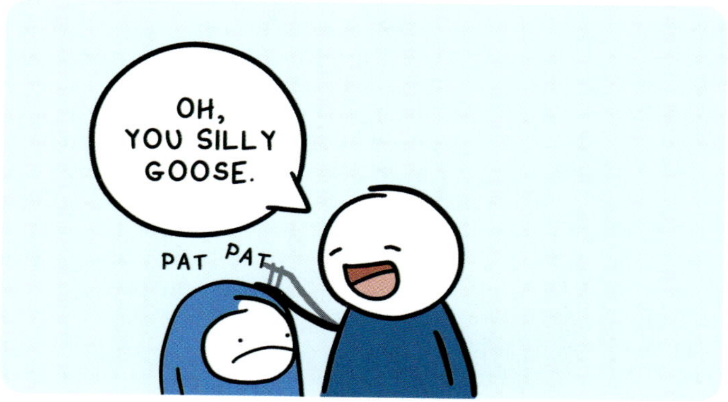
OH, YOU SILLY GOOSE.
PAT PAT

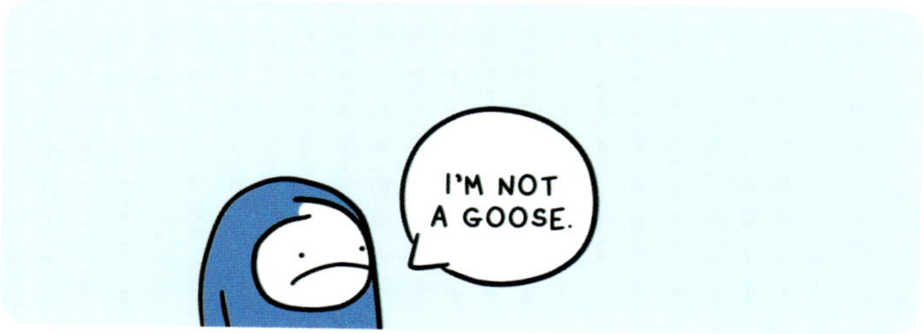
I'M NOT A GOOSE.

But maybe it's a good thing—this maddening cycle of self-doubt that ebbs and flows with time. Maybe it's the universe's way of keeping us humble, keeping us in check, and reminding us that we've still got quite a ways to go.

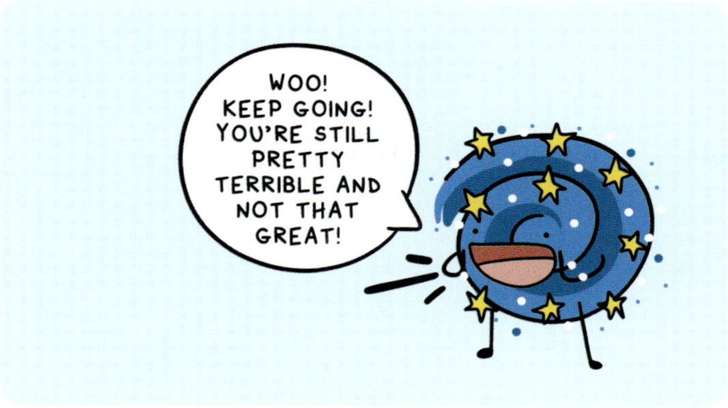
WOO! KEEP GOING! YOU'RE STILL PRETTY TERRIBLE AND NOT THAT GREAT!

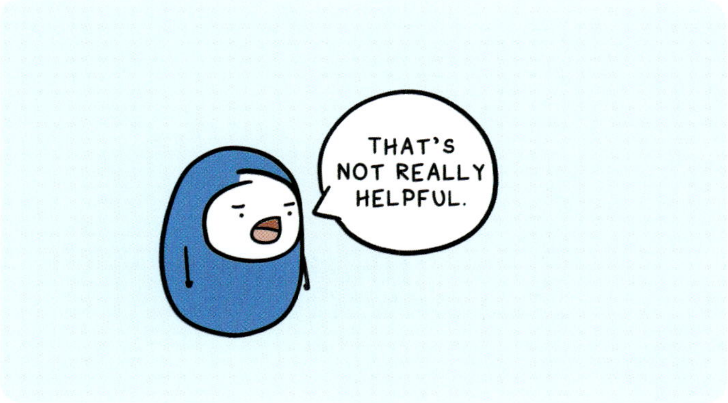
THAT'S NOT REALLY HELPFUL.

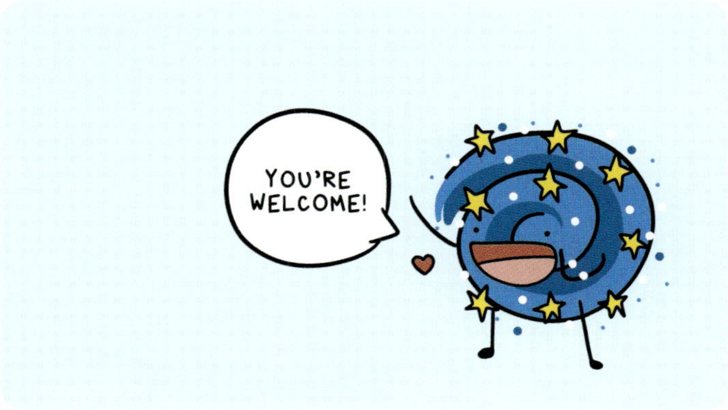
YOU'RE WELCOME!

CHAPTER 7

# OLDPOC-ALYPSE

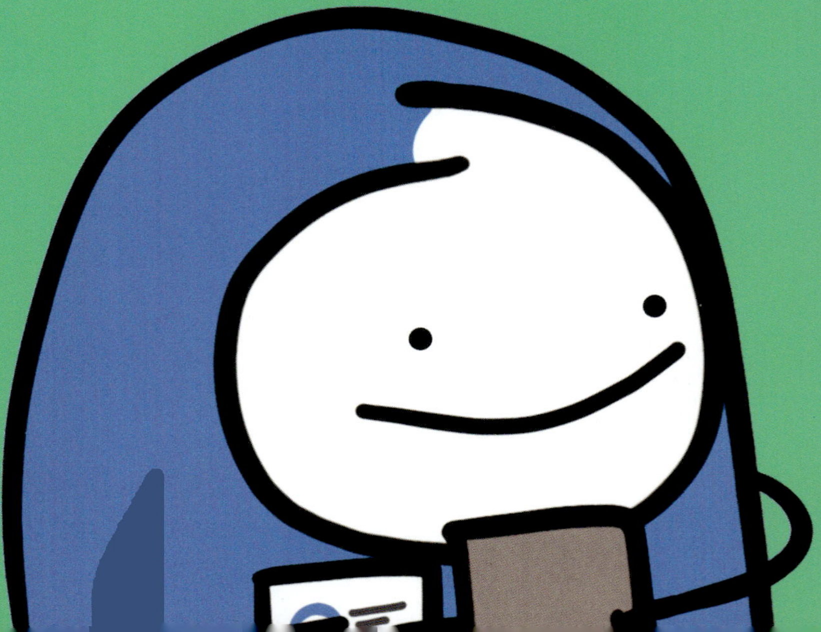

**A**nd what can I get the two of you to drink today?" our waitress asked warmly. She seemed excessively chipper for 4 p.m. on a Thursday, but then again, maybe I was just having a long week. I scanned the happy hour list for a good cocktail and came up short.

"Um . . . what can you recommend?" I asked, before swiftly and intensely regretting this decision as the waitress launched into a list of various aged whiskeys I could not have cared less about.

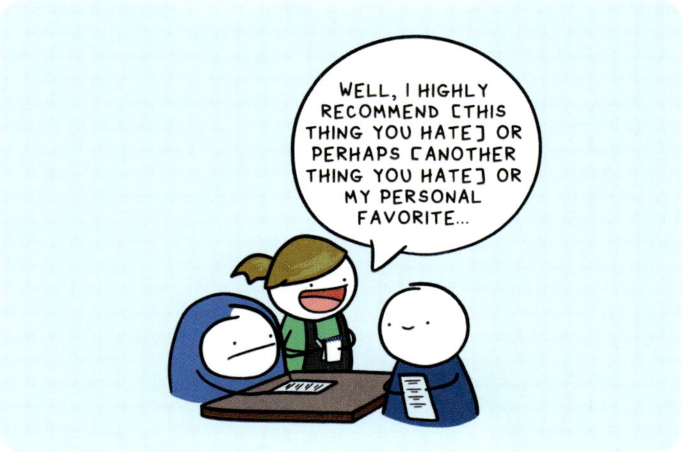
WELL, I HIGHLY RECOMMEND [THIS THING YOU HATE] OR PERHAPS [ANOTHER THING YOU HATE] OR MY PERSONAL FAVORITE...

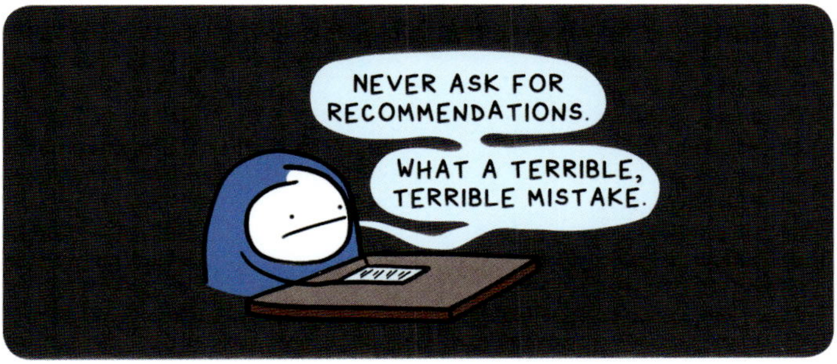
NEVER ASK FOR RECOMMENDATIONS.
WHAT A TERRIBLE, TERRIBLE MISTAKE.

Sensing my indecision, my friend decided to order first.

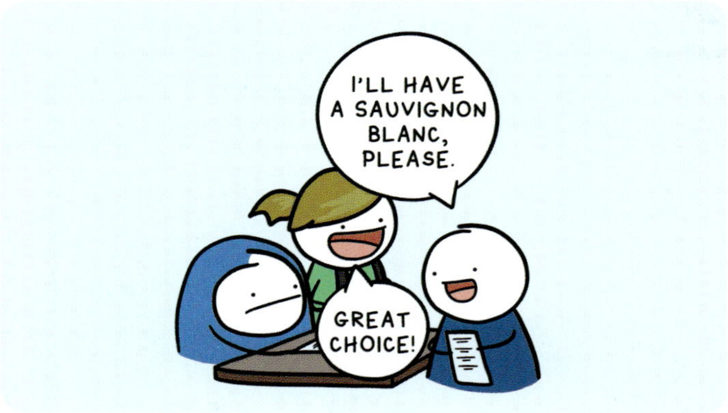
I'LL HAVE A SAUVIGNON BLANC, PLEASE.
GREAT CHOICE!

She always orders wine, she's sensible like that. The waitress nodded with an approving smile as she jotted down her request.

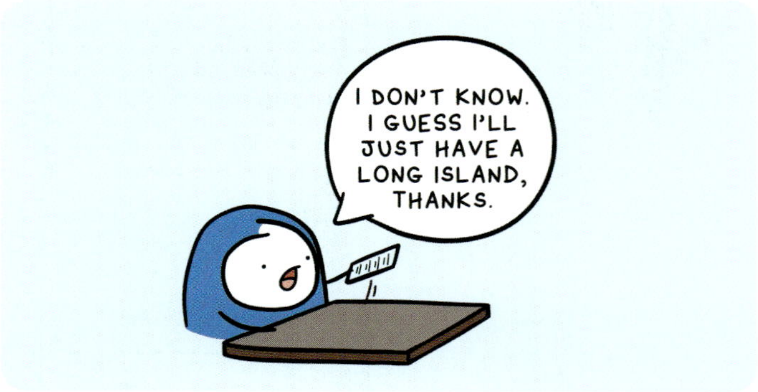
I DON'T KNOW. I GUESS I'LL JUST HAVE A LONG ISLAND, THANKS.

I handed the menu of stodgy aged whiskeys back to the waitress. She didn't move to take it.

"A . . . *what*?" the waitress asked, all remnants of hospitality gone.

"Um . . . a Long Island iced tea?" I repeated, slightly taken aback and unsure if explaining how to make one would be perceived as condescending or helpful.

My friend was now hiding, rather poorly, a look of palpable delight as her eyes darted between the waitress and me with unadulterated glee.

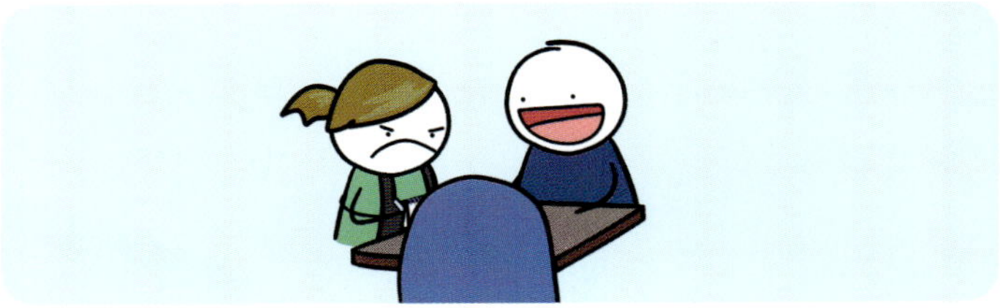

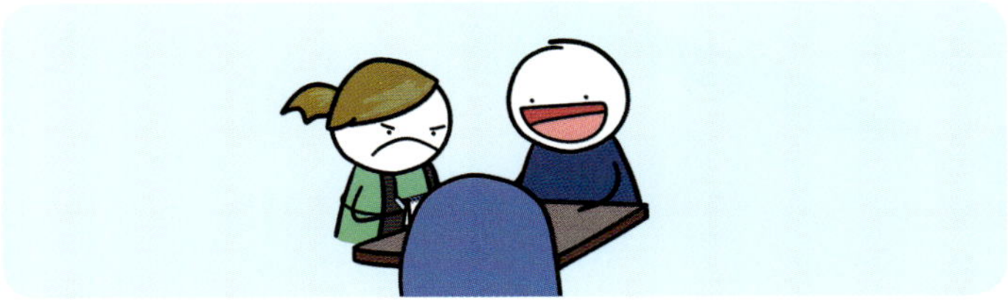

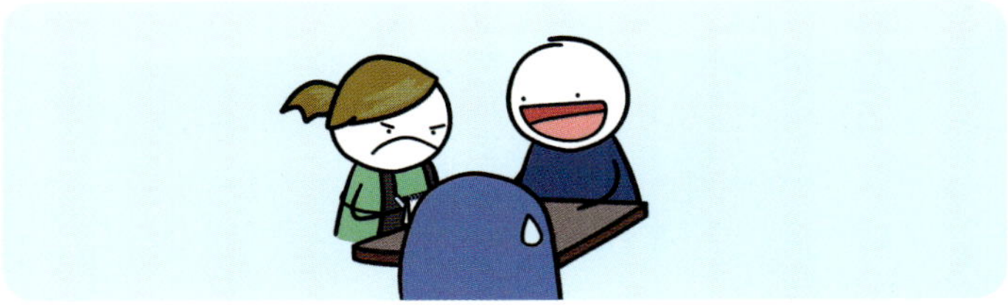

I didn't understand what was happening, so I hesitated for a second before offering another olive branch. "Is . . . your bar able to make it for me? Or maybe I could pick something else that's . . ."

The waitress slammed her notepad shut.

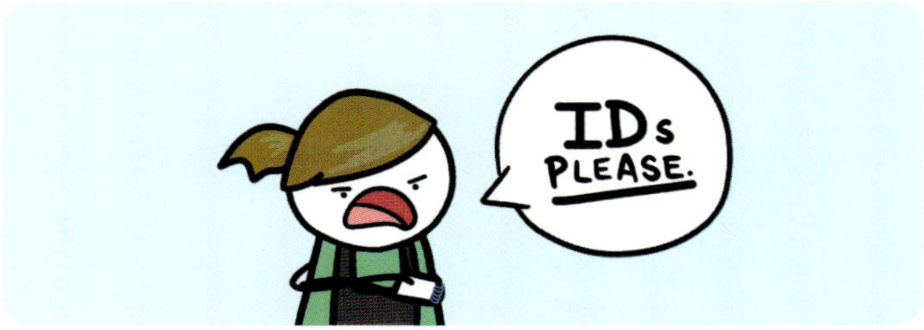
IDs PLEASE.

Clearly struggling to contain her amusement at this point, my friend flashed a wry smile before deftly handing her ID to the waitress. I did the same.

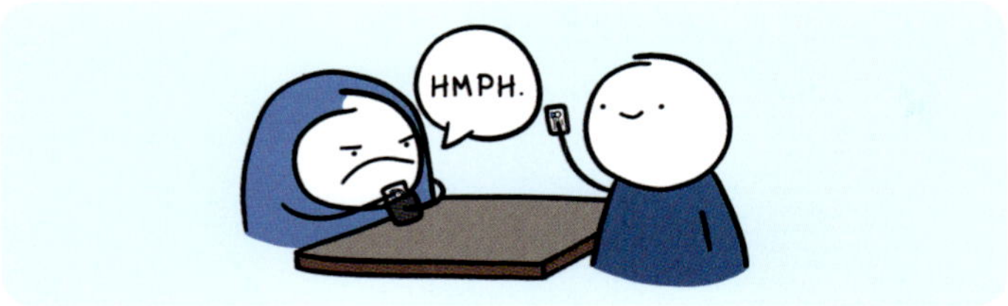
HMPH.

After much scrutiny, the waitress tossed our cards back onto the table and stormed off. "What the hell was that!" I asked. I was still unsure if they were going to make my drink and this bothered me almost as much as the waitress' unseemly reaction.

"You can't just *order* a LONG ISLAND!" my friend explained as she burst into laughter.

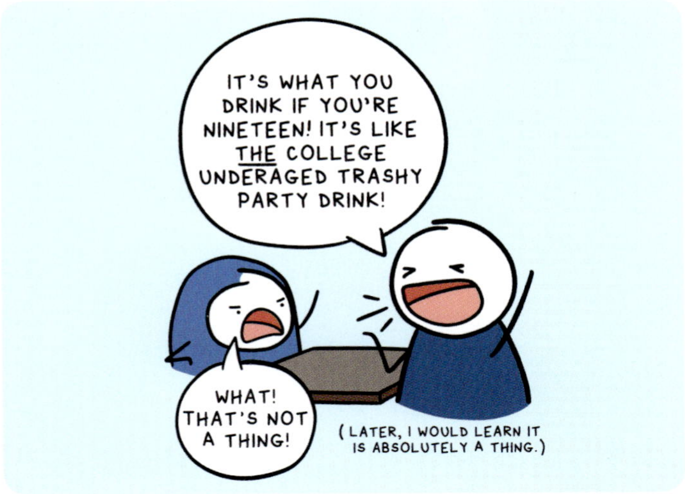
IT'S WHAT YOU DRINK IF YOU'RE NINETEEN! IT'S LIKE THE COLLEGE UNDERAGED TRASHY PARTY DRINK!
WHAT! THAT'S NOT A THING!
(LATER, I WOULD LEARN IT IS ABSOLUTELY A THING.)

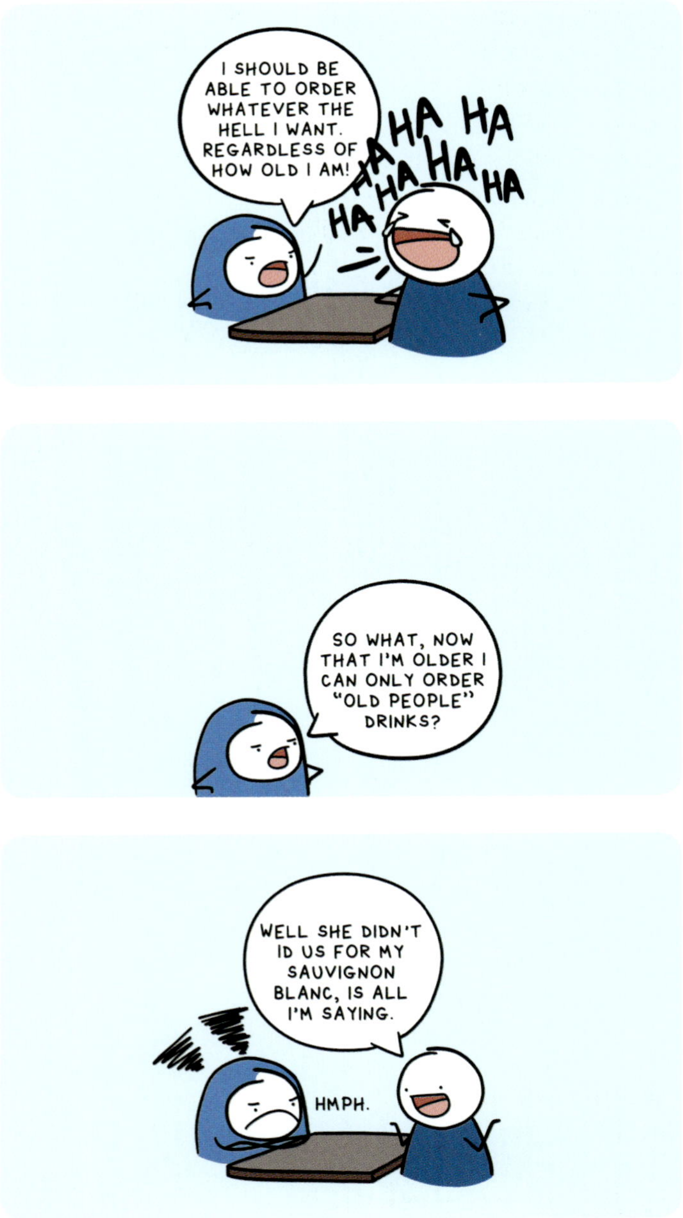
I SHOULD BE ABLE TO ORDER WHATEVER THE HELL I WANT. REGARDLESS OF HOW OLD I AM!
HA HA HA HA HA HA HA HA HA
SO WHAT, NOW THAT I'M OLDER I CAN ONLY ORDER "OLD PEOPLE" DRINKS?
WELL SHE DIDN'T ID US FOR MY SAUVIGNON BLANC, IS ALL I'M SAYING.
HMPH.

I had never identified as an "adult" despite having an ID that proved otherwise. The notion of being an adult just seemed like such a dreary badge to slap on. It also carried this connotation of being someone immutably stuffy and incapable of having fun—neither of which I was particularly inclined to relate to. And while I made the effort to be dependable and responsible when necessary, I always made sure to leave a small margin for joy—a slight, yet critical barrier to separate myself from the *real* adults of the world.

CRITICAL
BARRIER

ME
REAL
ADULTS.

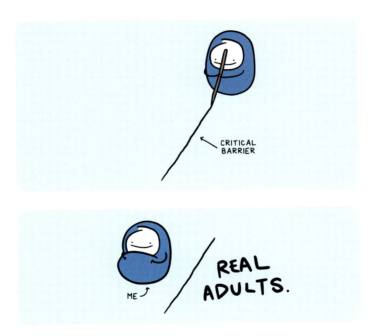

My friends shared a similar philosophy, and this unified pledge towards the conservation of our youth kept the plague of aging at bay for many years. But all paradise is eventually lost, and ours was not immune to the tides of time.

The initial signs of infection were first seen among my closest friends. Their decision-making became uncharacteristically responsible and their risk tolerance skewed disturbingly conservative. Like the lone protagonist of a postapocalyptic story, I was the only one who saw the emergence of rational thinking for what it truly was—an early symptom of aging souls.

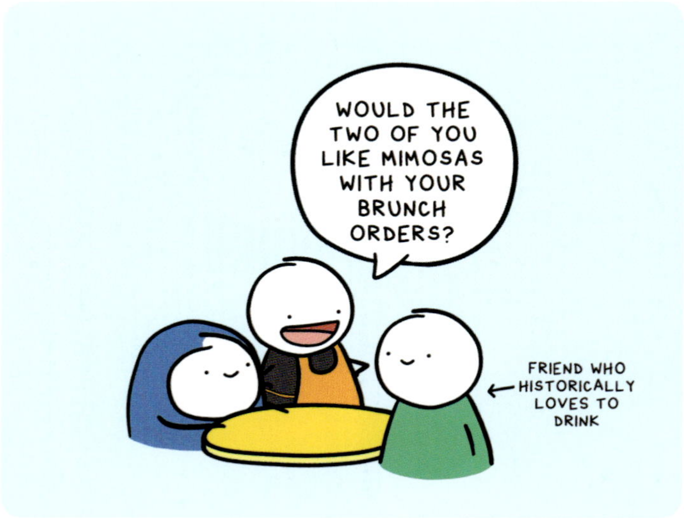
WOULD THE TWO OF YOU LIKE MIMOSAS WITH YOUR BRUNCH ORDERS?
FRIEND WHO HISTORICALLY LOVES TO DRINK

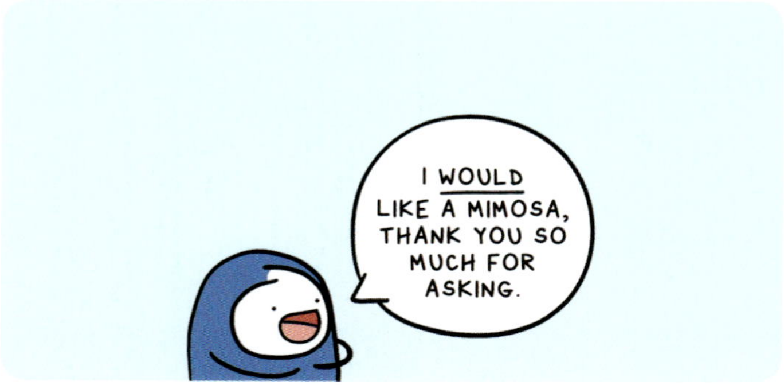
I WOULD LIKE A MIMOSA, THANK YOU SO MUCH FOR ASKING.

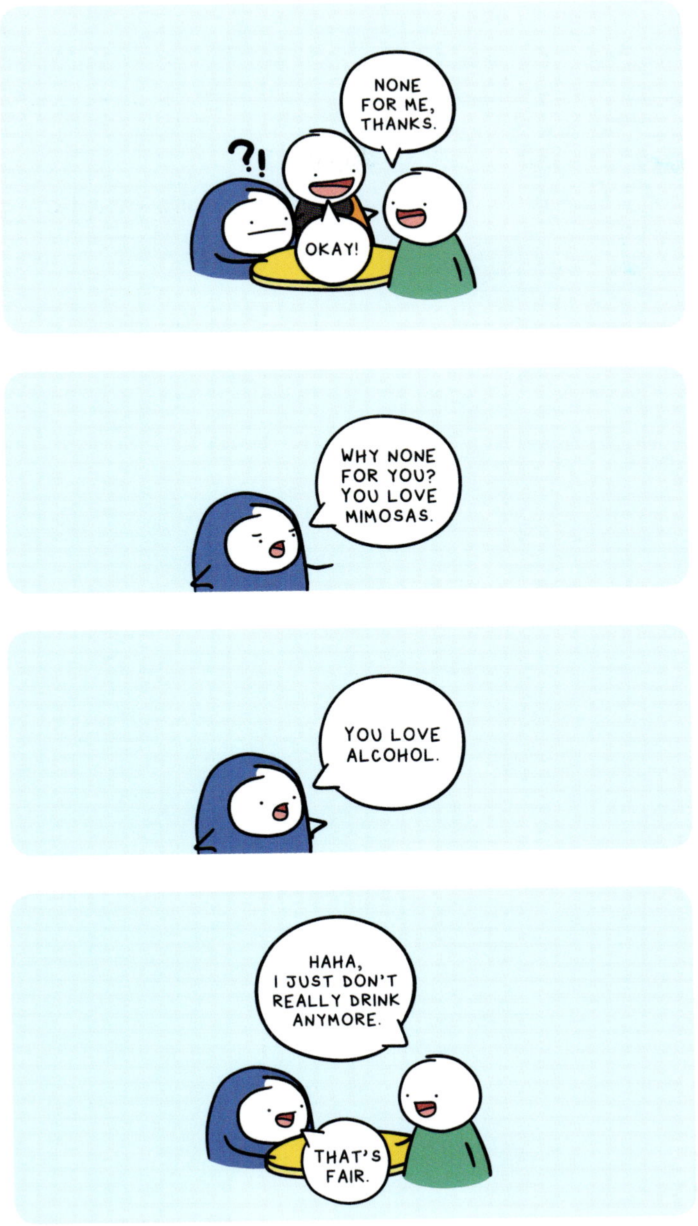
?!
NONE FOR ME, THANKS.
OKAY!
WHY NONE FOR YOU? YOU LOVE MIMOSAS.
YOU LOVE ALCOHOL.
HAHA, I JUST DON'T REALLY DRINK ANYMORE.
THAT'S FAIR.

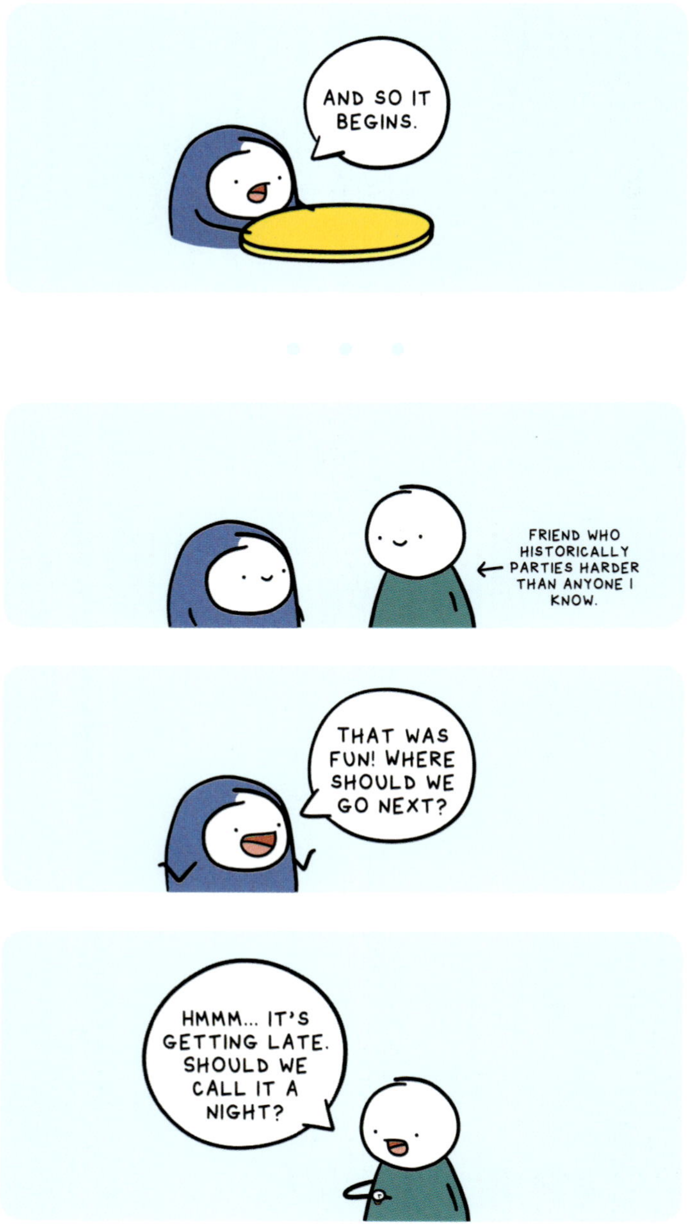
AND SO IT BEGINS.
FRIEND WHO HISTORICALLY PARTIES HARDER THAN ANYONE I KNOW.
THAT WAS FUN! WHERE SHOULD WE GO NEXT?
HMMM... IT'S GETTING LATE. SHOULD WE CALL IT A NIGHT?

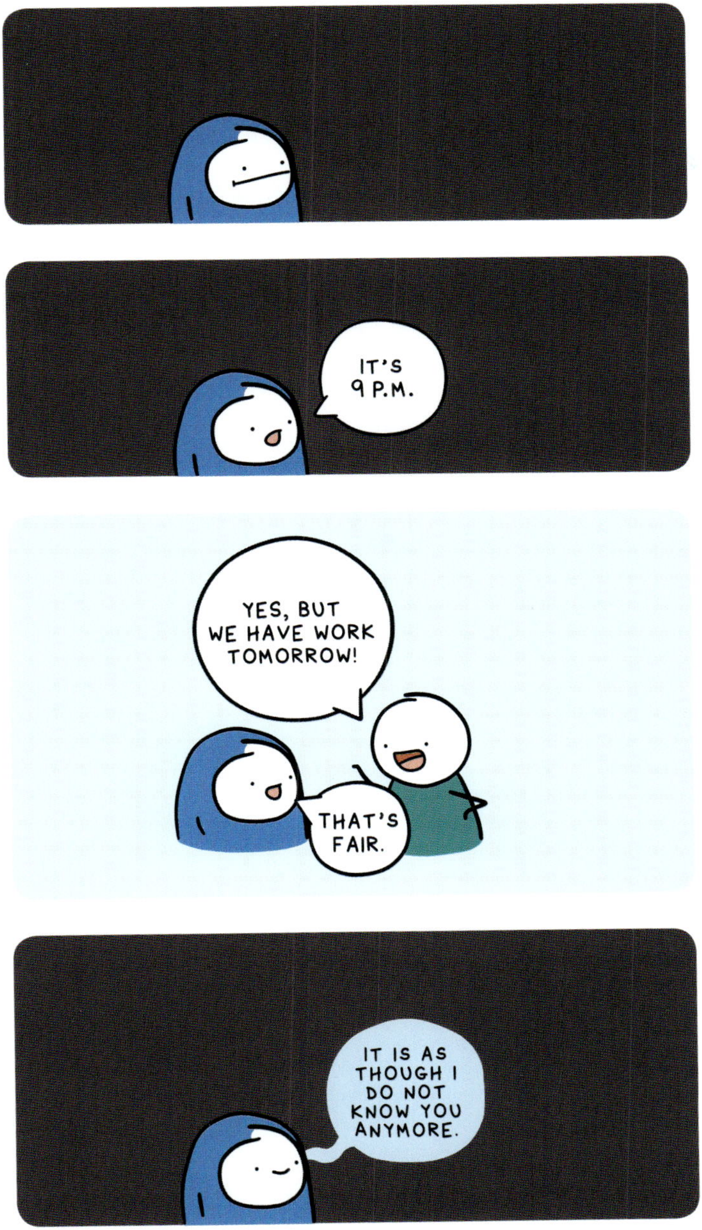
IT'S 9 P.M.
YES, BUT WE HAVE WORK TOMORROW!
THAT'S FAIR.
IT IS AS THOUGH I DO NOT KNOW YOU ANYMORE.

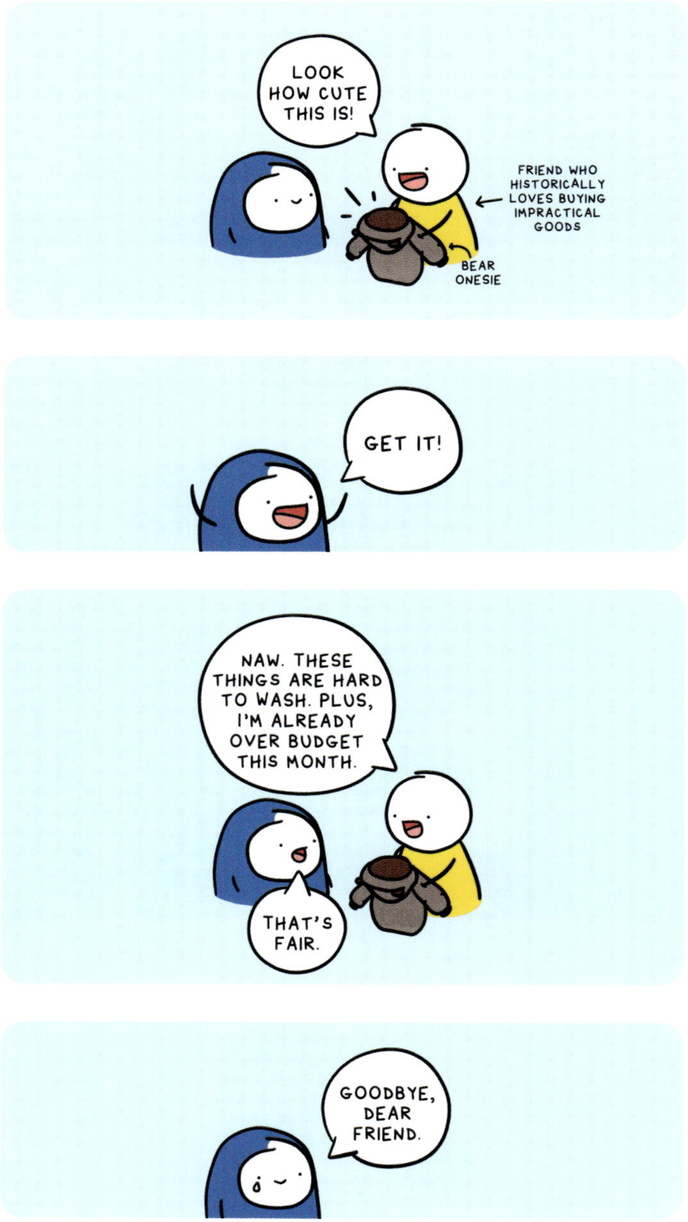
LOOK HOW CUTE THIS IS!
FRIEND WHO HISTORICALLY LOVES BUYING IMPRACTICAL GOODS
BEAR ONESIE
GET IT!
NAW. THESE THINGS ARE HARD TO WASH. PLUS, I'M ALREADY OVER BUDGET THIS MONTH.
THAT'S FAIR.
GOODBYE, DEAR FRIEND.

It was hard to watch.

One by one, my friends became unrecognizable monsters as they evolved from their beautiful, barely functional selves into deplorably responsible humans.

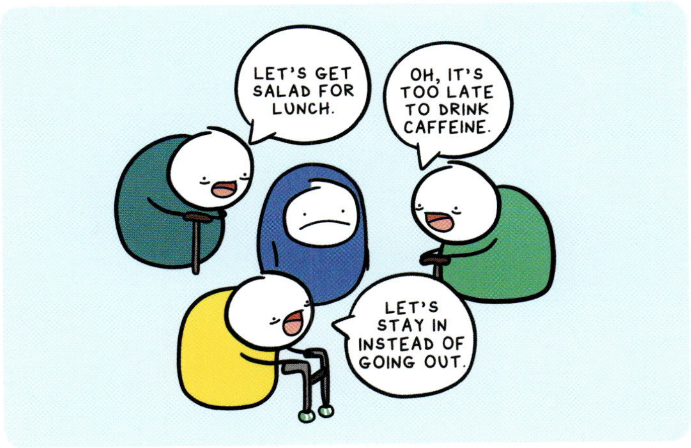
LET'S GET SALAD FOR LUNCH.
OH, IT'S TOO LATE TO DRINK CAFFEINE.
LET'S STAY IN INSTEAD OF GOING OUT.

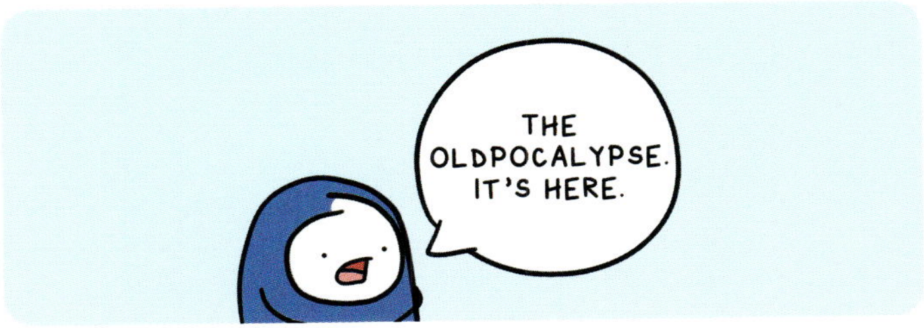
THE OLDPOCALYPSE. IT'S HERE.

I, on the other hand, had no intention of surrendering my youth. If my previously cool best friends wanted to be painfully sober, fiscally responsible, well-rested adults, that was fine.

To each their own.

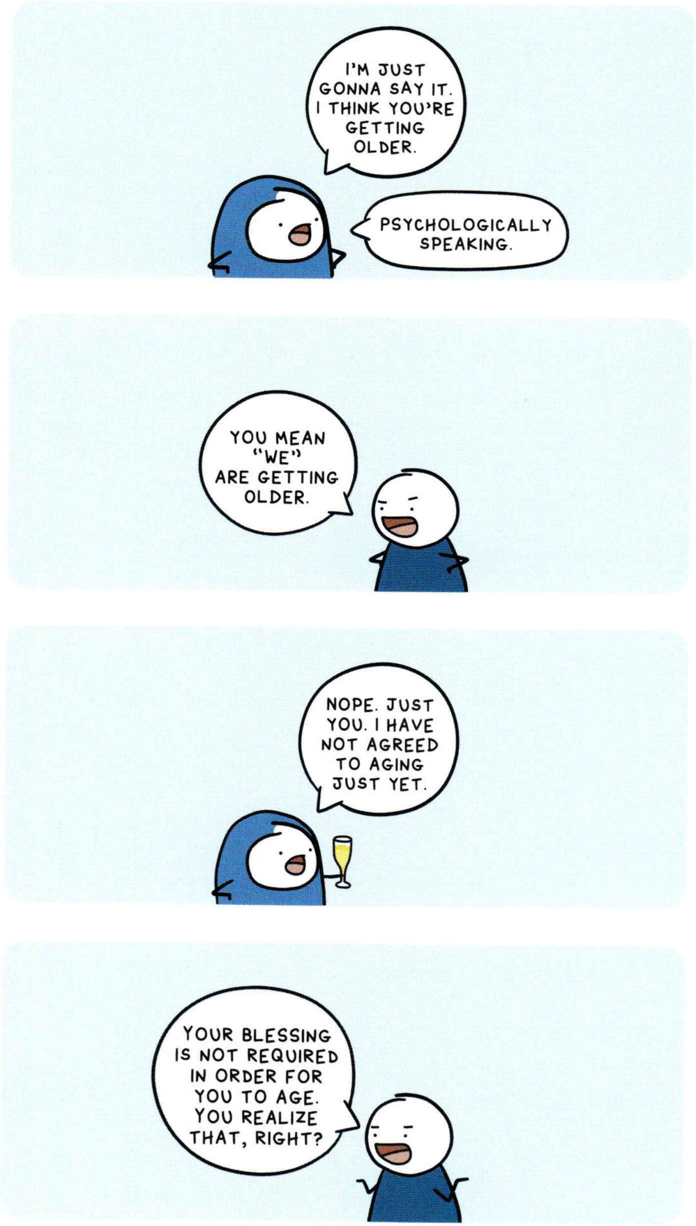
I'M JUST GONNA SAY IT. I THINK YOU'RE GETTING OLDER.
PSYCHOLOGICALLY SPEAKING.
YOU MEAN "WE" ARE GETTING OLDER.
NOPE. JUST YOU. I HAVE NOT AGREED TO AGING JUST YET.
YOUR BLESSING IS NOT REQUIRED IN ORDER FOR YOU TO AGE. YOU REALIZE THAT, RIGHT?

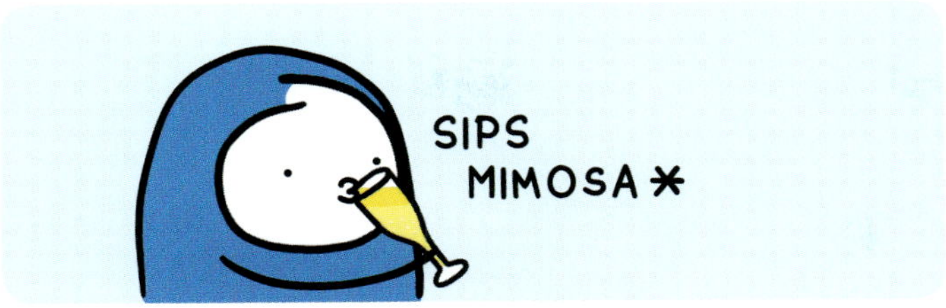
SIPS
MIMOSA *

Let's face it, my friends were bringing me down. Well, technically, they were raising me up, but I was a reluctant passenger on this spaceship to monotony. I wasn't ready to be steadily responsible, not yet at least. I *barely* had enough fun in the last decade of my life and was expecting at least a few more rounds of reckless adventures.

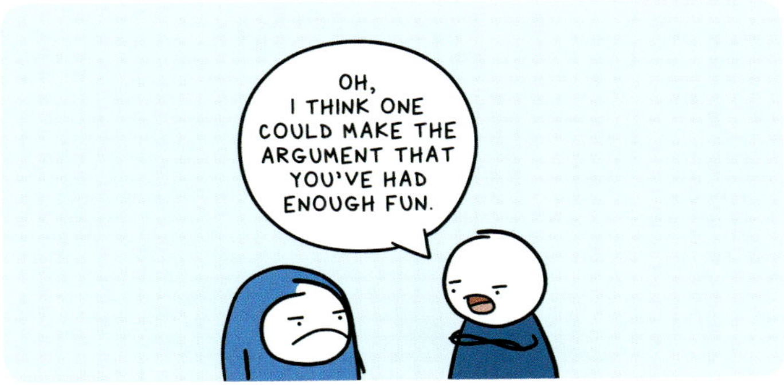
OH, I THINK ONE COULD MAKE THE ARGUMENT THAT YOU'VE HAD ENOUGH FUN.

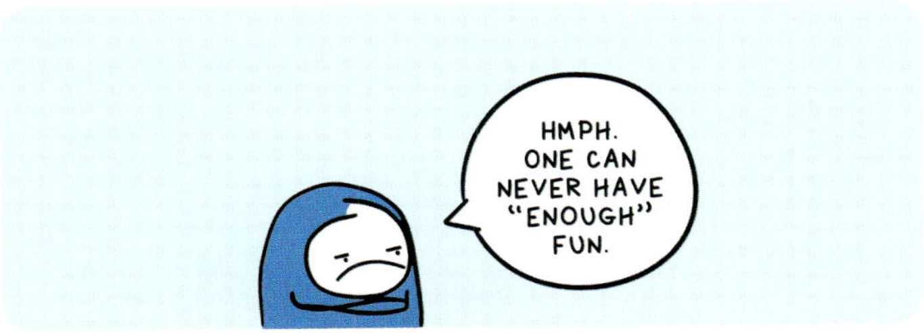
HMPH. ONE CAN NEVER HAVE "ENOUGH" FUN.

It was just too soon.

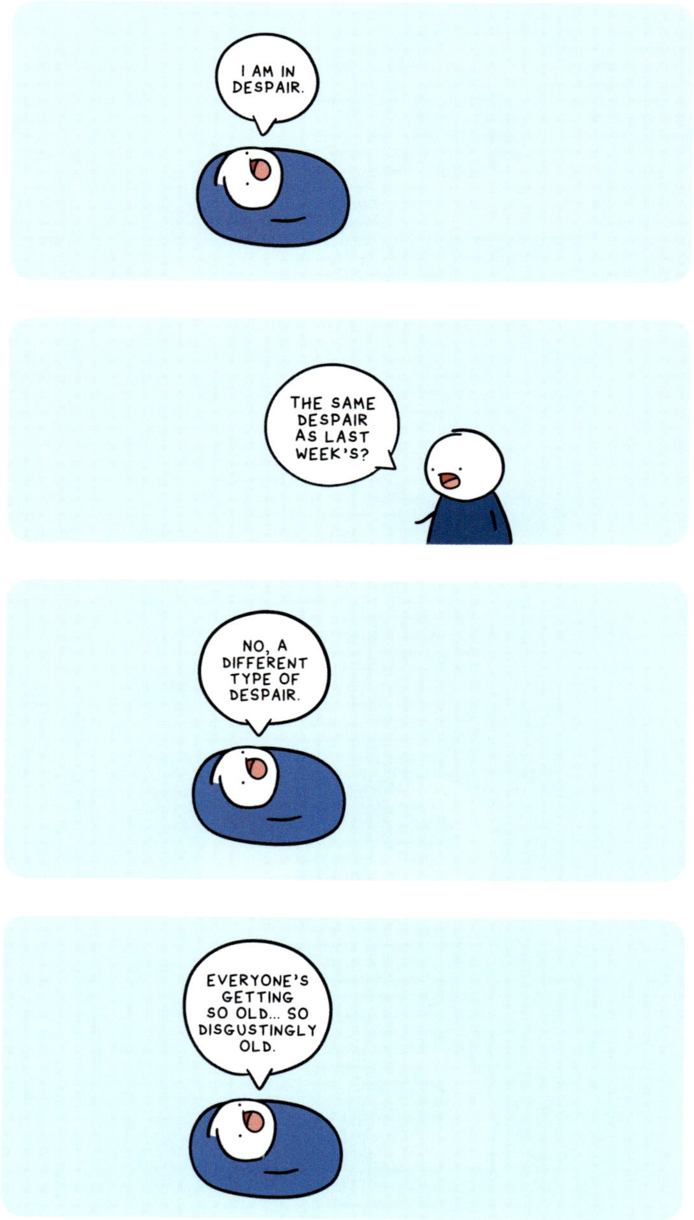
I AM IN DESPAIR.
THE SAME DESPAIR AS LAST WEEK'S?
NO, A DIFFERENT TYPE OF DESPAIR.
EVERYONE'S GETTING SO OLD... SO DISGUSTINGLY OLD.

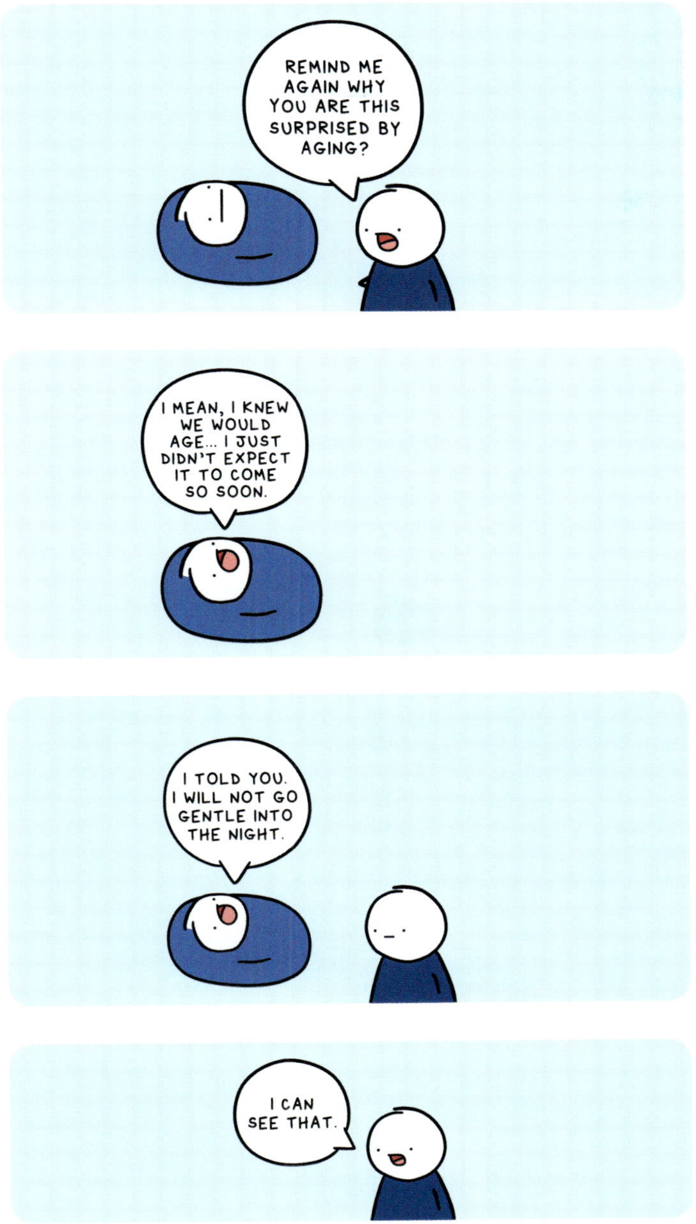
REMIND ME AGAIN WHY YOU ARE THIS SURPRISED BY AGING?
I MEAN, I KNEW WE WOULD AGE... I JUST DIDN'T EXPECT IT TO COME SO SOON.
I TOLD YOU. I WILL NOT GO GENTLE INTO THE NIGHT.
I CAN SEE THAT.

I tried my best to fight it, this inescapable eclipse of old age—this encroaching burden of rational thinking—but tragically, it wasn't long before I too started exhibiting symptoms.

Everywhere I went, I found myself in conversations that didn't feel quite like my own.

SHOPPING DAY!!!
WHAT SHOULD WE SHOP FOR?
OH, I NEED A NEW VACUUM!

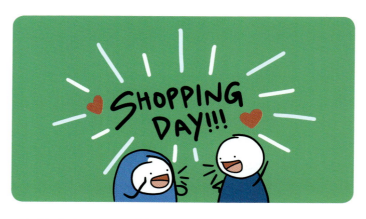

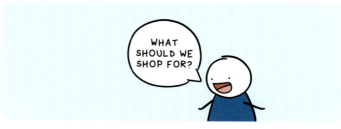

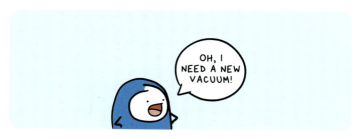

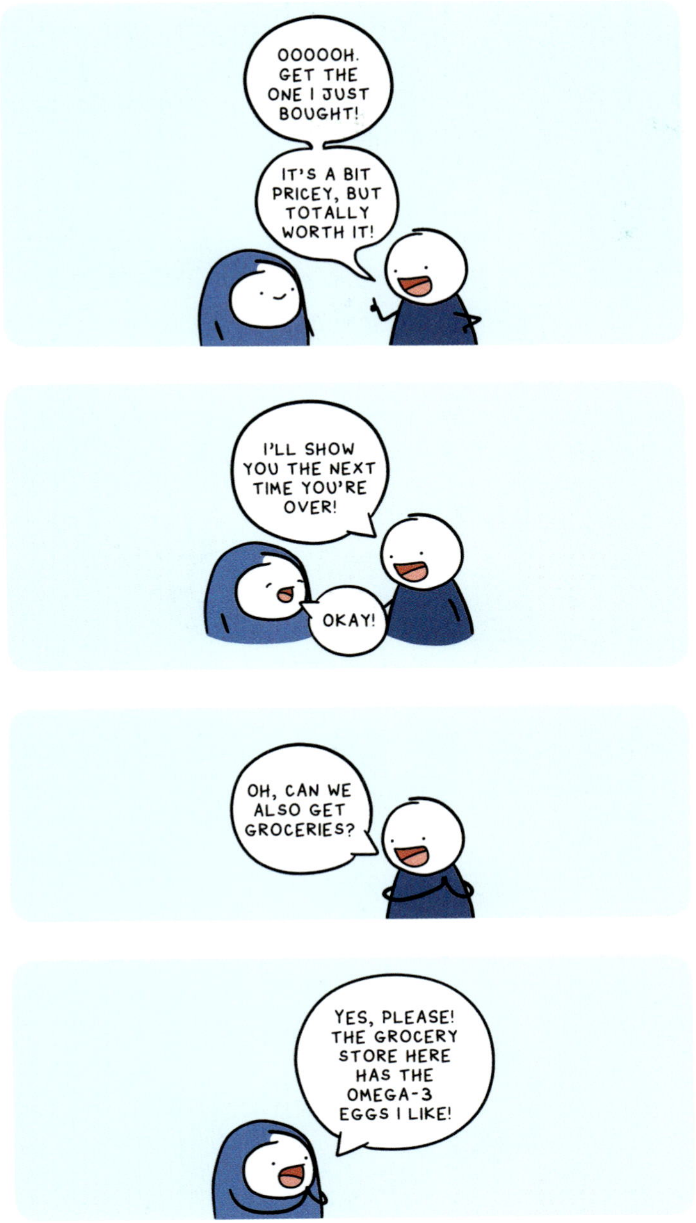
OOOOOH. GET THE ONE I JUST BOUGHT!
IT'S A BIT PRICEY, BUT TOTALLY WORTH IT!
I'LL SHOW YOU THE NEXT TIME YOU'RE OVER!
OKAY!
OH, CAN WE ALSO GET GROCERIES?
YES, PLEASE! THE GROCERY STORE HERE HAS THE OMEGA-3 EGGS I LIKE!

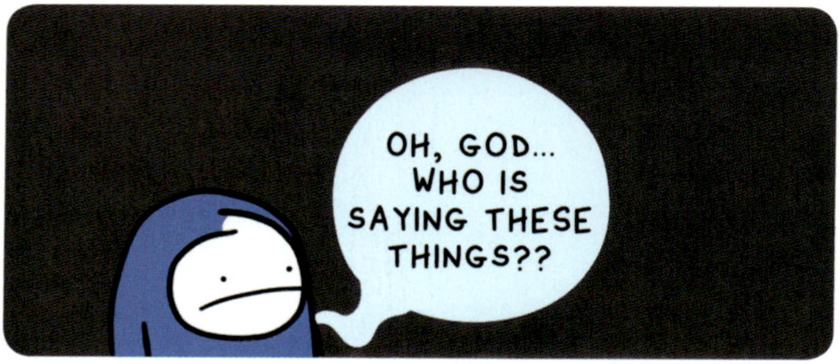
OH, GOD...
WHO IS
SAYING THESE
THINGS??

Surely it wasn't *I* who was saying these things. Surely it wasn't *I* who was meticulously comparing various vacuum models and grocery shopping with the same friends I used to stay out until all hours of the night with.

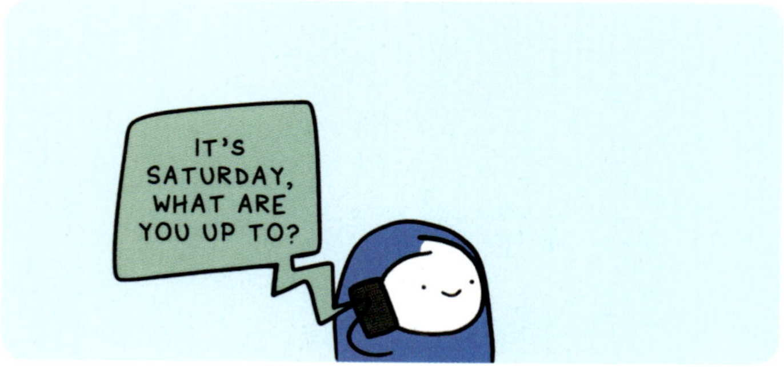
IT'S
SATURDAY,
WHAT ARE
YOU UP TO?

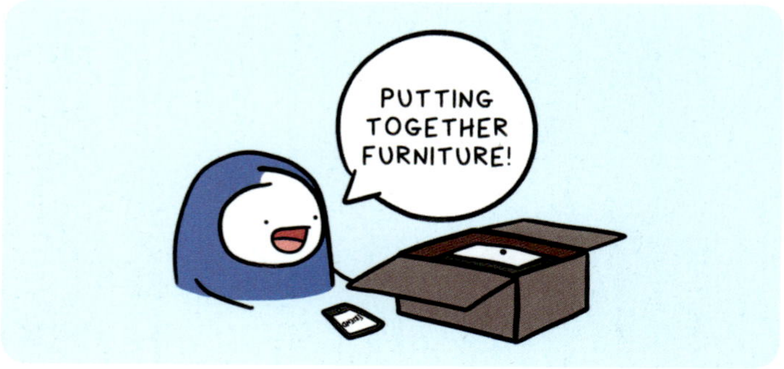
PUTTING
TOGETHER
FURNITURE!

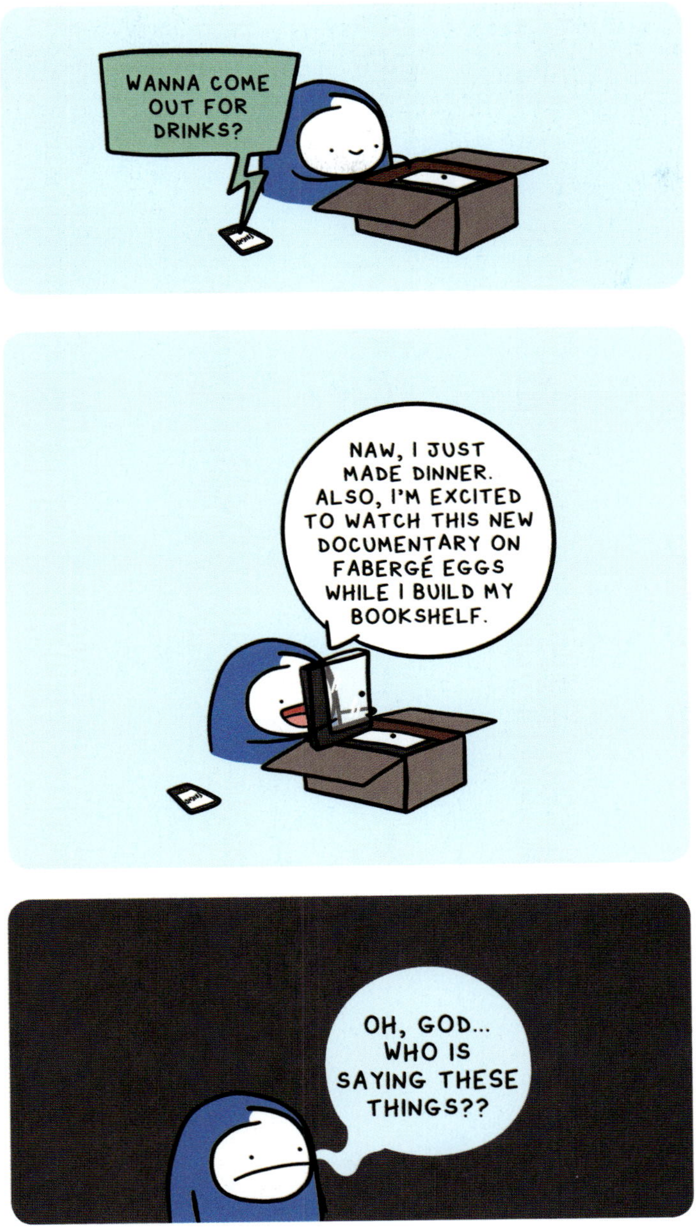
WANNA COME OUT FOR DRINKS?
NAW, I JUST MADE DINNER. ALSO, I'M EXCITED TO WATCH THIS NEW DOCUMENTARY ON FABERGÉ EGGS WHILE I BUILD MY BOOKSHELF.
OH, GOD... WHO IS SAYING THESE THINGS??

But it *was* me. Those *were* my thoughts. And true devastation was in how much I actually enjoyed that Fabergé documentary.

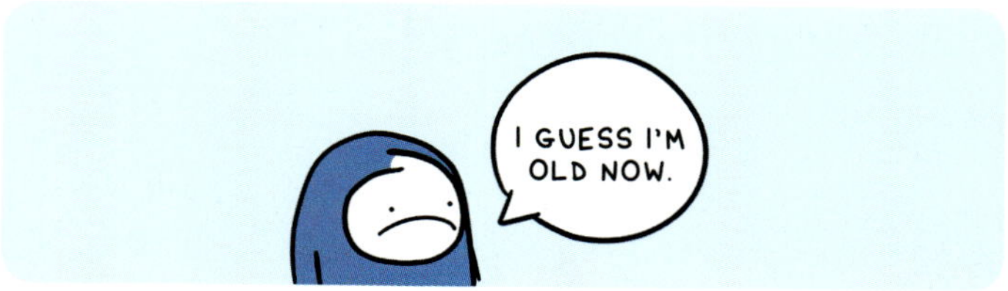
I GUESS I'M OLD NOW.

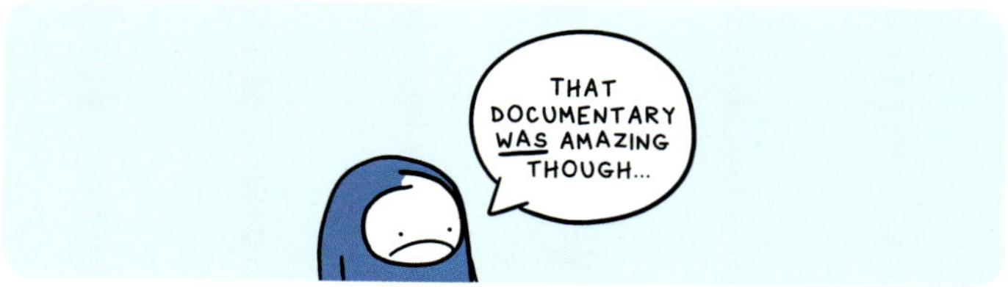
THAT DOCUMENTARY WAS AMAZING THOUGH...

My friend's wretched prophecy was coming true.

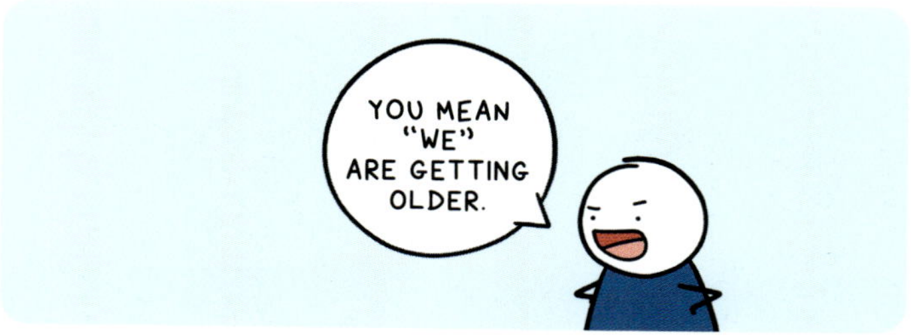
YOU MEAN "WE" ARE GETTING OLDER.

*Stupid* friend.

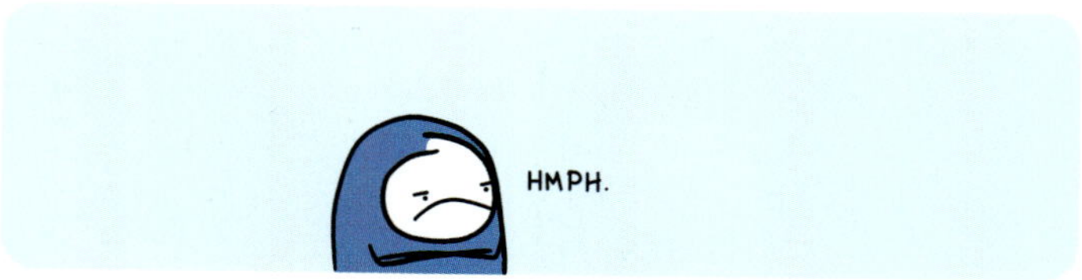
HMPH.

As my thoughts rewired without my blessing, I found my decisions becoming increasingly sound and conscientious each day. It was as though I were a hostage on a bullet train, and every time I looked outside, we were already in a different phase of life.

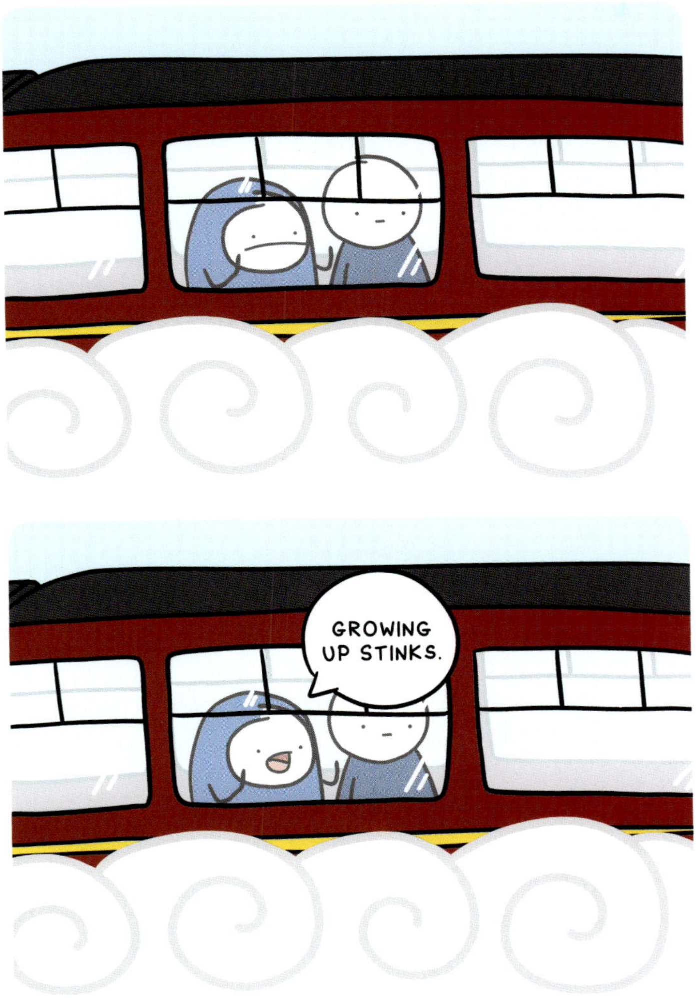
GROWING UP STINKS.

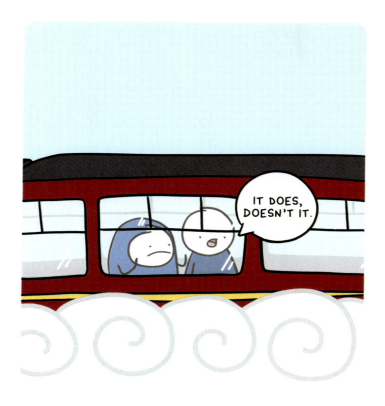

*Am I boring now? Am I old? Should I buy two of these meticulously carved, hand-painted tree ornaments?*

These questions loomed over my thoughts as I fluttered my fingers across the wall of Christmas trinkets dangling before me. My friends and I had specifically met up on this occasion with the singular mission to shop for decorative holiday knickknacks and trinkets together. It wasn't even Christmas—we were just *that* prepared.

Part of me recognized this moment as a new low.

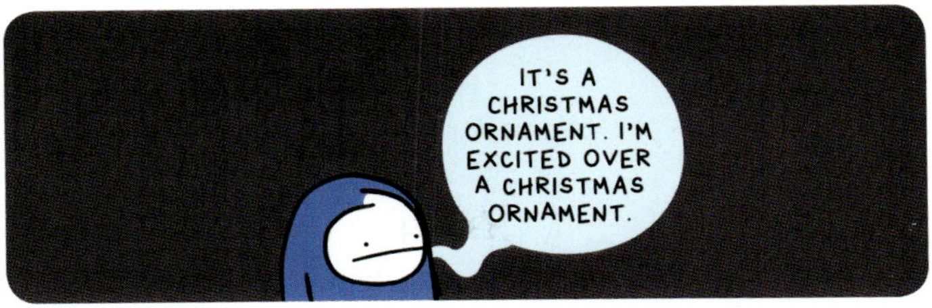
IT'S A CHRISTMAS ORNAMENT. I'M EXCITED OVER A CHRISTMAS ORNAMENT.

But a bigger part of me reveled in this new high.

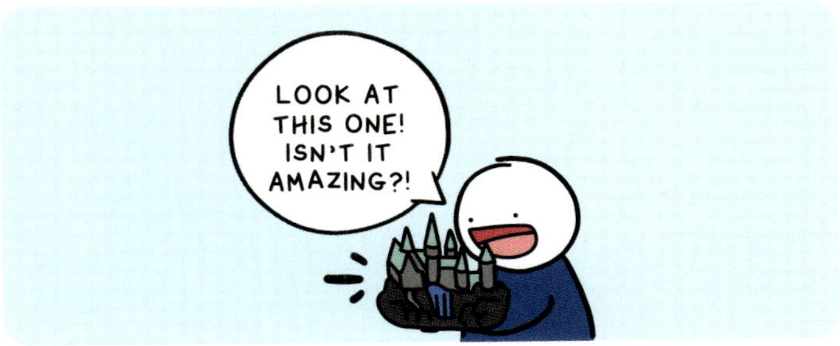
LOOK AT THIS ONE! ISN'T IT AMAZING?!

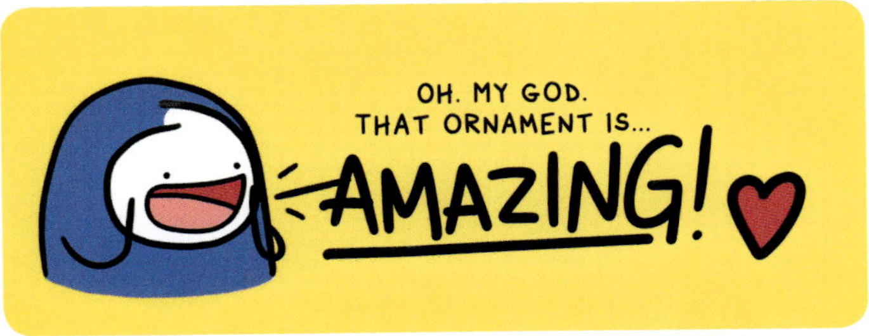
OH. MY GOD. THAT ORNAMENT IS...
AMAZING!

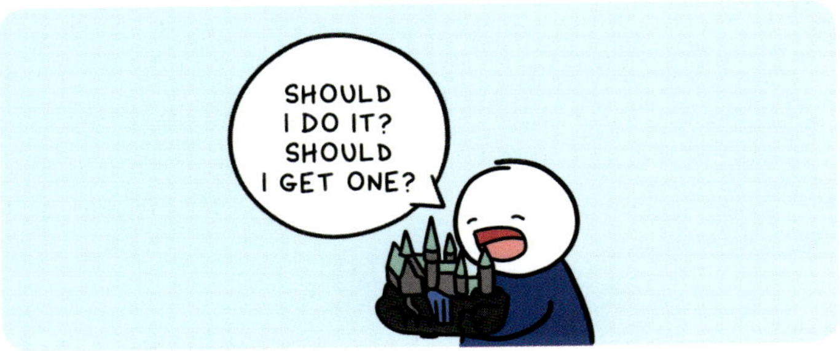
SHOULD I DO IT? SHOULD I GET ONE?

BUY. IT.
BUY IT ALL!
I SAY!!!

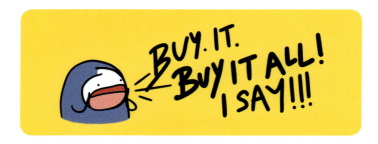

It was not lost on me that we were marveling at the same objects as seniors in the store, just with significantly less grace and decorum. And if it had just been the Christmas ornaments, I wouldn't have been that concerned. But I had a disturbing change of heart in other things as well. Music in public spaces suddenly started feeling too loud too often.

IS IT JUST ME, OR IS THE MUSIC TOO LOUD HERE?

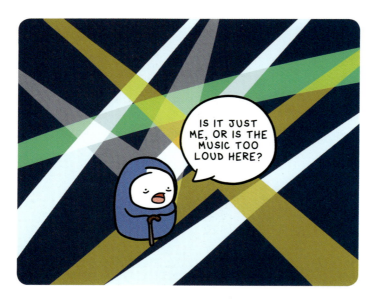

Youth and pop culture became an enigma.

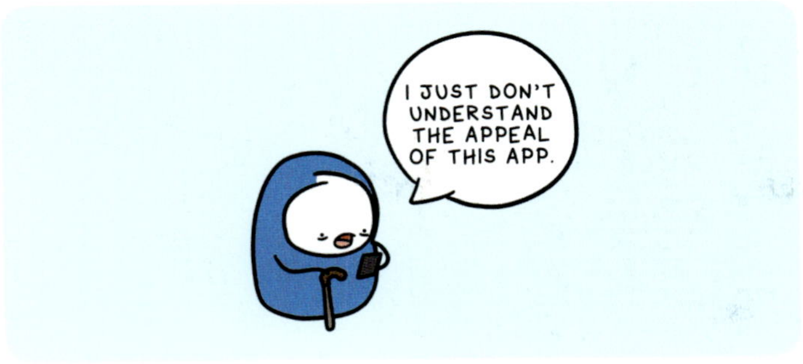
I JUST DON'T UNDERSTAND THE APPEAL OF THIS APP.

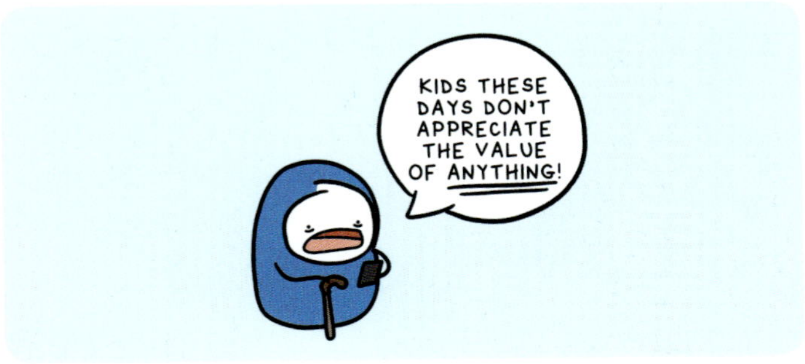
KIDS THESE DAYS DON'T APPRECIATE THE VALUE OF ANYTHING!

Tasteful furniture purchases became personal treats, and decorating my home with trees and plants brought me an unsettling level of joy. I stopped knowing what was "in" because all I did was stay in, even when I was spending time with my friends.

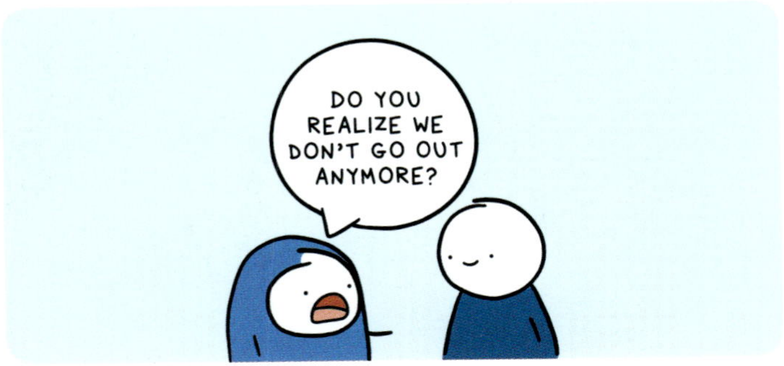
DO YOU REALIZE WE DON'T GO OUT ANYMORE?

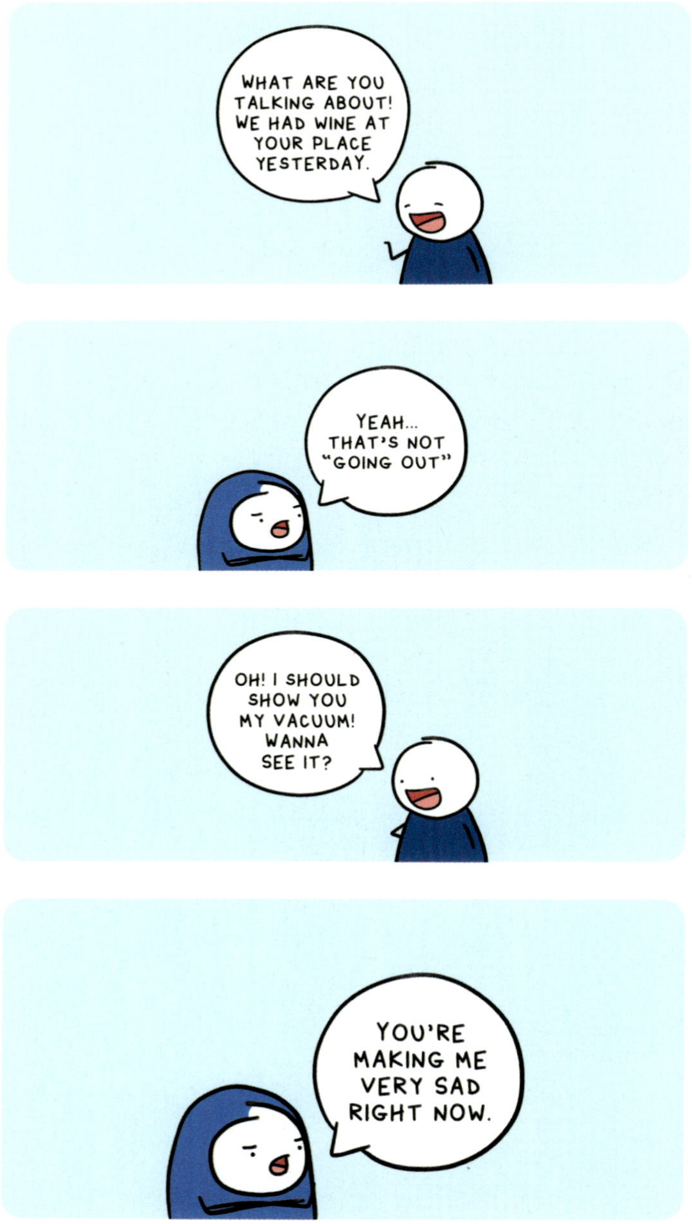
WHAT ARE YOU TALKING ABOUT! WE HAD WINE AT YOUR PLACE YESTERDAY.
YEAH... THAT'S NOT "GOING OUT"
OH! I SHOULD SHOW YOU MY VACUUM! WANNA SEE IT?
YOU'RE MAKING ME VERY SAD RIGHT NOW.

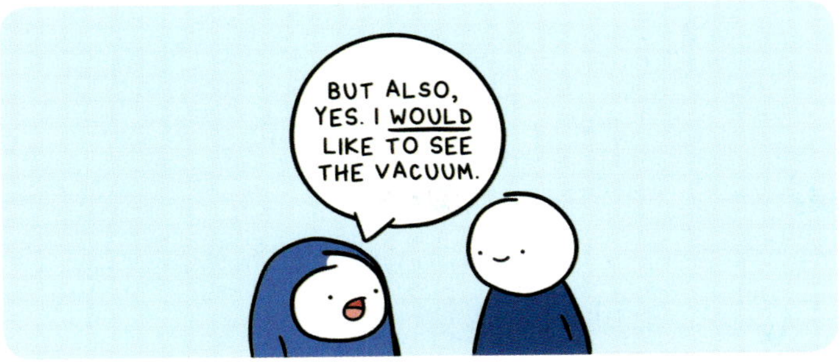
BUT ALSO, YES. I WOULD LIKE TO SEE THE VACUUM.

The worst part was that I actually *liked* it. I liked these frumpy interests that I had previously deemed mundane and elderly. I *liked* staying in, I *liked* being well-rested, and it grew increasingly difficult to find things that were worth staying up for.

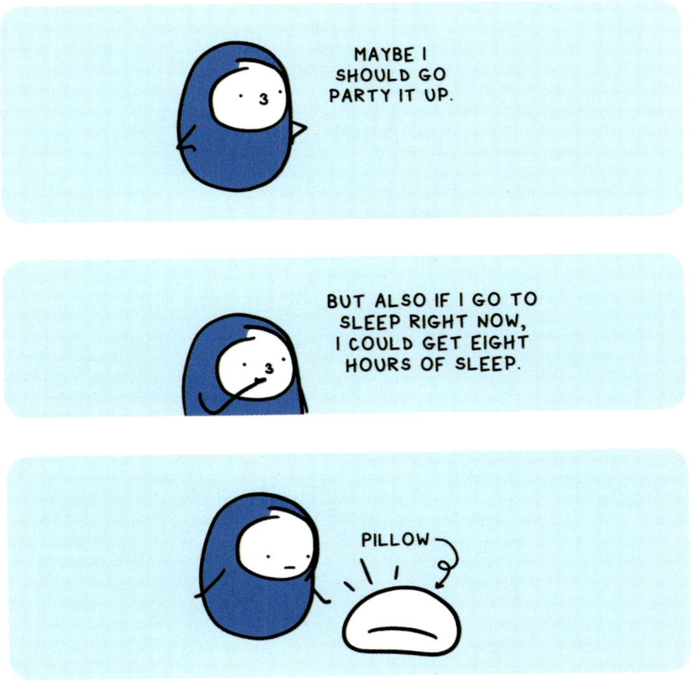
MAYBE I SHOULD GO PARTY IT UP.
BUT ALSO IF I GO TO SLEEP RIGHT NOW, I COULD GET EIGHT HOURS OF SLEEP.
PILLOW

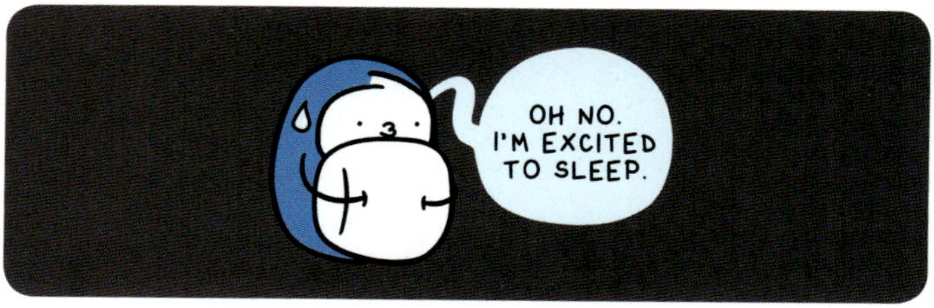
OH NO.
I'M EXCITED
TO SLEEP.

What was especially disturbing was that while I still had the memories of my younger, less responsible self, there was simultaneously this budding voice of wisdom that always seemed to know a *tiny* bit better.

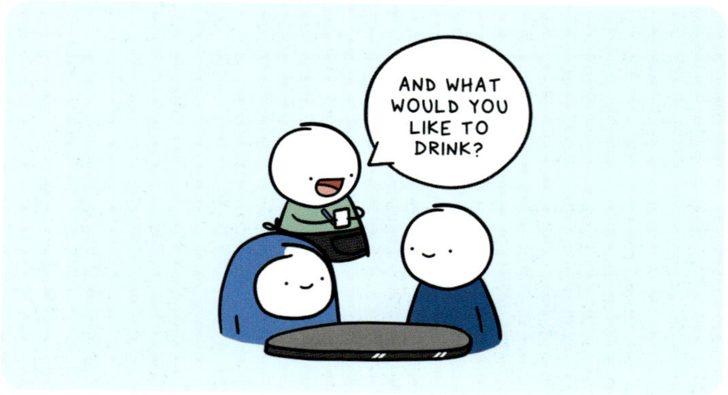
AND WHAT
WOULD YOU
LIKE TO
DRINK?

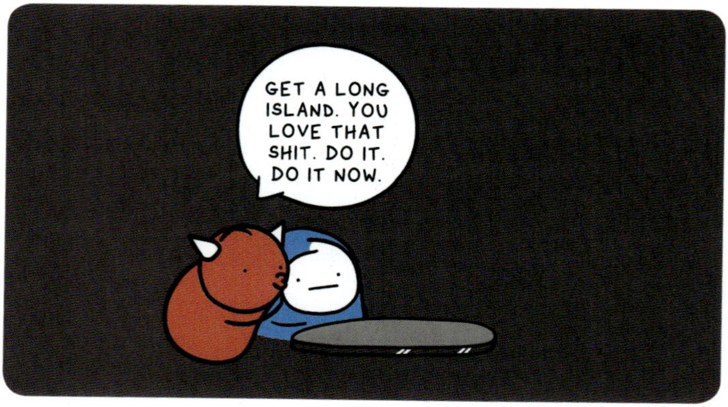
GET A LONG
ISLAND. YOU
LOVE THAT
SHIT. DO IT.
DO IT NOW.

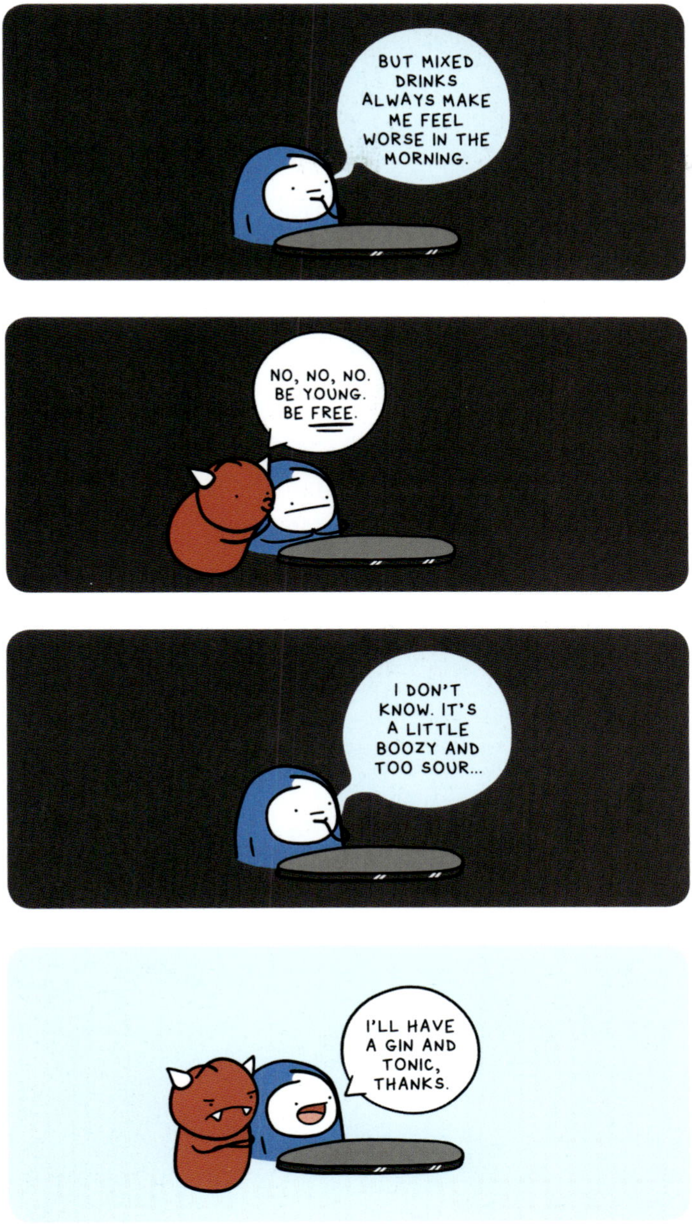
BUT MIXED DRINKS ALWAYS MAKE ME FEEL WORSE IN THE MORNING.
NO, NO, NO. BE YOUNG. BE FREE.
I DON'T KNOW. IT'S A LITTLE BOOZY AND TOO SOUR...
I'LL HAVE A GIN AND TONIC, THANKS.

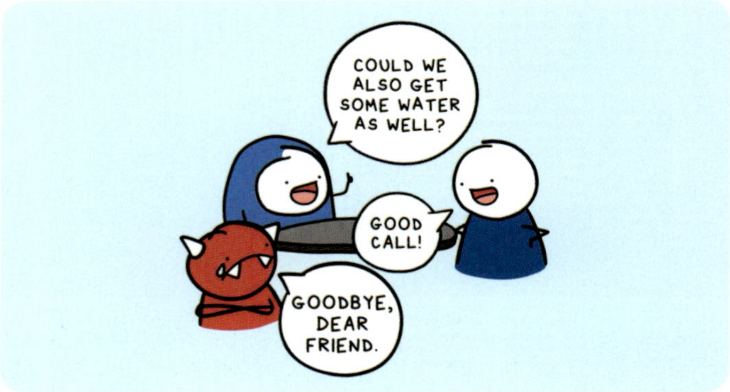
COULD WE ALSO GET SOME WATER AS WELL?
GOOD CALL!
GOODBYE, DEAR FRIEND.

Thinking about how old you are is like opening up a can of psychological glitter: it doesn't really bother you until you start mucking around in it. But once you open that thought, once you grab a fistful of sparkling dust and scatter it in the atmos, that anxiety is in your lung cavities forever—it's here to stay.

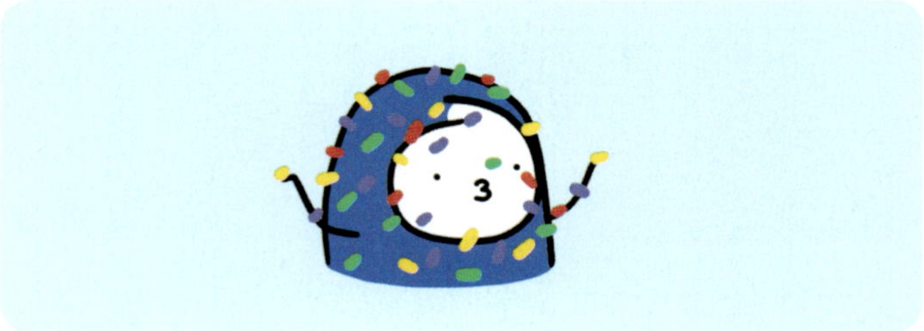

*Oh God, am I old now? Is that why everything is changing? Is that a wrinkle?*

These thoughts ran circuits around my head as I stood brushing my teeth in front of the bathroom mirror. Self-reflection—*what a wild ride.*

BRUSH
BRUSH

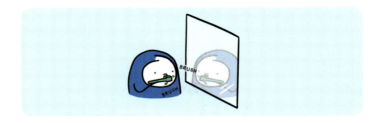

Sure, it *does* take me a lot longer to recover from a night out, and I *did* find an unverified wrinkle the other day, but I didn't know that it meant that I was old, I just assumed it meant I was not young. I wasn't so much bothered by the fact that I was aging, I was simply bothered by the fact that I didn't know how to feel about it.

I FEEL LIKE WE'RE IN THIS WEIRD AGE WHERE WE'RE NOT YOUNG, BUT ALSO NOT OLD.

LIKE IT'S INSENSITIVE TO CLAIM WE'RE OLD, BUT ALSO INACCURATE TO CLAIM TO BE YOUNG.
RIGHT, IT'S LIKE WE'RE IN AN IN-BETWEEN STATE.

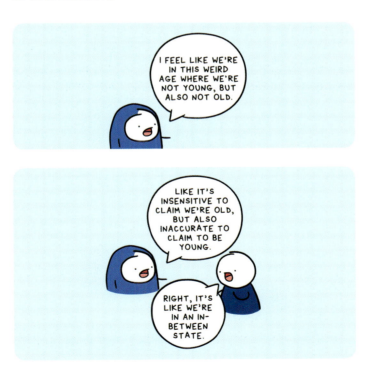

EXACTLY. WE'RE IN AGE LIMBO.

In an effort to better understand how I felt about being in *Age Limbo*—this period of not old and not young—I looked back at the past decade of my life to see what had transpired. Turns out, a lot had changed. Friends, jobs, loves, homes . . . everything had shuffled around substantially. My life looked nothing like it did a mere decade ago.

In the rearview mirror I saw all the things I knew before I knew better. My friends aren't the reckless human beings they were when we first met, but perhaps neither was I. Maybe somewhere along the way, we all got suckered into growing up.

DO YOU REALIZE OUR FAVORITE BAR FROM COLLEGE IS NOW CLOSED?

PROBABLY BECAUSE IT WAS A SHITTY DIVE BAR.

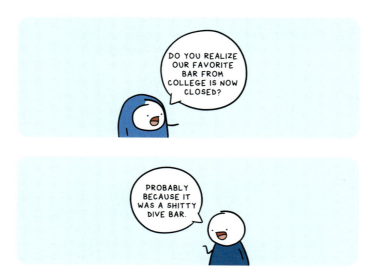

YES, BUT IT STRANGELY NEVER FELT SHITTY BACK THEN, YOU KNOW?
YEAH, I GUESS WE HAVE STANDARDS NOW.
EXCEPT I STILL DON'T HAVE STANDARDS THOUGH.

The more I thought about it, the more it made sense. It made sense that we stay in more because we live in nicer homes now. It made sense that we do mundane things like grocery shopping because that's how you get to bask in the glory of a fully stocked fridge. And for the most part, we eat healthier, sleep earlier, and take better care of ourselves because—simply put—*it's nice to not have to feel like shit.*

And then I thought about the other side of it all—the perks of being older—the ability to travel, the freedom to do all the things we've always wanted to do but never could, and the wisdom to understand and appreciate everything just a tiny bit more.

It almost made me wonder if growing (just a little bit) older isn't all that bad.

• • •

I have since suspended my despair when it comes to getting older—at least, for now. Don't get me wrong, I still dry heave from thinking about it every now and then, but for the most part, it's under control. And in my *graceful* embrace of the Oldpocalypse, I take comfort in knowing one thing in particular—that our prerogative to do wonderful and stupid things will always be there no matter how old we get.

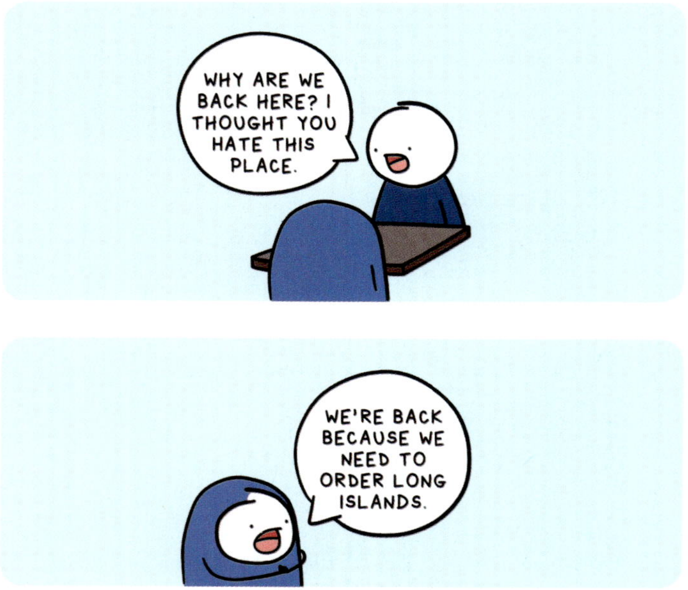
WHY ARE WE BACK HERE? I THOUGHT YOU HATE THIS PLACE.
WE'RE BACK BECAUSE WE NEED TO ORDER LONG ISLANDS.

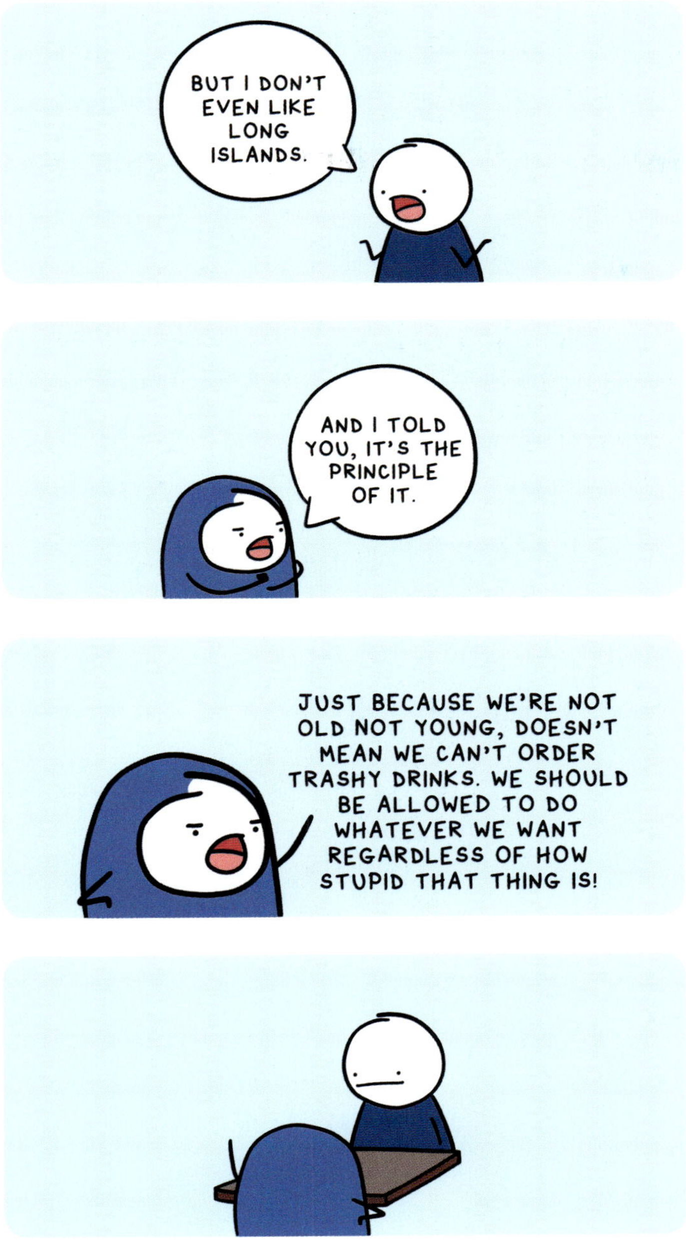
BUT I DON'T EVEN LIKE LONG ISLANDS.
AND I TOLD YOU, IT'S THE PRINCIPLE OF IT.
JUST BECAUSE WE'RE NOT OLD NOT YOUNG, DOESN'T MEAN WE CAN'T ORDER TRASHY DRINKS. WE SHOULD BE ALLOWED TO DO WHATEVER WE WANT REGARDLESS OF HOW STUPID THAT THING IS!

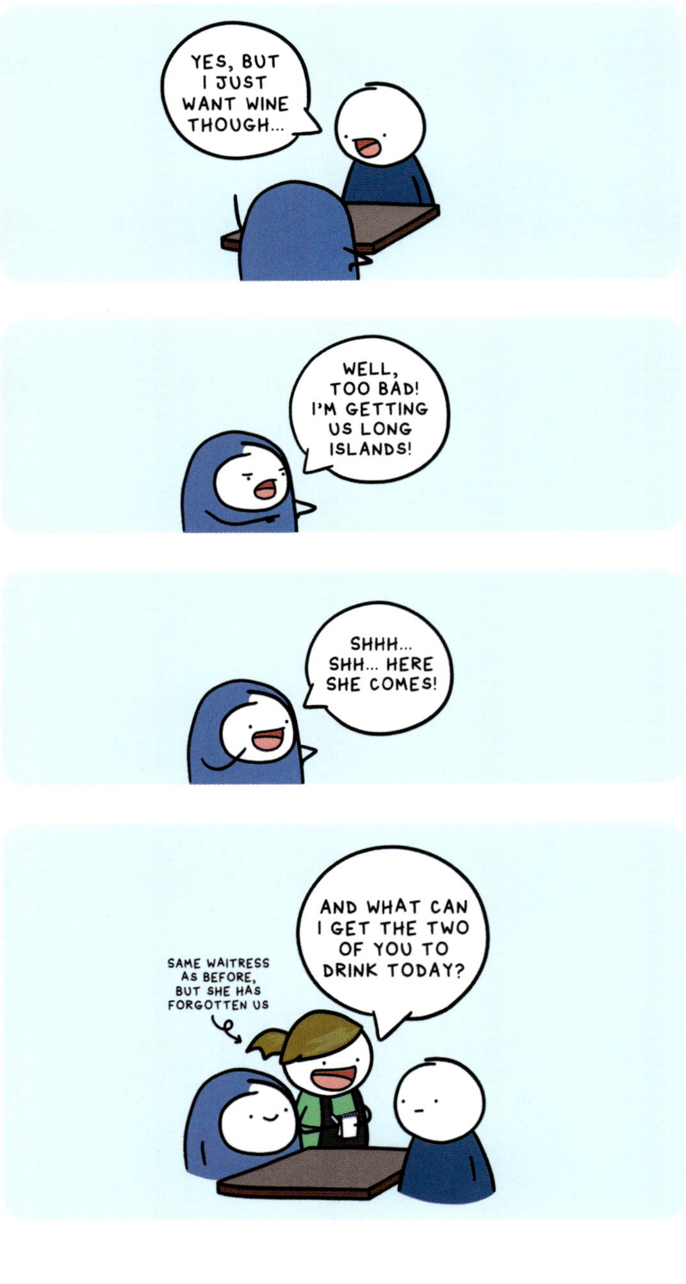
YES, BUT I JUST WANT WINE THOUGH...
WELL, TOO BAD! I'M GETTING US LONG ISLANDS!
SHHH... SHH... HERE SHE COMES!
SAME WAITRESS AS BEFORE, BUT SHE HAS FORGOTTEN US
AND WHAT CAN I GET THE TWO OF YOU TO DRINK TODAY?

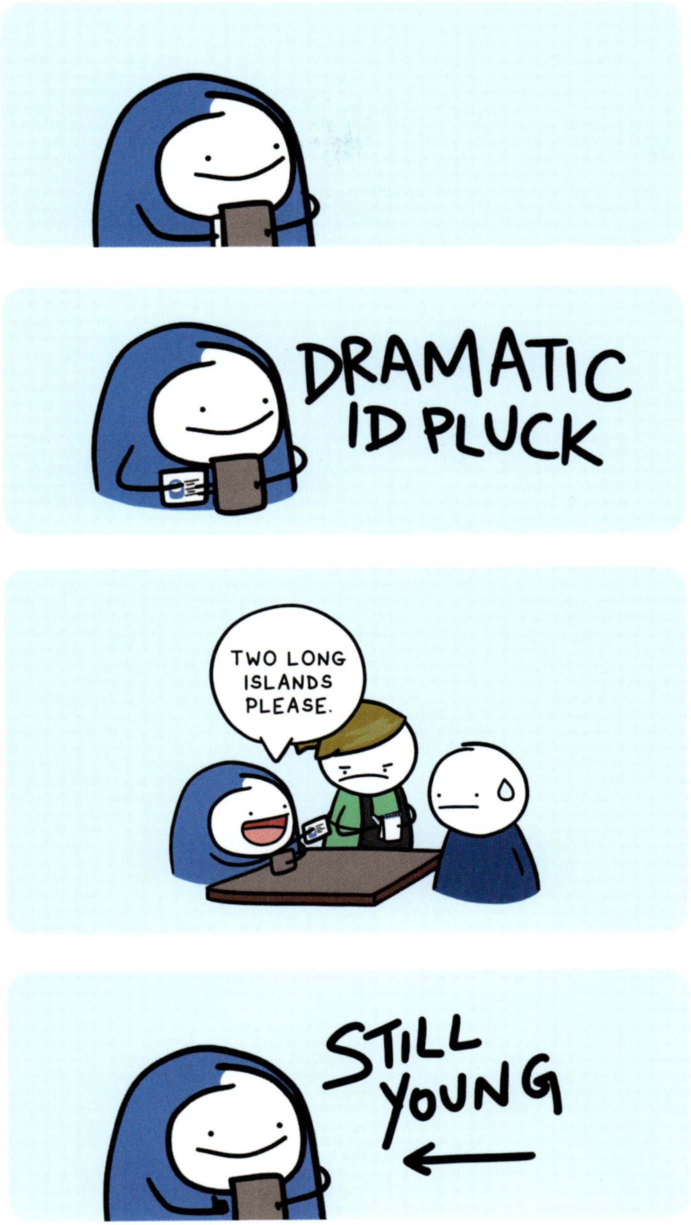
DRAMATIC ID PLUCK
TWO LONG ISLANDS PLEASE.
STILL YOUNG

# CHAPTER 8

# THE GRASS ON THE OTHER SIDE

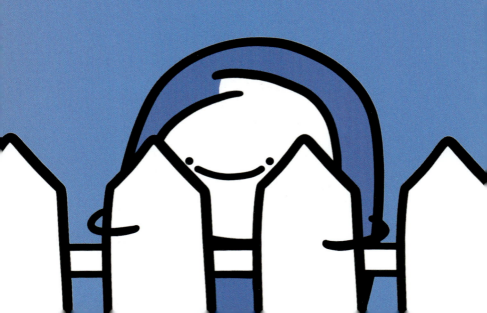

"I'm telling you guys, it's going to be worth it!" my uncle shouted with glee from the top of the pebbled slope he had just scampered up. Even from the bottom of the hill, I could see the fervent glint in his eyes as he eagerly waved for us to follow.

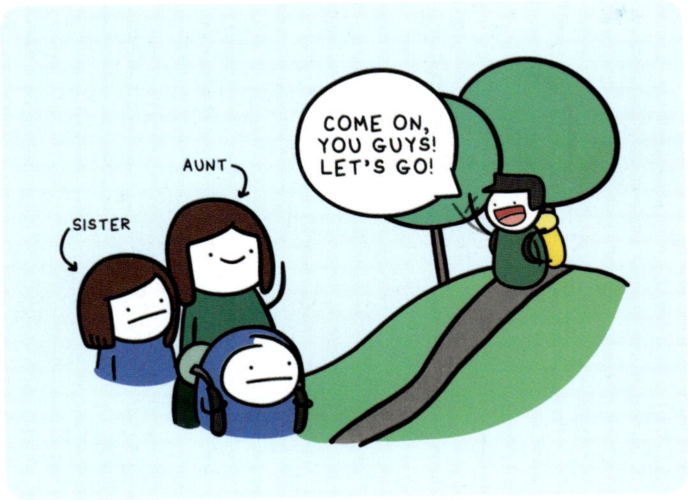
COME ON, YOU GUYS! LET'S GO!
AUNT
SISTER

It was a balmy October morning, and my uncle had somehow managed to trick us into yet another hiking trip. The bold expedition had been pitched to us as something that would later become the "highlight of our trip," but I had my doubts.

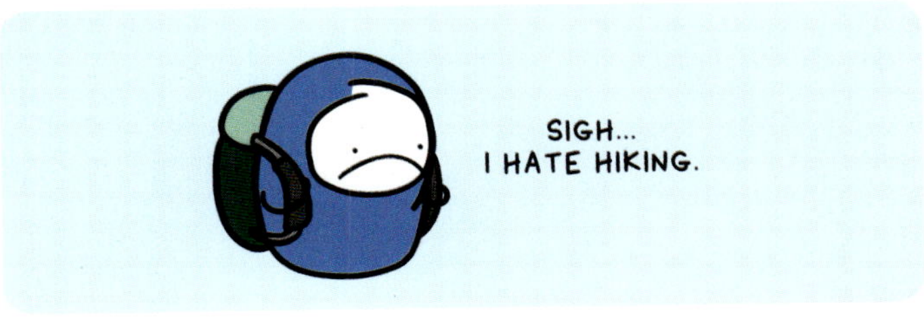
SIGH...
I HATE HIKING.

BUT SOMEHOW I AM ALWAYS HIKING.

HOW AM I CONSTANTLY TRICKED INTO HIKING?

"So . . . where are we going, exactly?" I asked my uncle as we plodded up the hill.

"We're following the trail on this map so that we can get to the peak!"

"What's at the peak?"

"Exquisite beauty," he whispered dramatically with barely contained delight.

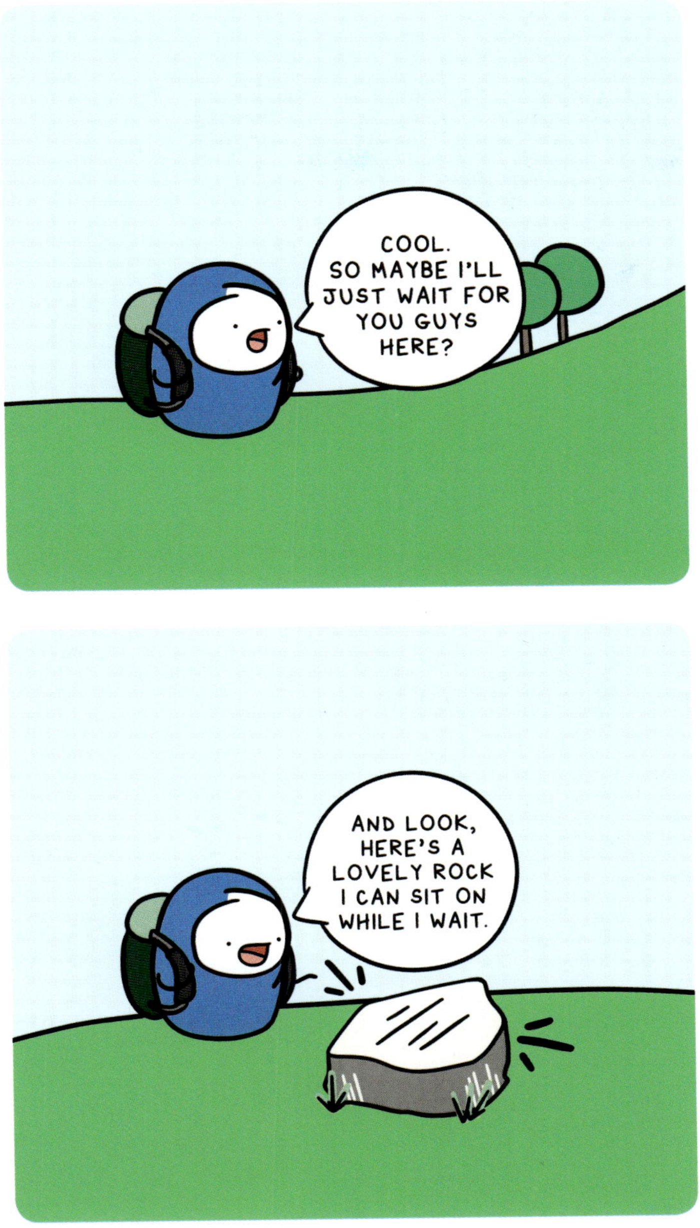
COOL. SO MAYBE I'LL JUST WAIT FOR YOU GUYS HERE?
AND LOOK, HERE'S A LOVELY ROCK I CAN SIT ON WHILE I WAIT.

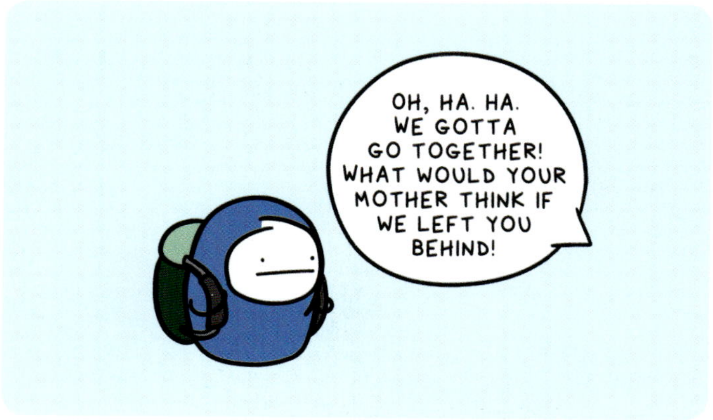
OH, HA. HA. WE GOTTA GO TOGETHER! WHAT WOULD YOUR MOTHER THINK IF WE LEFT YOU BEHIND!

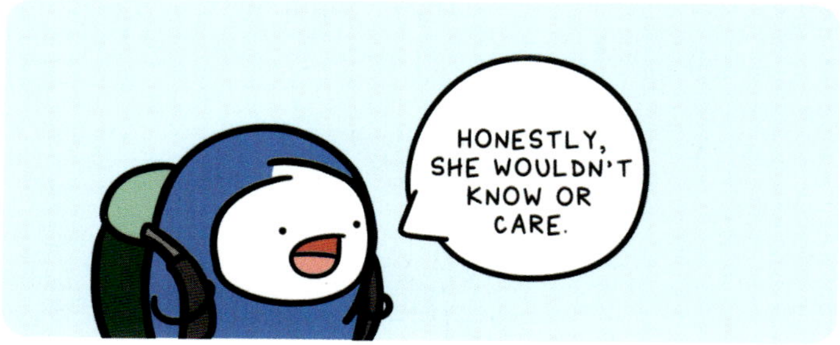
HONESTLY, SHE WOULDN'T KNOW OR CARE.

Four and a half grueling hours of hiking later, we were finally there.

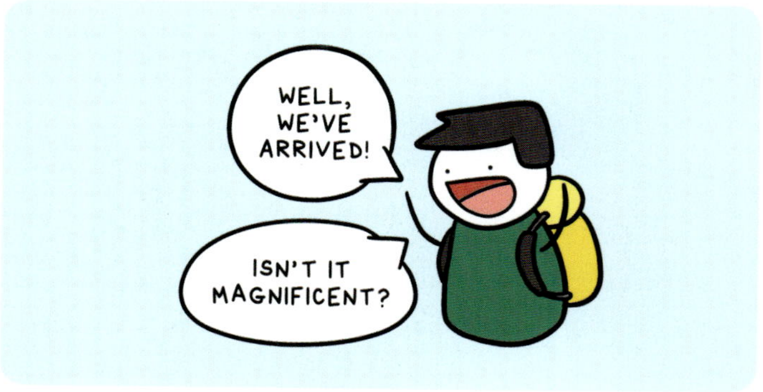
WELL, WE'VE ARRIVED!
ISN'T IT MAGNIFICENT?

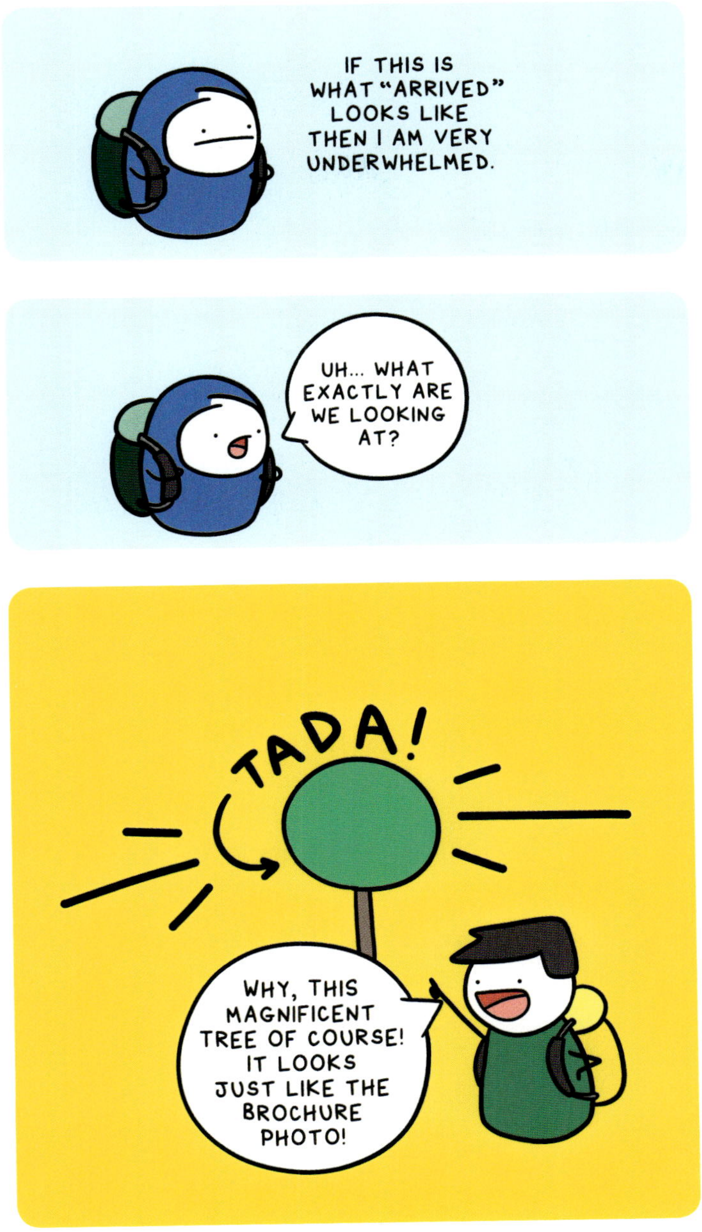
IF THIS IS WHAT "ARRIVED" LOOKS LIKE THEN I AM VERY UNDERWHELMED.
UH... WHAT EXACTLY ARE WE LOOKING AT?
TADA!
WHY, THIS MAGNIFICENT TREE OF COURSE! IT LOOKS JUST LIKE THE BROCHURE PHOTO!

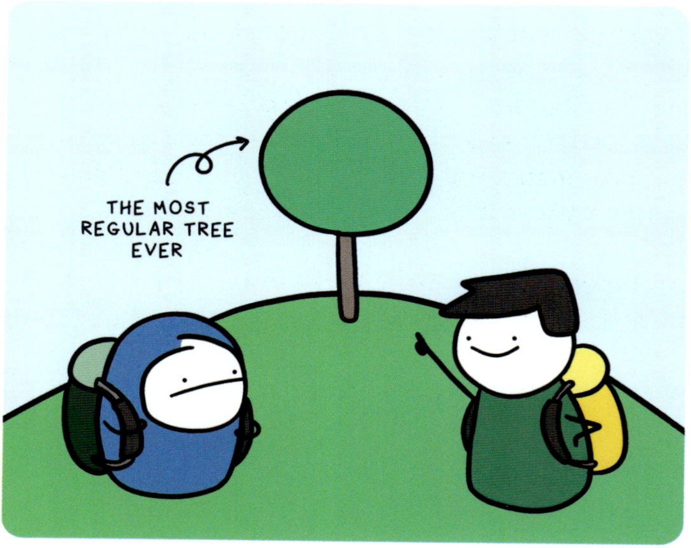
THE MOST
REGULAR TREE
EVER

For context, I am someone who *loves* trees. Trees are majestic beings—nature's historians who silently safeguard the riddles of our universe. But this tree before me, this tree I had just hiked *four and a half hours* for, was indisputably the same as the hundreds of trees we had just marched past.

"Isn't it just magnificent?" my uncle repeated.

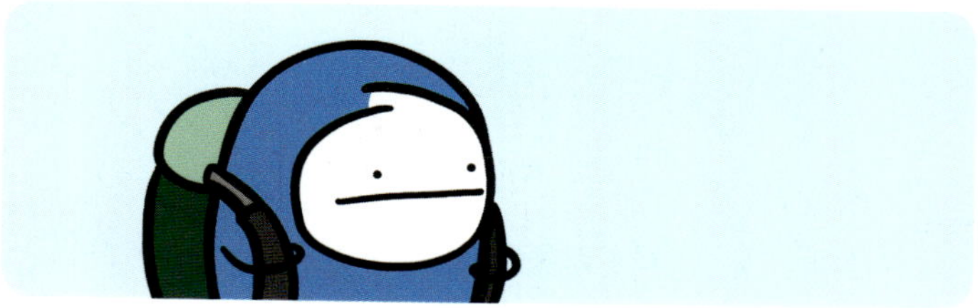

I reminded myself how unbecoming it would be to strike my elders.

Standing next to this unexceptional tree in the parching midday heat, I started to fantasize of a different life. Perhaps a life where I had persevered a bit more and sat on that lovely little rock at the beginning of the hike instead of embarking on this pointless trail to nowhere. But I dream . . . oh, how I dream.

And then I saw it. In the just-visible distance, a large black boulder was waddling along a grassy slope.

It was a cow.

A wild friggin' cow.

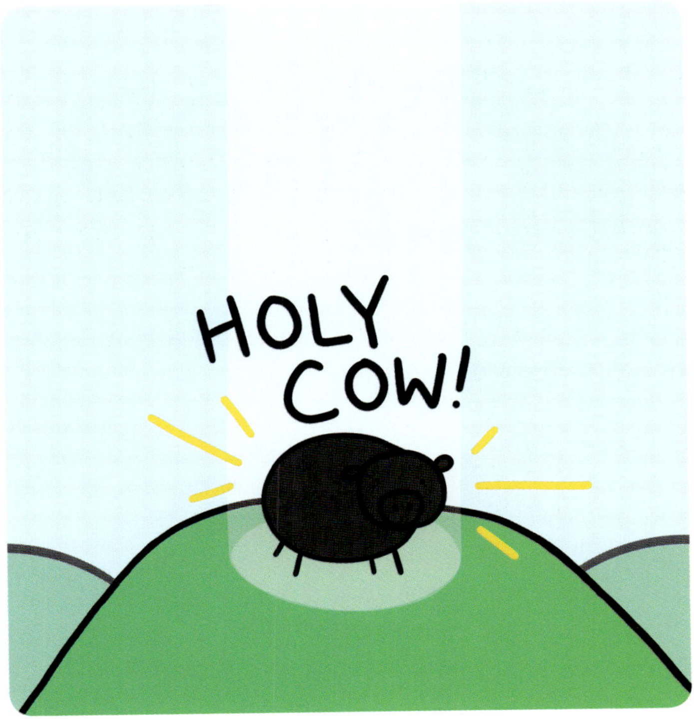
HOLY COW!

"Oh yeah, there are cows here," my uncle muttered, visibly disinterested in my discovery as he continued to study the map. "But be careful not to . . ."

I started sprinting to my new best friend before my uncle could even finish that sentence. Bolting through the grassy knolls, I was a few degrees from spraining my ankles with every leap in the air. I could hear myself squealing with delight as the wind plastered the manic smile onto my face. When I was finally close enough to see the look of absolute boredom on the cow, I slowed to catch my breath.

Upon closer inspection, I noticed that a swarm of flies had taken up residence on the cow's muddy black coat. Nevertheless, I was delighted.

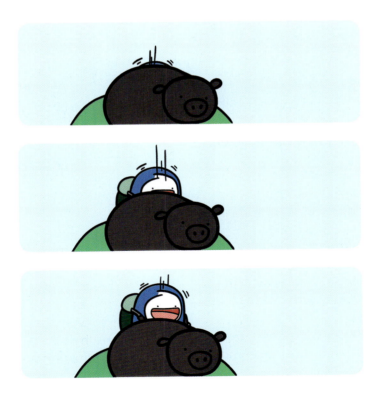

I felt a deep and immediate connection.

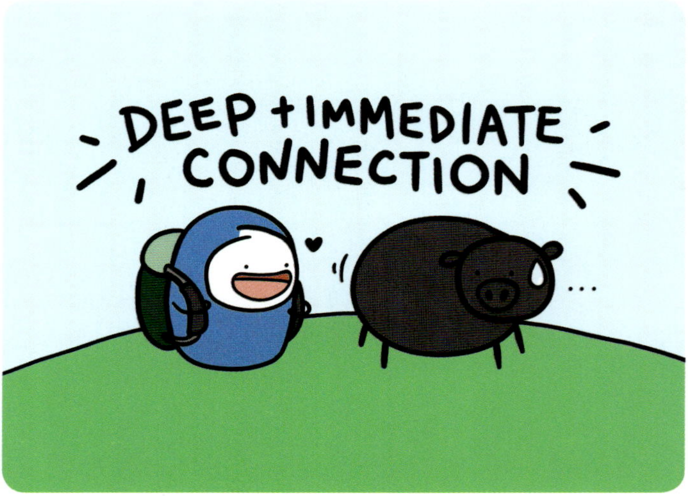
DEEP + IMMEDIATE CONNECTION
...

My feelings of wonder and reverence were, however, very much unreciprocated, for the cow was visibly disinterested in my existence and barely acknowledged me at all.

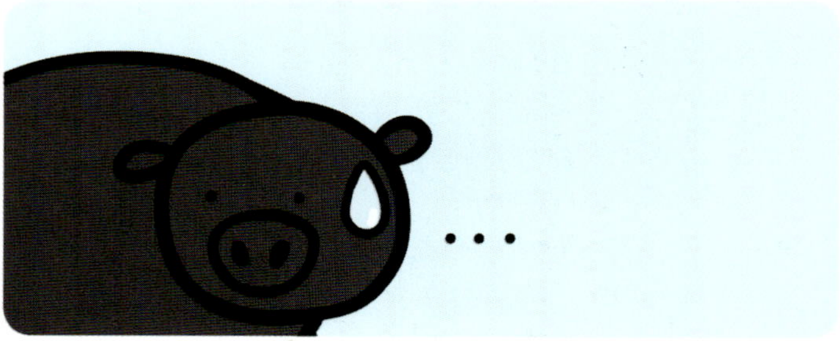
...

I had seen cows before, but I had never seen one while hiking on a mountain. And in that moment, I realized my uncle was right. This hike *was* remarkable. There would be *no* topping this. There would be no better discovery than this one, specific black cow from . . .

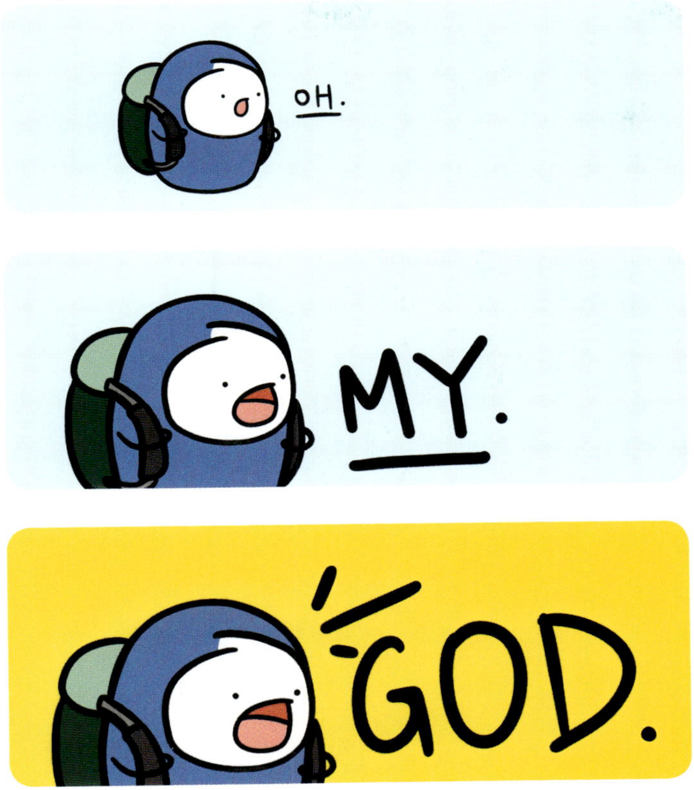
OH.
MY.
GOD.

There was another cow.

At the edge of the trees stood a new cow, even more striking and perfect than the one I was standing next to. I mean, I couldn't really tell because the new cow was so far away, but I was pretty sure she was better.

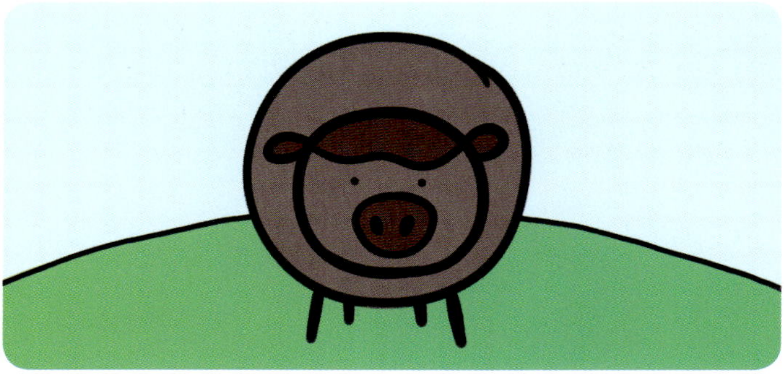

I began bounding towards this second cow with the fervor of someone discovering a new continent. The second cow was actually a lot farther than I had anticipated, and by the time I reached her, the first cow was just a black speck in the distance.

Upon closer inspection, I discovered the second cow had a velvety tan coat with a single splotch of brown at the top of her head. It made her look rather silly, as though she were wearing a strangely misshapen beret. *How peculiar*, I thought.

I loved this second cow and felt a deep and immediate connection.

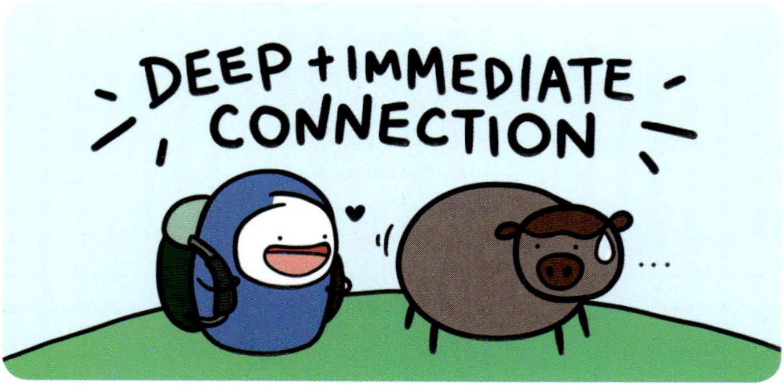
DEEP + IMMEDIATE CONNECTION
...

Once again, this new cow barely acknowledged my existence, and within a few seconds, it started trotting away. Having no sense of personal boundaries, I followed the cow.

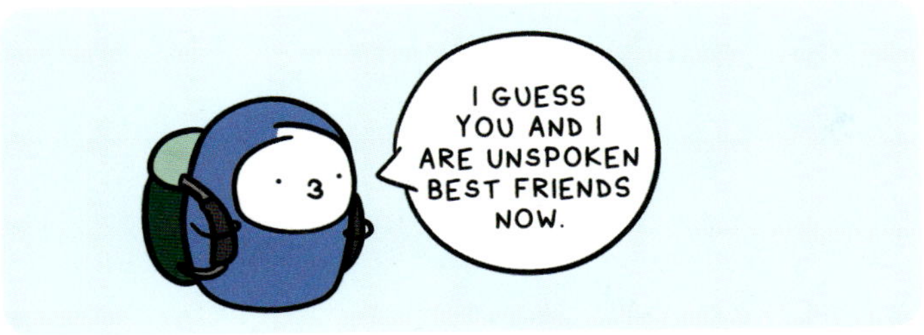
I GUESS YOU AND I ARE UNSPOKEN BEST FRIENDS NOW.

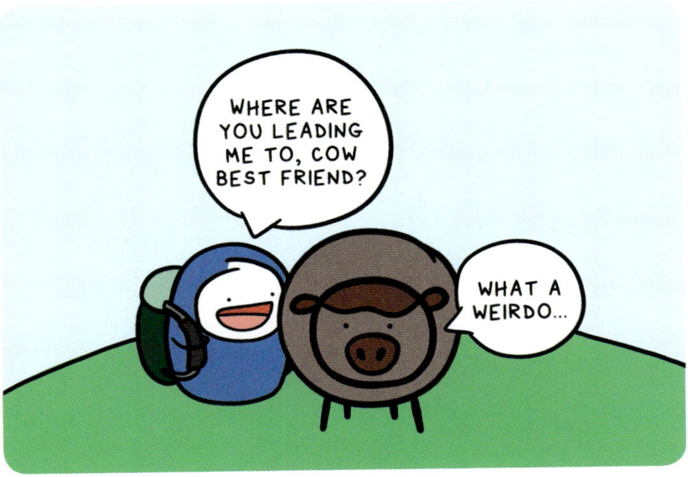
WHERE ARE YOU LEADING ME TO, COW BEST FRIEND?
WHAT A WEIRDO...

The cow didn't seem particularly interested in my company, but tolerated me enough to let me follow.

To this day, I still have no idea how long I followed that cow—but I'm guessing any amount of time was probably too long. As we made our way through the trees, I started telling the cow deeply personal secrets.

"And you see, *that* is when I knew I had moved on. When I felt the slow, deep rumbling of the pedestal crashing down . . ." I explained.

The cow probably hated it.

When we finally stopped, I found myself and my cow best friend standing at a clearing with a single tree at the center of it—the tree looked exactly like the tree my uncle had led me to earlier.

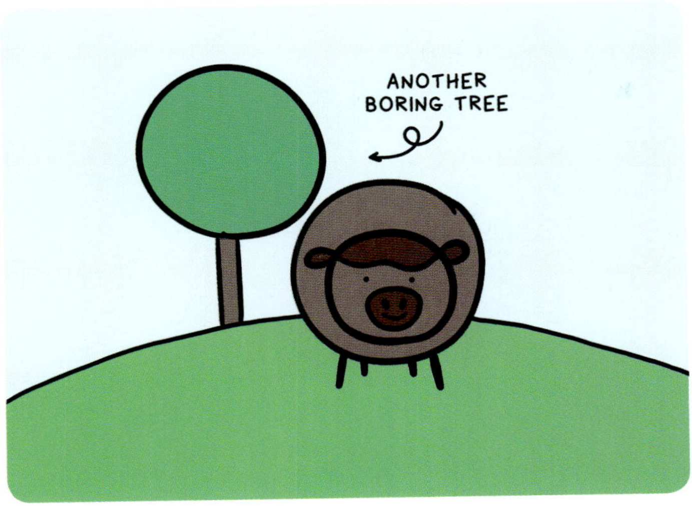
ANOTHER BORING TREE

I began to wonder if I was missing something. Clearly, if both cows and uncles have made it their life's goal to get to this particular type of tree, there must be some merit to it. But the tree had no significance to me and no matter how long I stared at it, I was still unable to conjure the same appreciation or delight everyone else seemed to have towards it.

I just didn't get it.

Unlike me, my cow best friend seemed extremely pleased with herself for having reached her destination. She trotted over, plopped down beneath the shade of the tree, and gave me a meaningful look as if to announce that she had arrived.

To each their own.

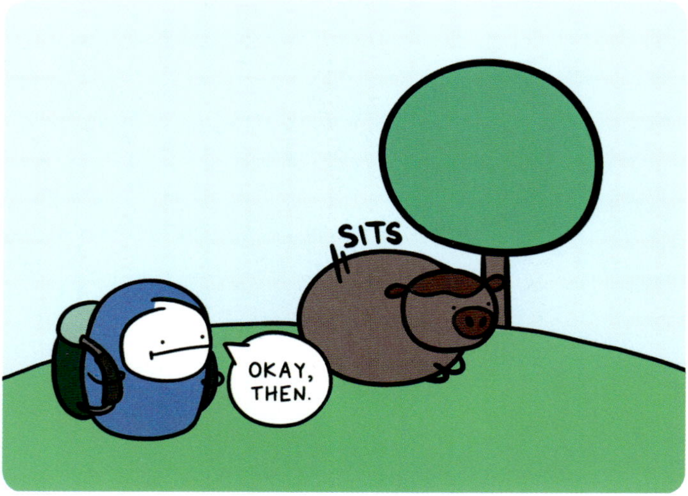
SITS
OKAY, THEN.

Not wanting to be rude, I politely thanked the cow for her hospitality before turning to leave.

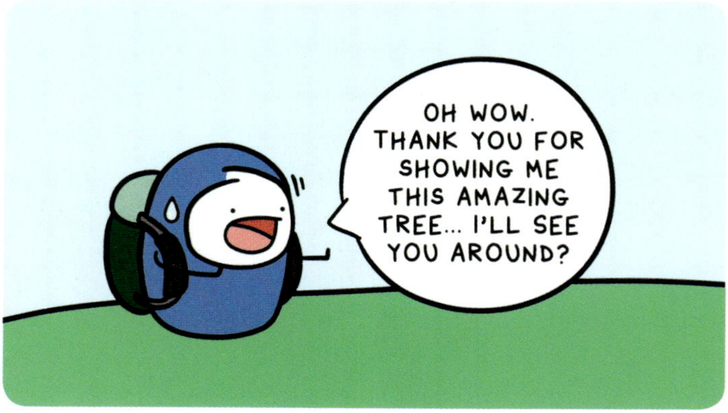
OH WOW. THANK YOU FOR SHOWING ME THIS AMAZING TREE... I'LL SEE YOU AROUND?

As I began to meander away from the boring tree and the now-dozing cow, I realized I wasn't entirely sure which way I had come from. I looked around and began searching for any recognizable trees, but of course, all the trees looked the same.

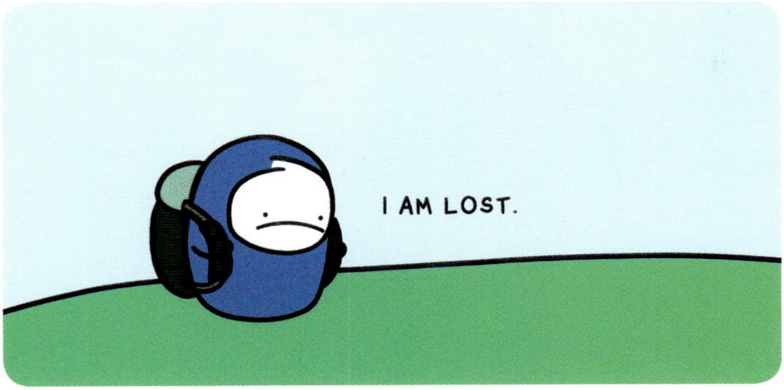
I AM LOST.

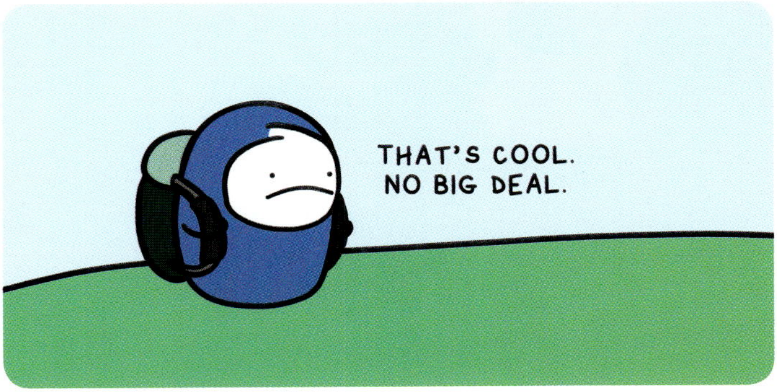
THAT'S COOL.
NO BIG DEAL.

Getting physically lost has never really bothered me. Perhaps because when I was young, I would wander away from my parents a lot. It wasn't that I didn't like them, I was just perpetually distracted by everything else the world had to offer.

My mum noted this as a red flag early on.

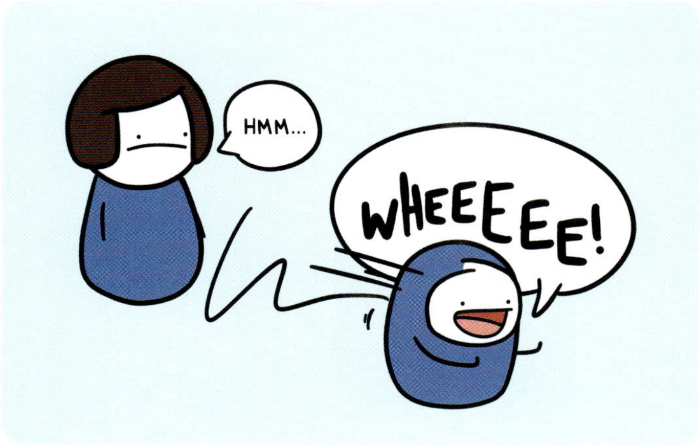
HMM...
WHEEEEEE!

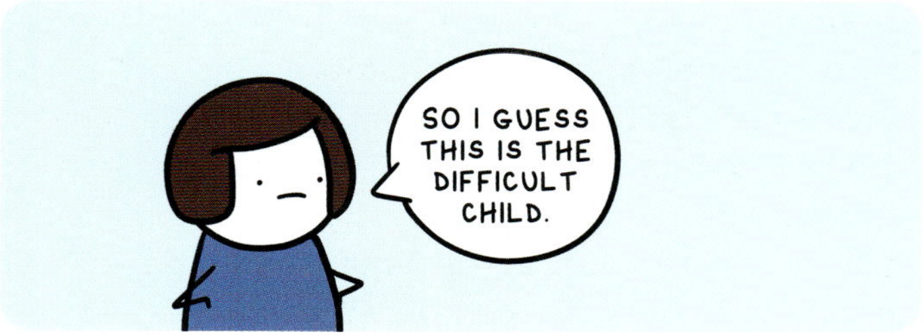
SO I GUESS THIS IS THE DIFFICULT CHILD.

In hopes of curbing future chaos, she told me what parents always tell their kids, that if I were to ever get lost, I ought to stay put and wait until someone can come find me.

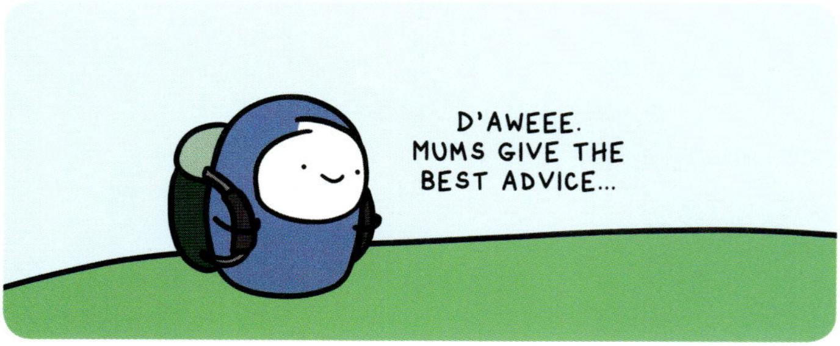
D'AWEEE.
MUMS GIVE THE BEST ADVICE...

I started walking in an arbitrary direction.

• • •

For what felt like an hour, I aimlessly trudged through piles of rocks, mud, and nature gunk. This would have continued much longer had I not been interrupted by the sound of waves.

*Wait . . . how are there waves at the top of a mountain?*

I must be imagining things. But as I continued forward, I heard it again; just beyond the clearing ahead came the unmistakable sound of waves lapping against a shore. I picked up the pace and started galloping—the kind of awkward gallop you do when you're too impatient to walk but not fully committed enough to run—I was essentially thrashing on land. It was incredibly attractive.

A few gallops later, I found what I was looking for.

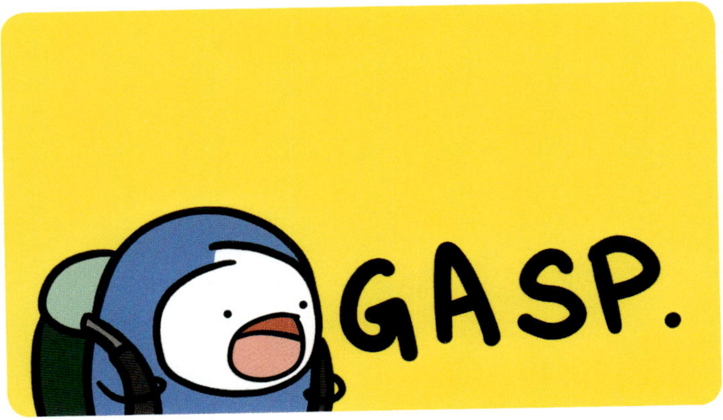
GASP.

There must have been . . . fifty cows in that cove and not a single human in sight. I would later confirm the number at sixty-eight as I thrashed across the beach to do a headcount.

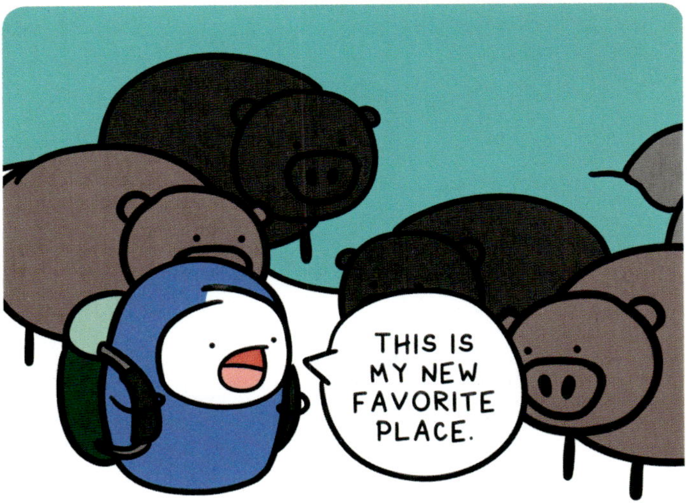
THIS IS MY NEW FAVORITE PLACE.

I loved these cows and felt a deep and immediate connection with every single one of them.

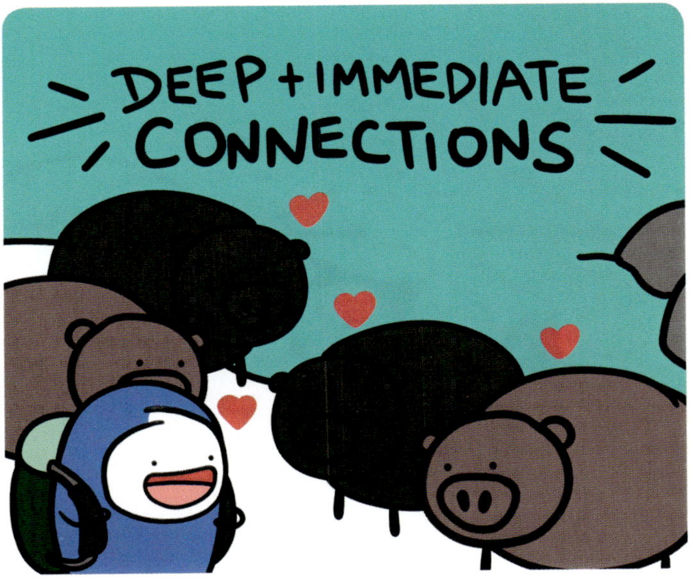
DEEP + IMMEDIATE CONNECTIONS

A few hours later, my aunt, uncle, and sister found me sitting on the beach, talking with cows like some sort of vagrant who had completely detached from reality.

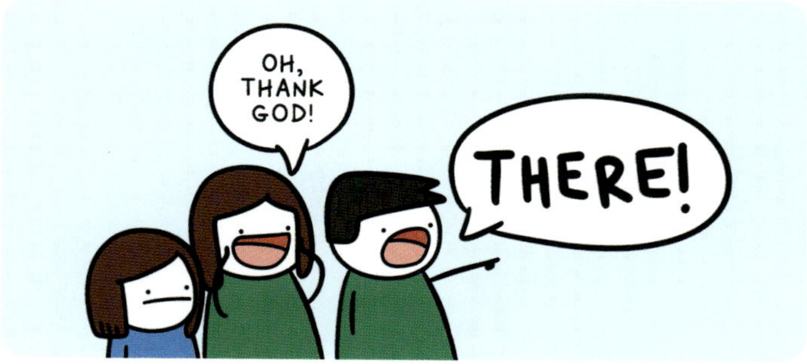
OH, THANK GOD!
THERE!

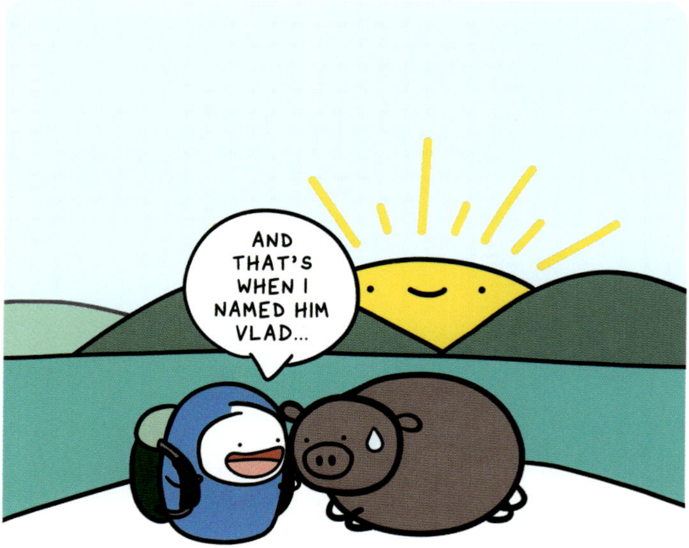
AND THAT'S WHEN I NAMED HIM VLAD...

My aunt and uncle were visibly relieved. My sister simply looked bored—her expression reminded me of the cow with the beret.

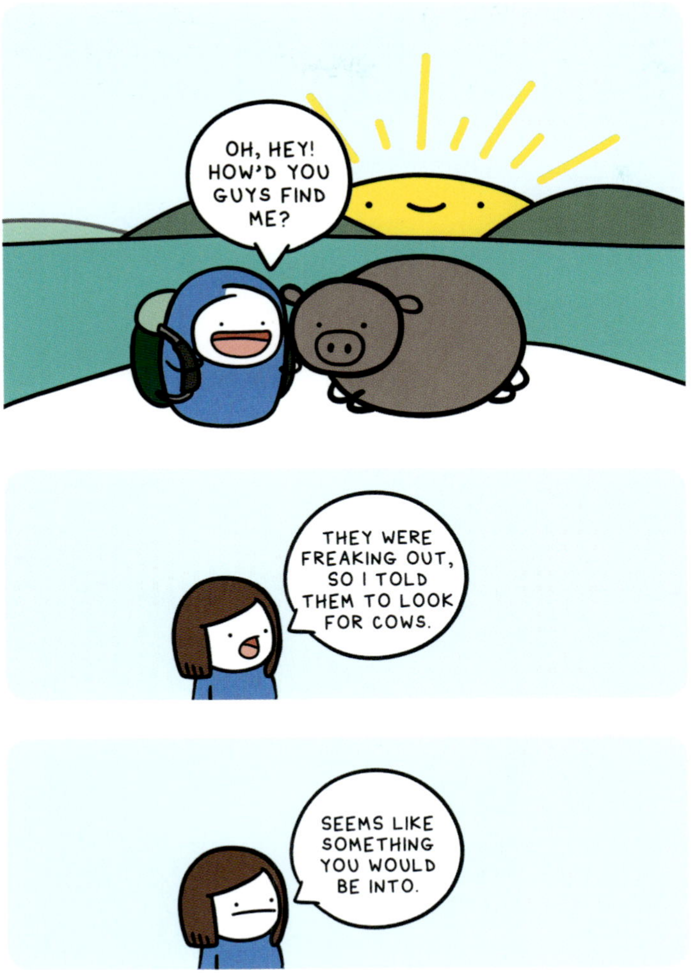
OH, HEY! HOW'D YOU GUYS FIND ME?
THEY WERE FREAKING OUT, SO I TOLD THEM TO LOOK FOR COWS.
SEEMS LIKE SOMETHING YOU WOULD BE INTO.

In true younger-sibling-unsolicited-storytelling-mode, I blurted out everything that had happened to me since I had wandered away. I told my sister how I had hiked for hours following my cow best friend, how I had gotten myself hopelessly lost, and how I ended up here in this secluded cove.

Looking down at the overexcited, insane little grin I was wearing while sitting next to sixty-eight wild cows on a beach, my sister simply said,

"Well, you don't look lost to me."

· · ·

One Saturday afternoon, I woke up feeling incredibly lost.

And not just lost in the fleeting sense that one sometimes feels when they wake up and don't know where they are—but *lost* in a bigger sense—lost in the celestial sense.

I don't know what it was exactly, but as I sat up in my bed, I looked around and thought . . .

OH, DEAR.

LOOKS LIKE SOMEONE DOESN'T KNOW WHAT THEY'RE DOING WITH THEIR LIFE...

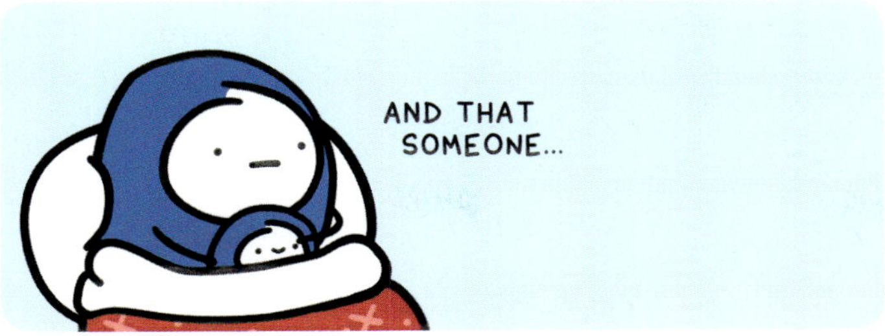
AND THAT
SOMEONE...

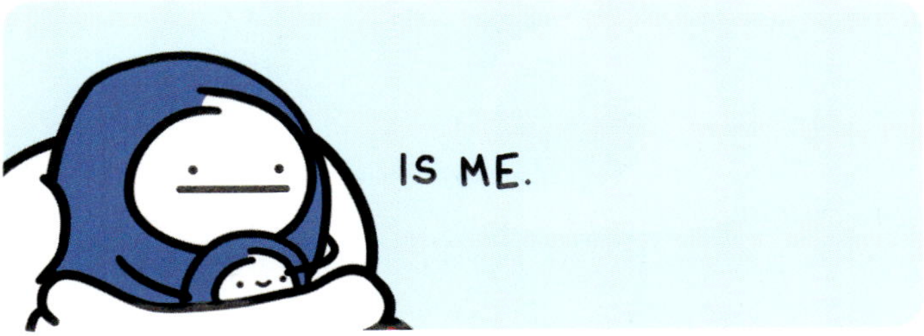
IS ME.

In retrospect, this feeling probably stemmed from a myriad of things: Karlie Kloss staring me down on the cover of *Forbes* "30 Under 30," work being impossibly disheartening all summer, and the loose pile of birthday cards from the night before, silently taunting me from the wooden stool on which they sat next to my bed.

A wonderful symphony of reminders as to how my life had thus far failed to meet expectations.

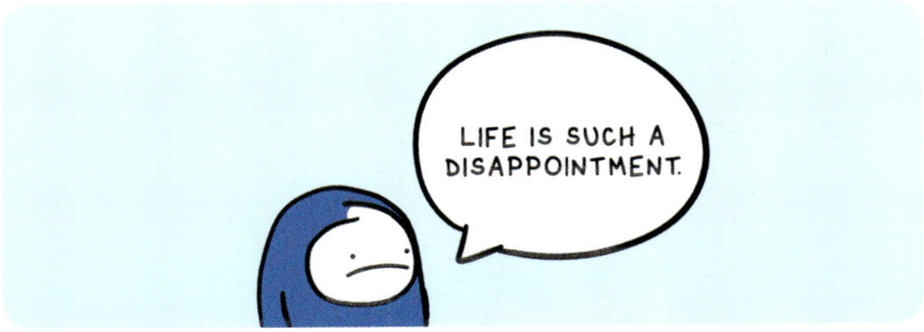
LIFE IS SUCH A
DISAPPOINTMENT.

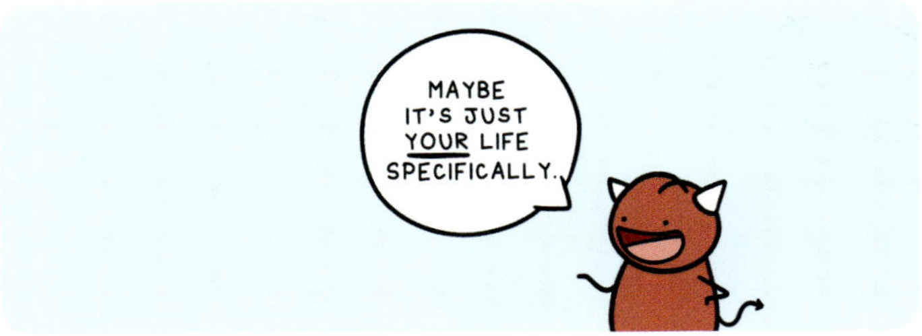
MAYBE IT'S JUST YOUR LIFE SPECIFICALLY.

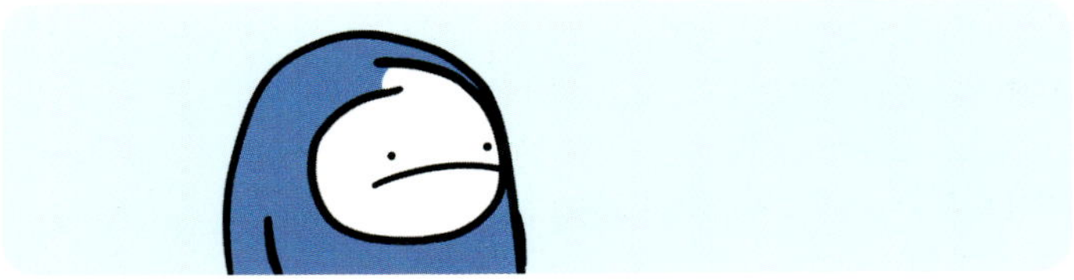

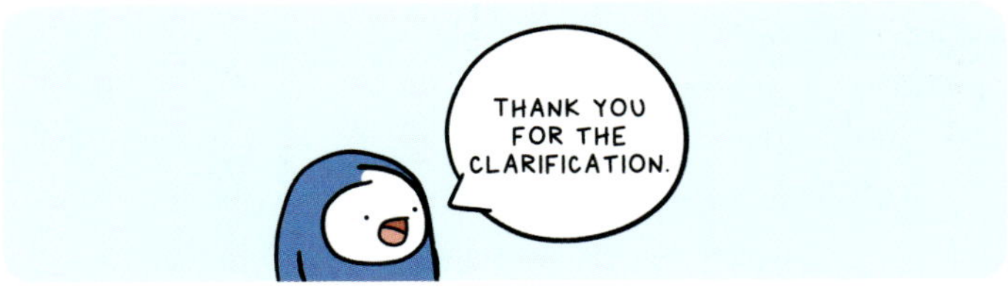
THANK YOU FOR THE CLARIFICATION.

The problem with getting older is that you start asking yourself increasingly annoying questions—questions like: *What am I doing with my life? What am I supposed to be doing with my life? Where is this all even going?*

Younger me would have rattled off answers without missing a beat. Older me wasn't so sure.

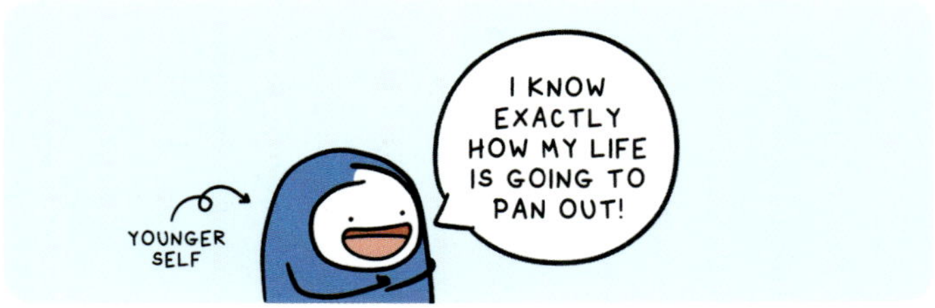
YOUNGER SELF
I KNOW EXACTLY HOW MY LIFE IS GOING TO PAN OUT!

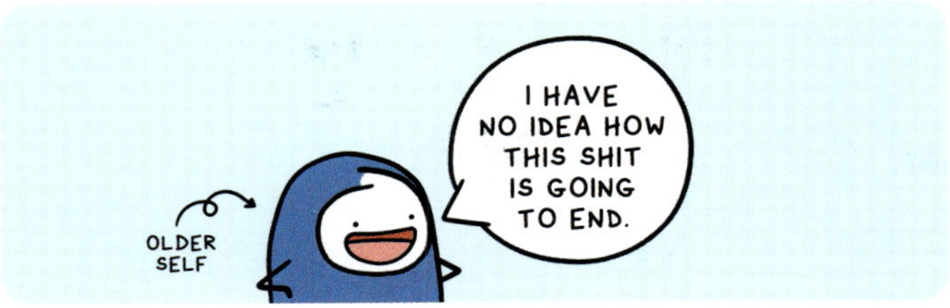
OLDER SELF
I HAVE NO IDEA HOW THIS SHIT IS GOING TO END.

It had been quite a few years since I had last experienced this particular gradient of despair—but I guess despair has a tendency of finding its way back to us.

I was at a point in my life where I had already checked off most of the easy milestones—school, graduation, a stable job—but the path ahead held much less clarity and I couldn't help but feel as though I was running out of directions.

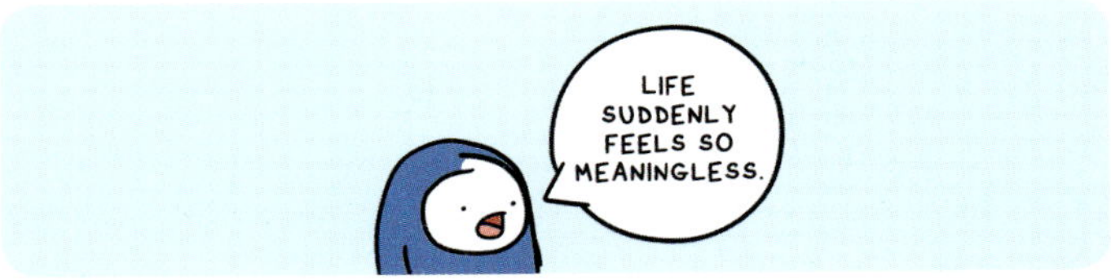
LIFE SUDDENLY FEELS SO MEANINGLESS.

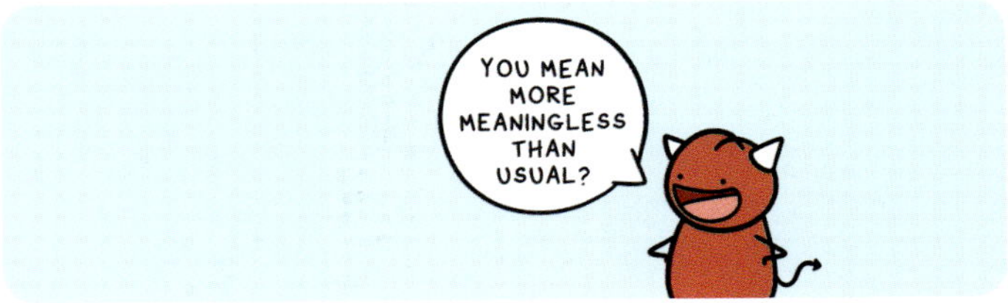
YOU MEAN MORE MEANINGLESS THAN USUAL?

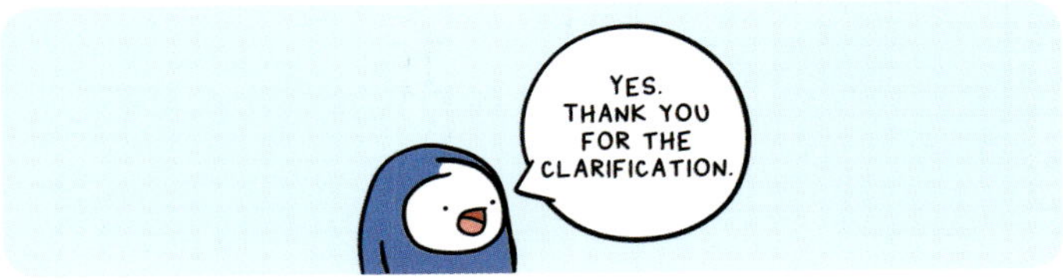
YES. THANK YOU FOR THE CLARIFICATION.

It was as though I were treading water—neither sinking nor swimming—simply anchored in place with nowhere to go.

TREAD.
TREAD.
TREAD.
TREAD.
TREAD.
TREAD.
SO...
WHAT THE HECK
AM I SUPPOSED TO
DO NOW?

In hopes of figuring out what I was supposed to be doing with my life, I looked to my friends for clues. Surely, *someone* knew what we were all supposed to be doing.

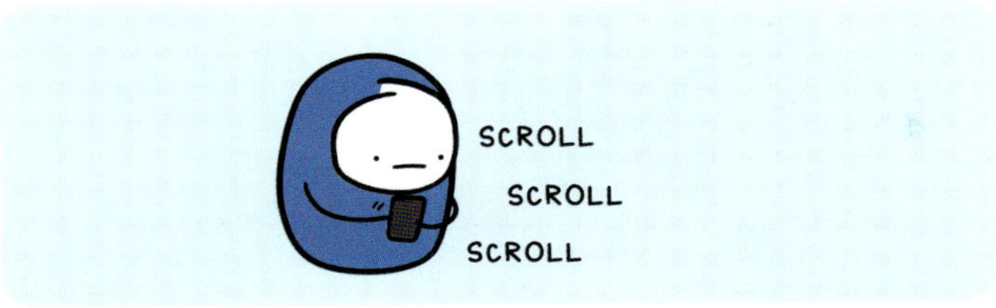
SCROLL
SCROLL
SCROLL

The results were varied and inconclusive.

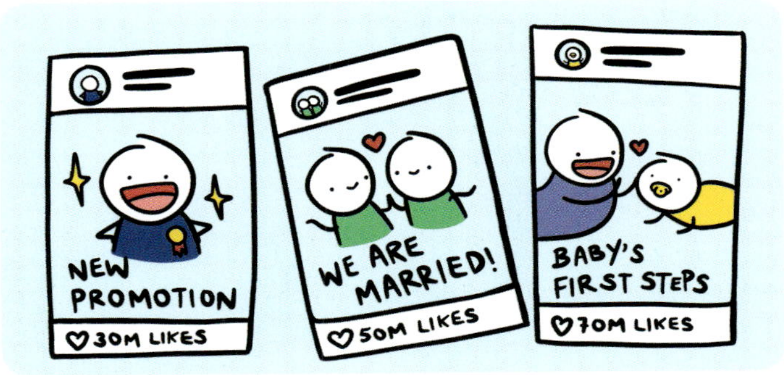
NEW PROMOTION
30M LIKES
WE ARE MARRIED!
50M LIKES
BABY'S FIRST STEPS
70M LIKES

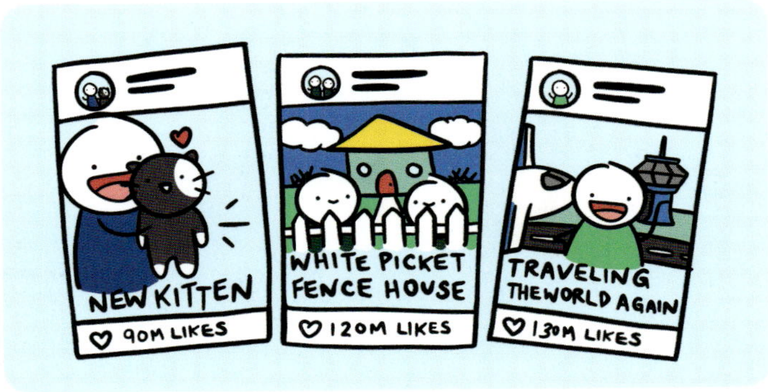
NEW KITTEN
90M LIKES
WHITE PICKET FENCE HOUSE
120M LIKES
TRAVELING THE WORLD AGAIN
130M LIKES

Maybe I was supposed to have a cat?

WHITE PICKET FENCE
MEOW.

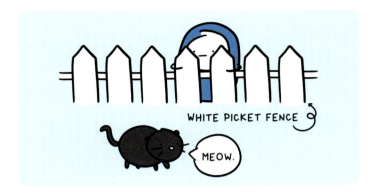

But I didn't have a cat. I had two frogs.

*Maybe I was supposed to have a white picket fence?*

But I didn't want a white picket fence. They attract weirdos.

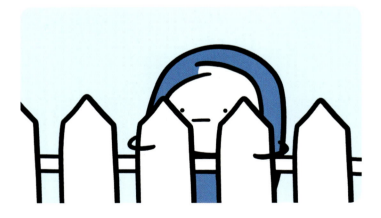

Once again, the all-too-familiar seeds of despair started to take root.

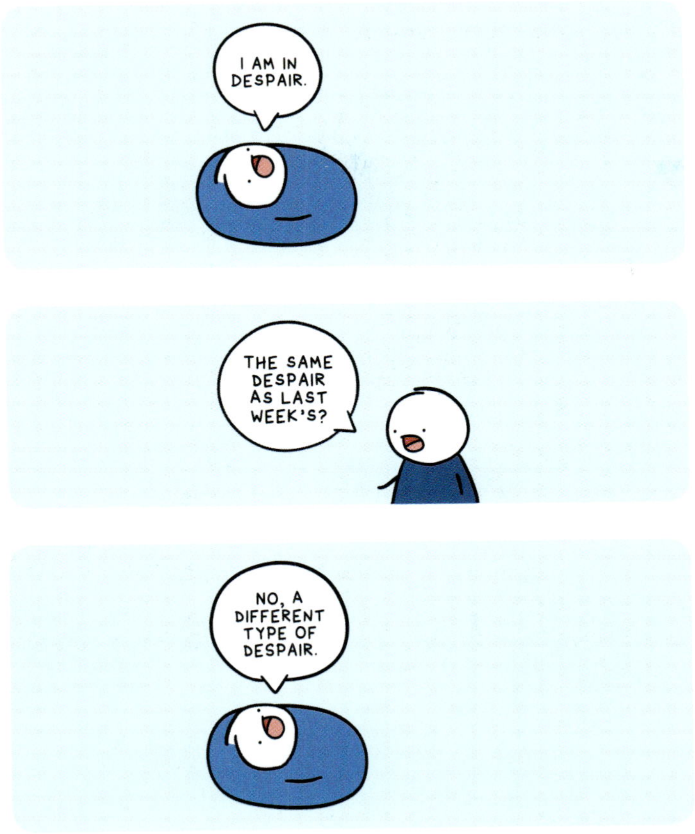
I AM IN DESPAIR.
THE SAME DESPAIR AS LAST WEEK'S?
NO, A DIFFERENT TYPE OF DESPAIR.

In need of direction, I went back to my milestone checklist. There was one thing I had always known was missing—the coveted dream job checkbox. I knew I was probably at an age where I was supposed to be at my dream job by now, but reality had not aligned with expectations (surprise!) and my dream job was still just that—a dream.

I had always told myself I would one day apply to the perfect job when I was good enough, but the problem was that I never felt good enough. I was good, not great, and "good" doesn't get you anywhere. Greatness was like the sun, always in sight but never within reach.

GREATNESS
CAN'T TOUCH THIS.
TRIES!
HUT!
FAILS.

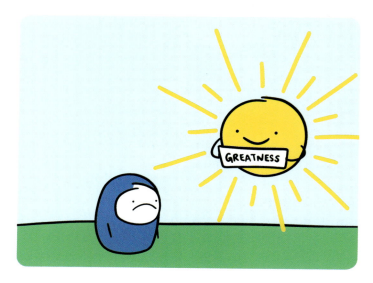

HAHA, WHAT A LOSER.
TRIES AGAIN.
HUT!
FAILS AGAIN.

I knew I wasn't good enough to get any of my dream jobs, but something about never having even tried seemed inexcusably pathetic.

I'M NOT GOOD ENOUGH YET.

I'M NOT THERE YET.

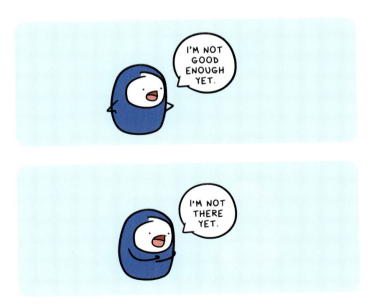

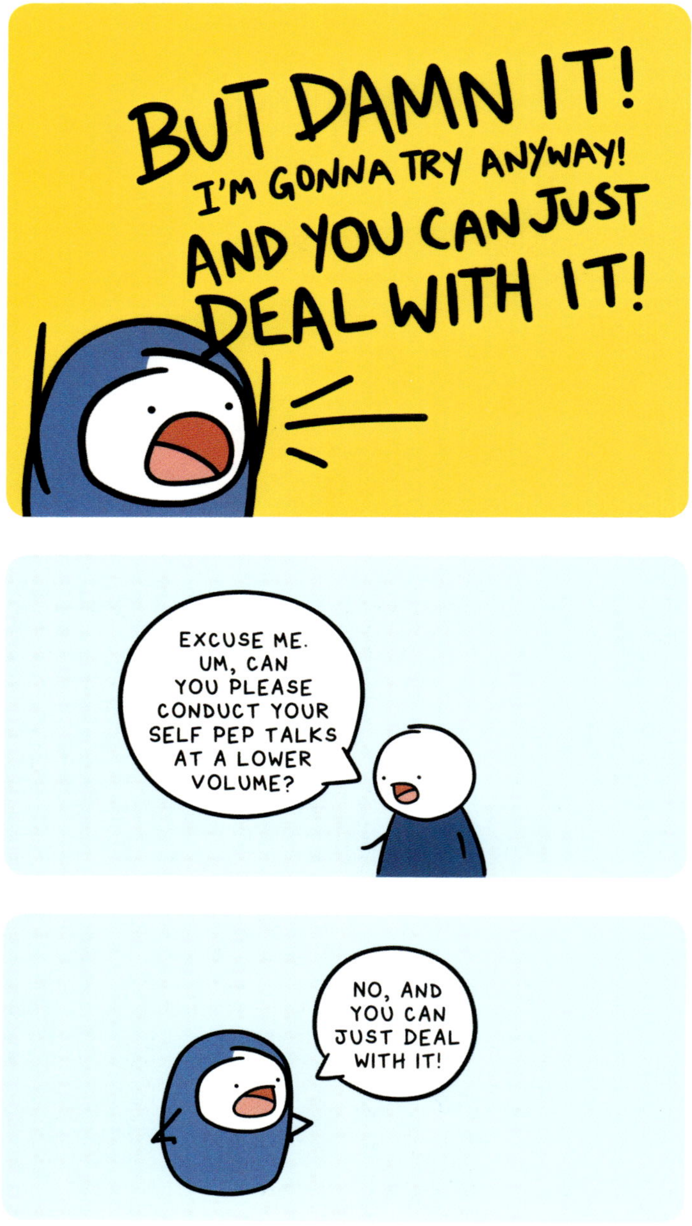
BUT DAMN IT! I'M GONNA TRY ANYWAY! AND YOU CAN JUST DEAL WITH IT!
EXCUSE ME. UM, CAN YOU PLEASE CONDUCT YOUR SELF PEP TALKS AT A LOWER VOLUME?
NO, AND YOU CAN JUST DEAL WITH IT!

And so that night, in a rare moment of determination, I submitted my application to work as a designer at Google.

• • •

When Google responded, I didn't open their email for a week.

The only thing that separates you from the inevitable pain of an email you don't want to read is your blatant refusal to open it.

SEES EMAIL
I DO NOT WANT
TO READ.

NO CLICK.

FEW DAYS LATER

STILL NO CLICK.

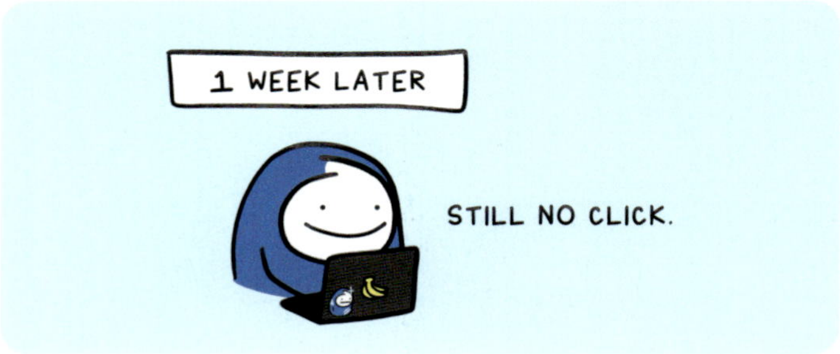
1 WEEK LATER
STILL NO CLICK.

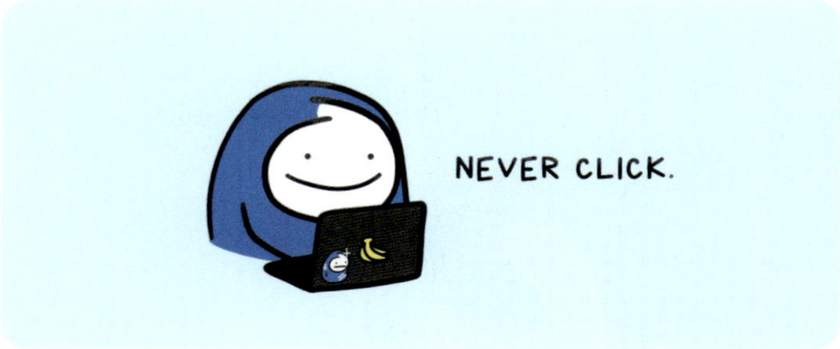
NEVER CLICK.

When my friend found out about this insane little game I was playing, she rightly yelled at me to get it together. A true friend is someone who is willing and able to scold you when you're being a total frickin' idiot.

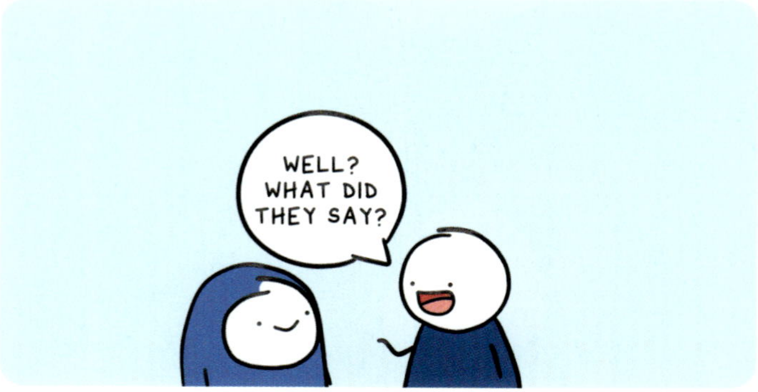
WELL? WHAT DID THEY SAY?

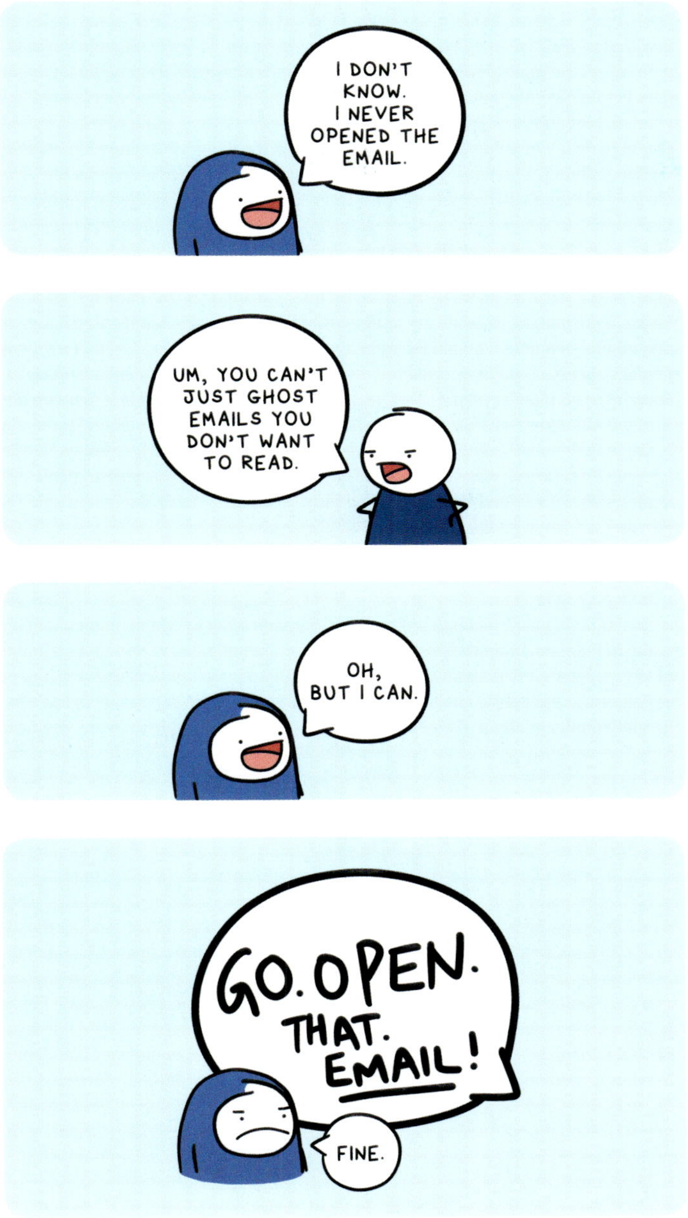
I DON'T KNOW. I NEVER OPENED THE EMAIL.
UM, YOU CAN'T JUST GHOST EMAILS YOU DON'T WANT TO READ.
OH, BUT I CAN.
GO. OPEN. THAT. EMAIL!
FINE.

The next few months of my life were sacrificed to the Google interview gods.

Step 1: Phone interview with a recruiter.

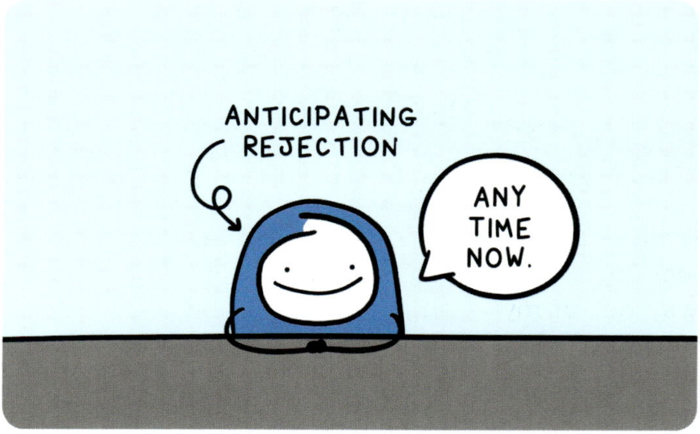
ANTICIPATING REJECTION
ANY TIME NOW.

Step 2: Phone interview with a Google designer.

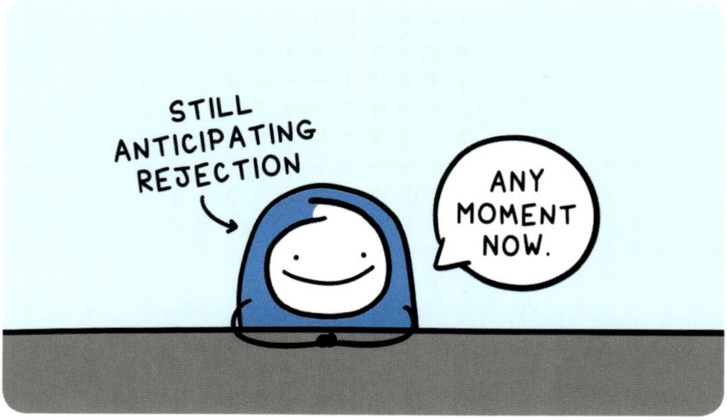
STILL ANTICIPATING REJECTION
ANY MOMENT NOW.

Step 3: Design exercise where I had to create, document, and present a concept.

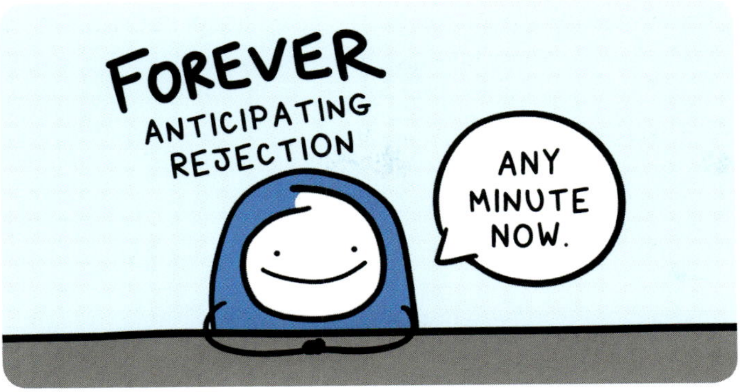
FOREVER
ANTICIPATING
REJECTION
ANY
MINUTE
NOW.

It was the longest I had ever spent anticipating rejection. It was as though I were dating someone way out of my league, and failure just seemed the most reasonable and expected outcome.

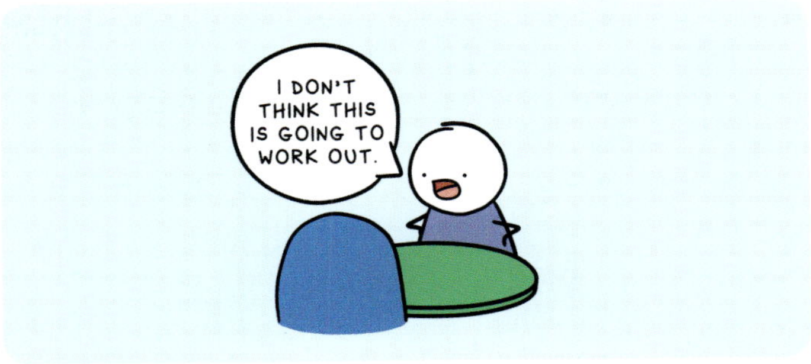
I DON'T THINK THIS IS GOING TO WORK OUT.

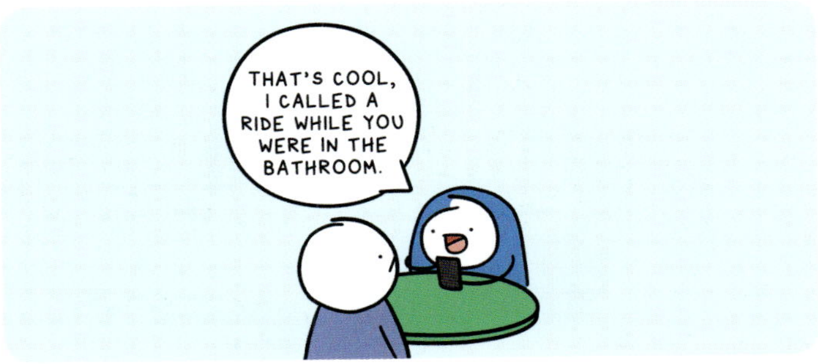
THAT'S COOL, I CALLED A RIDE WHILE YOU WERE IN THE BATHROOM.

I guess when you really want something, it's just easier to assume you won't get it. I wasn't consciously lowering my expectations, it was just the ol' defense mechanism kicking in on its own. For the most part, I didn't even tell my friends and family I was applying because I didn't want to disappoint both myself *and* them. Not getting something you really want is disheartening enough without also having to be consoled by others.

A few months of anxiety later, I found myself heading down to my last round of interviews at Google's global headquarters—otherwise known as Googleplex—in Mountain View, California. I had hoped for an easy journey, but the universe was not having it. My afternoon flight from Vancouver was delayed repeatedly and when I finally landed in California, it was close to 2 a.m. Batches of delayed flights flooding in at the same time also translated into a two-hour lineup for taxis at the airport. Exhausted and overwhelmed, I counted the long stretch of people in front of me over and over again until I was at the front of the line. By the time I arrived at my hotel, I had two hours left to sleep before having to get up for a full day of interviews.

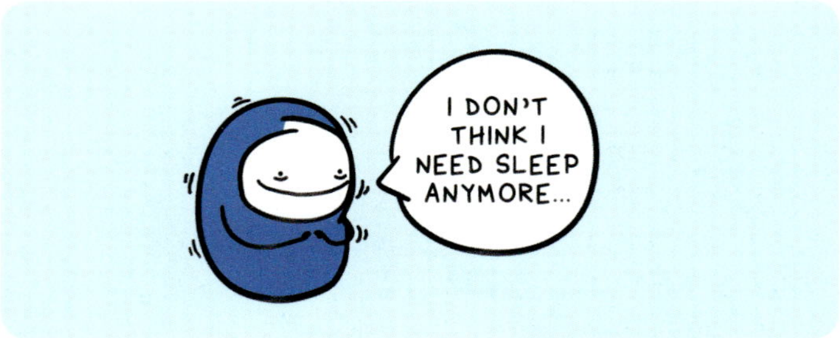
I DON'T THINK I NEED SLEEP ANYMORE...

I THINK I'VE TRANSCENDED MY BIOLOGICAL NEED FOR SLEEP.
AM I... INVINCIBLE? AM I... LIMITLESS?
DUDE. YOU'RE SHAKING.
I AM LIMITLESS.

Walking into Googleplex felt like strolling into a storybook or toy box. Everything was so playfully pristine it almost didn't feel real. Having immediately gotten lost the second I arrived, my first set of directions came from a kindly security guard who told me to "keep walking until you hit the T. rex skeleton and then turn right."

"Wait, a T. rex skeleton? Like a life-sized one?" I asked. It's important to clarify such things.

"Yep," he replied, giving no additional context.

Under the eternal rays of the California sun, Googlers cheerfully propelled past me on brightly painted yellow bikes fitted with charming turquoise fenders and red wired baskets. The campus was filled with curved glass buildings, perfectly manicured lawns, and pops of candy-colored hues.

It was as though I had stumbled onto the filming of *The Good Place* and anytime now, Kristen Bell would mosey on by with a frozen yogurt in hand, politely asking me to get off the set. Later on, I would learn that there actually *is* frozen yogurt at Google.

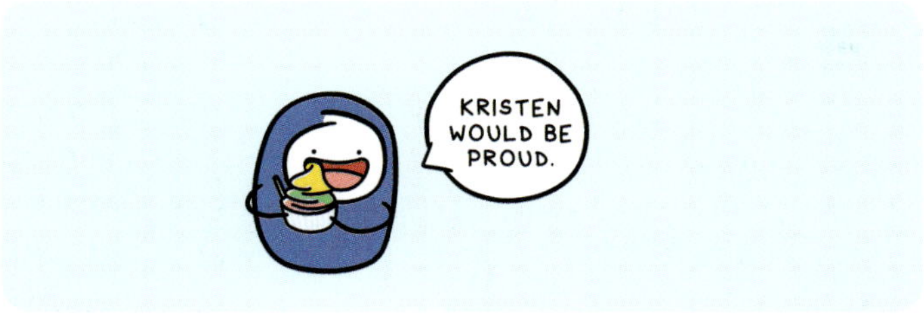
KRISTEN WOULD BE PROUD.

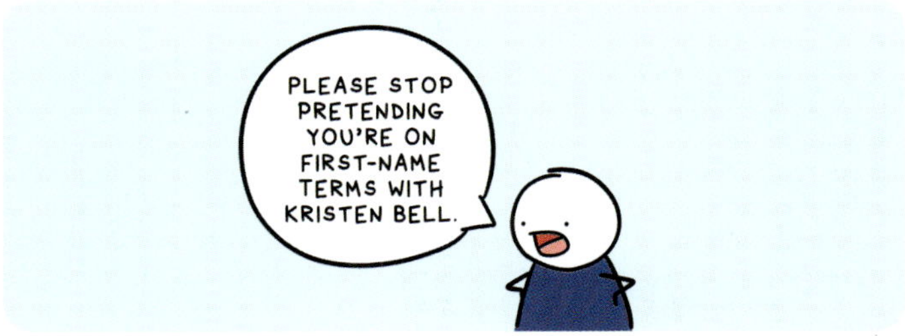
PLEASE STOP PRETENDING YOU'RE ON FIRST-NAME TERMS WITH KRISTEN BELL.

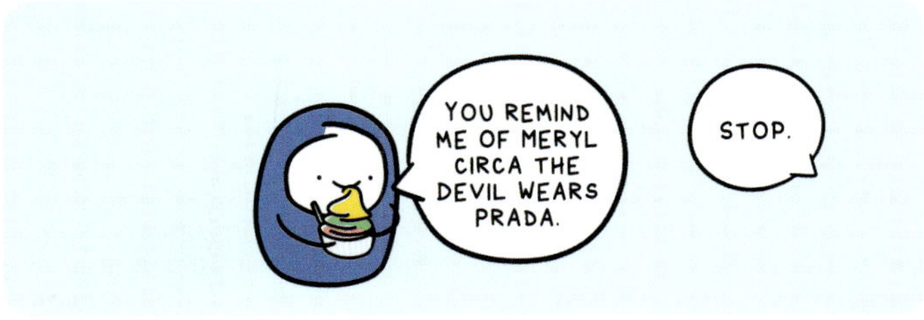
YOU REMIND ME OF MERYL CIRCA THE DEVIL WEARS PRADA.
STOP.

I ended up meeting five different interviewers that day, each invoking an entirely different sense of anxiety within me.

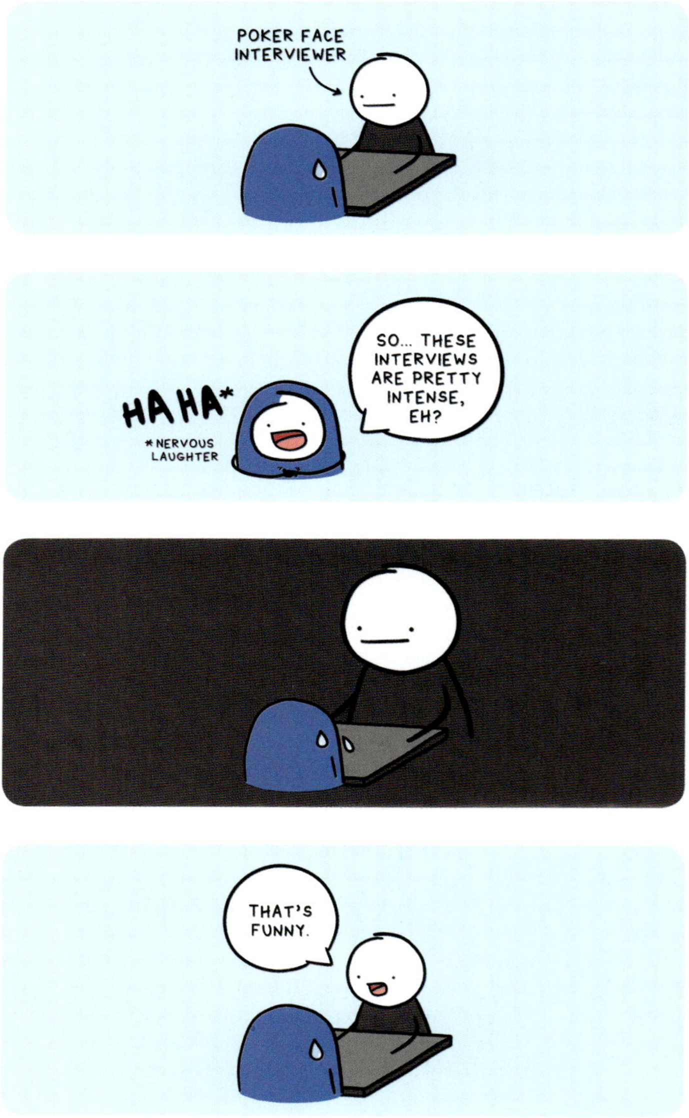
POKER FACE INTERVIEWER
HAHA*
*NERVOUS LAUGHTER
SO... THESE INTERVIEWS ARE PRETTY INTENSE, EH?
THAT'S FUNNY.

By the time I returned home, I was ready to call a wrap on my great Google adventure.

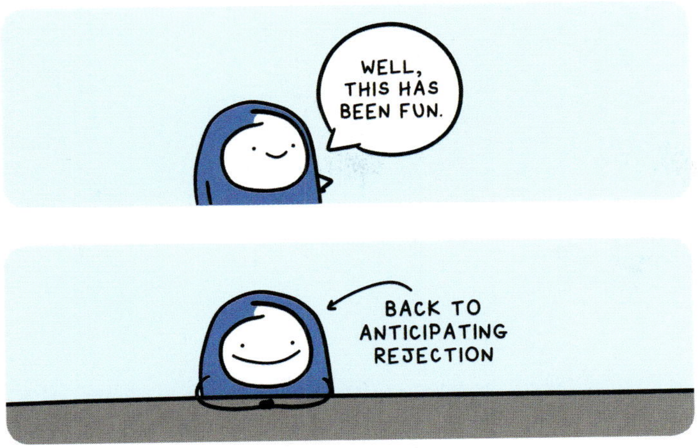
WELL, THIS HAS BEEN FUN.
BACK TO ANTICIPATING REJECTION

A week later, I received the official offer to work at Google.

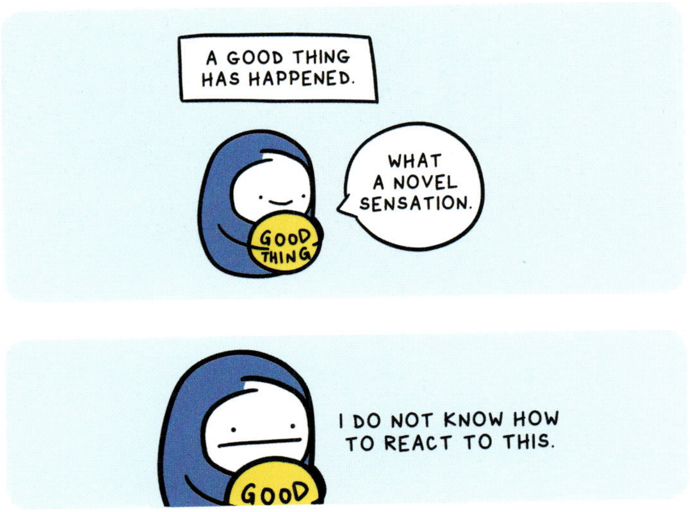
A GOOD THING HAS HAPPENED.
GOOD THING
WHAT A NOVEL SENSATION.
GOOD
I DO NOT KNOW HOW TO REACT TO THIS.

Google offered me the job I had always wanted—the *dream* job. All I had to do was leave everyone and everything I knew and loved to move to a new country.

*No. Big. Deal.*

I was scared, but I also knew this was my opportunity to shake the feeling of being lost and unfulfilled—so I rolled the dice and braced myself for the other side.

• • •

In the weeks leading up to moving day, my friends and family kept asking me if I had packed yet. And for weeks, I responded with:

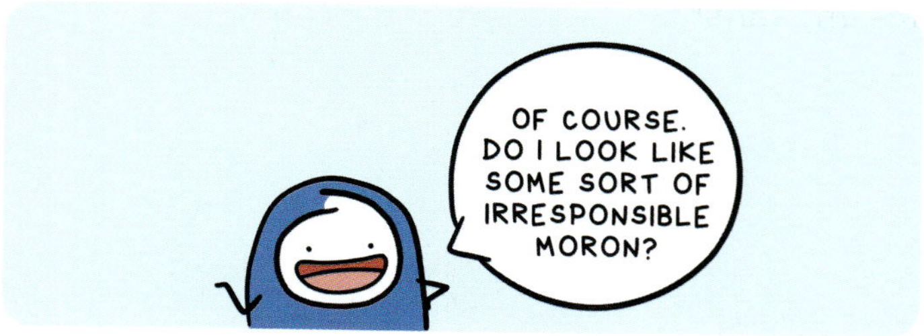
OF COURSE.
DO I LOOK LIKE SOME SORT OF IRRESPONSIBLE MORON?

I started packing two days before I had to move.

I had generously allotted myself two days because I lived in a 400-square-foot studio apartment with *barely* anything in it.

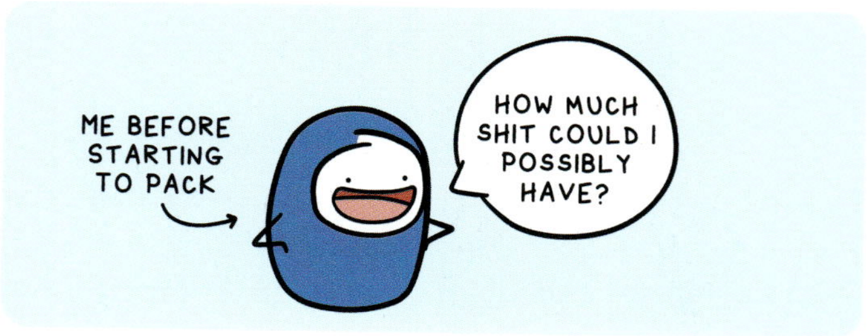
ME BEFORE STARTING TO PACK
HOW MUCH SHIT COULD I POSSIBLY HAVE?

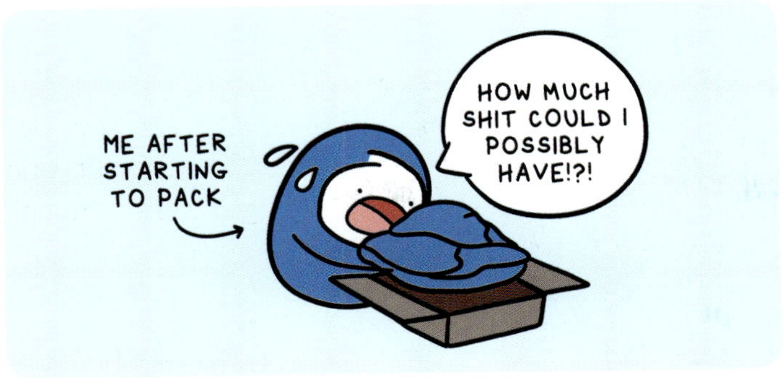
ME AFTER STARTING TO PACK
HOW MUCH SHIT COULD I POSSIBLY HAVE!?!

When my friends offered to help me pack, I declined. I assumed it wouldn't be a fun task, so instead, I enlisted the best free labor I had access to—my family.

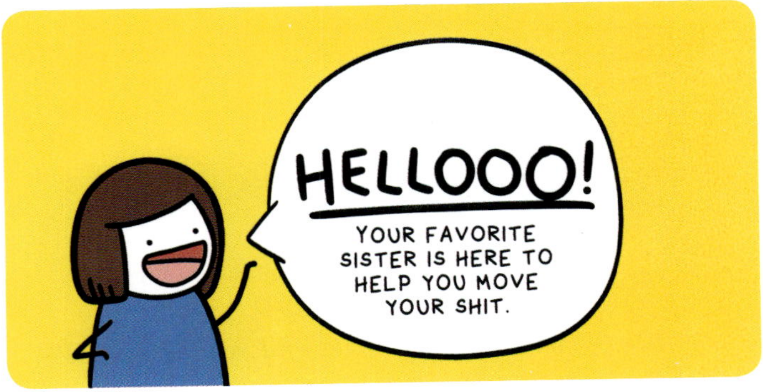
HELLOOO!
YOUR FAVORITE SISTER IS HERE TO HELP YOU MOVE YOUR SHIT.

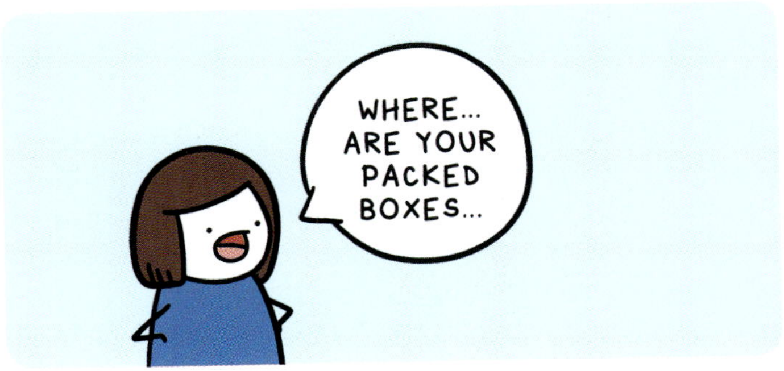
WHERE... ARE YOUR PACKED BOXES...

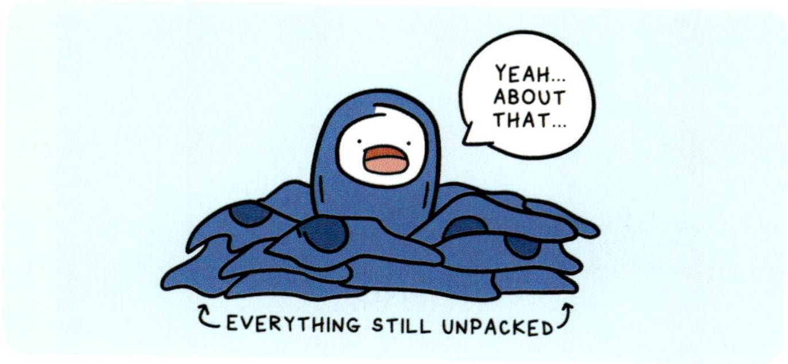
YEAH... ABOUT THAT...
EVERYTHING STILL UNPACKED

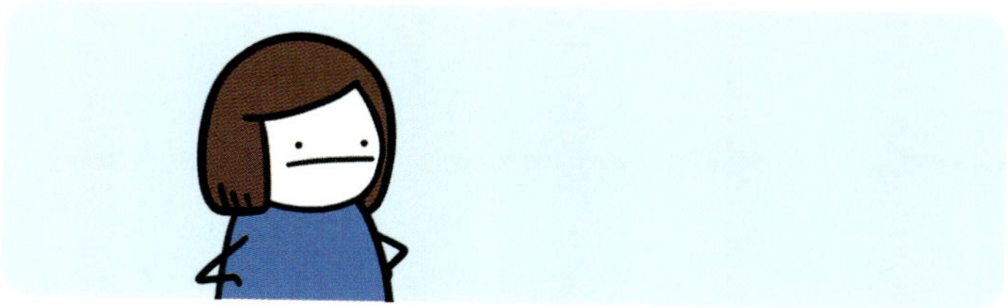

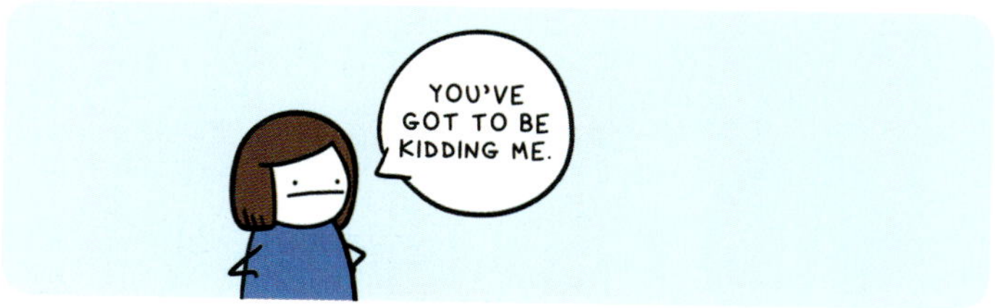
YOU'VE GOT TO BE KIDDING ME.

My mum and dad helped too. They were much more tolerant of my packing ineptitude than my sister was because they had always known I would be the difficult child. I was simply fulfilling the prophecy.

Even with all the extra hands on deck, packing everything in my apartment was exhausting. Make someone pack eight wine glasses, twelve plates, ten bowls, and nine oddly shaped novelty mugs (without any proper packing supplies) and their love for you will definitely be put to the test.

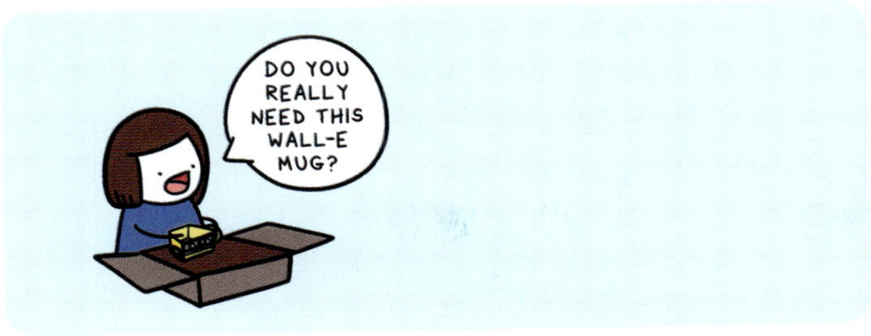
DO YOU REALLY NEED THIS WALL-E MUG?

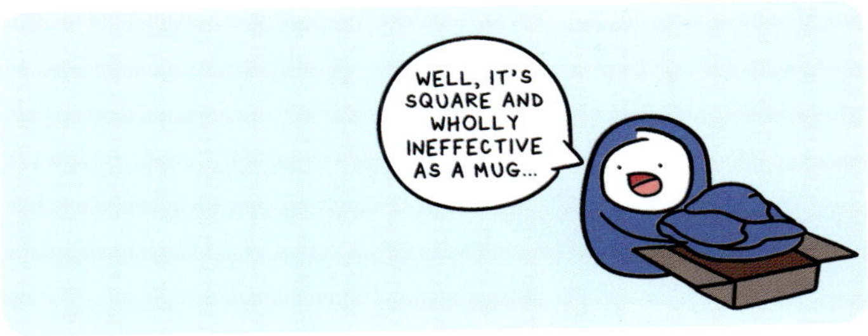
WELL, IT'S SQUARE AND WHOLLY INEFFECTIVE AS A MUG...

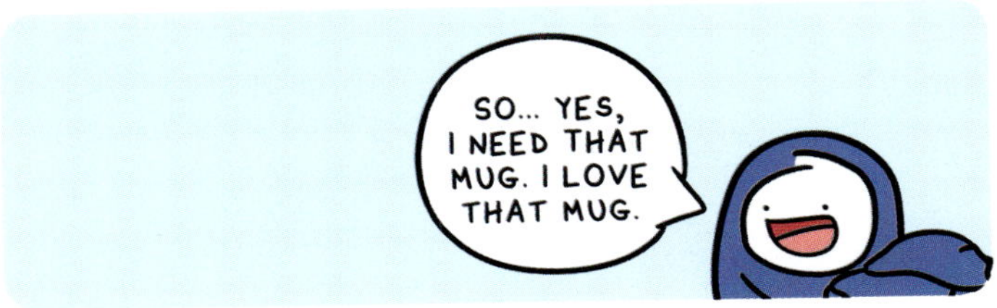
SO... YES, I NEED THAT MUG. I LOVE THAT MUG.

In an effort to be helpful, I tried to brainstorm solutions to lighten our workload.

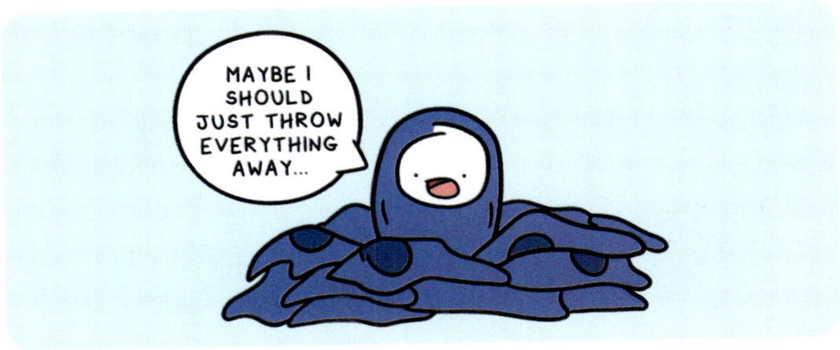
MAYBE I SHOULD JUST THROW EVERYTHING AWAY...

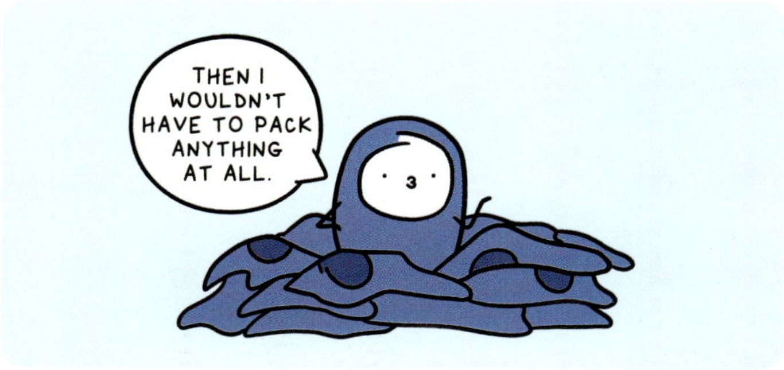
THEN I WOULDN'T HAVE TO PACK ANYTHING AT ALL.

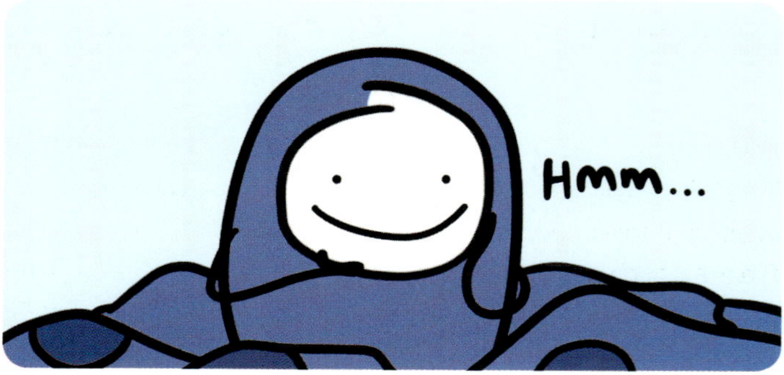
Hmm...

My sister did not appreciate my nonsense.

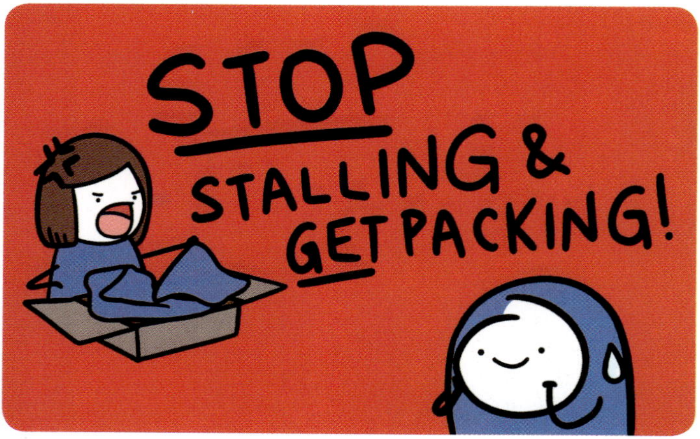
STOP STALLING & GET PACKING!

I think a large part of it was that I didn't actually want to move. I had lived in Vancouver most of my life and had serious doubts about my ability to survive in a new country. Eventually, after a lot of needless angst and struggle, we packed everything. It was packed poorly, it was packed inefficiently, but nobody cared anymore. When we finally got everything into the car—everyone was done.

In retrospect, I probably should've packed earlier.

The first month at Google was perfect. Everyone was brilliant, competent, and kind. The food was free and the work was challenging. I realized I had finally done it. I had finally *arrived*.

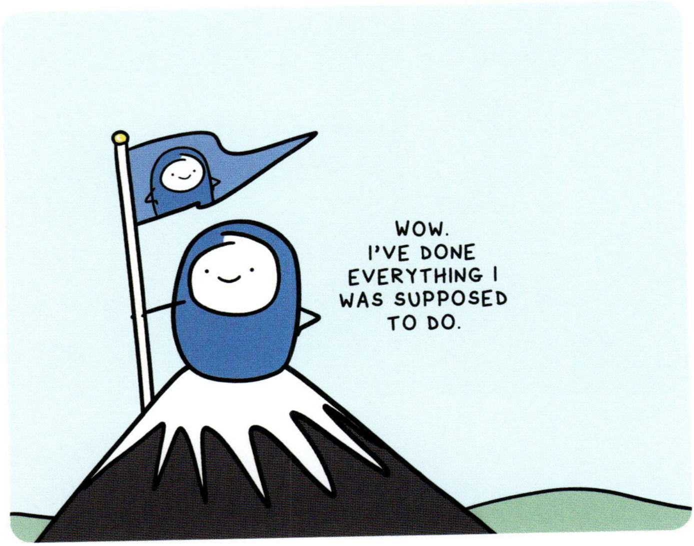
WOW.
I'VE DONE EVERYTHING I WAS SUPPOSED TO DO.

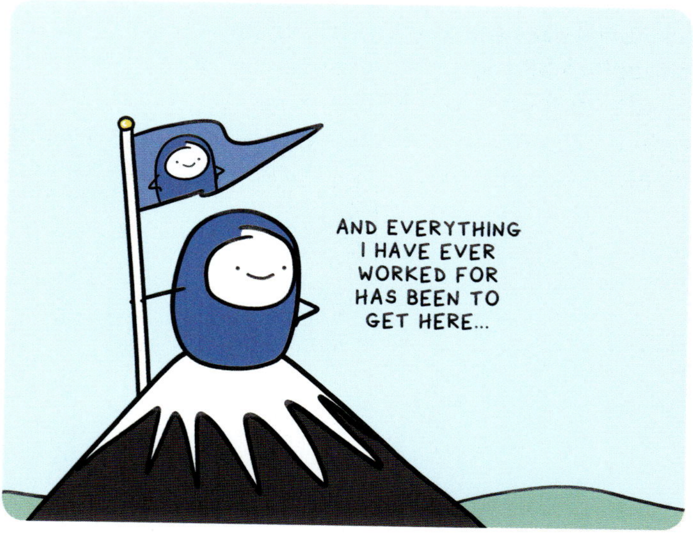
AND EVERYTHING I HAVE EVER WORKED FOR HAS BEEN TO GET HERE...

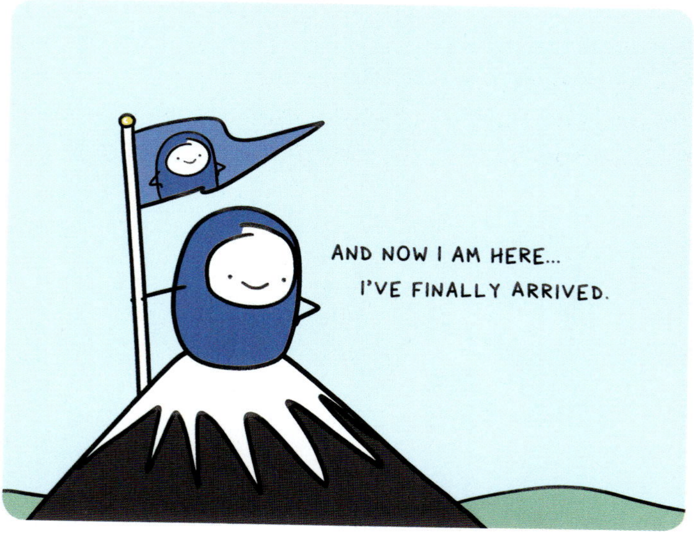
AND NOW I AM HERE...
I'VE FINALLY ARRIVED.

Google's perks lived up to its legend. There were salmon benedict breakfasts and buffet lunches five days a week. There were massage chairs, nap rooms, and Skee-Ball machines. The air *literally* smelled like chocolate all the time because our office was right next to a chocolate factory. It was so perfect that it didn't feel real. It was more than I had ever dreamt of, and certainly more than I ever deserved.

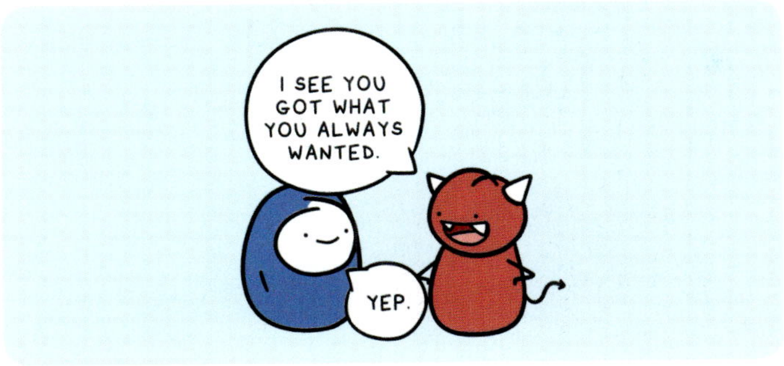
I SEE YOU GOT WHAT YOU ALWAYS WANTED.
YEP.

But when the pixie dust settled, when I finally had everything set up in my apartment, I looked at my life and I heard it—that pesky little voice in my head that whispered the most dangerous of questions . . .

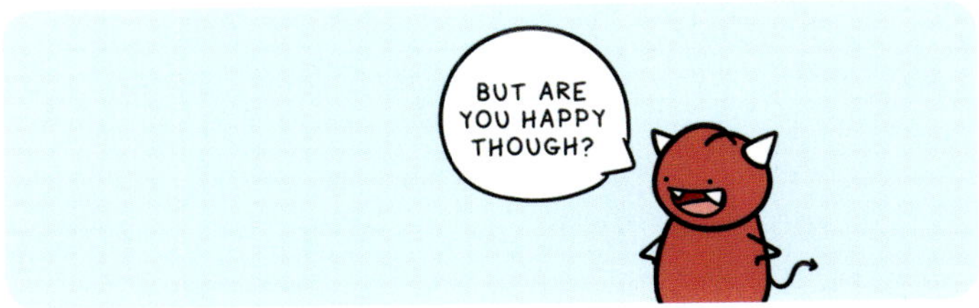
BUT ARE YOU HAPPY THOUGH?

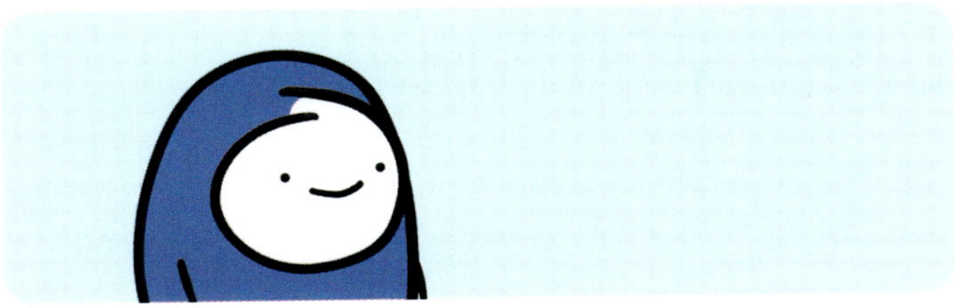

In the months that followed, the glitz of Google gradually faded, and work slowly became just work. Eventually, there were normal work struggles—just like any other place. And as much as I was grateful for all the new wonders in my life, I somehow managed to find myself feeling lost yet again.

I didn't understand what was happening. How was I *still* having this existential crisis? I had done what I had set out to achieve, I had done everything I was supposed to do. I'm not *supposed* to feel lost. More importantly . . . I'm not *allowed* to feel lost.

When things are overtly terrible and you feel lost, you understand how to fix it. The remedy may not be easy, but the remedy is clear. But when things are seemingly perfect, when you've done all the things you set out to do, and you *still* feel lost—that's a much more unsettling realization.

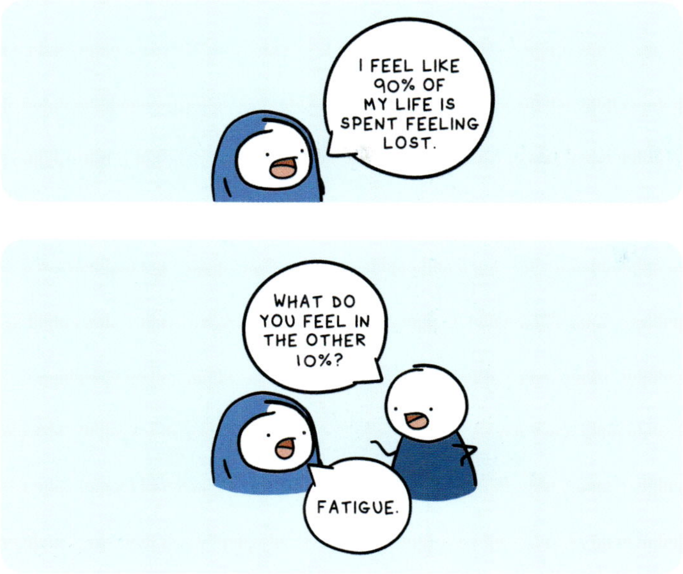
I FEEL LIKE 90% OF MY LIFE IS SPENT FEELING LOST.
WHAT DO YOU FEEL IN THE OTHER 10%?
FATIGUE.

Whenever I spoke with close friends and family back home, they would always ask me how I was doing.

"I'm good," I would say, with as genuine of a smile as I could muster. I didn't want to be disillusioning.

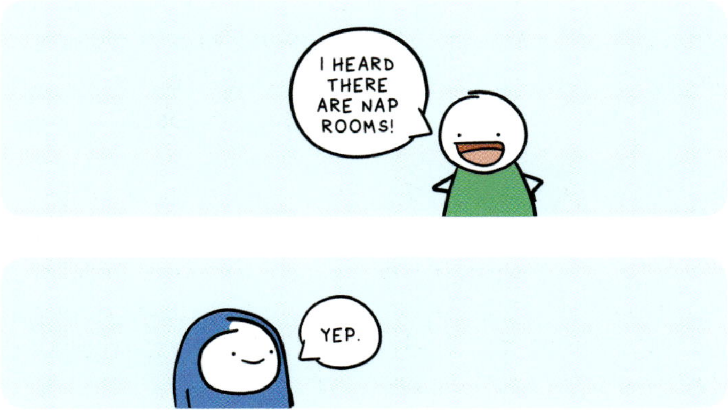
I HEARD THERE ARE NAP ROOMS!
YEP.

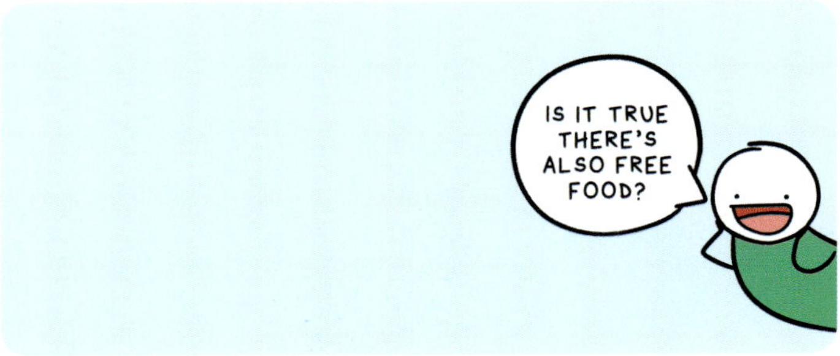
IS IT TRUE THERE'S ALSO FREE FOOD?

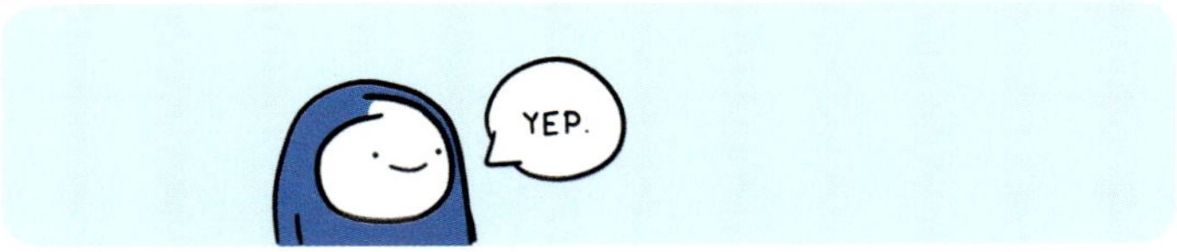
YEP.

I was always grateful to be asked about the food, as it allowed me to launch into a well-practiced story about how wonderful the food was. *You don't need to worry about me, you see, there's food here!* Talking about free food was a lot easier than talking about real things—real things like feeling lost and not knowing why. Real things like wondering why you've arrived but also still haven't.

• • •

A few months later, I found myself eating lunch with a coworker I was meeting for the first time. She asked me how I was feeling about life since moving for the job, and I gave her my well-rehearsed, pleasant answer. She nodded sagely in response.

And then out of the blue, she asked me something so off-script that I felt strangely compelled to answer:

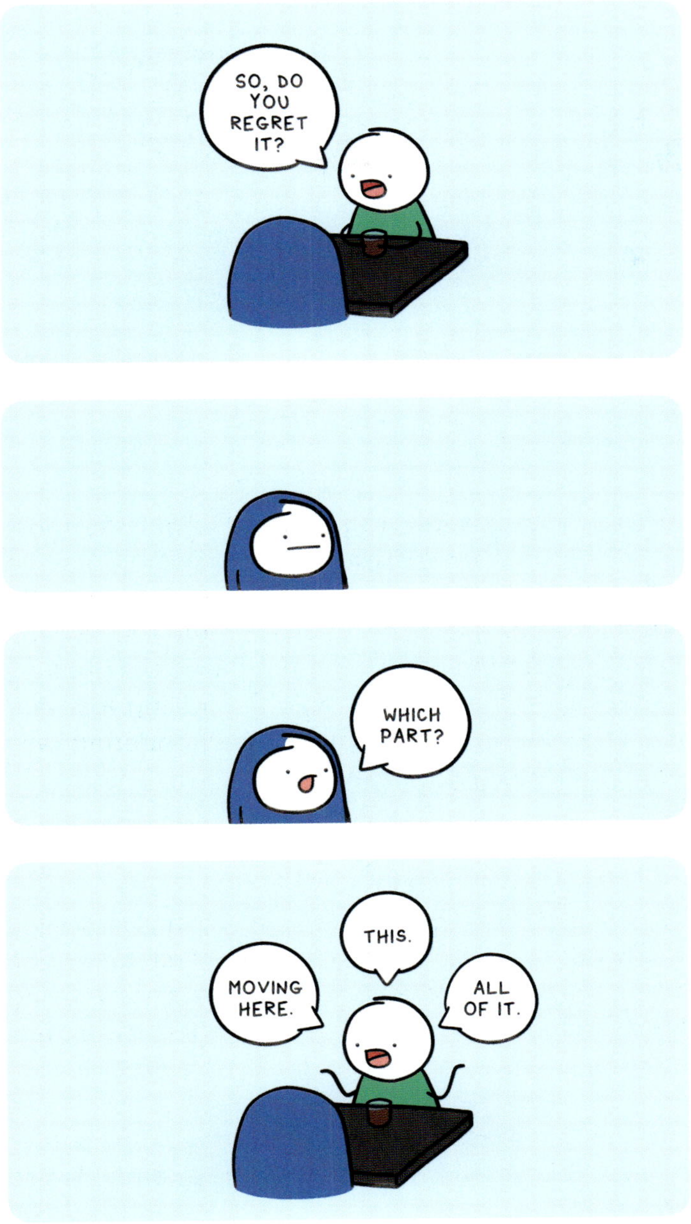
SO, DO YOU REGRET IT?
WHICH PART?
MOVING HERE.
THIS.
ALL OF IT.

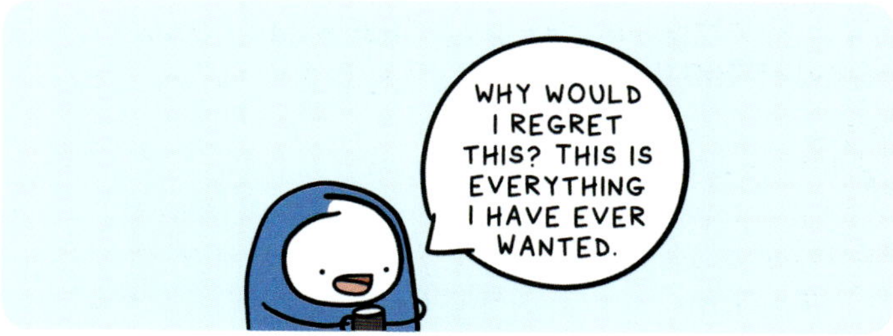
WHY WOULD I REGRET THIS? THIS IS EVERYTHING I HAVE EVER WANTED.

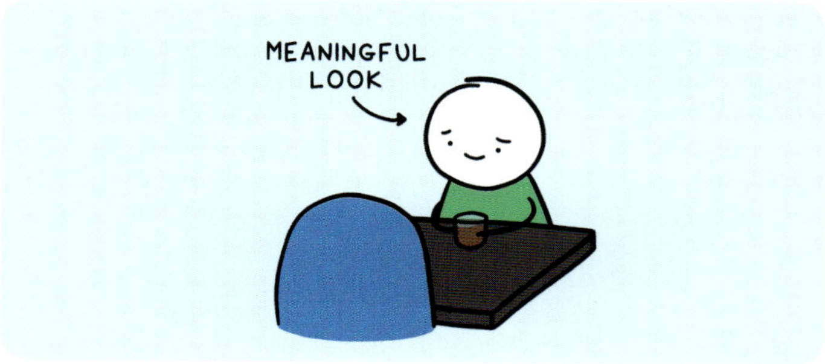
MEANINGFUL LOOK

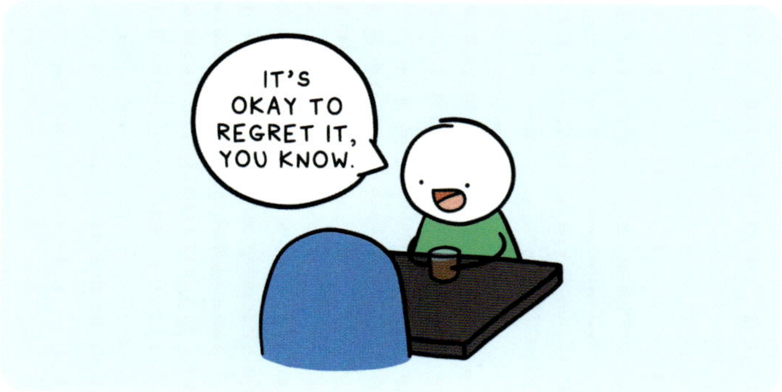
IT'S OKAY TO REGRET IT, YOU KNOW.

Sometimes when people tell me it's okay to feel a certain way, I get annoyed. *Don't tell me how to feel!* I'll silently retort in my head. Yes, I know, I have issues—see chapters one to seven for details. But when my coworker said, "It's okay to regret it, you know," I felt a sudden sense of relief. It was as though

I had been holding my breath for months, and someone finally gave me the green light to exhale.

I think a part of me had always wondered if there was a bit of regret, but I just never allowed myself to fully explore the feeling because I was scared of what I might find. I didn't think I was allowed to feel anything *but* happiness over something that's supposed to make me feel happy. It almost seemed ungrateful to let myself feel what I actually felt—ungrateful to whom, I couldn't say.

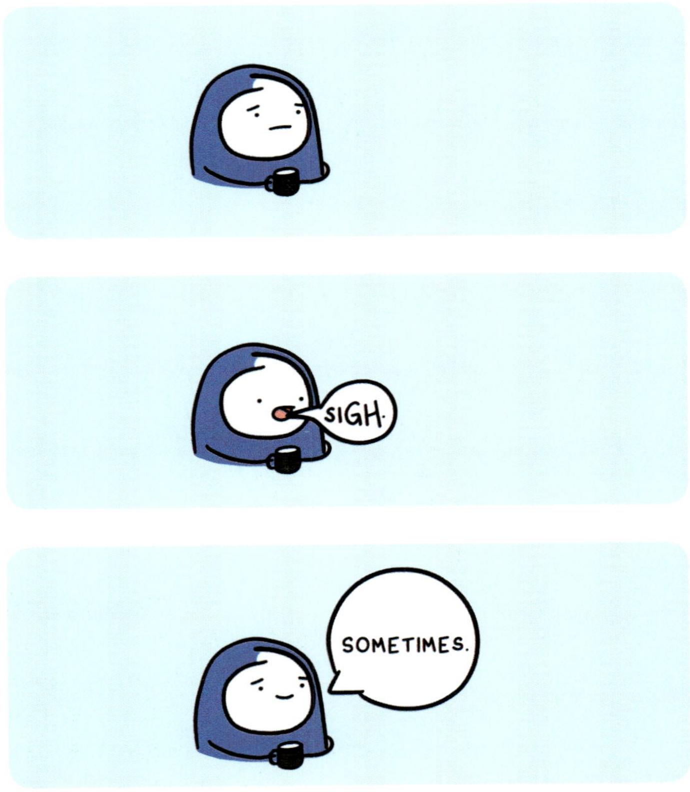
SIGH.
SOMETIMES.

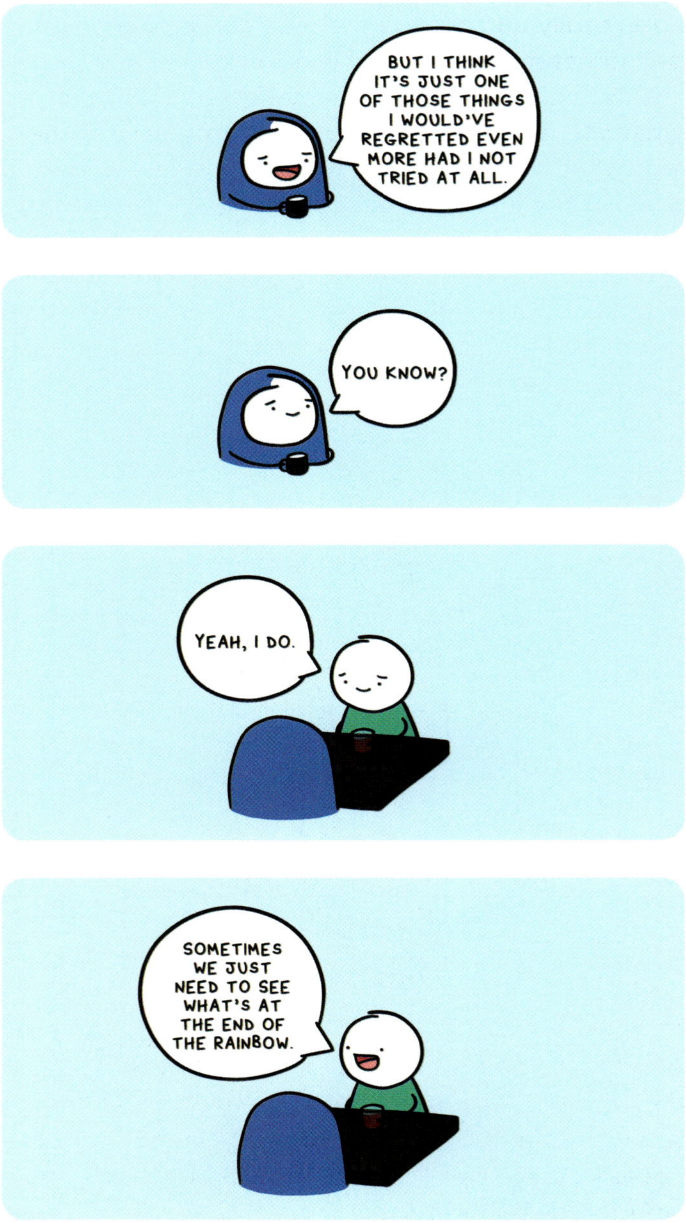
BUT I THINK IT'S JUST ONE OF THOSE THINGS I WOULD'VE REGRETTED EVEN MORE HAD I NOT TRIED AT ALL.
YOU KNOW?
YEAH, I DO.
SOMETIMES WE JUST NEED TO SEE WHAT'S AT THE END OF THE RAINBOW.

I don't fully understand the magic or logic behind it, but sometimes a stranger, with no sense of boundaries, asking you deeply personal questions is *exactly* what you need to hear in order to rethink your life.

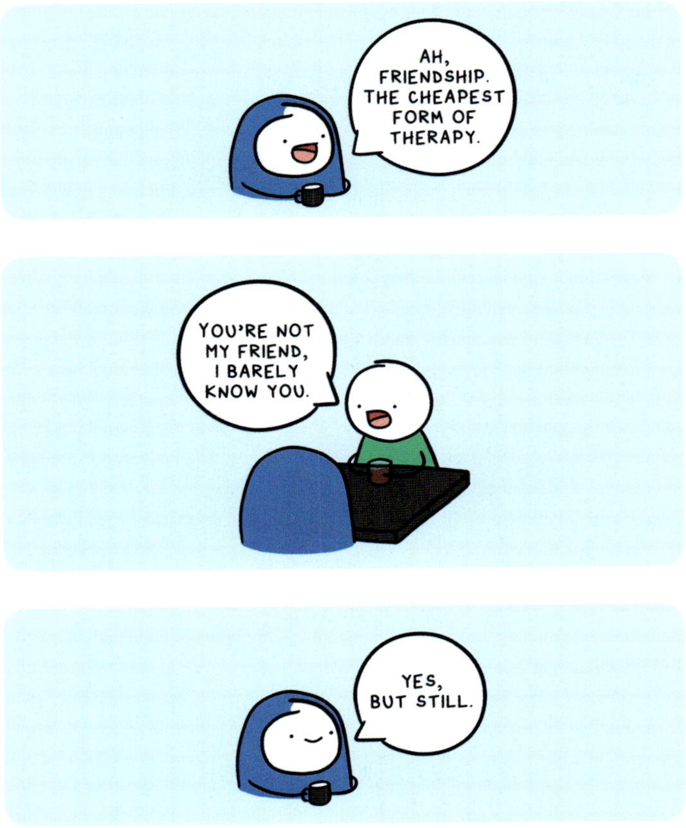
AH, FRIENDSHIP. THE CHEAPEST FORM OF THERAPY.
YOU'RE NOT MY FRIEND, I BARELY KNOW YOU.
YES, BUT STILL.

After I got home that day, I stood and stared out the window for a really long time. It was unnecessarily dramatic, but that just made it all the more necessary. As my eyes scanned the city below me, I wondered if I could fight crime.

After my voice of reason rightfully shut down the terrible crime-fighter idea, my trail of thought went instead to everything that had led me to this moment in time. The relentless need to figure out what I was *supposed* to be doing with my life, the expectations of happiness, both self- and socially imposed, and the worry of feeling lost in a world where everyone else seemed found.

It all felt so misguided.

I had spent so much time focusing on what I was *supposed* to do, and how I was *supposed* to feel, I never really stopped to think about what it was that I actually wanted to do.

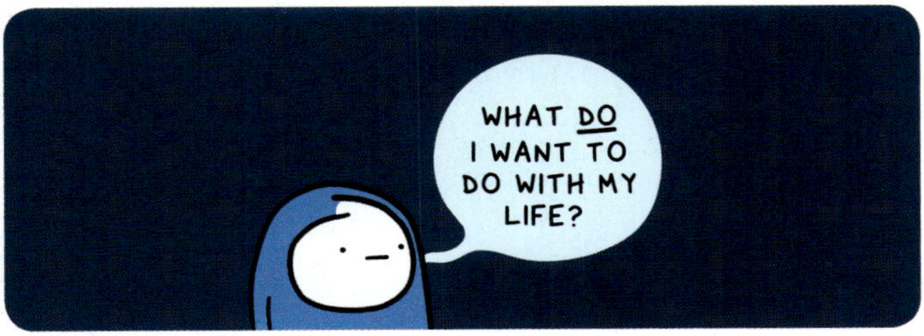
WHAT DO I WANT TO DO WITH MY LIFE?

I didn't have an answer, but it finally felt like the right question. And that seemed good enough for the day.

• • •

I don't think we're *supposed* to be doing anything with our lives.

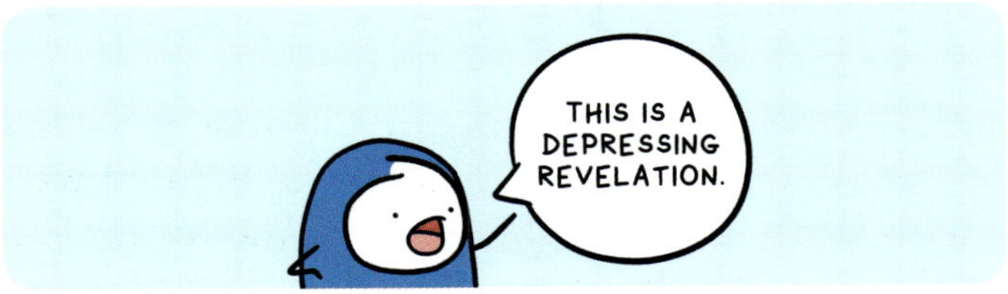
THIS IS A DEPRESSING REVELATION.

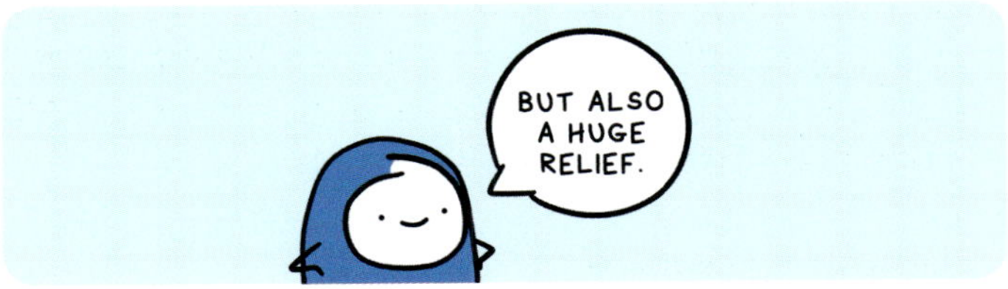
BUT ALSO A HUGE RELIEF.

I think we're allowed to just . . . do whatever it is that we *want* to do. Whatever it is that makes us happy.

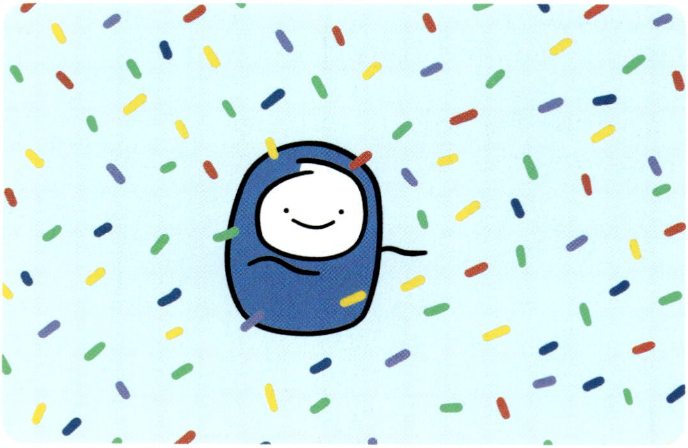

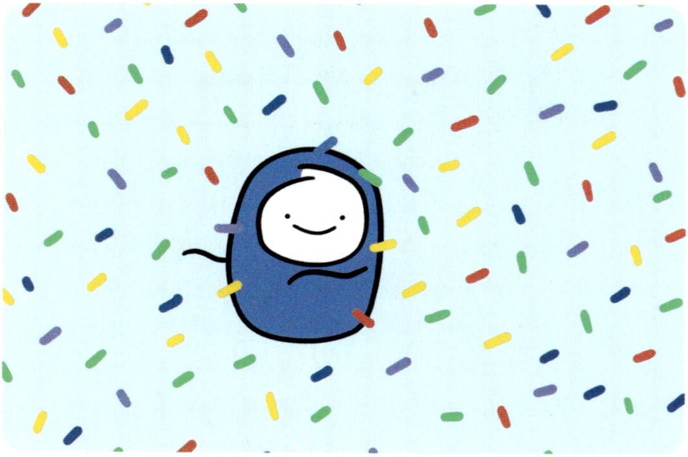

And in trying to figure out what we want to do, in trying to figure out what makes us happy, we're bound to feel a little lost at times. But maybe this sense of feeling lost is necessary. Maybe feeling lost is what pushes us to keep exploring. It's the ethereal song that awakens our curiosities and drives us to follow cows, discover hidden coves, and find remnants of good in a world that so often feels too dark and broken.

Maybe feeling lost is just the prerequisite of adventure—the first chapter of any good story.

SO... WHAT NOW?

WHAT ARE YOU GOING TO DO WITH YOUR LIFE?

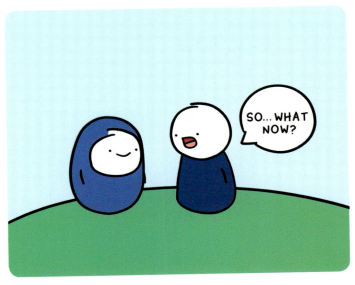

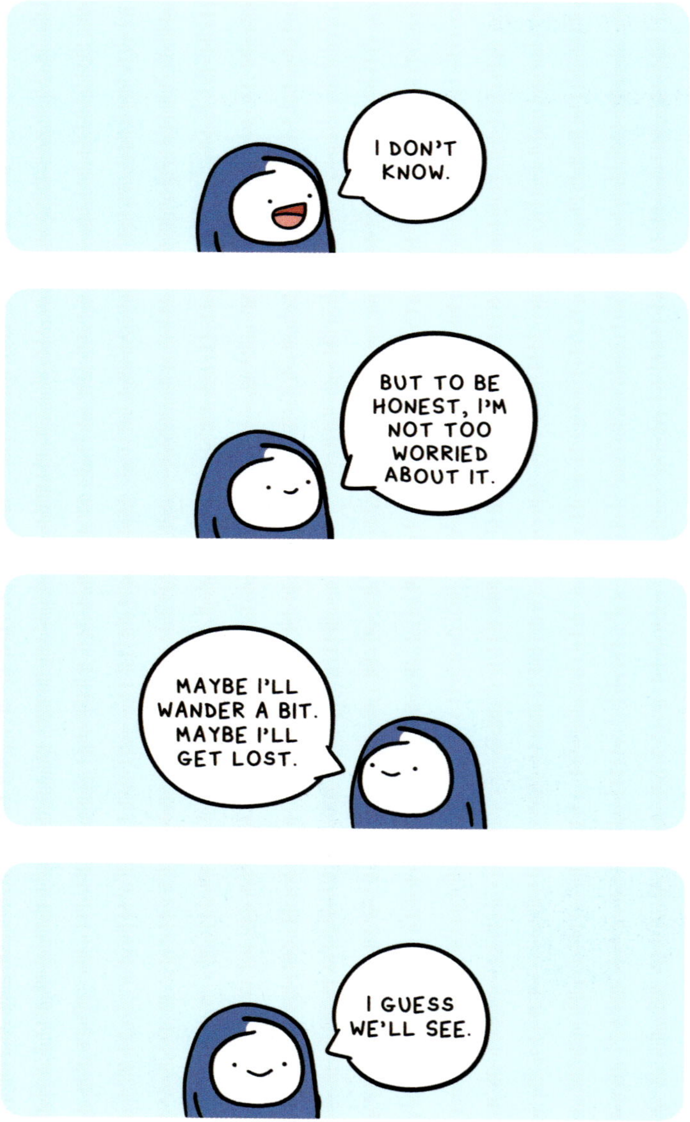
I DON'T KNOW.
BUT TO BE HONEST, I'M NOT TOO WORRIED ABOUT IT.
MAYBE I'LL WANDER A BIT. MAYBE I'LL GET LOST.
I GUESS WE'LL SEE.

I think at the end of it all, I just want to be able to look back and know that I enjoyed my time here.

And who knows?

Maybe it'll all make sense eventually.

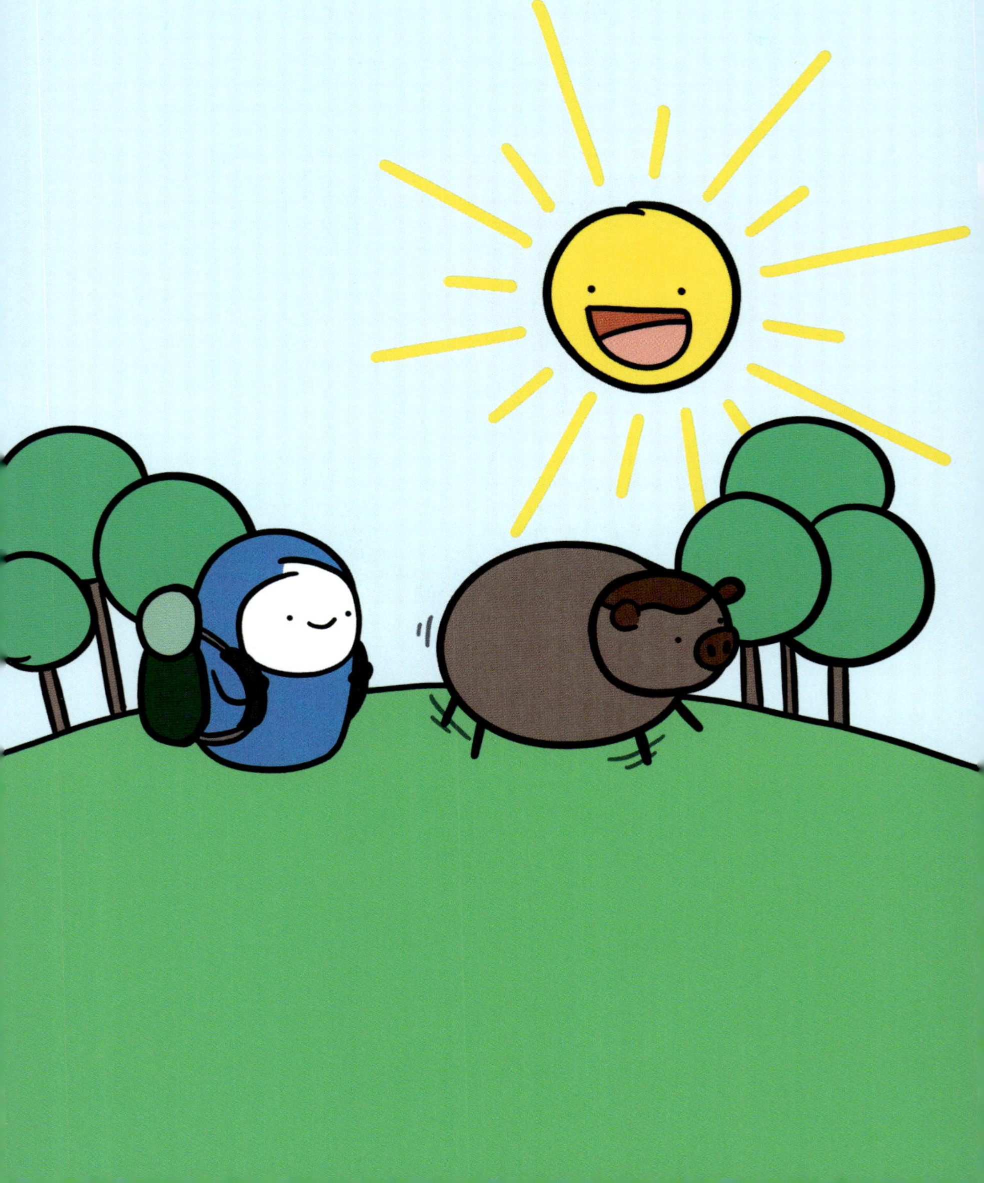

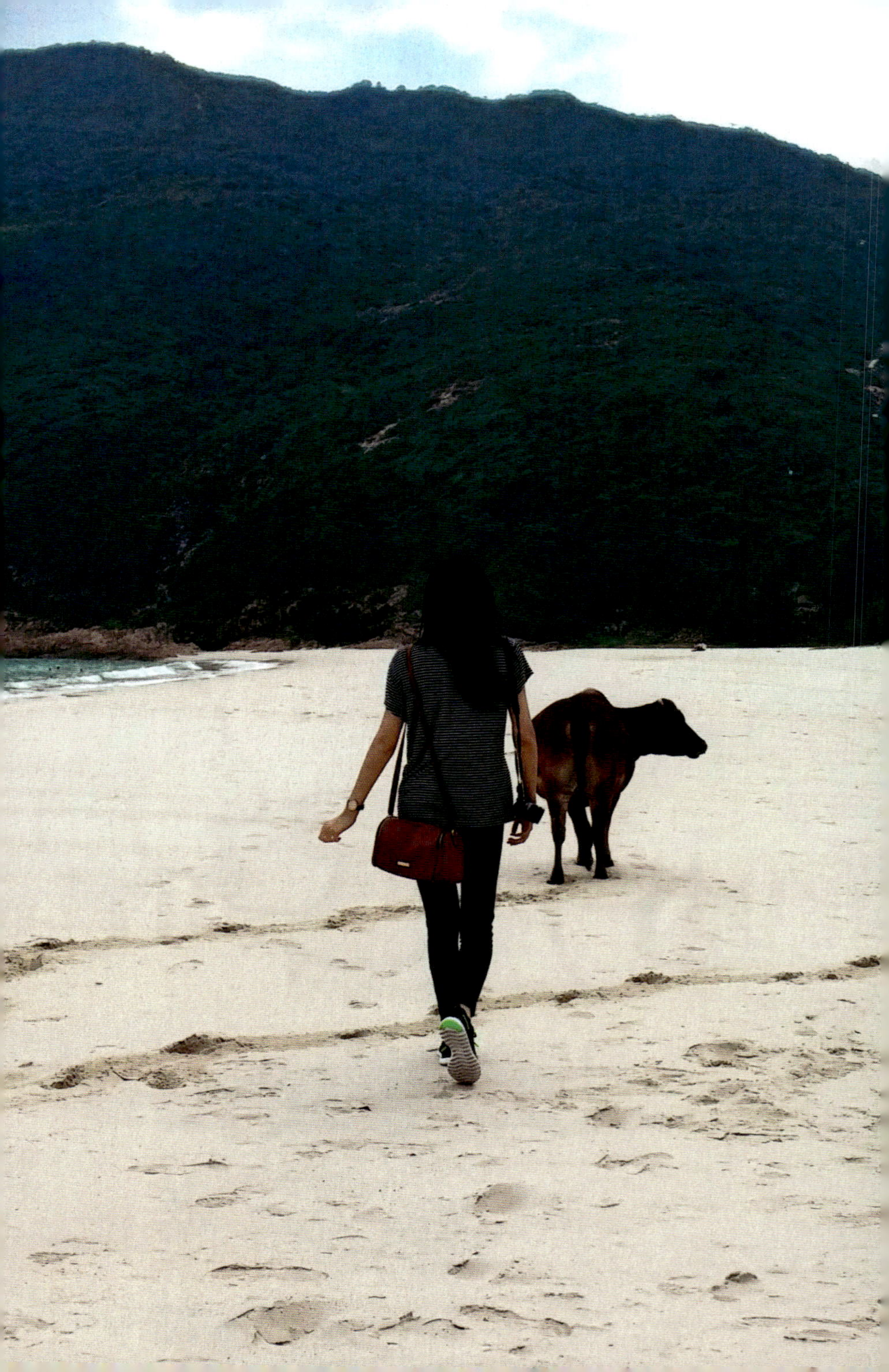

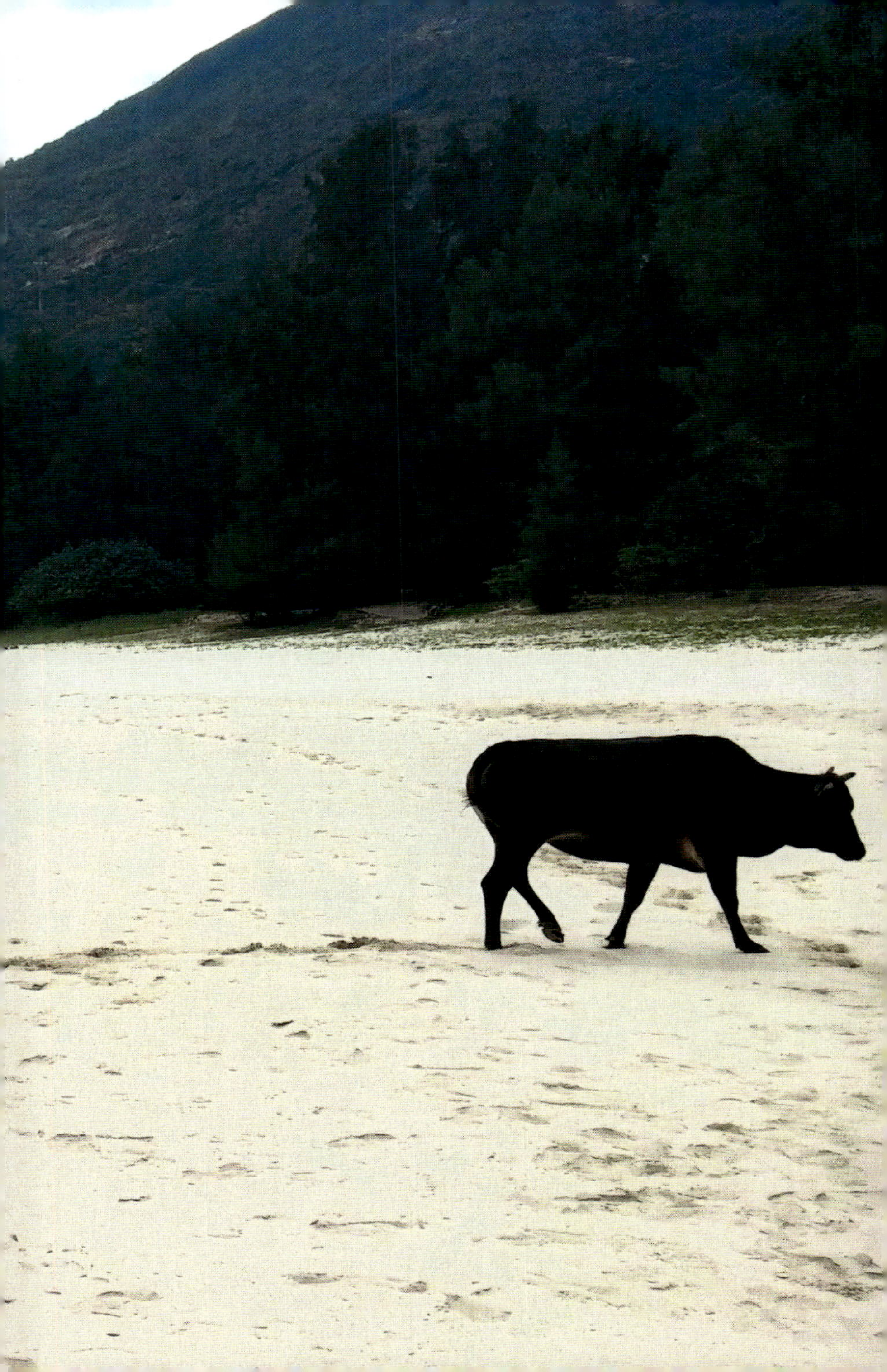

# ACKNOWLEDGMENTS

Like most children who spent their summers in the sacred arms of public libraries, I have always wanted to write a book.

I thought writing a book would be fun—a neat little one-year project from start to finish.

I was wrong. It took over three and a half years, and was the hardest thing I've ever had to do.

During these years, A LOT of people helped bring this book to life. People like:

- My agent, Cindy Uh, who (in my opinion) really rolled the dice when she plucked me out from a sea of comic artists. I would not have had the opportunity to write this book without her.

- My editor, Sarah Ried, who always kept the ship afloat and sailing beautifully, from the start, right to the very end.

- Jen Overstreet, Andrea Guinn, and Suzette Lam, who assembled the pieces of this book more beautifully than I ever could.

- Megan Looney, Kristin Cipolla, and the legion of talent at Harper Perennial—it takes a team of people to bring a book to life and into the reader's hands.

- My friends and family, who were subjected to years of me in panicky book-writing form and still stayed my friends and family.

- And finally, my unofficial editors, Jamie Alexis Goco, Caryn Wille, Bianca Wong, and Jenny Ng, who were forced to read a litany of early first drafts filled with questionable writing and still found the kindness in their hearts to encourage me to keep going.

Thank you for all your love and support, and for helping me move the nonsensical stories from my head onto the nonsensical pages of this book.

# ABOUT THE AUTHOR

MEICHI NG is the creator of *Barely Functional Adult,* a comic she started back in 2015. She tells nonsense stories from a teeny tiny apartment in Vancouver, British Columbia.

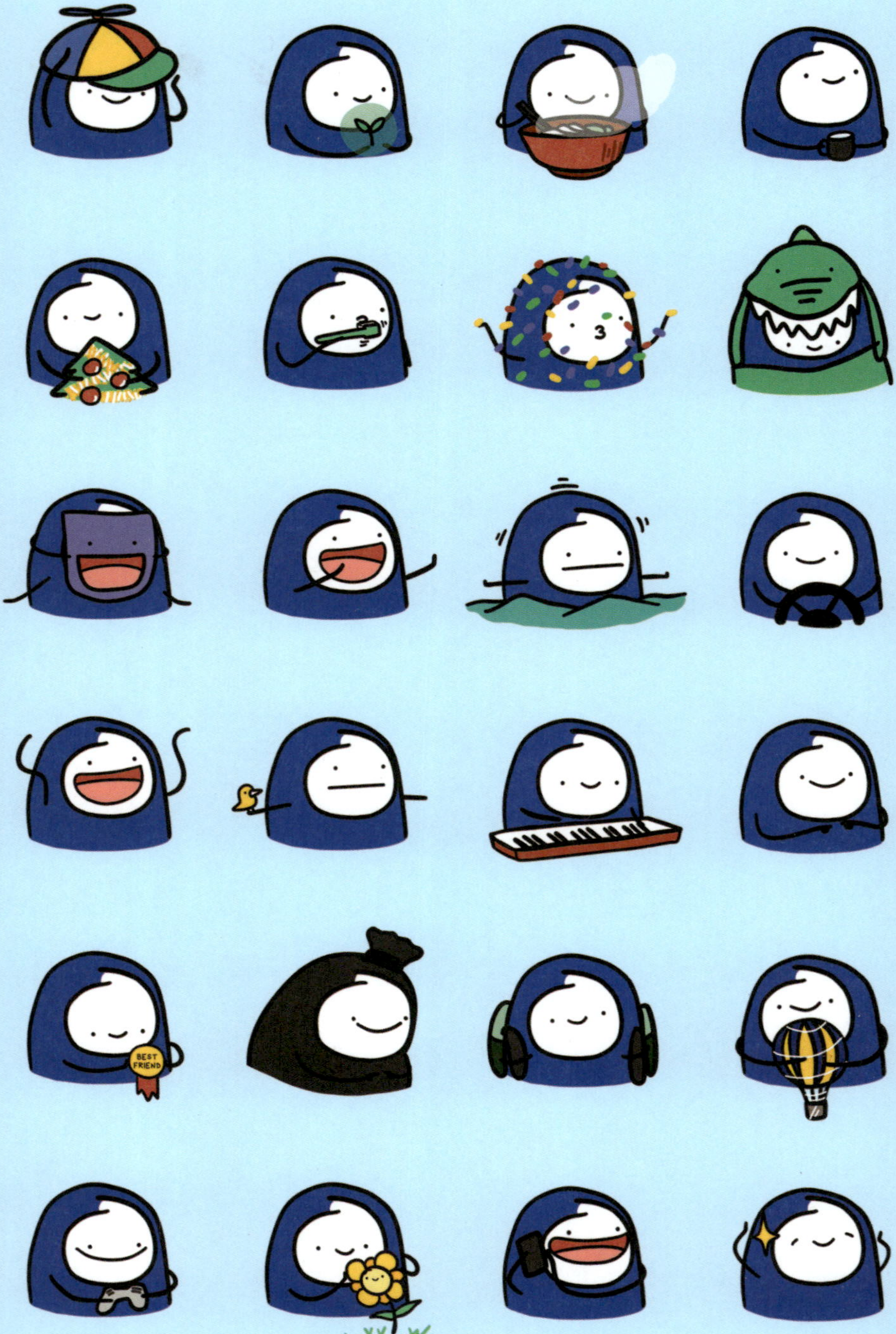
BEST FRIEND